WITHDRAWN

# ALPINE PLANTS
## OF NORTH AMERICA

# ALPINE PLANTS

## OF NORTH AMERICA

AN ENCYCLOPEDIA OF
MOUNTAIN FLOWERS FROM
THE ROCKIES TO ALASKA

## GRAHAM NICHOLLS

Rick Lupp, Consulting Editor

*Foreword by Bobby Ward*

TIMBER PRESS
*Portland • Cambridge*

Published in 2002 by

Timber Press, Inc.
The Haseltine Building
133 S.W. Second Avenue, Suite 450
Portland, Oregon 97204, U.S.A.

Timber Press
2 Station Road
Swavesey
Cambridge CB4 5QJ, U. K.

Printed in Hong Kong

Library of Congress Cataloging-in-Publication Data

Nicholls, Graham
    Alpine plants of North America: an encyclopedia of mountain flowers from
    the rockies to Alaska / Graham Nicholls: Rick Lupp, consulting editor;
    foreword by Bobby Ward.
        p. cm.
    Includes bibliographical references (p. ).
    ISBN 0-88192-548-9
        1. Mountain plants—West (U.S.)—Encyclopedias. 2. Mountain plants—
    Canada, Western—Encyclopedias. 3. Wild Flowers—West (U.S.)—
    Encyclopedias. 4. Wild flowers—Canada, Western—Encyclopedias. I. Title.

QK133.N53 2002
582.13753'0978—dc21                                              2002023199
                                                                        CIP

Frontispiece: *Castilleja scabrida* var. *barnebyana*, Burr trail, Utah. Photo Chris Norton.

*To Ev Whittemore, the "crazy New Englander," without whose friendship and enthusiasm this book would never have been written, and to my wife, Iris, who has had the patience of a saint during almost five years of suffering as a computer widow.*

# CONTENTS

# ACKNOWLEDGMENTS

AT THE COMMENCEMENT of this project I thought I would not need any help. After all, had I not been growing and writing about these plants for years? I just needed a little time to sit at the computer and the book would be written. Well, that thought did not last very long and now almost five years later I realize how many people have assisted me.

Primarily my thanks must go to Anne Spiegel, with whom I share an affinity for western alpines. Anne, in addition to checking and editing so much for me, also turned my writing completely on its head almost from day one. Her e-mail must have been overloaded on many occasions, and her many valuable comments have had a great impact on this book.

My thanks also go to Rick Lupp, nurseryman and plantsman extraordinaire, whose friendship and skill have furthered my knowledge of western plants. To Verna and Frank Pratt, Tass Kelso, and Carolyn Parker for their invaluable knowledge and assistance in checking the *Androsace*, *Douglasia*, and *Primula* chapters, particularly the Alaskan species, and also for supplying so many good photographs of Alaskan flora. To Roger Barlow, Phyllis Gustafson, Dave Joyner, Bill King, and Jay Lunn for checking parts of the manuscript. Likewise I have to thank John Andrews, Shirley Barber, Bruce Barnes, Peter Downe, Ed Godleski, Jane Grushow, David Hale, Russ Jolley, Dave Joyner, Ned and Betty Lowry, Jay Lunn, Neal Maillet, Chris Norton, Ron Ratko, Fermi de Sousa, and Ev Whittemore for allowing me the use of their slides.

Finally my thanks go to Neal Maillet of Timber Press for believing in me.

# FOREWORD

GRAHAM NICHOLLS has been growing and showing alpines for 40 years, including serving as show secretary for the West of England Show of the Alpine Garden Society, picking up awards and honors along the way, such as the prestigious Farrer Medal for Best Plant in Show. His first trip to the western United States in 1982 opened his eyes to western American alpines, and he has maintained an enduring, passionate relationship with them. After retiring in 1990, he opened a mail-order nursery, Graham's Hardy Plants, to allow him time to focus more extensively on North American alpines, particularly the xeric or dryland area species, which are his main interest. In Timsbury (near Bath), Somerset, England, he gradually mastered techniques for managing them in pots, raised beds, sand beds, and troughs. As an exhibitor, he established credible and convincing evidence of his propagation and cultivation skills.

I first met Graham when he came to North Carolina in 1994 to attend the annual meeting of the North American Rock Garden Society (NARGS) in Asheville. His long-term plant pal and organizer of the meeting, Ev Whittemore, invited him to relate his experience in starting his alpine nursery, which was then about four years old. I remember a witty, light-hearted talk detailing the good, bad, and the ugly of plant nursery management. Bulging trays of plants crammed into the back of a van (used for trundling them from show to show) indicated his attempts to boost sales to customers who were leery of their (and his) ability to cultivate North American alpines in the United Kingdom. Graham also showed pans of his immaculately grown North American alpines at Alpine Garden Society (AGS) shows, the zenith for worldwide exhibition and competition of alpine and rock garden plants because of the exacting show standards.

During the next several years I read articles that Graham sent to Ev Whittemore, which she published in the newsletter of the Southern Appalachian Chapter of NARGS. In these dispatches from Somerset he continued to detail his expanding knowledge in culturing across-the-ocean alpines. At the Alpines 2001 Conference in Edinburgh, Scotland, in July of that year, I attended the opening session of the decennially held conference titled "All the Way from America" in which Graham shared billing with Verna Pratt of Alaska and Baldassare Mineo of Oregon, both experts in North American alpines. He gave a breathless, fast-paced talk with slides of *Astragalus*, *Eritrichium*, *Hymenoxys*, *Silene*, and *Townsendia*—all of which he grows at his nursery and garden. At the session break, Graham held court in the plant sales room as attendees admired his stock of *Talinum* 'Zoe' or *Aquilegia grahamii* and conversed with him about successfully cultivating North American alpines.

Graham has now set down his accumulated knowledge and experience in *Alpine Plants of North America: An Encyclopedia of Mountain Flowers from the Rockies to Alaska*. The book took Graham five years to produce, which is not unreasonable considering refinements he made to early drafts of the manuscript, including adding descriptions by mountain range of alpine habitats from Alaska's Brooks Range southward to Oregon's Coast Range and the California Sierra and eastward to the Front Range of the Rocky Mountains. This "massive piece of real estate" is the source of the plants with which Graham is smitten, and the inclusion of this information in the book is an immense, worthy addition because Graham knows the difference between some deep-rooted "alpines" of the desertlike Great Basin, where hot summer temperatures and low rainfall is the norm, and the saxatiles of the Cascade and Olympic mountains, whose winter snow cover keeps them dry. Plants in the Pacific Northwest have mild but wet winters, and Graham tells us that to know how to grow a plant you must first know the habitat where the plant grows. I believe that admonition is the great merit and benefit of *Alpine Plants of North America*, and we should follow his example by knowing the plant in its habitat and full seasons, as well as the local meteorology, and extrapolate his successful container culture experience to our own native conditions.

*Alpine Plants of North America* is an alphabetical coverage of 54 genera from *Androsace* to *Zauschneria* with treatment of not only the most horticulturally worthy species but also some of the new, popular, and easy to grow cultivars. Many entries include anecdotes on field observations of the species, cultivation and propagation information, and details of the geographical range and localized habitat. Graham does not mind revealing that he has trouble over-wintering a plant such as *Campanula lasiocarpa* 'Talkeetna'. Nor does he shy from making unabashed, enthusiastic comments on *Castilleja* (Indian paintbrush) when he sees them light up the scenery, "the top of their stems like ragged brushes dipped in red paint," or from admitting his long-term love affair with *Lewisia*.

Graham's North American alpine knowledge was complemented by counsel from other stateside aficionados including Rick Lupp of Washington, an experienced plantsman who ably assisted Graham as consulting editor. The result is a largely comprehensive compendium of choice or signature alpine and saxatile plants from the North American West (the eastern mountains of North America are excluded from this treatment because of their limited alpine areas and because most of them are an extension of Arctic flora). Of particular note is Graham's coverage of *Phlox* (40 species), the often overlooked *Claytonia*, and the underappreciated *Talinum* and *Lesquerella*. There is, as expected, generous coverage of *Draba*, *Eriogonum*, *Gentiana*, *Penstemon*, and much more, particularly those species that grow in Alaska and its range of habitat extremes. Graham has included a general chapter on cultivation of alpines with recommendations for soil mixtures and a useful glossary to tease apart thorny alpine plant terms. He includes a generous collection of almost 500 photographs of alpines in both their natural habitat and cultivation.

Growing alpines is a challenge—a delicate high-wire act requiring the careful balance of moisture, drainage, and soil type with the plant's requirements. That lesson is the linchpin of Graham's *Alpine Plants of North America*. May we all grow alpines now *in excelsis*.

BOBBY J. WARD
*Bobby J. Ward is the president of*
*the North American Rock Garden Society*

*Hulsea nana*, Mount Shasta, California. Photo John Andrews.

# PREFACE

WHAT IS AN ALPINE PLANT? In the strictest *botanical* sense it is any plant that grows above the tree line in subalpine and alpine zones in mountainous regions. Owing to the harsh conditions that exist in arctic areas like Alaska, not all alpinelike, treeless habitats are mountainous. Furthermore, a large number of plants that grow below the tree line are just as attractive and as suitable for growing in an alpine or rock garden as the true alpines; such plants may come from habitats ranging from woodland to desert. Even though some can be fairly tall it is generally accepted that to be classed as an alpine plant in the *horticultural* sense they have to be small, no taller than 30–40 cm (12–15¾ in.) high. Although many plants I describe in this book originate in true alpine areas, others are alpines only in the horticultural sense. Those in the horticultural category can be just as difficult to cultivate successfully as the true alpine plant because of the conditions (such as high light levels and the type of rock in the soil) that exist in their natural habitat. Most plants I discuss in this book do grow at least a few thousand feet above sea level, but as I point out in the Introduction, a wide range of factors govern the growth of alpine plants.

I have been growing alpines from all parts of the world for over 40 years, but my first trip to the western United States in 1982 sold me on western alpines. Cultivating these wonderful plants has become part of my life ever since. I exhibit them at Alpine Garden Society shows, which means they have to be cultivated to a high standard. In attempting to meet these standards I have learned propagation and growing techniques not available in many books. In addition, since I am a nurseryman specializing in North American alpines, I have been able to study and grow many more genera than I otherwise would have.

I have excluded the limited alpine areas of the eastern mountains of North America, most notably those of the Appalachian and Adirondack Mountains. The tallest of these mountains would rank as relatively small peaks if they occurred in the West, and their floras are mainly an extension of the arctic tundra. As such, these mountains have few affinities with the areas described in this book.

## HOW DID THIS BOOK COME ABOUT?

The seed was sown during that first western trip. When I asked for a book on North American plants at a national park visitor center, I was presented with a variety of publications on local flora. Some were badly written and many had poor photographs. After explaining that I grew these plants and also photographed them in the wild, I asked for one book that would cover the majority of the high-altitude plants I would likely see in the West. Not only was I told there was no such book, but I was also told to write one myself since one was greatly needed. Thinking the task an impossibility because I would have to live in the United States for a long time to produce such a book, I left it at that. Although I purchased many books, most were written with the average tourist or plant hunter in mind; naturally, cultivation and propagation information was missing. My attempts to identify a plant were often frustrated, despite the library of books I had to help me.

The situation remained that way for another 12–13 years, and it probably would have done so for a lot longer but for a chance remark I made to Ev Whittemore in 1995. Ev, formerly of New England, is a friend of over 20 years, who now lives and gardens with her husband, Bruce, in Penrose, North Carolina. I complained to her that there was no single book possessing information on the majority of the popular western plants. Back came a short, typical New Englander answer: "Then write it yourself, Graham!" And so it began.

This is a book intended for plant hunting enthusiasts, growers, and anyone else interested in North American alpines. It contains much more than descriptions and photographs of plants—I have included information on propagation and cultivation of each individual genus that I describe. The book also contains anecdotes of how I discovered a lot of this information, and there is a general chapter on cultivation with suggestions of how to grow western alpines. The altitude information I provide is approximate, particularly since each measurement had to be converted to its imperial or metric equivalent. Although I have indicated the main states in which each species grows, they, like many plants in this book, overlap into neighboring states. Anyone wishing to grow alpines will find that the majority of those I describe are available from seed exchanges, commercial seed lists, or nurseries. All the knowledge I have gained while growing these plants has gone into this book, resulting in what I hope is not only easy reading but also a high quality reference book.

How did I select the genera for inclusion in the book? I may have been a bit selfish by including all my personal favorites, but I have also consulted other growers and plant hunters in the United States and have written up the genera generally considered to be signature flowers of the alpine West. Unfortunately the constraints on the size of the book would not allow the inclusion of every genus in the western United States. Ferns, for example, are absent from the book as these nonflowering plants are mainly the province of specialists. I have deliberately omitted bulbs because they have been discussed at length in the excellent volume *Bulbs of North America* by the North American Rock Garden Society (NARGS). During the writing of this book, my eyes were opened to much of the beautiful flora of Alaska and so I included many of these Alaskan species, not only in the text but also in the photographs.

As far as possible I have been botanically correct, and all those who have kindly checked portions of the manuscript have kept me on track. Nevertheless it must be remembered that this book has been written primarily from the viewpoint of an enthusiastic plant hunter, grower, and nurseryman, not a botanist.

## PLANT NAMES AND NAMING

I have taken great pains to insure that the scientific plant names listed in the book are as accurate as possible. Please note that any common names listed in the book are offered for convenience only; one reader's trout lily is another's dog's-tooth violet. It is impossible to list every common name for the plants included here, and I have not tried to do so. However, I have attempted in the index to cross-reference from well-known common names to their corresponding botanical names.

Please note also that not everyone agrees on the correct botanical name for a given plant. First, plants have no idea that we human beings are traveling about attaching names to them and they are remarkably proficient at resisting the nice, neat categories we impose on them. Furthermore, newcomers to plant taxonomy are often surprised that there is no central governing board to decide on whether the Rocky Mountain fringed gentian is *Gentiana detonsa* var. *unicaulis*, *Gentiana elegans*, or *Gentianopsis thermalis*. As a rule, older names fade away as newer names are published and supported scientifically. Unfortunately, scientists and the editors of botanical publications do not always agree. As a non-botanist, I have tried to follow the most current and recognized thinking, but some are sure to disagree with the choice of this or that plant name. I can only vouch that every name included here has been validly published in accordance with the *International Code of Botanical Nomenclature*. I have often included alternative scientific names as synonyms whenever I thought that other names are still in use.

Those who are unfamiliar with scientific plant names may benefit from a brief explanation of the system of botanical Latin.

The primary scientific means of referring to a plant species is to use its Latin binomial, which is formed by combining its genus name and specific epithet. The scientific name *Aquilegia caerulea* is such a binomial. All columbines throughout the world are members of the genus *Aquilegia*, of which there are approximately 70 species. However, *Aquilegia caerulea* is a single species growing from Idaho to New Mexico; all members of this species share certain characteristics. The epithet *caerulea* (Latin for deep blue) denotes only the columbines that exhibit the characteristics of this species.

Often, however, there may be a certain amount of variation within a given species. Some examples of *Aquilegia caerulea* that grow in Colorado are spurless and receive their own designation as a variety of *Aquilegia caerulea*, such as *Aquilegia caerulea* var. *daileyae*. Other individuals of *Aquilegia caerulea* that are somewhat white and found in the Rocky Mountains have been described as *Aquilegia caerulea* var. *ochroleuca*. Such names under a species name are described as infraspecific. In other cases, an infraspecific name may be described as a subspecies rather than a variety, such as *Lewisia rediviva* subsp. *minor*.

When an infraspecific group is named for the first time, the names of all the other plants within that species must change slightly to be distinct. All the plants within *Aquilegia caerulea* that are not *Aquilegia caerulea* var. *ochroleuca* or *Aquilegia caerulea* var. *daileyae* should be called *Aquilegia caerulea* var. *caerulea*. Such an infraspecific name in which the specific epithet is repeated is called an autonym, which is also known as the type variety. This is a confusing concept because people sometimes informally use the Latin binomial alone to mean the type variety or subspecies without saying so. The binomial *Aquilegia caerulea* in this example should be understood to encompass all three varieties, not just the type variety.

Throughout my book I have carefully spelled out the autonym when listing all infraspecific taxa *except* when there is only one variety or subspecies besides the type. At the risk of being somewhat inconsistent I have bowed to common usage to avoid looking too fussy. Since *Lewisia rediviva* has only one subspecies, I have neatly divided the species into *Lewisia rediviva* (implying the autonym *Lewisia rediviva* subsp. *rediviva* as well) and *Lewisia redivia* subsp. *minor*. *Lewisia columbiana* has two varieties besides the type, and I have been careful to spell out *Lewisia columbiana* var. *columbiana* whenever I mean the type. This may seem confusing at the start, but I hope this system will be understood without too much difficulty.

Finally, please note that I have indicated the family to which each genus belongs next to the genus heading. The genus *Aquilegia* belongs to the family Ranunculaceae, as do genera such as *Clematis* and *Anemone*.

## ETHICS FOR ALPINE TRAVELERS

It is sad to note that in years past visitors to wild areas considered it their right to dig up and collect the plants they found there. Thankfully, such practices are now prohibited both by law and common sense.

For all its ruggedness and raw force, the alpine zone is an extremely fragile habitat that is easily damaged by insensitive visitors. Even the smallest ground-covers and cushions may be hundreds of years old; in harsh, alpine conditions, it may take many years for a plant to achieve decent size, and the line between life and death can be razor thin. Alpine plants dug from the wild almost never adapt to human cultivation, and there is therefore no point in doing so even if the chance of being caught is remote. Be aware that even seed collecting is prohibited on some public lands without the proper permits, and remember to inquire of the local authorities before you plan to take any plant materials from common lands. Regulations tend to be strictest within areas administered by the National Park Service—federal law prohibits the removal of even a twig or pebble from protected areas no matter the circumstances. Be aware, also, that many large private landholdings are scattered among the government-owned lands of the West. Respect posted signs and tread lightly so that others may enjoy the same access to private areas that you have. Take nothing away with you except happy memories.

# INTRODUCTION

## Principal Alpine Habitats of Western North America

Western North America encompasses a huge area extending from the Brooks Range of Alaska to the southern Sierra of California and from the Coast Range of Oregon to the Front Range of the Rockies. This massive piece of real estate contains some of the most varied and extreme alpine habitats in the world, and an equally large number of alpine plants makes their home here. Given the diverse nature of this huge piece of land, anyone with a serious interest in learning to grow these marvelous plants needs at least a basic understanding of the wild habitats where they grow and prosper.

Many factors come together to produce a given habitat, including climatic variations such as rainfall, temperature, snow cover, wind exposure, and humidity. Other factors are soil types, soil structure, altitude, and even latitude and its effect on photoperiod, which is the interval in a 24-hour period during which a plant is exposed to light. Although a lifetime of work and study is not long enough to document all the factors that form the habitat for each individual species and subspecies of alpine plants, we can nevertheless obtain a general understanding of a plant's needs when we know something of its habitat.

## ALASKA

When it comes to extremes of habitat in western North America, Alaska, which comprises over 880,000 square kilometers (550,000 square miles), is very difficult to beat. It spans 20 degrees of latitude and 48 degrees of longitude, which means that its extent east to west and north to south is about the same as the contiguous 48 states of the United States. Alaska can be divided into four general areas of alpine habitat for the purpose of our discussion.

### Interior Alaska and the North Coast

The area contained by the Alaska Range to the south and the Brooks Range to the north is known as the interior, and the coastal area to the north of the Brooks Range is the north coast. Almost all the north coast plants that are of interest to alpine gardeners are also found in interior Alaska, so I will treat this area as one habitat.

The summits of the Alaska Range generally vary from 3075 to 3690 m (10,000 to 12,000 ft.), but this range is also home to Mount McKinley (Denali), the highest peak in North America at 6250 m (20,320 ft.), and to other giant peaks such as Mount Foraker at 5230 m (17,400 ft.). The area between the Alaska Range and the Brooks Range is a huge plateau that is 615–923 m (2000–3000 ft.) high and cleft by numerous river valleys. Most alpine plants are found growing at 615–1540 m (2000–5000 ft.). The Brooks Range to the north rises to about 1845 m (6000 ft.). The entire area is primarily metamorphic rock.

The mean annual air temperature of Alaska's interior ranges from about −6°C (21°F) in the north to −2°C (28°F) in the south with extremes of as much as 35°C (95°F) in the summer to −63°C (−82°F) in winter. The area has 40–60 frost-free days per year with a growth period of 120–140 days. Wind is almost constant and sometimes severe. Total mean precipitation is approximately 40 cm (15¾ in.), and during the growing season it is approximately 15 cm (6 in.).

The photoperiods of this area range from 24 hours of daylight during the height of summer to no daylight in winter in the Brooks Range. Further south in the Alaska Range the photoperiods are more like 22 hours of daylight during summer to two hours in winter. The significance of these photoperiods becomes apparent when trying to grow plants from this area such as *Douglasia gormanii* (synonym *Androsace constancei*). I have grown plants from seed of this species many times, and although the seed germinates well and produces strong, healthy looking plants, I have never been able to get the plants to bloom. Other growers around the world I have shared the seed with have had the same results, a fact that I can only attribute to the difference in photoperiods. This failure to produce bloom is by no means a consistent feature of the flora of this area; most genera will produce bloom at lower latitudes, although often it is not as good as that in the plant's native habitat.

Some plant associations in this area's alpine screes are *Androsace chamaejasme* subsp. *lehmanniana*, *Lesquerella arctica*, *Saxifraga eschscholtzii*, *S. oppositifolia* subsp. *smalliana*, and *Silene acaulis* subsp. *subcaulescens*. The grassy areas are home to such plants as *Aconitum delphiniifolium*, *Campanula lasiocarpa*, *Cassiope tetragona*, *Rhododendron lapponicum*, and *Vaccinium caespitosum*.

### The West Coast and Aleutian Islands

The west coast extends southward from near Point Hope in the north to the Aleutian Islands in the south and from the Bering Sea to the eastern boundary of the low Kigluaik Mountains east of Point Hope and the Seward Peninsula. The Seward Peninsula, the Aleutian Islands, and the shores of the Bering Sea support a treeless vegetation similar to the lowland arctic tundra of the north coast. The mountains in this area are low, generally less than 1540 m (5000 ft.), and alpines grow from sea level to near the summits of these mountains. The predominant soil types in this area are derived from glacial deposits and volcanic rock.

Temperatures are more moderate than in the interior. Even near Nome and Point Hope, winter lows reach only about −34°C (−30°F). Winter low temperatures in the Aleutians reach about −17°C (2°F). The mean annual air temperature of the west coast ranges from about −4°C (24°F) in the north to about 2°C (36°F) in the Aleutians. The mean July air temperature is about 10°C (50°F) in Nome and the Aleutians. Total mean precipitation is approximately 40 cm (15¾ in.) near Nome and as much as 254 cm (100 in.) in parts of the Aleutians. Photoperiods near Nome are similar to the interior and are less extreme in the Aleutians.

A typical plant association near the shores of the Bering Sea includes *Artemisia borealis*, *Aster sibiricus*, *Chrysanthemum arcticum*, *Primula nutans*, and *Rhododendron camtschaticum* subsp. *glandulosum*. The montane screes near Nome are home to *Artemisia senjavinensis*, *Campanula uniflora*, *Dryas integrifolia*, *Erigeron hyperboreus*, and *Eritrichium aretioides*. Plants found in nearby grassy areas include *Cassiope tetragona*, *Diapensia lapponica* subsp. *obovata*, *Gentiana algida*, and *Primula cuneifolia* subsp. *saxifragifolia*.

## The South Coast

The south coast extends from the Aleutians in the west to the St. Elias Mountains in the east and from the Alaska Range in the north to the Gulf of Alaska. The highest peaks in this area rise to 5075 m (16,500 ft.) in the St. Elias Mountains. Large volcanic peaks are found in the Wrangell Mountains north of the St. Elias Mountains and on the southern part of the Alaska Peninsula to the west. The Chugach Mountains around Anchorage and the Talkeetna Range, which runs south from the Alaska Range, are of nonvolcanic origin.

The south coast's climate is also much more moderate than the interior's. Winter low temperatures range from about −22°C (−8°F) near the coast to about −34°C (−30°F) inland. The mean annual air temperature ranges from −1°C (30°F) in the north to 2°C (36°F) in the south. The mean July air temperature is about 13°C (55°F). Total mean annual precipitation ranges from about 60 cm (24 in.) in the north to as much as 245 cm (96 in.) in some coastal areas. Photoperiods in this area are pronounced but still much less extreme than in the interior. Much of the coastal region is covered by a blanket of coniferous forest made up of Sitka spruce, Alaska cypress, western hemlock, and mountain hemlock. Plants such as Sitka alder predominate at subalpine elevations.

Typical plant associations found in the screes in this area include *Draba stenoloba*, *Potentilla fruticosa*, *Potentilla villosa*, *Saxifraga bronchialis* subsp. *funstonii*, and *Silene acaulis* subsp. *acaulis*. Growing in nearby grassy areas are plants such as *Campanula lassiocarpa*, *Cassiope stellariana*, *Corydalis pauciflora*, and *Potentilla palustris*.

**The Southeast Coast**

The southeast coast includes the area extending from the city of Yakutat to the Queen Charlotte Islands and includes the coastal mountains, the narrow strip of land along the coast, and a large number of both large and small islands lying off this narrow strip of coast. The coastal mountains rise to over 4310 m (14,000 ft.) at Mount Fairweather and are among the most heavily glaciated in the world. These mountains are of nonvolcanic origin. The coastal strip and the offshore islands are blanketed by coniferous forest.

The southeast coast has a temperate maritime climate featuring plenty of rain and cloudy weather with much less extreme temperatures than those further north. The mean annual air temperature is about 2°C (36°F), though it is slightly higher for the offshore islands. The mean July air temperature for the area is about 16°C (60°F), and total mean annual precipitation is about 254 cm (100 in.). The effect of photoperiod on plant bloom is not much of a factor in this area.

Typical plant associations from the montane screes here include *Antennaria pallida*, *Lupinus nootkatensis*, *Saxifraga tolmiei*, and *Veronica wormskjoldii*. Plants found in the alpine meadows include *Arnica latifolia*, *Cassiope lycopodioides*, *Erigeron peregrinus* subsp. *peregrinus*, and *Phyllodoce aleutica*.

# THE PACIFIC MOUNTAIN SYSTEM EXCLUDING ALASKA

The Pacific mountain system extends from Alaska to Mexico and includes the Olympic Mountains in Washington, the Coast Mountains of Canada, the Cascade Range, the Sierra Nevada of California, the Coast Ranges of Oregon and California, and numerous smaller ranges. All these ranges run from north to south, thus presenting their western flanks to the full force of the Pacific storms that bless their windward slopes with dependable precipitation in the form of rain and snow. The rainfall is heaviest on the western slopes of the Olympics of Washington in the north and gradually decreases further south into Oregon and California. Temperatures also moderate as we move southerly through this mountain system.

**The Olympic Mountains and the Coast Ranges of Oregon and California**

The coastal ranges of Washington, Oregon, and California share many common habitat features. They are all of nonvolcanic origin and contain the first peaks to intercept the rain that blows inland from the Pacific storms. They receive more precipitation than any other mountain range in America, and the temperatures of all of these ranges is moderated by the influence of the Pacific Ocean. Some of these ranges also have significant rain shadow areas on their leeward slopes. Sequim, Washington, which is located south of the northeastern slopes of the ·Olympic Mountains, has a mean annual precipitation of 43 cm (17 in.), while Quillayute, Washington, on the west side of the Olympics has a mean annual precipitation of 258 cm (103 in.). The rainforests slightly to the east of Quillayute get as much as 500 cm (200 in.) of rain a year. Temperatures are approximately the same on both the east and west sides of the Olympics—maximum mean July temperatures are 22°C (71°F) and minimum mean January temperatures are 2°C (36°F). The highest peak in the Olympics is Mount Olympus at 2428 m (7965 ft.), roughly the same height as the peaks of the coastal ranges.

Typical plants in the high screes of the eastern Olympics are *Campanula piperi*, *Douglasia laevigatia* var. *ciliolata*, *Lewisia columbiana* var. *rupicola*, and *Viola flettii*. Plants typical of the high meadows in the Olympics include *Anemone multifida* var. *saxicola*, *Aquilegia formosa*, *Erigeron flettii*, and *Erythronium montanum*.

The climate and flora of the northern Coast Range of Oregon are very similar to that of the Olympics but both change considerably as we move south to the Siskiyou Mountains in the Coast Ranges of southern Oregon and northern California. The climate here is drier with very moderate temperatures in both summer and winter. On the west side of the range, the difference between the daytime high temperature and the nighttime low temperature averages only about −7°C (20°F). North Bend, Oregon, has a maximum mean July temperature of 19°C (67°F) and a minimum mean January temperature of 5°C (40°F). The mean annual precipitation is 158 cm (63 in.) The Siskiyou Mountains also create a substantial rain shadow effect; the mean annual precipitation in Sexton, Oregon, on the east side of the mountains is only 90 cm (36 in.). Serpentine soils are common throughout this region.

Scree plants commonly found in the Siskiyou Mountains include *Fritillaria glauca*, *Horkelia hendersonii*, *Lewisia cotyledon*, *L. leeana*, and *Lupinus aridus* subsp. *ashlandensis*. Other plants in the higher grassy areas include *Dicentra formosa* subsp. *oregana*, *Dodecatheon hendersonii*, *Erigeron bloomeri*, and *Erythronium citrinum* subsp. *citrinum*.

## The Canadian Coast Range and the Cascade Range
The Canadian Coast Range and the northern Cascade Range have very similar flora and habitat. Most peaks in the range are 1845–2460 m (6000–8000 ft.) and are of nonvolcanic origin. However, the highest peaks are volcanoes. Mount Rainier in Washington is the highest at 4392 m (14,411 ft.), while Mount Shasta at the south end of the Cascades in northern California rises to 4355 m (14,160 ft.). Many other volcanoes are scattered throughout the Cascades including two that erupted during the twentieth century, Lassen Peak and Mount St. Helens. These volcanoes have produced many areas of habitat

where the predominant soils are volcanic scoria. Areas where limestone predominates are rare.

The Cascades receive substantial precipitation, although less than on the coast. Most falls as snow as the annual precipitation occurs predominantly between the months of October and May. The world record annual snowfall is currently held by Mount Baker in the north Cascades at over 2795 cm (1100 in.). Stampede Pass weather station in the heart of the Washington Cascades has a mean annual rainfall of 221 cm (87 in.) and snowfall of 1115 cm (439 in.). The mean July daily high temperature is 21°C (70°F) and the mean January daily low is −7°C (20°F). Extreme lows can drop to −29°C (−20°F). On the rain shadow side of the Cascades in Wenatchee, Washington, which lies in the heart of the Wenatchee Mountains, the mean annual precipitation is only 20 cm (8 in.). Mean July daily high temperatures are 32°C (90°F) and mean daily January low temperatures are −7°C (20°F). The total annual precipitation drops off somewhat in the southern Oregon Cascades, and the mean daily high temperatures are slightly higher.

Some of the plants found growing in the screes of the high Cascades include *Arenaria capillaris*, *Erigeron aureus*, *Ivesia gordonii*, *Penstemon davidsonii*, and *Phlox hendersonii*. The screes on the east slopes or rain shadow side support such plants as *Campanula scabrella*, *Collomia debilis*, *Draba paysonii*, *Erigeron linearis*, and *Phacelia sericea*. Plants found in the meadows of the Cascades include *Caltha biflora*, *Cassiope mertensiana*, *Erythronium grandiflorum*, *Polygonum bistortoides*, and *Pulsatilla occidentalis*.

## The Sierra Nevada

The Sierra Nevada extends over 640 km (400 miles) or most of the length of eastern California beginning near Susanville in the north and extending almost to the Gulf of California. It is primarily a range of granitic peaks with some old volcanic flows in the northern and southern ends of the range. The range tilts to the west with the steepest slopes on the east side of the range. It consists mainly of peaks ranging from 1845 to 2743 m (6000 to 8915 ft.) but is also home to over a half dozen peaks that exceed 4310 m (14,000 ft.). Mount Whitney at 4418 m (14,491 ft.) is the highest peak in the range and the highest peak in the lower 48 states.

This range covers so many different climatic areas that I must generalize when giving data regarding precipitation and temperatures. Most precipitation in the range falls as snow. Mean annual precipitation in the northern end of the range is between 76 cm (30 in.) and 152 cm (60 in.), with mean annual temperatures of 7°C–13°C (45°F–55°F). The central and north portions of the range have about the same mean annual precipitation with mean annual temperatures of −1°C–5°C (30°F–40°F) around the Lake Tahoe area. The southern end of the range near the Kern Plateau has mean annual precipitation of 25–76 cm

(10–30 in.) and a mean annual temperature of 2°C–13°C (35°F–55°F). The flora is quite different from the north to the south end of the range.

Some plants growing in screes in the north include *Leptodactylon pungens*, *Lewisia sierrae*, *Pellaea bridgesii*, and *Penstemon heterodoxus* var. *heterodoxus*. Growing in the southern end of the range are *Eriogonum kennedyi*, *Heuchera abramsii*, *Lupinus excubitus* var. *austromontanus*, and *Nama rothrockii*.

## THE GREAT BASIN

The Great Basin is another very large area of alpine habitat. It covers about 492,100 square kilometers (190,000 square miles) and is home to about 400 separate mountain ranges with most of these ranges running on an east to west axis and forming a sort of washboard topography. This area received its name because it has no outlet to the sea and so all the precipitation runoff collects in terminal lakes and marshes such as the Great Salt Lake. The general boundaries of the Great Basin are the Columbia Plateau of Washington and Oregon to the north, the Rockies and the Colorado Plateau to the east, the Sonoran Desert to the south, and the Sierra Nevada to the west. These boundaries are well defined in the east and west but are more subtle with broader transition zones in the north and south. The Great Basin includes the entire state of Nevada and parts of Oregon, Utah, Arizona, and California. At the point where Mount Whitney in the Sierra Nevada drops off to Death Valley in the Great Basin lies one of the greatest extremes in topography in the United States—a difference of about 4494 m (14,740 ft.) in only 134 km (84 miles).

The mountains of the Great Basin are home to hundreds of species of alpine plants including more than 74 species and subspecies of *Eriogonum* and many of the finest species of *Penstemon*. These dryland species thrive here because of the low annual precipitation and high solar radiation at the higher elevations. The Sierra Nevada intercepts most of the moisture from the Pacific Ocean, and the southern Rockies block most of the moisture from the Gulf of Mexico, and yet the peaks of the eastern Great Basin receive more moisture from the Gulf than the Great Basin's peaks in the west receive from the Pacific. The Great Basin receives an average annual precipitation of 18–30 cm (7–12 in.) with more falling in the mountains than on the desert floor.

The mountains of the Great Basin have been referred to as montane islands in a sea of desert shrubs. These mountains are home to many endemic plants that have been unable to spread to other ranges because of the areas of dry desert that lie between the peaks. The mountains are also refuges for the alpine plant communities of the Pleistocene epoch. These communities were much more widespread during the wetter, cooler conditions that prevailed during the Pleistocene epoch, which occurred between 10,000 and 1.6 million years ago and was characterized by widespread glacial ice. Only one true glacier now remains in the entire Great Basin. True alpine tundra occurs in small local areas of the highest ranges such as the Toiyabe, the White Mountains, the Sweetwater Range, and the Toquima Range. Alpinelike conditions where talus slopes and rocky ridges prevail are found in the Spring Mountains, the Santa Rosa Range, and Steens Mountain. The most diverse alpine plant communities are found in the White and Spring Mountains.

A great diversity exists in the makeup of these isolated ranges. The western peaks are predominately granite, as is the adjoining Sierra Nevada. The peaks in the northwest are mostly basalt. Rhyolite predominates in the central peaks, and we find limestone in the eastern and southern ranges. The highest peaks in the Great Basin are about 3660–4260 m (11,895–13,845 ft.). None of these ranges is of recent volcanic origin.

Just as there is a steady decrease in precipitation from north to south, there is a concurrent rise in mean annual temperatures. Salt Lake City, Utah, has a mean annual precipitation of 41 cm (16¼ in.) with mean annual high temperatures in July of 33°C (92°F) and mean annual lows in January of −6°C (21°F). Las Vegas, Nevada, has mean annual precipitation of 9 cm (3½ in.) with mean annual high temperatures in July of 38°C (100°F) and mean annual lows in January of 2°C (35°F).

Among the best known alpine plants in the Great Basin include *Aquilegia scopulorum*, *Erigeron compactus* var. *consimilis*, *Gilia caespitosa*, *Lepidium nanum*, *Lesquerella tumulosa*, *Penstemon leiophyllus* var. *francisci-pennellii*, and *Townsendia condensata*.

## THE ROCKIES

The Rockies are among North America's most spectacular geographical features. Often referred to as the "backbone of America," the Rockies extend for over 3200 km (2000 miles) from northern British Columbia to New Mexico. They are relatively young, which accounts for the abundance of very high peaks with steep, jagged features. The vast reach of mountains from north to south ensures a great diversity of climate and habitat. Most authorities divide the Rockies into four general areas, the northern Rockies, the middle Rockies, the southern Rockies, and the Colorado Plateau.

### The Northern Rockies
The northern Rockies stretch from near the Yukon—British Columbia border in the north to the Montana—Wyoming border in the south and range from about 120 km (75 miles) wide in the far north to about 400 km (250 miles) wide in the south. The highest peak here is Mount Robson at 3955 m (12,855

ft.). Almost all the peaks of the northern Rockies are alpine tundra with winter lows of as much as −46°C (-50°F) and precipitation ranging from about 50–140 cm (20–50 in.). The northern Rockies receive more precipitation on average than the southern regions with most of the precipitation falling in the form of snow. Many large glaciers and ice fields are still found here, although areas in western Idaho are relatively mild owing to the influence of the Pacific Ocean.

Included within the northern Rockies are parts of British Columbia and Alberta, Canada, portions of Washington, Idaho, and Montana, and a small area of Wyoming. The mean annual precipitation for Spokane, Washington, which lies near the center of this area, is 42 cm (16½ in.). The mean annual July high temperature is 29°C (85°F) and the mean annual January low temperature is −6°C (21°F).

Plants found growing in the far north of this region include such arctic alpines as *Arnica lessingii*, *Delphinium glaucum*, *Potentilla biflora*, and *Rhododendron lapponicum*. In the southern end of this region we find *Aquilegia jonesii*, *Douglasia montana*, *Dryas octopetala*, *Phyllodoce glanduliflora*, and *Smelowskia calycina*.

## The Middle Rockies

The middle Rockies are home to some of the most beautiful peaks in North America and include the Teton Range, the Beartooth Range, and the Bighorn Mountains. The highest peak in the region is Gannett Peak at 4208 m (13,804 ft.) in the Wind River Range of Wyoming. Almost all the higher peaks in the middle Rockies contain areas of alpine tundra, which is generally found between 2155–3075 m (7000–10,000 ft.). This region is generally drier than either the northern or southern Rockies and hosts large areas of sagebrush between the major ranges.

The middle Rockies include portions of the states of Montana, Colorado, Idaho, and Utah. The mean annual precipitation for Sheridan, Wyoming, near the middle of this region is 37 cm (14½ in.). The mean annual July high temperature is 31°C (88°F) and the mean annual January low temperature is −12°C (10°F).

Alpine plants that grow in this region include *Antennaria lanata*, *Erigeron humilis*, *Pedicularis oederi*, *Shoshonea pulvinata*, and *Telesonix jamesii*.

## The Southern Rockies

Most of the highest peaks in western North America are found in the southern Rockies. More than 50 peaks in the Rockies exceed 4310 m (14,000 ft.) and all are in the state of Colorado. The highest of these is Mount Elbert with an elevation of 4400 m (14,433 ft.). This region includes large, flat, parklike areas at about 3075 m (10,000 ft.) in elevation that are surrounded by higher peaks.

Portions of the southern Rockies were never buried under the glaciers of the Ice Age and so are home to older flora than the northern and middle Rockies.

This region features a classic continental climate with rather low precipitation that falls as torrential thunderstorms and then runs off before it can be utilized by the plants. Bright sun and windy conditions contribute to a high evaporation rate that leaves little moisture for the plants. This region is also characterized by frequent winter warm spells followed by intense cold. Denver, Colorado, has a mean annual precipitation of 39 cm (15½ in.) with a mean annual July high temperatures of 32°C (90°F). Mean annual January lows are −8°C (18°F).

The alpine plants in the southern Rockies include *Erigeron pinnatisectus*, *Eritrichum nanum*, *Hymenoxys grandiflora*, *Phlox condensata*, *Potentilla nivea*, and *Thlaspi montanum*.

### The Colorado Plateau

The Colorado Plateau is located at the southern end of the Rockies and includes portions of the states of Utah, Colorado, Arizona, and New Mexico. The area is made up mostly of high table land cut through by deep canyons, including the Grand Canyon. The highest peaks are found in ranges scattered throughout the region; among the highest is Humphreys Peak at 3851 m (12,633 ft.) in the San Francisco Mountains of Arizona.

This is an arid region with most precipitation falling at higher elevations, primarily as winter snow. The city of Flagstaff, Arizona, has mean annual precipitation of 58 cm (23 in.) with a mean annual July high temperature of 28°C (82°F). The mean annual January low temperature is −8°C (18°F).

Plants in the region of the Colorado Plateau include *Hymenoxys acaulis*, *Penstemon eatonii*, *P. utahensis*, *Phlox longifolia*, and *Townsendia incana*.

### Summary

Western North America is home to some of the finest and most demanding alpine plants in the world. Anyone who is interested in growing these plants successfully and in character should attempt to learn as much as possible about each plant's natural habitat. (In order to help you do that, I provide information on a plant's flowering time as it occurs in its native habitat.) A difference of just 48 km (30 miles) from the west to the east side of a mountain range can mean the difference between 254 cm (100 in.) and 38 cm (15 in.) of precipitation a year as well as a difference of 25 degrees in winter low temperatures. A basic knowledge of these variations can make the difference between success and failure for the grower.

# AN ENCYCLOPEDIA OF MOUNTAIN FLOWERS FROM THE ROCKIES TO ALASKA

Mount Goliath Pesman trail, Colorado.

# A

## ANDROSACE
### Primulaceae
*rock jasmines*

Whether as mats, cushions, or mounds, androsaces have always been favorites among alpines. Europe abounds with androsaces, some of which are classics. My focus is on the American species that can be listed among the classics.

*Androsace chamaejasme* is circumpolar and grows not only in the Rockies but also in Alaska, although its forms vary from location to location. It spreads by short stolons with new growth emerging each year, and the height of the flower stem varies from 2.5 to 8 cm (1 to 3 in.).

I once found a superb plant of subsp. *lehmanniana* at the edge of the lower parking lot on the Mount Goliath Pesman trail, Mount Evans, Colorado. It was growing on an embankment created by the waste soil thrown there when the lot was built, and snowmelt runoff at the bottom of the embankment keeps the soil moist. The plant makes a mat about 50 cm (20 in.) long and 25 cm (10 in.) wide and is covered with almost stemless white flowers, most of which have a yellow eye. The rosettes are tightly packed, and flowers that were past their best had turned pink or red. Although I also saw *Hymenoxys acaulis* and *Polemoniun viscosum* during my hike, *Androsace chamaejasme* subsp. *lehmanniana* stood out as the best.

Although the plant I saw on Mount Evans had quite short stems, the form of *Androsace chamaejasme* I grow has 7.5-cm (3-in.) tall stems and large white flowers.

Some publications list this species as subsp. *carinata* or just *A. carinata*, but see the entry on *A. chamaejasme* subsp. *lehmannian*a and Sylvia (Tass) Kelso's observations.

*Androsace lehmanniana* also causes some confusion. It is closely related to *A. chamaejasme*, and the *Flora of Alaska* records it as *A. chamaejasme* subsp. *lehmanniana*. It forms loose tufts, close mats, or cushions with white flowers that are either stemless or on very short stems.

I grow only one plant each of *Androsace chamaejasme* and *A. lehmanniana*, so it is difficult to observe many differences between them. However, the *A. lehmanniana* I have grown from seed collected in Alaska is not stoloniferous and increases by rosettes each year unlike my plant of *A. chamaejasme*.

Tass Kelso, professor of botany at Colorado College, notes that the Rocky Mountain representatives of *Androsace chamaejasme* have previously been classified as subsp. *carinata* on the basis of a single character, an apparently prominent keel on the leaf blade occurring on tight leaf rosettes. Although this character does appear on the type from Pikes Peak in Colorado as well as on other plants growing in similarly exposed

*Androsace chamaejasme* subsp. *lehmanniana* near the parking lot at Mount Goliath Pesman trail, Colorado.

sites on the tundra, it disappears as the leaves flatten and the rosettes expand when plants are transplanted to protected sites in low elevation gardens. In environmentally benign habitats, the leaves become identical to those of subsp. *lehmanniana* that grow in protected sites in Alaska, Canada, and the Rockies. Since the distinguishing character of keeled (carinate) leaves is environmentally induced, it is best to treat all of the North American individuals as *A. chamaejasme* subsp. *lehmanniana*.

### Propagation

When it is available, you can propagate plants of this genus by seed that you sow in spring and then make a selection from the variety of forms that are produced. Germination is a bit spasmodic so be careful not to disturb seedlings about to germinate when you are pricking out other seedlings.

Propagation by cuttings is quite simple. New rosettes start to grow when flowering finishes, and as soon as they are large enough (around June or July), cut them off with a piece of stem attached and insert them into moist sand in a cutting frame. They usually root in four to eight weeks.

I also take androsace cuttings in autumn since some root over winter and I repot them in spring. Those that have failed to root do so as soon as spring arrives.

The *Androsace* Society offers a very good seed exchange of not only American species but also rarities from around the world.

### Cultivation

The best way to grow androsaces in the open garden is on a piece of tufa in either a trough or on a small rock garden. Many of us are reluctant to grow androsaces outside rather than inside an alpine house, especially if we have only a few plants. Nevertheless, they do grow much better in the open air, especially when rain falls during the growing season and good air circulation is maintained. Protect the plants during winter by constructing some form of cover or moving them inside. Androsaces make excellent pot plants, and the North American species are no exception as long as they have deep enough top dressing or rock tucked under their rosettes to allow air to circulate freely.

Aphids, especially whiteflies, can be active all year round on plants in the alpine

*Androsace chamaejasme* subsp. *lehmanniana*, Kantishna Hills, Alaska. Photo Carolyn Parker.

*Androsace chamaejasme* subsp. *lehmanniana*, St. Paul Island, Bering Sea. Photo Carolyn Parker.

house, so check the leaf undersides as often as possible (these pests are not as prevalent in the open garden). The only way to get rid of them is with a weak drench of a systemic insecticide. Plants in the alpine house are also more likely to suffer a fungus attack during autumn and winter, although with enough air movement this is less likely. Remove any affected rosettes immediately.

## ANEMONE
Ranunculaceae
*windflowers*

Some 120 species of *Anemone* are widely distributed around the world but most are in the Northern Hemisphere. Approximately 14 species grow in the Rockies. Anemones are either rhizomatous or tuberous with mostly palmately or pinnately divided basal leaves. The flowers do not have petals but are composed of sepals that look much like petals and range in color from white to cream, yellow, blue, or purple The fruiting heads can be oblong or rounded, very woolly or silky. This most attractive plant does well in the open garden.

*Anemone canadensis* grows on grassland and in woody areas from Labrador to Colorado. It has long, stalked, basal leaves and a stout stem that grows to 60 cm (24 in.) with white star-shaped flowers 2.5–3.8 (1–1½ in.) across in spring through summer. This vigorous plant is more suitable for the woodland garden than the rock garden.

*Anemone drummondii* grows on dry, rocky ledges, scree slopes, and fell-fields to around 3690 m (12,000 ft.) from Alaska to California and the Rocky Mountain areas of Idaho and Montana. It has finely divided basal leaves and stems 20 cm (8 in.) tall, and

the solitary white flower in May through August is 1–3.5 cm (½–1.4 in.) across and tinged green, blue, or lavender on the underside. The fruiting head is rounded, densely woolly and silky. In Alaska this species is very blue on the underside; it was named for Thomas Drummond, a Scottish botanist who collected plants in the early 1800s.

*Anemone globosa*, a species closely related to *A. parviflora*, ranges from Alaska to California and New Mexico in high valleys and mountain areas. The basal leaves are divided and lobed with slender stems to 30 cm (12 in.), and the flowers are greenish yellow to deep purple. The fruiting head is globose.

*Anemone multiceps* grows in Alaska and is very rare. Originally thought to be a color variation of *A. drummondii* as it inhabits the same area, it is much smaller and looks like a tiny pulsatilla. Blooming is late May through early August.

*Anemone multifida* grows in rocky soils and rock crevices at high elevations from Alaska and the Yukon to California, southern Nevada, Arizona, and New Mexico. It is also found in southern South America. It is tufted with long-stalked, trilobed basal leaves that are further lobed and toothed.

*Anemone drummondii*, Denali National Park, Alaska. Photo Verna Pratt.

Hairy stems grow 5–50 cm (2–20 in.) tall, each with one to three white, cream, or pale yellow to yellow flowers in May through August that are tinged with red, blue, or purple. A wide variation in color within a population may occur, and one form in cultivation has reddish flowers. The fruiting head is rounded and woolly haired.

*Anemone narcissiflora* inhabits high mountain meadows, often on limestone, in Colorado, north-central Wyoming, Alaska, and the Aleutian Islands. It also grows in central and southern Europe. The basal leaves are deeply divided with hairy stems growing 10–40 cm (4–15¾ in.) tall. Whitish to lemon-yellow flowers in early June through mid-August are occasionally flushed pink on the exterior. The flowers have yellow anthers and may be solitary or in umbels of three to eight. The fruiting head is

glabrous and globose with smooth black fruits.

Subspecies *monantha* (synonyms subsp. *alaskana*, subsp. *interior*) inhabits dry heaths and stony slopes in Alaska. It grows to 15 cm (6 in.) tall with a slender stem and mostly single flowers that are white on the outside.

Subspecies *villosissima* grows in Alaska's meadows, primarily in the Aleutian Islands. A coarse plant that grows to 35 cm (14 in.) tall, it has several spreading basal leaves that are ciliated in the margin, orbicular or kidney-shaped in outline, and divided into five sessile parts. There are several large white or creamy white flowers.

*Anemone oregana*, which is similar to *A. nemorosa*, ranges from northern Washington to central Oregon, inhabiting open woods and brushy hillsides. It spreads by

*Anemone multiceps*, Eagle Summit, Alaska. Photo Verna Pratt.

*Anemone narcissiflora* subsp. *monantha*, Denali National Park, Alaska. Photo Verna Pratt.

underground stems and grows 10–30 cm (4–12 in.) tall. It has one leaf at the base and three deeply divided and toothed leaves in a whorl on the stem. The bluish lavender to reddish lavender or pale pink flowers in March through June are 2.5–3.8 cm (1–1½ in.) wide.

Variety *felix* has a limited range in Oregon, where it is considered very rare, but is more plentiful in Washington's bogs and marshy areas. The leaves are ternate and the stems grow 15–30 cm (6–12 in.) tall. White flowers in March through June have purplish areas on the exterior. More than 60 stamens help distinguish it from the type.

'Ellensburg Blue' with dark blue flowers is a Rick Lupp selection of the species from the eastern Washington Cascades at 1230 m (4000 ft.).

*Anemone parviflora* is circumboreal, ranging from Alaska and the Yukon to Oregon, Idaho, Utah, and Colorado. Alaskan habitats include meadows, heaths, stony slopes, and snowbeds at 615 m (2000 ft.) in the St. Elias Mountains. It also grows as far down as the upper reaches of the forest region. South of Alaska it grows to 3050 m (9915 ft.) in spruce and fir communities and along mountain streams and meadows. Dark green basal leaves are lustrous, glabrous, and divided into trilobed, bluntly toothed parts. The stems are white-pubescent and grow 5–20 cm (2–8 in.) tall. Small white to cream flowers in June through August are solitary and have a bluish underside. The fruiting head is globose or ovoid and densely woolly.

Variety *grandiflora* usually grows in Alaska and has larger flowers 3–4 cm (1¼–1½ in.) in diameter.

*Anemone richardsonii* grows in the mountains of Alaska to at least 1000 m (3250 ft.), where it inhabits moist woods, thickets, and meadows. From underground horizontal rhizomes grow stems 7.5–15 cm (3–6 in.) tall with long-stemmed, trilobed leaves. The lobes are divided again and have shallow teeth. Single flowers in May through late July are bright yellow, and the sepals are brownish on the underside. The fruiting head is globose.

*Anemone tuberosa* grows in Utah, California, Arizona, and New Mexico. It grows in mixed desert scrub and juniper at 800–1650 m (2600–5365 ft.) and is quite common in California's deserts. It has silky, hairy to glabrous basal leaves 5–15 cm (2–6 in.) long that are ternate with deeply parted leaflets. Stems grow 8–50

Cream form of *Anemone parviflora* var. *grandiflora*. Chugach Mountains, Alaska. Photo Verna Pratt.

White form of *Anemone parviflora* var. *grandiflora*. Denali National Park, Alaska. Photo Verna Pratt.

cm (3–20 in.) tall from tuberous rhizomes and have light pink, upright flowers in March through May. The fruiting head is cylindrical.

**Propagation**

Propagate these species by seed, preferably as soon as it is ripe, although you might struggle to separate the woolly seed. The seedlings grow very slowly and are best left in the seed pot for a couple of years before pricking out. You can increase the rhizomatous species by lifting and dividing the rhizomes in autumn or early spring before growth commences.

**Cultivation**

Most species grow well in the rock garden with no special care, and plants left

*Anemone richardsonii*, Chugach Mountains, Alaska. Photo Verna Pratt.

undisturbed grow into large clumps. If *Anemone oregana* gets too wet over winter the rhizomes rot off; however, it requires plenty of moisture in the spring while in growth.

Slugs are the only pest problems I have encountered.

## AQUILEGIA
Ranunculaceae
*columbines*

*Aquilegia* is a circumpolar genus of great beauty and variety. Columbines are fixtures not only of wild places around the upper latitudes of the world, but also of gardens everywhere. Many of you are familiar with showy hybrid columbines, some of which are related to the *Aquilegia* species I describe. You should, however, also consider the merits of some American species as many are suitable for woodland gardens and may grow to 60 cm (24 in.). Others are lovely alpine species suitable for troughs or cultivation in the alpine house and may challenge your growing skills. Challenging or not, aquilegias are undeniably beautiful whether in the wild or in a garden.

Group of *Aquilegia caerulea*, Red Mountain Pass, Colorado. Photo Chris Norton.

*Aquilegia barnebyi*, the shale columbine, is endemic to Utah's Uinta Basin, where it grows in the oil shale barrens at an altitude of 1675–2255 m (5445–7330 ft.). It has very distinctive blue, sticky, glaucous foliage and small flowers in mid-June through early July with yellow petals and pink sepals. It usually grows 20–30 cm (8–12 in.) tall but occasionally reaches 80 cm (32 in.). Very similar in appearance to *A. flavescens*, it has a shorter tuft of basal leaves and the sepals are shorter than the spurs. A fairly easy species to grow in a rock garden, it probably needs winter protection in wet areas. This species is sometimes available from the commercial seed lists, but most seed is from garden-grown plants.

*Aquilegia brevistyla* grows from western Canada to Colorado. Will Ingwersen (1978) describes it as a "rather undistinguished American species with small, short-spurred cream and blue flowers." Barr (1983) reported it being plentiful from near the northern Canadian border to the Yukon Territory as well as in the Black Hills. A rarely cultivated species, it grows 20–80 cm (8–32 in.) tall and is reportedly closely related to *A. saximontana*.

*Aquilegia caerulea*, a true alpine, inhabits the Rockies from Montana to Arizona and New Mexico to 3550 m (11,540 ft.). Although growing to a roadside height of 60 cm (24 in.) at lower elevation, at high altitudes it normally grows no more than 20 cm (8 in.) high; on exposed alpine slopes, however, it occasionally reaches 40 cm (15¾ in.). Some reports state that the high-altitude plants are more colorful. It is the famous Colorado state flower, and photographs of this plant appear on the cover of many wildflower books. In addition to seeds from plants with blue and white flowers,

Close-up of white form of *Aquilegia caerulea*. Brighton, Utah. Photo Peter Downe.

*Aquilegia caerulea* at the roadside near Vail, Colorado.

seeds of white forms have been available in at least one commercial list, although I have had limited success with the white forms. *Aquilegia caerulea* is used as a parent for many long-spurred hybrid aquilegias, including the Scott-Elliott strain. A spurless mutant of this strain is improperly named *A. clematiflora* and it grows 20–40 cm (8–15¾ in.) in height with deep reddish purple flowers.

Two varieties include the spurless var. *daileyae* that was named for plants in the Estes Park area of the Rocky Mountain National Park, Colorado, and var. *ochroleuca*, which grows on the Wasatch Plateau in Utah at 3260 m (10,600 ft.), that has huge white flowers with orange-yellow anthers and is well worth cultivating.

'Crimson Star' has red and white flowers.

*Aquilegia chaplinei* is a moisture lover, and although a close relative of *A. chrysantha*, grows further south in the mainly shady, moist cliff faces of New Mexico. The pale yellow flowers with long spurs are on stems that, at 30 cm (12 in.) tall, make it look like a smaller form of *A. chrysantha*.

*Aquilegia chrysantha* occurs throughout the Southwest at an altitude of about 1340 m (4355 ft.) inhabiting stream and seep margins and other moist sites. It is consequently more tolerant of sun and heat than many other species. I once saw this plant's large golden flowers glowing against a background of wet, deep green leaves on 90-cm (36-in.) stems tucked alone between two rocks near Weeping Rock in Zion Canyon, Utah. Water dripped onto every part of the plant from the overhanging rock face.

This species hybridizes with *Aquilegia formosa*, and multicolored populations hang in damp gardens such as the one in Zion Canyon. A cultivar of this species named 'Yellow Queen' has soft yellow flowers.

*Aquilegia elegantula* grows on moist slopes and woods throughout the southern Rockies in Colorado, New Mexico, and Utah at an altitude of 1735–2745 m

*Aquilegia elegantula*, Sierra Blanca, New Mexico. Photo Ev Whittemore.

Close-up of *Aquilegia chrysantha* at Weeping Rock, Zion National Park, Utah.

(5640–8920 ft.). It reaches 10–30 cm (4–12 in.) in height and has red and yellow flowers similar to the eastern *A. canadensis*, although some reports describe plants with pure red flowers. It is rarely seen in cultivation.

*Aquilegia flavescens* grows throughout the Southwest, extending much further north than *A. chrysantha* into Washington, Oregon, Utah, and Colorado at an altitude of 1370–3265 m (4450–10,610 ft.). It has short, pale, yellow, or sometimes pink flowers. A close relative of *A. formosa* but a little shorter at 20–70 cm (8–28 in.), this species grows in alpine meadows and screes and is among the easiest to grow in either sun or shade.

Variety *rubicunda* grows at 2255–2500 m (7330–8125 ft.) and is endemic to Emery and Sevier counties of Utah. It has smaller flowers, and a lovely dwarf form grows in Glacier National Park.

*Aquilegia formosa* is perhaps the most widespread species in the West. In the Sierra Nevada it grows at an altitude of 1230–3075 m (4000–10,000 ft.). In 1990 I traveled to Summit Meadow in Yosemite Park where the previous year's good snowfall meant the meadow was full of *Camassia leichtlinii*, *Dodecatheon jeffreyi*, and *Polygonum bistortoides*. As I was leaving a flash of red and yellow caught my eye—a delightful *A. formosa* tucked away at the foot of a tree near the road, the long-petalled flowers seeking the attention of a hawkmoth for pollination. The stems were quite tall at 100 cm (39 in.) but they can grow to 120 cm (48 in.). I was lucky to find it here as it normally grows along seeps and mountain streams. This species is a good one for the perennial border, where it usually grows to only 90 cm (36 in.).

Variety *truncata* (synonym *A. eximia*) grows in southern Oregon, Nevada, and California. A very elegant though rarely cultivated plant, it has long stamens that protrude from the delicate flowers.

Variety *wawawensis* has pale salmon or yellow flowers and grows to 35 cm (14 in.). Seed of this subspecies collected at an elevation of 1000 m (3250 ft.) from Snake River

*Aquilegia flavescens* growing in Cooke City, Montana. Photo Peter Downe.

*Aquilegia formosa* near Hemlock Butte, Oregon.

Canyon, Washington, was offered by Rocky Mountain Rare Plants.

*Aquilegia grahamii* is endemic to eastern Utah's shaded canyons at 2320 m (7540 ft.). Originally thought to be a pink form of *A. scopulorum*, it has since been identified as *A. grahamii*. It is 25–60 cm (10–24 in.) tall when growing beneath the wet, hanging gardens that spill from Weber sandstone cliffs but in cultivation it is only 15 cm (6 in.). It has pink-white blooms with some yellow markings and very long spurs. Superb in a sunny crevice or scree, its flowering season is long and it sets a reasonable amount of seed.

*Aquilegia jonesii*, the limestone columbine, grows at high altitudes throughout the

Rockies on exposed limestone screes. Undoubtedly the star of the genus, it is the smallest of the alpine columbines with tiny blue-green, lobed leaves in dense tufts and stems growing 2.5–10 cm (1–4 in.). The terminal, purple to deep blue solitary flowers look straight up at you and sometimes seem lost in the foliage. Even without the flowers, the foliage is superb.

Jerry DeSanto (1991) has written of a form of *Aquilegia jonesii* growing in Glacier National Park, Montana, that has a variation in color. He reported seeing plants that have white flowers with lavender tips as well as a pure white form, and he speculates that *A. flavescens* may have had some influence since it occurs together with *A. jonesii* at lower elevations within the park. His splendid photos accompanying the article are of plants we all would love to grow whether or

*Aquilegia grahamii.*

*Aquilegia jonesii* in a typical limestone scree area in the Big Horn Mountains, Wyoming. Photo Ev Whittemore.

*Aquilegia jonesii*, Hunt Mountain, Big Horn Mountains, Wyoming. Photo Chris Norton.

not they are hybrids. *Aquilegia jonesii* is a
beauty for the trough or piece of tufa, and
except for *Eritrichium* must be the biggest
challenge to alpine growers.

*Aquilegia laramiensis* is an endemic of
the Laramie Mountains of Wyoming and
covers a wide range of altitudes from
coniferous woodlands to 3000 m (9750
ft.). At high altitudes it grows in granite
rock fissures. It keeps a neat and compact
habit in cultivation and thus is perfect for
troughs. One reference gives the height as
5–25 cm (2–10 in.) but all the plants I have
grown have been under 15 cm (6 in.). In
April, small, pure white flowers hang
downwards like lanterns, although sometimes they can become hidden in the
foliage. Seed is set freely and the resultant
plants come true.

*Aquilegia longissima* grows in New
Mexico and western Texas. Although
usually short-lived, it is a spectacular plant
that blooms during summer with large,
bright yellow flowers and spurs that can be
as long as 8 cm (3 in.) on stems 40–60 cm
(15 ¾–24 in.) tall. It is easy in cultivation as
it does not require alpine house treatment
and is such a lovely plant that I grow several
of them in pots around the patio. It also sets
plenty of seed.

The $F_1$ hybrid 'Music' has larger
flowers.

*Aquilegia micrantha* is endemic to the
Colorado Plateau, where it inhabits the
shady seeps in sandstone rock crevices on
canyon walls at 1125–1895 m (3655–6160
ft.). Growing 30–60 cm (12–24 in.), it has
sprays of small, pale blue, cream, or white
flowers. It rarely appears in seed lists.

*Aquilegia pubescens* is native to high-
altitude regions at 2770–4000 m
(9000–13,000 ft.) of the Sierra Nevada,
where the purple-tinted cream blooms
appear from June through August. It is often
found in close proximity to *A. formosa* and in
Yosemite's rock crevices above the tree line.
Occasionally the hawkmoth lands on the
pale yellow stamens of *A. pubescens* after visiting *A. formosa*; the resulting hybrids can
occur in a variety of colors from creamy
white to pink, yellow, or lavender. Although
*A. pubescens* is shorter than *A. formosa* at
10–60 cm (4–24 in.), it has larger flowers
that are 3.8–5 cm (1½–2 in.) across.

*Aquilegia saximontana*, the Rocky
Mountain columbine, is found in the wild
throughout the Rocky Mountain screes and
alpine regions of Colorado. Growing 10–15
cm (4–6 in.) tall among rocks that shelter it
from harsh conditions, it resembles a dwarf

*Aquilegia laramiensis.*

*Aquilegia longissima*, Royal Botanic Gardens,
Kew.

version of *A. caerulea* with blue and yellow-ish white flowers in July. In spite of this harsh habitat, it is an easy selection for the scree garden or trough. Plants more than five years old grow in one of my alpine beds, and the clump increases in size each year. This is another species that crosses freely in the garden, and seed offered from garden-grown plants often results in hybrids.

*Aquilegia scopulorum* grows in Utah and Nevada among the alpine tundra communities of limestone screes at 2100–3400 m (6825–11,050 ft.). Although it grows 5–45 cm (2–18 in.) high in the wild, it is the dwarf form we all recognize. The bluish foliage, spurs that are the longest in the genus, and pink to lavender-blue to rich blue flowers with yellow stamens make it a most desirable plant. Some say it is easier to grow than *A. jonesii* but in my experience it has been easier only to flower; both species need careful treatment in cultivation. *Aquilegia scopulorum* grows well in a trough or scree bed but does not like too much winter moisture. I tried growing it in tufa, and although it does well there, it still needs winter protection. Although seed of *A. scopulorum* is often offered in seed exchanges, it is very rarely correct, and like *A. saximontana*, is

usually a hybrid of some form. I recommend you buy it from a commercial list that offers wild-collected seed.

*Aquilegia shockleyi* grows to 20–30 cm (8–12 in.) in California. It is a dainty plant with yellow and red flowers similar to those of *A. elegantula* and *A. canadensis*. Once quite rare, it is now in general cultivation and appears to be easy to grow.

**Propagation**

Seed is the only realistic way of propagating the alpine species of this genus. However, obtaining true seed is always a problem. So much seed in the exchanges comes from garden-collected seed of uncertain origin, but *Aquilegia laramiensis* from garden-collected seed has always come true for me.

For seed of these alpine species I highly recommend the commercial lists for their offerings of wild-collected seed. If you already have the plant of a herbaceous species and it has made a reasonable clump, divide and replant it very carefully in spring. Divisions do not always grow readily so be prepared for some fatalities. Sow wild-collected seed of the herbaceous species in autumn for spring germination; I find that seed I sow in the spring rarely germinates

*Aquilegia saximontana.*

*Aquilegia scopulorum*, Mount Washington, Nevada. Photo David Hale.

until the following year. If you want to collect your own seed, periodically check the pods by squeezing them between your thumb and forefinger. Although the pods may still be green, once they split the seeds are ripe. Cut the pods from the stems, turn them over into a seed packet, and leave them to dry off. All the seed eventually falls out. Many pods are quite sticky when green, and if you try to remove seed then it can get tricky. If you wait until the pods are brown before picking them, much of the seed has probably fallen out and blown away.

## Cultivation

All the species die back in winter. Most herbaceous species are happy in a sunny position with well-drained soil that does not dry out. Even the exceptions I have mentioned that grow naturally in shade can take some sun.

*Aquilegia scopulorum* grows best in the alpine house or in a trough that can be protected from winter wet. A gritty, well-drained soil mixture is required, as is a situation in full sun. There is no trouble in flowering this species, and it makes a good exhibition plant.

*Aquilegia jonesii*, as well as being the smallest in the genus, presents the biggest problem when it comes to blooming. For a

start, the plant is slow growing, so it is difficult to know its age and whether it is mature enough to bloom or not. I recommend you keep a record of sowing and germination dates. Over winter it dies down to a tiny twiggy clump. Do not overwater it otherwise the plant will rot off from the center.

I always assume that once the plant is two or more years old it should bloom, and although my rule of thumb is not foolproof, it has given me some success. In Timsbury where I live, I grow *Aquilegia jonesii* in a pot in the alpine house, but as soon as it comes into growth in spring I put the pot up against the glass facing the sun so it can get as much sun as possible. I give it about 0.6 liter (½ pint) of water every day, and as the soil mixture is very gritty the water practically runs straight through. I use plenty of limestone chippings in the soil mixture and feed the plant monthly with a tomato fertilizer or something similar. Lincoln Foster (1968) suggests feeding *A. jonesii* with bone meal and dry manure. Another method worth trying is neglect. A customer bought a plant from me in about 1998, potted and then plunged it in his alpine house, and forgot about it. After a while the bottom roots

Blue form of *Aquilegia scopulorum*. Butch Cassidy Draw, Utah. Photo Chris Norton.

Pink form of *Aquilegia scopulorum*.

grew into the sand plunge. The plant grew well for two years, eventually becoming pot bound. In the third year it flowered with 24 blooms, proving that the other vital ingredient you need is luck!

Powdery mildew seems to be the biggest problem and not only in the alpine house, although it is more prevalent there especially in a damp atmosphere. In the open garden slugs may nibble the new growth in spring, and when the plants are in full growth, caterpillars can strip a plant's foliage down to a skeleton. If you systematically spray at the first sight of the pest, you will prevent your plants from such a stripping.

## ASTRAGALUS
Leguminosae, or Fabaceae
*locoweeds, vetches*

I cannot think of any other genus that produces as many species and satisfies as many tastes as astragalus. Flower color varies from a vivid scarlet to a delicate shade of lavender with yellows, whites, and purples in between, and the leaves, whether on buns, mats, or upright stems, can be a beautiful silky silver. Many species have attractive inflated seedpods, some of which are horned or curved and brightly mottled in a range of vivid colors. Several species have huge pods resembling birds' eggs. The wild habitat for most *Astragalus* species is dry, gritty sandstone or limestone soils in exposed places. Poisonous chemicals in the soil give rise to one of the common names for the astragalus, locoweed. Most species grow in areas with arsenic or selenium in the soil, and the uptake of these chemicals makes the plant poisonous to man, cattle, and horses through its affect on the brain. The Spanish word *loco* means crazy. Another common

name—rattleweed—refers to the sound of ripe seeds in pods that are being shaken.

The majority of the astragalus species grow throughout Utah, Arizona, Nevada, California, and the Great Plains, although three species grow in Alaska. Those that inhabit Utah are not as compact as some Great Plains species but they are still dwarf enough to satisfy the most demanding plant hunter.

The genus contains so many different species that to cover all of them would be impractical. Instead I describe species that either I have grown or that are considered the most desirable. They can be divided into those that are cushion, bun, or mat forming and those that are more upright.

*Astragalus amphioxys* grows among desert shrub and sagebrush at 670–1530 m (2178–4975 ft.) in Nevada, Utah, Arizona, and New Mexico. Although it reaches a height of 35 cm (14 in.), the compact forms can be as short as 2.5 cm (1 in.). They are beautiful plants with racemes of 2–13 large purple flowers with a banner twice as long as the calyx.

*Astragalus amphioxys* var. *amphioxys* in Utah.
Photo Chris Norton.

Variety *amphioxys* (synonym *A. short-ianus*) has a banner twice as long as the calyx.

*Astragalus aretioides* grows in the Great Plains and the Rocky Mountain foothills of Wyoming at around 2000 m (6500 ft.) on steep, eroded clay slopes. Among the most desirable species, its solid silver, silky mound is covered with stemless flowers of an intense carmine-purple. Although reputed to be difficult in cultivation, I find this species fairly easy to grow; however, it will rot off with too much winter moisture. It has never set seed for me but is nevertheless worth searching for and treasuring.

*Astragalus asclepiadoides* is a rare species that grows to 15–20 cm (6–8 in.) among desert shrub communities on clay or badlands in the Uinta Basin, the northeast of Utah, and Colorado at 1475–1910 m (4795–6200 ft.). Erect stems have glaucous, blue-green leaves that are also large, thick, and roundish. Vivid rose-purple flowers in May through June are in erect, axillary inflorescences exserted beyond the leaves, and the seedpods that follow are large, erect, and mottled. This species does not look like a typical astragalus.

*Astragalus austinae* grows in Nevada and the Sierra Nevada among stones on exposed summit ridges at approximately 2770–3385 m (9000–11,000 ft.). It forms lovely, silver-haired mats with whitish, purple-veined flowers in June through September. Unfortunately, like many really choice species, seed is rarely available from commercial lists.

*Astragalus barrii* is a Great Plains endemic in Montana, Wyoming, and South Dakota, where it grows on dry, rocky prairie knolls, hillsides, and barren areas. Similar in size to *A. gilviflorus*, it has gray, soft leaves with large pink to purplish flowers in April through June. It is named after the wonderful plantsman and pioneer of Great Plains flora, Claude Barr. Barr (1983) described walking one sunlit May morning down a cattle trail in the badlands of South Dakota, and as he stepped between the many flowering cushions of *A. gilviflorus* he spotted plants with rose-colored flowers. On closer inspection, however, Barr found further differences. Although initially identified as *A. tridactylicus*, Rupert Barneby (1964) later concluded that it was indeed a new species and gave it the specific name *barrii* to honor the finder.

*Astragalus bolanderi* is native to California and grows mainly in the east, ranging from Tulare county to Plumas county. Its habitat includes dry conditions in meadows, flats, and mixed coniferous forests at 1600–3075 m (5200–10,000 ft.). It grows 15–45 cm (6–18 in.) tall with hairless stems and whitish, pink-tinted flowers in June through August.

This astragalus was named for Henry Bolander, who made extensive botanical collections from 1863 to 1875 during his work on the California Geological Survey with William Brewer.

*Astragalus bolanderi* seedpods.

*Astragalus calycosus* is among the most dwarf in the genus and grows in Utah, Wyoming, Idaho, Nevada, California, and Arizona at 1430–2730 m (4650–8870 ft.). It has pads of tiny, gray-white leaves and whitish yellow to pink and blue-purple flowers that are either stemless or on thin stems that grow to 5 cm (2 in.). It makes a good trough plant. The type has pinkish blue flowers.

Variety *mancus* is a rare alpine endemic from the Deep Creek Mountains of western Utah and into Nevada, where it grows on ridge tops at 2650–3660 m (8610–11,895 ft.). It has much shorter leaflets.

*Astragalus ceramicus* grows in sandy soils, occasionally on stream banks, at 1270–2360 m (4130–7670 ft.) over a wide area in Utah and the Great Plains. Its name makes you think of something delicate and decorative, and the species lives up to that name. In May through early June it has insignificant purplish to pink or white flowers on slender, rushlike stems to 25 cm (10 in.) long that are occasionally sprawling. However, it produces superb inflated pods of yellowish green parchment blotched with crimson that sometimes look like Christmas tree decorations.

*Astragalus chamaeleuce* is a rare and unusual species growing in the Uinta Basin, the northeast of Utah, Colorado, and Wyoming at 1530–2310 m (4975–7500 ft.).

*Astragalus ceramicus* in seed. Photo Chris Norton.

*Astragalus coccineus*, Westgard Pass, White Mountains, California. Photo Chris Norton.

Site of *Astragalus coccineus*, White Mountains, California.

*Astragalus coccineus* in seed. Alabama Hills, California. Photo Chris Norton.

Small tufts of bluish green, finely haired foliage and small cream-white to lavender flowers in early April through July grow on stems 5–7 cm (2–2¾ in.) tall. The large seedpods that follow are attractively mottled. This species did not grow too well in a pot for me but was excellent in a trough until rotting off after continuous rainfall.

*Astragalus coccineus*, a legend among the species, grows on rocky, exposed, sunny positions in the White Mountains of California near the California–Nevada border at an altitude of 1400–2000 m (4550–6500 ft.). It makes hummocks of white woolly foliage from which grow stems 15–25 cm (6–10 in.) tall topped with huge elongated flowers of bright scarlet. Although the horned pods that follow are very striking, it is the flowers that make this astragalus among the best. Since the plant dies down soon after blooming in spring, you have to be very observant—and lucky—to actually notice this species in the wild. It had been rare in cultivation but the seed now appears in several commercial lists, making it more widely grown. I am proud to have been among the first in the United Kingdom to have recently grown and flowered it successfully. A plant from my nursery earned one of my customers an Alpine Garden Society Award of Merit in 1996. Though it is difficult to know when to reduce the amount of moisture you give this species and how best to repot it since it does not do well if disturbed, it is nevertheless well worth the challenge.

*Astragalus cymboides* is endemic to just Carbon, Emery, and Grand counties in Utah at 1600–2300 m (5200–7475 ft.) in silty lime or sandstone clay among salt-desert shrub and pinyon and juniper communities. As it is very similar to *A. chamaeleuce*, some consider it to be a synonym for that species. It grows 2.5–8 cm (1–3 in.) tall with flowers of yellowish white to pink-purple.

*Astragalus detritalis* is endemic to the Uinta Basin, growing in the northeast of Utah and northwest Colorado at 1725–2770

Bristlecone pines in the White Mountains, California.

*Astragalus detritalis* in cultivation.

m (5600–9000 ft.) among desert shrub and pinyon and juniper woodlands. Among the most choice species, its leaves are silvery with one to five small narrow leaflets clumped in tight, caespitose cushions. Stems grow to 10 cm (4 in.) and bear six to eight large, vivid pink-purple flowers in April through May that remain tight to the foliage before elongating as the quill-like seedpods ripen.

*Astragalus gilviflorus* is another wonderful silver bun from Alberta to Wyoming at about 2000 m (6500 ft.). This species is usually the first to flower, sometimes as early as late March, showing off the large, stemless white blooms that are sometimes tinted lavender. The trifingered foliage is quite large for the size of the plant as it rarely exceeds 10 cm (4 in.) in height but can grow to 20–25 cm (8–10 in.) across. A most striking plant that is useful for pot cultivation, it has also flowered for me out of season in autumn. Seed usually sets quite generously.

*Astragalus hyalinus* is another species ranging over the Great Plains on rocky prairie knolls and open hillsides, but it is one that could only be loved by the astragalus enthusiast. In spite of the large, prostrate, silver cushion, which gives it the nickname of the "silver vegetable sheep," the tiny white flowers tinged with lilac that appear in summer are a great disappointment.

*Astragalus kentrophyta* is a mat-forming species that is widely distributed from the West Coast and in the Rockies. It makes upright, shrubby growth that disappears underground after seed has set. Its habitat is the same as that of var. *jessiae*, and the flowers, which I find nondescript, range from cream to yellow to a rich carmine-pink in June through August.

Variety *implexus*, although a rare Great Plains plant, is fairly abundant where it grows in Oregon, California, and the Uinta Mountains of Utah at 2770–3300 m (9000–10,725 ft.). A somewhat disappointing variety that forms gray, hairy, flat mats with prickly leaves, it grows in exposed positions on rocky prairie hilltops but looks lovely when it spills over rocks. Many plants in the wild flower the first year and then die, while others may live two to four years.

Variety *jessiae* is a little known relative that grows at the lower elevation of 1785–2645 m (5800–8600 ft.). Not a particularly attractive species, it has similar flowers in July through September depending on the elevation, and it makes a mat of sage green leaves.

*Astragalus lentiginosus* var. *fremontii* ranges from the southwest corner of Utah into California and Nevada. It grows 15–60 cm (6–24 in.) tall with leaves 2.5–15 cm (1–6 in.) long, each with 9–23 leaflets. The racemes are of pink-purple or whitish yellow flowers that are variously suffused with pink or purple. Beautiful bulbous seedpods are green with scarlet pimples. I once collected seedpods from this species (it was growing among *Argemone munita* and *Stanleya elata*) at Westgard Pass while traveling to the Bristlecone Pines Reserve in the White

*Astragalus kentrophyta* var. *implexis*. White Mountains, California. Photo Chris Norton.

Mountains of California. I put the pods into my backpack and forgot them until, four or five days later, I noticed a vile smell coming from the car's trunk. The pods had been exuding an oily substance that not only stained my backpack but also created that terrible odor. I never noticed these problems with astragalus pods on cultivated plants so I can only assume that chemicals in the soil at the plant's location had been transferred to the pods and subsequently onto my pack.

*Astragalus loanus* is a lovely endemic that grows in Sevier county, Utah, on sliding volcanic rocky slopes at 1920–2075 m (6240–6745 ft.). It grows 2.5–5 cm (1–2 in.) tall and forms pads of silky, silver-green leaves covered with woolly hairs. White, lavender-tipped flowers are followed by beautiful beaked pods that are tinted red-purple and have long shiny hairs. This is an excellent, very showy pot plant.

*Astragalus lutosus* grows on inhospitable slopes of oil-rich shale at 1660–2645 m (5400–8600 ft.) in the Uinta Basin, northeast Utah, and Colorado. A dwarf species 2–10 cm (1–4 in.) tall, it forms mats of tiny, pleated, grayish leaves. Small white flowers are followed by large, shiny, papery pods that are red-hued and that look like sausages. This is a rare and beautiful astragalus.

*Astragalus musiniensis* is endemic to Utah's south-central counties, where it grows among salt and mixed desert shrub at 1430–2130 m (4650–6920 ft.). Similar to *A. loanus* in growth and size, it has tufts of silky gray foliage and racemes of pink and purple flowers on 2.5-cm (1-in.) stems. The large inflated pods are equally striking as they are a pinkish velvet.

*Astragalus newberryi* is another very attractive species from Nevada and Utah, where it occurs at approximately 1525–1725 m (4955–5600 ft.). It grows 2–12.5 cm (1–5 in.) tall and makes nice downy cushions topped with large purple-pink flowers. The beautiful large seedpods are clothed in white velvet.

Variety *castoreus* has vivid pink-purple flowers 2.5 cm (1 in.) across on dense tufts of white downy leaves that are similar to but smaller than those of *A. coccineus*. Although reputed to be a challenge and difficult to grow, seed became available in commercial lists in approximately 1999.

*Astragalus nutzotinensis* covers a wide range in Alaska and grows in the Brooks Range, southern Alaska Range, Talkeetna Mountains, and Wrangell–St. Elias Mountains, where it inhabits river bars and gravel soil. This weak, sprawling species has leaves

*Astragalus lentiginosus* var. *fremontii* in seed, Westgard Pass, White Mountains, California.

*Astragalus loanus* in cultivation. Photo Martin Sheader.

with 7–14 oval or pointed leaflets and two to four rose-purple, pink-based flowers per stem. The bright red seedpods are straight at first but gradually become sickle-shaped and they tend to lie on the ground.

*Astragalus piutensis* grows in Nevada at around 2090 m (6800 ft.) in fine, silty limestone soils and in Utah at 900–2430 m (2925–7900 ft.) among desert shrub. Growing 3–10 cm (1¼–4 in.) tall, the foliage is silky and the rose blooms are bright. It closely resembles *A. purshii* in habit. It could possibly be a very good show plant, and its seed is becoming available in commercial lists.

*Astragalus nutzotinensis*, Alaska Range. Photo Carolyn Parker.

*Astragalus nutzotinensis* in fruit, Alaska Range. Photo Carolyn Parker.

*Astragalus polaris* grows on the northwest coast of Alaska and along mountain streams in Denali National Park and the Aleutian Islands. It is similar to *A. nutzotinensis* but with one to two flowers. The leaflets may be cuneate at the tip and the seedpods are shorter and elliptical.

*Astragalus purshii* grows in the Great Basin and California northward from San Bernardino Mountains on the dry soil of plains, hills, and rocky ridges to around 3385 m (11,000 ft.). In Utah, variety *purshii* grows at 1530–2270 m (4975–7375 ft.) and has yellowish white flowers with purple tips.

Three other varieties are worth mentioning. Variety *glareosus* (which is very similar to *A. utahensis* in flower and habit) grows 5–12.5 cm (2–5 in.) tall among sagebrush communities in British Columbia and Nevada and at 1530–1830 m (4975–5950 ft.) in Utah. In Washington it grows at about 615 m (2000 ft.) in dry gravel soils on hilltops and north-facing slopes.

Variety *lectulus*, a small-flowered form of var. *glareosus*, grows in the Sierra Nevada at about 2815 m (9150 ft.).

Variety *tinctus* grows in the Sierra Nevada at 1725–3000 m (5600–9750 ft.)

*Astragalus purshii* var. *tinctus*.

and has very attractive mats that can be to 30 cm (12 in.) across with low tufts of gray-white foliage and purple-pink flowers in May through August.

*Astragalus sericoleucus* is a Great Plains species from Wyoming and Colorado that grows on flat, limestone ridges in full sun. The silky, silver cushion just 2.5–5 cm (1–2 in.) high and to 60 cm (24 in.) across is completely hidden with magenta flowers in early June and occasionally again in September through October. Use this plant to cover any barren rock you have since it brightens up the whole area, especially if the rock color acts as a foil to the leaves.

*Astragalus simplicifolius* grows in Utah on rocky or shallow soils at 1500–2460 m (4875–8000 ft.). It looks like a condensed form of *A. spatulatus*, and Goodrich and Neese (1986) suggest that *A. simplicifolius* is a synonym of that species. It is only 10 cm (4 in.) tall with a spread to 25 cm (10 in.), and it has tiny silver leaves and stemless purple-pink flowers. The bun is so tight and hard that it is almost impossible to push your finger into it. The specimen I grow is so much tighter than *A. spatulatus* that I believe it is a separate species.

*Astragalus spatulatus* is widespread in the Great Plains and into Utah. An ideal species for exposed, hot, dry scree areas, it forms hard mounds 12–13 cm (4¾–5 in.) high and 20 cm (8 in.) across with racemes of deep pink to purple flowers in May on short, wiry stems.

*Astragalus tridactylicus* has the same range as *A. sericoleucus* in that it extends from Wyoming into Colorado. Although very similar to that species, it has larger leaves. Pads of ternate leaves that are covered in a dense, white pubescence form a cushion that grows to a similar height and spread as

*A. sericoleucus*, but it has rich pink- or lavender-rose flowers. It must be among the very best astragali.

*Astragalus umbellatus* is a bright yellow-flowered species that is common on the rocky slopes and moist tundra of Alaska's mountains, where the small flowers in terminal clusters bloom mid-June through late July. The leaves are alternate on the stems, pinnately divided, and hairy underneath. Stems grow to 15 cm (6 in.) tall, and the pods are pointed at both ends and covered with black hairs.

*Astragalus uncialis*, long believed to be restricted to the vicinity of Currant, Nevada, has been found at 1400–1620 m (4550–5265 ft.) in Millard county, Utah; in fact the largest population grows in Millard. Jim Archibald (1989–1990) quotes Rupert Barneby who described this species as "one of the most ornamental and dwarf astragali with three to five silvery foliolate leaves and narrow, long, and showy purple flowers which seem quite disproportionately large for the plant's diminutive stature." I cannot argue with that description having grown this species myself from seed collected on the north side of Sevier Lake, Utah, at 1470 m (4780 ft.), where it grows in the stony washes that run into the dry lakebed. Unfortunately, my plant died soon after flowering but perhaps one day I will again obtain some seed. This is the species to look for if you want something really rare.

*Astragalus utahensis* is fairly widespread in Utah at 1250–2130 m (4060–6920 ft.), and the many colonies along the Wasatch front bloom in April through May. It also spreads into Idaho and Nevada. Although a lovely species, I cannot agree with Utah's pioneer of botany, Marcus Jones, who described it as the most beautiful flower in the state. It forms mats of white felty leaves with stems 2.5–12.5 cm (1–5 in.) tall that end in racemes of carmine-purple flowers. The shaggy pods that emerge later are covered in shiny, creamy white hairs.

I have grown this species for five years, albeit in an alpine house, and it has set plenty of seed each year. For newcomers to the genus, this species must be among the best to start with since it is easy to cultivate and sets seed regularly. The leaf texture, flowers, and early flowering also provide a great deal of pleasure.

*Astragalus whitneyi* grows on dry mountain slopes from the eastern side of the Cascades to the Sierra Nevada and in the Great Basin. Variety *whitneyi* is from the high Sierra Nevada at around 2985 m (9700 ft.); although nowhere near as robust as var. *lenophyllus*, the mat is small and prostrate, and the flowers are a pleasant rosy violet.

Variety *lenophyllus* grows in rocky, volcanic areas of the high Sierra Nevada at 2155–3690 m (7000–12,000 ft.). Extremely robust with large mounds of foliage that culminate in dense, showy racemes of white flowers, they become dwarf at alpine elevation. Large seedpods are inflated, yellowish, and heavily mottled with purple.

Variety *siskiyouensis* grows at approximately 2015 m (6550 ft.) in Trinity county, California, and probably has the largest and most inflated and mottled pods in the genus. Similar in habit to *lenophyllus*, it has yellow flowers.

Variety *sonneanus* grows farther north in Washington and Oregon and is similar to the California varieties with prostrate stems 10–15 cm (4–6 in.) long that have very finely haired, gray-green leaves. Small cream flowers with lavender markings are in a compact raceme. The seedpods that follow resemble large, translucent, reddish purple kidney beans.

*Astragalus zionis* grows 3.2–23 cm (1 1/4–9 in.) tall in sandstone and sandy gravel soils at 1340–2430 m (4355–7900 ft.) in southern Utah and Arizona. The prostrate to ascending stems grow to 11 cm (4¼ in.) long with pale to mid pink-purple flowers. Leaves are 2.5–15 cm (1–6 in.) long with 13–25 leaflets on each. The ovoid pods are curved, brightly mottled, and grow to 3.2 cm (1¼ in.).

**Propagation**

Propagate astragalus by seed. Since 1989, more and more seed has become available

Close-up of *Astragalus utahensis* in cultivation.

*Astragalus whitneyi* var. *lenophyllus* in seed. Squaw Valley near Lake Tahoe, California. Photo Chris Norton.

from the commercial lists, enabling us to experience the challenge of growing the really choice species. As with most seed of the genera in the pea family, astragalus seed is large enough to handle between thumb and forefinger so there is little chance of sowing the seed thickly. Astragalus seed germinates better in cold, moist conditions (not freezing), and if these conditions are present when sowing, germination takes place very quickly, in two to three weeks.

Once you sow the seed, cover it with a layer of grit and place the pot outside on a table or bench to suffer whatever the weather throws at it. Germination is very quick, so I try to sow before November to allow the seedlings to grow during winter. Whatever method you use to sow the seed, make sure you scarify it in some way and penetrate the hard coat of the larger seeds, especially those of *Astragalus coccineus*. While holding the seed down tightly on a flat surface with my fingernail, I use a sharp knife to nick the coat. When I work with smaller seeds I place them between two pieces of sandpaper that I then briefly rub together to wear away the seed coat.

A popular theory regarding seed germination from plants in the pea family states

*Astragalus zionis*, Kolob Canyons, Zion National Park, Utah. Photo Chris Norton.

that after the first seed germinates, chemicals are produced from the seed coating that inhibit germination of other seeds in close proximity. During the many years I have grown astragalus, however, I have rarely encountered this problem, no doubt because I scarify all my seed before I sow it. As the seed is fairly large, I sow each one singly, and the resultant germination is good. My theory is that since most astragalus seed has a hard coat, it needs assistance (such as scarifying) in getting moisture to the inside or germination will not take place. Only the seed with the thinnest coats will germinate without help. The seed coats of astragalus vary in hardness, and while some seeds can be scratched easily, others require two or three attempts before a piece can be chipped off with a knife.

If you are in any doubt about your astragalus seed germination, look at the ratio between the number of seeds you sow and the number that germinates. For example, seed collected from my own plant of *Astragalus utahensis*, once sown, always results in many seedlings germinating. When I purchase seed from a commercial list, however, I have less seed and as a result not as many seedlings.

If you sow seeds together in seed pots, keep a close watch on their growth after germination. Continually check the base of the pot for emerging roots. Just like townsendia seedlings, astragalus roots grow very fast compared with the growth taking place above soil level. If roots are coming through the holes in the base of the pot, consider pricking out into individual pots even though you may have to do this in midwinter. As long as the seedlings are growing they can be potted up. If there are a large number of seedlings, be careful with the roots as they become tangled and difficult to pull apart. Put the pricked out seedlings into the alpine house, frame, or some other protection until spring.

**Cultivation**

Plants of this genus need to grow in a sunny, dry spot, where they will provide so much pleasure over a growing season. Seedlings from the various astragalus species grow at different speeds in spring. Species that form small cushions, such as *Astragalus aretioides* and *A. gilviflorus*, grow quite slowly, and it is best to keep them in their pots for the first year, repotting into something larger only if necessary. Others such as *A. coccineus*, *A. loanus*, and *A. utahensis* grow a lot more quickly, and by summer are large enough to be planted out. In fact *A. coccineus* grows so fast that it makes a good-sized plant and flowers only 18 months after germination in early winter. If you grow astragalus for exhibition in a pot you can use the same method of cultivation, but wherever it grows, make sure the soil is deep, gritty, and free draining. The taproot grows straight down seeking any available moisture, especially in the growing season. I grow all my species in a pot of neutral soil mix that contains lime, and it appears that the lack of oil shale or sandstone is not a worry. Perhaps I have had success because all the plants that grow here have originated from seed—a good reason for not digging up plants in the wild.

Bob Nold of Denver, Colorado, finds *Astragalus utahensis* and *A. coccineus* impossible to grow in his climate without winter protection. Offering a different perspective, however, is Anne Spiegel of Wappinger Falls, New York state, who reports that she grows astragalus from seed and puts seedlings into the garden the first year. She does warn that a big temperature drop with lots of frost and wet weather after unseasonable warmth is an almost perfect formula for killing an astragalus. During one cold spell, the most established plants of *A. coccineus*, *A. purshii*, *A. simplicifolius*, *A. tridactylicus*, *A. utahensis*, and *A. whitneyi* were either lost to Anne or were severely damaged. One exception was *A. barrii*, which seems an exceptionally tough plant more tolerant of the inopportune rains of the Northeast. She promises to try open-sided rain shields on the troughs during future winters.

I am always being asked how to grow *Astragalus coccineus*, and so I turn to the example of Alan Papworth. He bought a plant from me in 1992, and in 1996 he received two awards when the mature plant boasted more than 30 flowering stems. He used clay pots with a mixture in equal parts of sharp grit and a soil-based mix with twice the amount of fertilizer normally found in a mix used for pot-grown plants (he used John Innes™ compost number 2, which is available in the United Kingdom). After keeping the plant in the alpine house on moist sand during the dormant period, he repotted it in a larger pot after it first flowered in 1993 and added only top dressing until its impressive flowering three years later.

Although *Astragalus coccineus* becomes severely desiccated during its dormancy period in nature and thus is difficult to find, in cultivation I give it a small amount of moisture during this period and so it does not go entirely dormant. Throughout winter and into early spring the plant looks quite dead except for tufts of small gray leaves at the tips of the main stems. Once growth is apparent, the plant can receive a reasonable amount of water—and the grower can heave a sigh of relief.

The stems of *Astragalus utahensis* in cultivation grow longer than they do in the wild, and the best way to counteract this is to trim the stems back to within 5 cm (2 in.) of the main stem after flowering and seed setting. New shoots appear in no time, and the plant stays compact.

The main pests that can strip a plant bare overnight are slugs and snails. They chiefly go for the young, potted up seedlings. Aphids on both young and mature plants, especially in the alpine house, can cause leaves to twist and plants to wilt. Red spider mite also causes mottling of silver leaves. A systemic insecticide or plant pin usually gets rid of both red spider mites and aphids.

Beware of overwatering, especially the seedlings as they are prone to damping off in early life even when under cover. Mature plants grown in pots do not usually require water until growth is evident.

# C

## CALYPTRIDIUM
Portulacaceae
*pussy paws, pussy toes*

Although Calyptridium has about six species in the Americas, only one is commonly seen in the western United States, and it is unmistakable. The flowers of *Calyptridium umbellatum* look like the upturned paws of a cat, giving it the common name pussy paws. It often grows in dusty parking lots and along roadsides or trails, the seed disbursed there by chipmunks partial to the plant's shiny black seeds. Although not an annual, it should be classed as a short-lived perennial in cultiva-

tion, and you should grow new plants every year from seed.

*Calyptridium umbellatum* (synonym *Spraguea umbellata*) grows in open, dry rocky places at 770–4000 m (2500–13,000 ft.) from British Columbia to California, Montana, Nevada, Utah, and northwest Wyoming. It has a basal rosette of bright green spatulate leaves to 7.5 cm (3 in.) long. Stems are 5–25 cm (2–10 in.) tall with dense umbellate cymes of white-pink to carmine papery flowers in May through August that look like the underside of a cat's paw. The stems tend to elevate themselves during the hottest part of the day (which protects the center of the rosette), and as the day cools, they return to their

*Calyptridium umbellatum*, Mount Pinos, California.

Close-up of *Calyptridium umbellatum* flowers.

prostrate position on the ground. Such stem action not only controls the temperature of the plant but also gives it the specific name *umbellatum*, meaning umbrella-like.

## Propagation
You can propagate this species by seed sown in autumn or spring and put the seed pots outside after sowing.

## Cultivation
It is possible to grow *Calyptridium umbellatum* in a sunny scree bed for a short while, especially if you protect it from the winter rains. If your winters are dry, you may be more successful. Of course if you treat it as an alpine house plant, the outside conditions will not matter. I occasionally see it as an exhibition plant, and usually the flowers are a rich carmine rather than the pale colors of those in the wild.

Rotting off, either in the alpine house because of overwatering or by excessive rain outside, is the only problem I have noticed.

## CAMPANULA
Campanulaceae
*bell flowers, bluebells, harebells*

Although many consider Europe's native campanulas to be among the finest, a number of campanula species that grow in the northwestern United States are equally attractive. Most are compact in growth and inhabit the mountain scree areas. A number of fine cultivars that have been selected from plants growing in the wild are well worth seeking out. Some North American species grow fairly well all year round in my alpine beds, while others, although quite happy outside during summertime, need protection against winter damp and humidity to prevent rotting off. Several of the North American species, *Campanula piperi* and *C. shetleri* for example, make excellent pot plants for exhibition and always feature at the Alpine Garden Society shows.

*Campanula lasiocarpa*, despite the common name of Alaska bluebell, grows not only in Alaska but also further south to the Cascades of central Washington and into the Olympics. It is much smaller than the Asian form and inhabits sandy, gravel slopes, thriving in scree areas and blooming July through August.

Although the stems can grow to 15 cm (6 in.), the form found by Rick Lupp at the western end of the Talkeetna Mountains in Alaska is very different. It is more condensed and makes a prostrate mat of tiny rosettes sparsely studded with large blue cups on stems 1–2 cm (½–¾ in.) tall. Given the cultivar name 'Talkeetna', it is an excellent introduction.

*Campanula lasiocarpa*, Kantishna Hills, Alaska.
Photo Carolyn Parker.

*Campanula parryi* grows in many states across the West, inhabiting moist subalpine and low alpine meadows. It makes a dense mat of neatly tufted foliage, and the blue, funnel-shaped, starlike flowers are upward-facing on 15-cm (6-in.) long stems. The plant increases by slender underground rhizomes. In cultivation it is among the easier western campanulas.

Variety *idahoensis* inhabits rocky subalpine meadows at 1970 m (6400 ft.) near Wenatchee in Washington. It has shorter stems than *Campanula parryi*—to 10 cm (4 in.) long—that carry solitary, erect, blue-purple bell flowers.

*Campanula piperi* from the Olympics in Washington grows in rocky, subalpine slopes and screes at about 1785 m (5800 ft.). The slender rhizomes run underground, emerging to form compact, tufted rosettes of shiny, dark green, leathery leaves that are toothed. Stems may be as short as 2.5 cm (1 in.) or to 8 cm (3 in.) tall. The upward-facing flowers of a flattish bowl shape are 2–3 cm (¾–1¼ in.) in diameter and bloom July through August. Flower color varies from lavender to deep blue to purplish blue.

Steve Doonan and Phil Pearson of Grand Ridge Nursery in Washington and Rick Lupp have given cultivar names to some of the best selections of this species. *Campanula piperi* in any form is an outstanding species, particularly since it has such a variety of flower form and color. In the early 1990s Steve Doonan of Grand Ridge Nursery found a white form named 'Townsend Ridge'. 'Snowdrift', another white cultivar with beautiful blooms that open quite flat, was found by Roger Whitlock of Victoria, Canada, in the Olympics at about the same time. Both cultivars are more vigorous than the blue forms and make lovely pot plants for exhibition.

Several other cultivars are worth mentioning. 'Marmot Pass' has blue flowers that open flat with a blush of lavender at the edge. 'Mt. Tahoma' has a dense compact habit and a reliable bloom of rich lavender-

Pale blue flowers of *Campanula piperi*. Olympic Mountains, Washington. Photo David Hale.

Mid-blue flowers of *Campanula piperi*. Olympic Mountains, Washington. Photo Jane Grushow.

blue. 'Townsend Violet' has lovely, soft violet blooms.

*Campanula prenanthoides* is a very close relative of *C. scouleri*. Although some sources describe taller stems, my own plants grown from seed collected in Oregon at 925 m (3000 ft.) have stems that are only 15 cm (6 in.) tall. It has bright blue flowers in a shape similar to *C. scouleri*.

*Campanula rotundifolia* is circumboreal in distribution and is a fairly easy species to grow. In the Rockies the common name is mountain harebell, and it grows in a wide range of moist habitats from lower mountain slopes to alpine zones. It spreads by small rhizomes that send up tufts of basal leaves and erect stems to 25 cm (10 in.) tall with several bell-shaped, erect or nodding blue flowers that appear in June through September.

'Ned's White', an excellent white selection, was discovered by Ned Lowry on Washington's Mount Townsend and named after him. Very large, cup-shaped flowers grow on 20-cm (8-in.) stems. One specimen I planted out in an alpine bed grew well alongside *Campanula parryi* for two years before succumbing to the damp winter. Although reputed to be quite vigorous, it does not increase as quickly as the blue form.

*Campanula scabrella* covers a wide range from Washington to California, Montana, and Idaho in screes and rocks at dry, exposed, subalpine levels. It has dense rosettes of spatulate, blue-gray foliage at the end of stolons that roam through the sunny and occasionally shifting screes. Stems are about 5 cm (2 in.) tall with one to six

*Campanula piperi* 'Townsend Ridge' in cultivation.

White form of *Campanula piperi*. Olympic National Park, Washington. Photo Jane Grushow.

*Campanula rotundifolia* at a Colorado roadside.

upward-facing, star-shaped flowers of blue-gray to violet. The flowers are 2.5 cm (1 in.) across. Although among the more challenging North American species, it is not impossible to grow and is worth the extra care required in cultivation, particularly as it is breathtaking in full flower.

*Campanula scouleri* grows in mountain woodlands and north-facing talus slopes from Alaska to California. It varies greatly in height from 10 to 30 cm (4 to 12 in.). The flowers are very attractive with nodding, pinkish lavender bells that have styles shaped like baseball bats.

*Campanula shetleri* grows in the Mount Shasta and Trinity Mountains area of California at about 1890 m (6140 ft.), usually in places that offer some shade.

It is often described as a compact version of *C. piperi* but I think it is much more delicate and attractive. The plant tucks itself into the crevices of north-facing granite cliffs, where it grows upside down like a dionysia plant. In this habitat it forms dense rosettes of spatulate, sharply toothed, dark green leaves and has the cool, moist root run needed for the woody rhizomes. Stems are 5–7 cm (2–2¾ in.) tall, and the small, bowl-shaped flowers can be white, pale to darker gray-blue, or a lovely deep blue. It is among the most beautiful North American campanulas I grow.

*Campanula uniflora* is a circumpolar and subarctic species that ranges from Alaska and the Yukon to Colorado and

Site of *Campanula scabrella*, a scree area on Burnt Mountain, eastern Cascades, Washington.

Mount Shasta, California.

*Campanula scabrella*, Burnt Mountain, eastern Cascades, Washington.

*Campanula shetleri* in cultivation.

Utah, where they grow in stony limestone formations and grassy tundra areas at 3630–3940 m (11,800–12,805 ft.). Decumbent to erect stems are 5–20 cm (2–8 in.) tall with single, funnel-shaped, mid-blue flowers that look like delicate harebells.

*Campanula* 'Bumblebee' is an excellent hybrid introduced by Rick Lupp of Mt. Tahoma Nursery in 1994 or 1995. Seedlings of *C. piperi* 'Mt. Tahoma' (from the Mt. Tahoma Nursery) were growing in close proximity to a tray of *C. lasiocarpa* when the bees carried out a natural cross. 'Bumblebee' is a lovely plant, with large, up-facing blooms of a deep blue on 15-cm (6-in.) long stems. This very vigorous plant quickly fills an 18-cm (7-in.) diameter pot, and it seems more agreeable in cultivation than either of the parents. It also grows well in a scree area or trough.

**Propagation**

*Campanula* seed varies from a recognizable size to something that is almost dustlike. When you collect seed from campanulas for the first time, be aware that unlike most plants the seed capsule is behind the flower and has pores at the base from where the seed is dispersed. Do not look for a seedpod

*Campanula* 'Bumblebee'. Photo Joan Beeston.

to open because as soon as the flower is over and the capsule starts to go brown, seed, especially very fine seed, is likely to disperse. You should cut off the capsules and either put them into a seed envelope or turn the capsules upside down and let the seed fall into the envelope.

*Campanula* seed that is very fine requires light to germinate and therefore must not be covered by grit or soil. I normally sow this seed on top of the grit and stand the pot in a saucer of water until the grit is obviously moist. Capillary action draws the seed slightly down into the grit, which is adequate for germination. Seed that is not as fine can be sown on top of the soil mixture and then covered with a light layer of grit.

Except for the white forms of *Campanula piperi*, all the North American species have set seed for me in cultivation. However, you must expect that plants grown from seed, as in the wild, will vary slightly in color and habit. Seed from *C. rotundifolia* 'Ned's White' has produced plants that have come true to color, the majority of which have large flowers. Stem height varies, although not by much. I have received wild-collected seed from white forms of *C. piperi*, but in each case the resultant plants had blue flowers.

You can vegetatively propagate most of the species by taking rooted pieces from the edge of the plant, potting them up, and keeping them in a closed frame for a couple of weeks. Vegetative propagation is ideal if you have a particularly good cultivar or a nice color form that you want to increase. *Campanula shetleri* and *C. piperi* in all forms can be quickly propagated using this method. I usually knock plants of these species out of their pots and shake off all excess soil. Using a pair of scissors, I cut off any piece with roots attached and pot it up; there may be a few failures but most pieces will grow. You can propagate plants this way from spring until early autumn. If vegetative propagation is done in spring and the pieces without roots are treated as cutting material in a frame, they will root in sand within five to six weeks. If your plants are growing in a trough or rock garden, take pieces from the edge of the plants by digging gently down and teasing rooted portions away from the main root system.

*Campanula scabrella* is more easily propagated by seed than cuttings. The stolons grow just underground but are not really suitable for vegetative propagation. However, Rick Lupp finds the plant can be increased by short divisions if it is left in a pot for a couple of years and the short stolons treated as cuttings, although this is not a quick way to build a stock.

*Campanula parryi*, and sometimes *C. rotundifolia*, can be propagated by removing the small rooted rhizomes where shoots have emerged from the soil and potting them up. These pieces are much larger than those in *C. piperi* and *C. shetleri*.

*Campanula* 'Bumblebee' is very quick to reproduce. A small piece potted up when the plant is in active growth grows so quickly that within a couple of months it can be divided yet again into a number of rooted pieces.

*Campanula lasiocarpa* 'Talkeetna' is more difficult than most to increase. Although propagation is by rooted pieces from the edge of the plant (as it is for the other campanulas), the roots of the mat are very near the surface and extremely tightly entwined so it is not easy to pull the rooted pieces away without damaging the root system. Once you

have potted up these rooted pieces, place them in a shady frame. Dieback occurs occasionally, but once the rooted pieces begin to grow, they do so very fast.

**Cultivation**

Campanulas are naturally greedy plants, and if you grow them in pots you must repot them every year and perhaps apply a liquid feed during the growing season. When repotting a plant grown for exhibition, squeeze any pieces popping up at the side of the pot and not used for propagation into the main central growth to make the plant appear more uniform.

*Campanula parryi* grows and slowly spreads in a scree bed without much fuss, but it is also among those deciduous campanulas that, because it dies down in winter, always makes the gardener worry until it appears again the following spring. Once it takes root, it begins to spread via slim rhizomes. This is an attractive, easy campanula for the rock garden.

Like *Campanula parryi*, *C. rotundifolia* and *C. scouleri* have no trouble growing in a gritty alpine bed, even one with alkaline soil. As long as the drainage is right and there is about 2.5 cm (1 in.) of top dressing, these campanula species grow well. One problem with *C. rotundifolia*, however, is that the tall stems are quite brittle where they join the main rootstock. In windy conditions these stems are blown around and sometimes break off. *Campanula scouleri* needs a spartan diet to keep it compact.

*Campanula lasiocarpa* 'Talkeetna', in spite of all my efforts, is impossible to keep going in my garden because of the high level of winter wet and humidity. In areas of winter rainfall, therefore, it must be grown in the alpine house where it is kept slightly moist over winter. During the spring to autumn growth period, it requires a fair amount of water to grow well, so you can place it outside in partial shade. This campanula also dies away completely in winter leaving only dead stems on the surface; it comes into growth quite late, the new green shoots emerging in late spring or even early summer.

Both the white and blue forms of *Campanula piperi* prefer gritty granite conditions. Although there are reports that this species is difficult to flower well, I have never found that to be a problem. The rosettes become brown in winter and some parts look dead, but a lot of live stems also turn brown, so be careful not to pull off the brown stems and leaves willy-nilly. You can remove any obviously dead foliage (use scissors and a great deal of care) but *be patient* and wait until growth restarts in early spring. If you cut away a stem and then spot a white milky substance oozing from the cut you know that you have blundered. *Campanula* 'Bumblebee' is very similar to *C. piperi* in winter appearance and soil requirements although I find it a much easier plant to grow, both in a scree or pot. It is an excellent plant for pot culture.

I tried several times to grow *Campanula shetleri* outside in a scree bed alongside other American alpines, and although it was doing well during the summer period, as soon as the cold rains arrived it rotted off. I now grow it in a pot with a soil mix that contains a fair amount of crushed granite and a top dressing of at least 5 cm (2 in.) of grit. Like *C. piperi*, it loves these conditions and spreads to the pots' edges throughout summer. I protect it during wintertime in the alpine house. In winter the green rosettes become brown around

the edges just like those of *C. piperi*, and they should be treated with the same judicious use of scissors. The flower stems, which also die back, can be removed with a *gentle* tug in spring. If it does not come away easily, use the scissors.

It is worthwhile growing plants of *Campanula shetleri* from seed and then selecting the best color forms. Make your selections by collecting seed from the best plants from which to grow into new plants. I now have a number of good compact plants with deep blue flowers. I am sure the various pollinators can do similar selections just as well in the wild—you simply have to keep hunting for the right color from which to start your own selections. This beautiful campanula species makes a great pot plant with alpine house or cold frame protection in the winter.

*Campanula scabrella* is the most difficult of all the North American campanulas to cultivate. Trying to simulate the soil conditions for this species is almost impossible, and to keep it in character you have to grow it in full sun with a very gritty soil mix and no additional fertilizer. The stems become a little lankier in any form of shelter, which means it has to spend a lot of time outdoors during the growing season if you grow it as a pot plant. I grow it in a pot using the same soil mix as I use on *C. piperi* and *C. shetleri*, and although I give it as much sun as possible, it still has stems 7–8 cm (2¾–3 in.) tall. I cannot grow and flower it to look like those on Burnt Mountain in the eastern Cascades.

Rick Lupp explains that he can keep his plant of *Campanula scabrella* in good character with stems less than 2.5 cm (1 in.) tall when it is grown with a very gritty soil mix and no additional fertilizer. He has not made any improvements in the original 1995 lean mix (although he occasionally gives the plant a very weak liquid feed), and it seems to get better and better. It grows in a large trough with *Penstemon caespitosa* var. d*eserti-picti*, which he says looks great.

Slugs are the worst enemies of campanulas; even in the alpine house I have to use slug bait. Unless there is a good flow of air around the plant, powdery mildew affects any plant that has dense foliage and becomes wet in the center. The problem of mildew is more prevalent in the alpine house where airflow is limited. Red spider mite also badly affects plants grown under glass unless the infestation is treated immediately.

## CASTILLEJA
Scrophulariaceae
*Indian paintbrushes*

Whether driving along a road or hiking the mountain trails throughout the West during early to late summer, you cannot help seeing castillejas lighting up the scenery, the top of their stems like ragged brushes dipped in red paint. Their botanical name comes from Domingo Castillejo, a Spanish botanist, and there are a variety of common names such as Indian paintbrush, painted cup, squaw-feather, or paintbrush. To the casual observer there are two colors, red and yellow, and although the dominant color is a deep red, the bracts (they are not flowers) are also white, pink, and pale green to yellow through to orange. The flowers are quite insignificant since they are almost completely hidden by the bracts. Castillejas are partially parasitic (hemiparasites) and grow on the roots of other nearby plants. These strange looking plants usually grow 5–90 cm (2–36 in.) tall. Various cultivation references contain similar negative comments, that these plants are not easily grown out of their natural habits or that they can scarcely live without the aid of other plants. Ingwersen (1978) states:

> *A race of handsome, but almost ungrowable, parasites from North America. Their beauty lies in the brilliantly colored bracts that surround the inconspicuous flowers. Occasionally unexpected successes lead to further attempts to cultivate them but they are unlikely to become good garden plants and it is pointless to describe the numerous species in detail.*

These plants are so attractive that some years ago I became determined to grow them in spite of the anticipated difficulties. In the spring of 1996, having finally germinated castilleja seed, I began thinking about which host plants to use, fully believing in the misinformation published about this genus. Then, like a breath of fresh air sweeping away all the old beliefs, came an article by Ken Sherman (1996). Ken had observed their growth in the wild and noted that although castillejas existed there with some form of hemiparasitic relationship, it was not a prerequisite to successful cultivation. He experimented with the genus and concluded that it is moisture that castillejas depend primarily on a host plant for. *Castilleja miniata*, the dominant castilleja species of the subalpine meadows, grows where the habitat is wetter and there is adequate moisture, although host plants such as *trifolium* species and other shallow-rooted perennials exist nearby. Ken also noted that pure stands of castilleja have been found on gravel bars and moraines with no encroaching roots from another plant within 2 m

(78 in.). During July 1996, I visited Ken at his home in Bend, Oregon, and he showed me how he grew and propagated a large number of castillejas in his garden.

There are around 200 species within the genus, 24 of which inhabit the Rocky Mountain area. Many are similar to one another, making identification in the wild extremely difficult. The list of species I describe includes the more common examples as well as those that have been successfully cultivated or whose seed is available in commercial lists.

*Castilleja applegatei* is a common species in Oregon, Idaho, California, Utah, and Nevada, where it grows to subalpine levels on dry mountain ridges. It varies in height—8–50 cm (3–20 in.)—with wavy leaf margins and bracts of yellow to reddish orange to bright red.

Variety *martinii* grows on Mount Pinos in California and is smaller—15–25 cm (6–10 in.) tall—with showy red bracts. Variety *pallida,* a really outstanding form, grows in the Sierra Nevada of California at around 2940 m (9555 ft.) and has dense spikes that vary in color from yellow to orange, copper, and red. Variety *viscida* has vivid red bracts.

*Castilleja arachnoidea* grows on ridges and slopes in the mountains of northern California and southwest Oregon. Stems

Close-up of *Castilleja applegatei* var. *viscida,* Uinta Mountains, Utah. Photo David Joyner.

Large clump of *Castilleja applegatei* var. *viscida.* Wasatch Mountains, Utah. Photo David Joyner.

*Castilleja arachnoidea* at the edge of Crater Lake, Oregon.

10–30 cm (4–12 in.) tall have troughlike, trilobed leaves, and the orange-yellow bracts are also trilobed with a wide, round-tipped central lobe. The flower spike has a thick, tight, rounded appearance, and the entire plant is covered with spiderweb-like hairs.

*Castilleja chromosa* is wide-ranging in Oregon, California, Wyoming, Nevada, Utah, Arizona, and New Mexico. It grows at 600–2610 m (1950–8480 ft.) among sagebrush and pine and juniper woodland. Although generally growing to 40 cm (15¾ in.), some good dwarf populations in Nevada are 10–15 cm (4–6 in.) tall. The bracts are bright red to orange- red,

*Castilleja chromosa* in grass, Uinta Mountains, Utah. Photo David Joyner.

although some are pale yellow to dark orange with bright scarlet tips.

*Castilleja cinerea* is a beautiful miniature from California at 3000 m (9750 ft.), where it grows in quartzite gravel among *Eriogonum kennedyi* varieties. Ideal in troughs at just 5–10 cm (2–4 in.) tall, it has blackish red bracts and greenish yellow corollas.

*Castilleja elegans* grows on rocky alpine slopes of western interior Alaska and coastal areas of northern and northwestern Alaska. It is branched and grows 10–25 cm (4–10 in.) tall with narrow, pointed, hairy leaves on purplish stems. Light pink to purple bracts in mid-June through July are hairy.

*Castilleja haydenii* grows in the high meadows and alpine tundra in Colorado and New Mexico. A dwarf species at 10–15 cm (4–6 in.) tall, it has very showy bracts that are a deep crimson, rose-red, or lilac.

*Castilleja latifolia* grows at the low altitude of 60 m (196 ft.) in California among the windswept colonies of *Gaultheria shallon* in well-drained sandstone soils. It has bright red bracts and pale greenish yellow corollas and is 25–30 cm (10–12 in.) tall. This species reportedly flowers in the first year from seed so it may be worth searching for in the seed lists.

*Castilleja elegans*, Yukon-Tanana Uplands, Alaska. Photo Carolyn Parker.

*Castilleja haydenii*. Mount Evans, Colorado.

*Castilleja miniata* grows in extreme south-eastern Alaska to California, British Columbia, New Mexico, Utah, and Arizona at 1765–3450 m (5735–11,210 ft.), usually near streams or other moist places. It is tufted with stems 30–80 cm (12–32 in.) tall and bracts that vary from orange to bright orange-red. This is among the easiest castillejas to grow in cultivation. I have grown it in a pot for exhibition and Jim Lever, a well-known plant exhibitor in the United Kingdom, has grown it in his garden for several years.

*Castilleja nana* grows in alpine meadows and on windswept ridges in gravel sand at 3200–3600 m (10,400–11,700 ft.) in Utah, Nevada, and California. A very compact plant at 3–9 cm (1¼–3½ in.) tall, it has dull yellow, purple-pink, or white spreading bracts.

*Castilleja occidentalis*, the western paintbrush, grows in the subalpine to alpine zones of New Mexico, Utah, Colorado, Montana, and Canada. Among the most common in the genus, it is 15–30 cm (6–12 in.) tall and has yellow bracts.

*Castilleja parviflora* var. *oreopola* grows in the Goat Rocks area of Washington, where it inhabits the volcanic talus and rocky alpine meadows at about 2150 m (6990 ft.). A true alpine, its stems are 10–15 cm (4–6 in.) tall with bracts of brilliant, glowing colors of scarlet, reddish purple, and magenta.

*Castilleja miniata*, British Columbia. Photo Peter Downe.

*Castilleja occidentalis* at the edge of Summit Lake, Mount Evans, Colorado.

*Castilleja nana*, White Mountains, California. Photo Chris Norton.

Summit Lake, Mount Evans, Colorado.

*Castilleja pulchella* occurs in Wyoming, Montana, Idaho, and Utah, and as it grows at 3325–3845 m (10,805–12,500 ft.), it can be classed as a true alpine. A real dwarf species growing only 5–15 cm (2–6 in.) tall, the bracts vary in color from maroon to yellow. I am currently having success with plants grown from seed that was collected in the Beartooth Pass in Wyoming.

*Castilleja rhexifolia* is the most common and widespread paintbrush in the northern and central Rockies, where it inhabits the alpine and subalpine meadows. It grows 10–30 cm (4–12 in.) tall with bracts of magenta to pink, green, orange, purple, and occasionally yellow.

*Castilleja scabrida* grows in Utah, Colorado, Nevada, and New Mexico and has two recognized geographical varieties. The type grows on most of the sandstone formations and sandy soils south and east of the Wasatch Mountains, and it ranges into Colorado and New Mexico at altitudes of 1340–2535 m (4355–8240 ft.). It grows 5–22 cm (2–8¾ in.) tall with bright red or orange, occasionally yellow, bracts that are deeply lobed with the lower one looking more leaflike.

Variety *barnebyana* inhabits rocky gravel ridges, slopes, and crevices of rhyolite and

*Castilleja rhexifolia*, Independence Pass, Colorado. Photo Chris Norton.

*Castilleja rhexifolia*, yellow bracts, Wasatch Mountains, Utah. Photo David Joyner.

*Castilleja rhexifolia*, pink and white bracts, Wasatch Mountains, Utah. Photo David Joyner.

*Castilleja rhexifolia* with *Potentilla diversifolia*, Uinta Mountains, Utah. Photo David Joyner.

dolomite limestone at 1890–2560 m (6140–8320 ft.) in Utah and Nevada. The stems are often purplish.

*Castilleja sulphurea* is wide-ranging from Montana to Utah and New Mexico, where it inhabits moist meadows and slopes at 2070–3175 m (6725–10,320 ft.). It grows 10–50 cm (4–20 in.) tall and has yellow bracts that resemble a ragged, pale yellow paintbrush. The lanceolate leaves grow to 7.5 cm (3 in.) long and are usually not cleft or lobed.

*Castilleja thompsonii* (synonym *C. villicaulis*) is a species with yellow bracts that grows in the Mount Adams and Burnt Mountain areas of Washington at an altitude of 1940–2250 m (6305–7310 ft.). It is 10–25 cm (4–10 in.) tall and prefers dry, alpine meadows and exposed rocky ridges.

*Castilleja unalaschcensis* inhabits woods and subalpine meadows in south-eastern coastal and south-central Alaska and the Aleutian Islands. It reaches 30–45 cm (12–18 in.) in height with long, pointed, and somewhat hairy leaves with three to five ribs. The yellow bracts cluster close to the ends of the stems.

**Propagation**

Every article I have read on castillejas recommends sowing seed outdoors in the autumn in order to cold stratify it over winter, and I treat mine no differently. I sow seed in 7-cm (2¾-in.) pots (just as I would any other seed) using a neutral, gritty,

*Castilleja scabrida*, Zion National Park, Utah. Photo Tony Barber.

*Castilleja scabrida* var. *barnebyana*, Burr trail, Utah. Photo Chris Norton.

*Castilleja sulphurea* in sand and dried mud habitat, Wyoming.

soil-based mixture, and I keep the pots outdoors until germination takes place. Jim Lever also sows his seed in pots but with a soil mixture of one part loam, one part peat, and two parts grit. To this he adds a very small amount of fertilizer and a dusting of magnesium carbonate. Others use different methods including cold stratification in a refrigerator, either together with or separately from the host plants.

Once you are successfully cultivating castillejas you can consider other methods of propagation. If you have a large specimen with multiple crowns you could, as Ken Sherman does, divide it by removing some crowns (still with a few roots attached), burying them in sand, and putting them into a closed cold frame. You can make these divisions in early spring, taking great care not to break off any of the tender buds. Growth usually restarts within three months, and flowering plants appear the following year.

Ken recommends taking heel cuttings of the nonflowering shoots in mid to late summer when these stems are about 5 cm (2 in.) long. Remove them from the caudex with a downward push and put them into your normal cutting mix. I use neutral horticultural grit and Ken uses horticultural-grade pumice, a more open material that makes it easier to examine the cuttings for rooting. Rooting is extremely fast, usually within three weeks. Be very careful when you check the cuttings for rooting as the stems are soft and the newly formed roots are hairlike and easy to break. Not long after roots have started to grow a new caudex forms and thin white shoots appear just above the surface. The cuttings remain like that until the following spring when the new plants can be potted up the way you pot rooted cuttings of other plants. Treat them with extreme care when potting up so as not to break off any of the new growth, and make sure that the new shoots and the caudex are planted just below the surface of the soil. Keep the cuttings in the shade for a few weeks, give them a little weak feed, and make sure they do not wilt. After they harden off they are ready to plant out. They should flower in the summer.

Regardless of the method you employ for seed germination, the postgermination care (germination is usually between March and May) that I describe is far more important.

## Cultivation

When you grow castillejas, ensure that they do not dry out. As Ken Sherman's

Overwintering stem buds of *Castilleja miniata* in cultivation. Photo David Joyner.

*Castilleja miniata* in cultivation showing that spring growth is starting. Photo David Joyner.

experiments show, castillejas require a host plant only as a means of obtaining moisture. However, if you cultivate them in the garden, make sure they do not receive too much moisture in the winter or the caudex will rot off.

I grow my plants in pots so it is easy to examine their growth up close. After the seedlings germinate I take the pots into the alpine house and allow them to continue growing until they have two or three shoots. When I prick out the seedlings into individual pots I make sure that they are planted at the same depth and that the roots are unbroken. The soil mix (a neutral, soil-based medium) is the same I use to sow the seed but I add extra grit for quick drainage and extra peat to conserve moisture. When you pot up these seedlings, you will notice that the shoots are growing from a "mini caudex." Do not worry when some shoots start to die back; as long as the soil mixture is kept moist, new shoots will grow again from below the surface of the soil.

Ken's research shows that the crown or caudex in mature plants is the center of growth and is usually buried about 2.5 cm (1 in.) underground. As autumn approaches, the shoots die down and new growth buds form at the base of the crown. If the winter is not very cold and the plant is kept moist, these new buds start to grow into shoots. Be careful that a sudden frost does not kill the shoots and prevent flowering. During the growing season you will notice that two forms of shoots are growing, those with buds and those without. The shoots with buds flower that year, and the shoots without buds form new flowering stems at their base for the following year. This continual formation of flowering shoots causes the caudex to become larger each year, and it

is from these aged plants with huge crowns that pieces with roots can be removed for propagation purposes.

Growing castillejas in pots makes it easy to miscalculate the amount of moisture in the pot and to let it dry out. I have grown *Castilleja applegatei*, *C. miniata*, *C. pulchella*, and an unidentified castilleja species, and all exhibited a similar reaction when on a hot day I accidentally withheld water or did so on purpose as an experiment. The stems flagged—some even died back—just as Ken suggested. On each occasion new growth appeared from the rootstock once I reapplied moisture.

Whitefly is the only pest I have experienced when growing plants of this genus. As I do with other plants suffering the same

*Castilleja miniata* in a garden replica of a montane meadow. Photo David Joyner.

problem, I give them a weak drench of systemic insecticide.

## CLAYTONIA
Portulacaceae
*springbeauties, purslanes*

The genus *Claytonia* was named after John Clayton (1686–1773), an English botanist from Virginia who was once described as the greatest botanist in North America. Claytonias grow throughout the West and range northwards into Alaska, inhabiting mainly alpine levels. The common name, springbeauty, aptly describes this early blooming genus that hardly waits for snowmelt before revealing five-petalled flowers.

*Claytonia acutifolia* grows in very wet places at high altitudes in Denali National Park and northwest Alaska. The long glabrous leaves are narrow, stiff, and pointed,

and they grow from a thick rootstock into a clump reminiscent of *Lewisia pygmaea*. The white flowers have a yellowish center.

*Claytonia exigua* is a wide-ranging annual with racemes 2.5–5 cm (1–2 in.) long of white-banded, rose-violet flowers growing from small tufts of linear leaves. A fine floriferous form grows on Mount Diablo, California, at approximately 1125 m (3655 ft.).

*Claytonia lanceolata*, the lanceleaf springbeauty, is widespread from Washington to southern California and the Rockies at 1385–2615 m (4500–8500 ft.), where it inhabits moist soils in shady woods, stream banks, and the alpine tundra, blooming soon after snowmelt. The stems have lanceolate leaves and grow from a deep underground corm to 5–25 cm (2–10 in.) tall; they are occasionally sprawling. As many as 15 pink or pink-veined white or violet flowers are in loose racemes and are 2 cm (¾ in.) or more across in May through July. The corm, when cooked, tastes like a potato.

Variety *chrysantha*, an extremely rare form with yellow flowers, grows on Chowder Ridge in the Mount Baker Wilderness area of Washington at 2000–2310 m (6500–7500 ft.).

*Claytonia acutifolia*, Kantishna Hills, Alaska. Photo Carolyn Parker.

*Claytonia lanceolata*, Rabbit Ears Pass, Wyoming. Photo Peter Down.

*Claytonia megarhiza*, the big-rooted springbeauty, has a wide range from Washington to New Mexico, where it inhabits high montane and alpine levels at 1910–3690 m (6200–12,000 ft.). Growing from a thick fleshy rootstock, it makes a rosette 10 cm (4 in.) high of succulent, spatulate leaves with 5-cm (2-in.) tall stems and white, five-petalled flowers in late June through August barely above the leaves. When I first saw this species near Summit Lake on Mount Evans, Colorado, it was tucked into rock crevices, making me think it was a lewisia, a close relation. Be careful when collecting seed as it tends to fall out of the pod easily and get lost in the dense clump of leaves.

Variety *nivalis* grows in the Wenatchee Mountains of Washington at around 1910

Site of *Claytonia megarhiza*, Summit Lake, Mount Evans, Colorado.

*Claytonia megarhiza*, Summit Lake, Mount Evans, Colorado.

m (6200 ft.), inhabiting screes and crevices in the magnesium-rich soil. A lovely plant of increasing popularity, it has large, rich pink flowers. It is more readily available in the trade than any other in the genus.

*Claytonia nevadensis* (synonym *Montia nevadensis*), the Sierra Nevada springbeauty, grows in wet areas at 2460–3690 m (8000–12,000 ft.) and at high elevations in the Steens Mountains of Oregon below springs or melting snow. This rhizomatous species spreads to make large patches. The two to six white to pink flowers in July through August are on stems 2–12.5 cm (1–5 in.) tall with succulent, ovate leaves that are dark green and occasionally reddish at the margins.

*Claytonia sarmentosa*, the Alaska springbeauty, grows throughout Alaska in meadows, tundra, and wet and rocky slopes, although it is not plentiful in Denali National Park. It makes clumps of fleshy, light green, long-stemmed, spatulate leaves, and the weak succulent stems have two opposite sessile leaves. Stems grow to 10 cm (4 in.) tall, and the five-petalled flowers in mid-June through mid-August are white to light pink with darker stripes.

*Claytonia scammaniana* grows throughout the Alaska Range in central Alaska including Denali National Park. The small

*Claytonia megarhiza* var. *nivalis* is deep pink in cultivation. Photo Rick Lupp.

reddish leaves are fleshy and narrow, and they form a clump to 6.3 cm (2½ in.) high. The flowers in mid-June through early August are bright to mid-pink with darker veins.

*Claytonia tuberosa* grows in the mountains of central Alaska and is a slender species, usually with a single flowering stem 4–10 cm (1½–4 in.) tall that has two short, narrow leaves. The flowers are white with a pale yellow center.

### Propagation

Propagate claytonias as you would lewisias, that is by sowing seed in the autumn or removing offsets as cuttings.

### Cultivation

*Claytonia megarhiza* and *C. megarhiza* var. *nivalis* both grow well in a sunny scree, a trough, or as a pot plant. They require a free draining situation where they can make a large clump. Although they can be short-lived—they rot off at the neck or die for no apparent reason—they nevertheless usually set plenty of seed.

*Claytonia lanceolata* and *C. nevadensis* need a moist but well-drained soil. They seem to be more difficult to grow than plants of *C. megarhiza*.

Overwatering causes neck rot especially in pot-grown claytonias. Aphids are the main pests, especially in the alpine house, and slugs partially eat the leaves on garden-grown plants.

## COLLOMIA
Polemoniaceae
*mountain trumpets*

There are approximately 15 species of *Collomia* throughout the Americas, and of these about 10 grow in the Rockies. The majority of these are either annuals or too tall for a rock garden, but one perennial species has several varieties that make it suitable for cultivation. The annual species I describe is a desirable plant for the xeric garden.

*Collomia debilis* inhabits alpine areas and shifting talus slopes at 1985–3660 m (6450–11,895 ft.) in Washington, Idaho, Montana, California, Nevada, Wyoming, and Utah. A loose tufted mat to 30 cm (12 in.) across consists of numerous sprawling stems. The flowering stems grow 2.5–12.5 cm (1–5 in.) tall with cream, white, pink, lavender, or blue flowers. Flowers are 2 cm (3/4 in.) wide, trumpet-shaped with five

*Claytonia sarmentosa*, Alaska Range. Photo Carolyn Parker.

*Claytonia scammaniana*, Alaska Range. Photo Carolyn Parker.

lobes, and 1.2–3.8 cm (½–1½ in.) long. Solitary or few in compact terminal clusters, flowers bloom June through August. *Debilis*, meaning weak, refers to the sprawling stems, although in a sense they are the strongest parts because they protect the plants from the icy mountain winds as they cling to the rocks in the scree areas.

Variety *ipomoea*, occasionally included in var. *debilis*, grows in west-central Wyoming and has beautiful, bright, rose-pink flowers. Variety *larsenii* (synonym *Collomia larsenii*) ranges from Washington to California at 1985–2185 m (6450–7100 ft.) on constantly moving talus slopes, the thong-like roots remaining anchored uphill. The gray foliage is beautifully filigreed and finely haired. Tubular flowers with flaring lobes are white to apricot-pink and blue-violet to deep violet in color. I consider it another gem of the alpine screes.

Variety *trifida* comes from central Idaho, northern Nevada, and the Cascades. Similar to *Collomia debilis* var. *debilis*, it has shorter, broader leaves, some of which can be deeply lobed, and smaller flowers to 2.5 cm (1 in.) long.

*Collomia debilis* var. *larsenii*, Burnt Mountain, eastern Cascades, Washington. Photo Rick Lupp.

*Collomia grandiflora* is an annual and ranges from British Columbia to California, Montana, Wyoming, and Arizona. It grows in dry, open or lightly wooded places from low to moderate elevations. Within the Columbia River Gorge it grows at 30–1200 m (100–3900 ft.). It has single, or occasionally several, stems that grow 15–55 cm (6–22 in.) tall with a dense terminal cluster of trumpetlike, salmon to orange flowers 1.2–2 cm (½–¾ in.) long. Narrow, linear leaves grow to 5 cm (2 in.) long and are only on the stem.

**Propagation**

Propagate collomias by sowing seed in autumn or as soon as it is ripe since seed sown in spring may not germinate until the following year.

**Cultivation**

*Collomia grandiflora* does best in a xeric flower garden. *Collomia debilis* and the varieties grow well in a sunny scree but tend to be short-lived, perhaps for two to three years at most. *Collomia debilis* var. *larsenii* makes a good exhibition plant and may be cultivated in an alpine house or frame.

Aphids and red spider mites are common pests to plants growing under glass.

# D

## DELPHINIUM
Ranunculaceae
*larkspurs*

There are approximately 250 species of *Delphinium* distributed throughout North America, Europe, and Asia, and there are many other hybrids of garden or horticultural origin. They are beautiful and elegant plants with flowers of various colors, and many have stems growing 2–2.4 m (6–8 ft.) tall. Although I describe only the North American species that grow to approximately 60 cm (24 in.), the small stature does not detract from their beauty. Many species die down after blooming, and you should take great care to prevent a cultivated plant from rotting off during its dormant period. Delphiniums are very poisonous, especially to cattle and horses, so if you are trail riding be careful where you tether your pony. The name *delphinium* means dolphin, which refers to the buds that are shaped like a dolphin.

*Delphinium alpestre* grows in Colorado and New Mexico in high mountain areas. Thin, weak stems are 10–15 cm (4–6 in.) tall with congested, much dissected leaves, and a short inflorescence of dark, dull flowers in May through July. The flowers are not very showy and barely reach above the leaves.

*Delphinium andersonii* is a common plant in the Great Basin and in southern Montana, where it grows in loose, sandy soils, sagebrush, mixed desert shrub, and open pine forests to 2340 m (7600 ft.). The mainly basal leaves are sparse and deeply divided. Smooth red stems grow 10–60 cm (4–24 in.) tall with bilobed flowers in dense spikes during April through June.

There are two very similar varieties that are often confused with one another where their ranges overlap, and some authorities consider them to be of specific rank only. Variety *andersonii* ranges from Oregon, to Montana, California, Nevada, and Utah and is subscapose with pale blue flowers. Variety *scaposum* grows in Colorado, New Mexico, Arizona, Utah, and Nevada but is not

particularly subscapose. The flowers are usually dark blue.

*Delphinium bicolor* occurs in grassland and pine forests of the northern and western Rockies to subalpine levels. Stems 15–40 cm (6–15¾ in.) tall grow from a cluster of woody, fibrous roots. The basal leaves are deeply cut, and the blue flowers in midsummer have yellow or white upper petals with blue veins.

*Delphinium brachycentrum* grows in Alaska inhabiting scree or rocky slopes and meadows along tundra to 1200 m (3900 ft.). This species is not often seen but is plentiful in Denali National Park. The leaves are alternate, palmate, and have three to five deeply toothed, rounded lobes. The hairy stems are 10–60 cm (4–24 in.) tall, and the creamy white to royal blue flowers bloom in mid-July through mid-August.

*Delphinium decorum* (synonym *D. orfordii*) is a beautiful dwarf plant ranging from southern Oregon to the California coastal region, where it grows in light woodland. Although references give the height as 10–40 cm (4–15¾ in.), my own plant never grows more than 15 cm (6 in.) high. Glabrous leaves with three to five segments may be lobed or entire, and hairy stems have

*Delphinium brachycentrum*, Denali National Park, Alaska. Photo Verna Pratt.

large, deep blue-purple blooms in many flowered racemes in May through July.

I once made the almost fatal mistake of throwing an apparently dead plant of this species onto a heap of plant debris (it was the plant's dormant period and I thought it was dead). The following spring I was amazed to see it growing—with a bud—at the base of the heap. Since this species makes a lovely pot plant, I potted it up and exhibited it two weeks later.

*Delphinium glareosum* inhabits talus slopes and alpine ridges in the Olympics. It has large, deeply lobed, fleshy basal leaves and grows 10–30 cm (4–12 in.) tall with rich, velvety blue, hairy flowers in 10 or more loose racemes. Blooming is June through August, and it dies down very quickly afterward.

*Delphinium hesperinum* comes from the Coast Ranges of California and is recognizable by the rust-colored veins on the underside of the narrowly divided leaves. Stems grow 30–60 cm (12–24 in.) tall with dark or pale blue flowers in May through July. The two lower petals are in a rounded dome and very hairy.

*Delphinium menziesii* grows on coastal bluffs, prairies, and low elevation meadows from British Columbia to northern California. It grows 15–60 cm (6–24 in.) tall and has hairs on its stems, leaves, and flowers. The leaves are in five segments, each trilobed, and blue flowers in April through July are in racemes of two to three on pedicels branching from the stem.

*Delphinium nelsonii* is common throughout the Rockies in woodland habitat. Unbranched stems 15–60 cm (6–24 in.) tall grow from tuberlike roots and have 3–10 rich blue-purple flowers with two white petals during midsummer. It is very similar in appearance and growth to *D. nuttallianum*.

*Delphinium nudicaule* grows in California on dryish slopes among scrub and open woodland to 2155 m (7000 ft.) and offers an interesting color break within the genus. It grows 20–60 cm (8–24 in.) tall with leafless stems and 2–10 orange to red flowers in March through June on long pedicels. Reputed to be short-lived in cultivation, it is possibly even a biennial. However, neither the color forms of *Delphinium nudicaule* or var. *luteum* has been short-lived with me. Perhaps this reputation arose as a result of growers mistakenly watering the plant too much (which results in rotting

*Delphinium decorum* in cultivation.

*Delphinium menziesii*, Washington.

off) during the dormant period, when it should be kept dry.

I saw this plant for the first time in the wild during a hike with Wayne Roderick and Janet Haden, Chair of the Western Chapter of the NARGS, on the Fire Interpretive trail in the beautiful Mount Diablo State Park, California. I had a difficult scramble on the scree slopes to photograph the plant, but it was worth it.

Variety *luteum* (synonym *Delphinium luteum*) is very similar in growth to *D. nudicaule* but has cream to deep yellow flowers. Both *D. nudicaule* and var. *luteum* come true to color from seed.

*Delphinium nudicaule*, Mount Diablo State Park, California.

*Delphinium nudicaule* var. *luteum* in cultivation.

*Delphinium nuttallianum* grows throughout the West in open, dryish habitats on meadow fringes and trailsides at 1500–3075 m (4875–10,000 ft.). Stems grow 15–50 cm (6–20 in.) tall with bright blue to pale purple flowers in March through July that have two white upper petals and two deeply bilobed lower petals. The few leaves are divided into three to five narrow divisions with sharp tips.

*Delphinium parishii* ranges from the Mojave and Colorado Deserts to the south-central valley of California among Joshua tree woodland, pinyon and juniper forests, and scrub. Stems grow 15–60 cm (6–24 in.) tall and have sky blue flowers in March through June with large, backwardly reflexed sepals. The leaves have three to five rectangular lobes.

*Delphinium patens* occurs in central and southern California on the fringes of woods below 1075 m (3500 ft.). The common name of zigzag delphinium refers to the unusual wiry, zigzag stem that grows 15–60 cm (6–24 in.) tall. The upper two petals of the dark blue flowers that bloom in March through May are white with blue streaks.

*Delphinium nuttallianum*, Yosemite National Park, California.

The leaves are divided into three to five simple segments.

*Delphinium pratense* grows in the southern Sierra Nevada in meadows and open woods at 1845–2615 m (6000–8500 ft.). The slender, hairy stems are 25–30 cm (10–12 in.) tall, and the blue-purple flowers bloom in June through July.

*Delphinium variegatum* occurs in the fields of California's Coast Ranges and the Sierra Nevada foothills. This striking species is aptly named the royal delphinium with its very large, royal blue flowers on stems that grow 30–60 cm (12–24 in.) tall. Leaves are divided into three narrow divisions that are again forked three to five times, and the leaf segments are densely hairy and folded together.

### Propagation

Seed sown during the autumn usually germinates the following spring. You can divide many species in early spring or increase them by taking cuttings of new growth.

### Cultivation

If you grow delphiniums in the garden, site them in a well-drained, open, sunny position. Delphiniums make good alpine house plants if you grow them in a gritty soil mix in full sun. Be aware, however, that some species, including *Delphinium decorum*, *D. glareosum*, *D. menziesii*, and *D. nudicaule*, require a dormant period after they die down. Some species are short-lived but are easily raised from seed.

The slug is probably the delphiniums' worst enemy. These pests love any new growth and will eat until the plant is completely distorted or dead. Aphids may attack plants grown under glass.

# DICENTRA
### Fumariaceae
*bleeding hearts, steers' heads*

There are about 20 species of *Dicentra* from Asia and the United States, most of which are herbaceous perennials. All are very attractive with dissected, ferny foliage and heart-shaped pendent flowers that hang in panicles or racemes. They bloom from early spring to summer. The species I discuss range mainly from Washington to California, although one extends eastwards and another grows in the eastern United States as well as the West. Dicentras are not plants for full sun; they generally grow on north-facing slopes when at altitude (though they are never at alpine altitudes) and are more commonly found in woodlands and other shaded areas.

*Dicentra chrysantha* grows on dry, brushy slopes below 1700 m (5525 ft.) from the southern two-thirds of California to northern Baja California in Mexico. Not as compact as the other species I describe, it grows 45–152 cm (18–60 in.) tall and has bilateral, bright yellow flowers in April through September with two petals bent at midlength that stick out sideways. Leaves are blue-green and fernlike. It is most common in areas that have burned as it quickly recolonizes those areas. This is not an easy species in cultivation.

*Dicentra cuccularia* grows in the eastern United States as well as in Oregon and Washington, where it inhabits moist woods. It has a rootstock of small tubers that are reminiscent of rice grains and from which grows a clump of finely dissected gray-green leaves and 20–30-cm (8–12-in.) tall stems. This species is the true dutchman's breeches, blooming with white, long-spurred flowers in March through May. It dies down very quickly after flowering and is often grown as a pot plant for exhibition.

'Pittsburgh' is a pink-flushed cultivar, and there are reports of a lemon-yellow form.

*Dicentra formosa* ranges from southern British Columbia to central California, growing in damp, shady places or wet, open woods below 2155 m (7000 ft.). From March through July deep rose-pink buds open to pink heart-shaped flowers that hang in racemes on stems 22–50 cm (8¾–20 in.) tall. Blue-green fernlike leaves have long stalks that form a basal clump. It self seeds quite readily, especially when assisted by ants that are attracted by the oil contained in the shiny black seeds.

Do not be confused, as I was during a hike to Bohemia Mountain in Oregon, if you see this species growing from a pile of rocks. *Erythronium grandiflorum* occurred nearby in a similar habitat, and although both species gave the appearance of being scree plants, they thrived in the damp, humus-rich soil that existed below the rocks. *Dicentra formosa* is very popular in cultivation and is sometimes confused with *D. eximia*, the species that grows in the northeastern United States. Some references even give it the synonym *D. eximia*. In the United Kingdom, *D. formosa* is micropropagated for sale in the trade.

*Dicentra cuccularia* in cultivation.

Close-up of *Dicentra formosa*.

*Dicentra formosa* in screelike conditions, Bohemia Mountain, Oregon.

A colony of *Dicentra formosa* subsp. *oregana* in the Siskiyou Mountains showing wide color variation. Photo Neal Maillet.

Subspecies *oregana* is endemic to serpentine soil or rock in southwest Oregon and California; the typically pink or yellowish white flowers are tipped rose-pink.

'Alba' has white flowers.

*Dicentra ochroleuca* grows in California below 1000 m (3250 ft.) on disturbed land or among scrub. Although similar to *D. chrysantha*, it has fewer, larger flowers that are off-white to cream with purple tips.

*Dicentra pauciflora* ranges from the Siskiyou Mountains to the Sierra Nevada in subalpine forests and alpine fell-fields at 1300–3300 m (4225–10,725 ft.). It is similar to *D. uniflora* but with two smaller, reflexed sepals that give it the common name, short-horn steer's head. The leaves are also more finely cut, and the white to pink flowers in June through July are on stems 2.5–7 cm (1–2¾ in.) tall.

*Dicentra uniflora* ranges from Washington to the Sierra Nevada of California, Idaho, western Wyoming, and northern Utah. It is common on gravel forest floors where the snowbeds persist or have just melted, typically at 460–3075 m (1495–10,000 ft.). This species is commonly called steer's head or longhorn steer's head because of the flattened, steerhead-like petals and

*Dicentra uniflora* in the Siskiyou Mountains, Oregon.

the two large reflexed sepals that give the flower the appearance of a Texas longhorn. Because it is small it is often hidden by the surrounding sagebrush making it difficult to spot. White to pink flowers in February through July are solitary on stems 5–10 cm (2–4 in.) tall, and the single, pinnate leaves grow separately to the stem. Dieback below ground level occurs quickly after blooming. Although a beautiful species, it is very difficult to grow.

### Propagation

If seed is available you should sow it as soon as it is ripe and expose it to the weather. You can also carefully divide the rhizomes or tubers in early spring.

### Cultivation

*Dicentra cuccularia* and *D. formosa* are easy to grow in a garden's gritty, humus-rich soil. The other species I mention, especially *D. uniflora*, may grow best in the alpine house where their individual requirements can be met.

Slugs are the biggest danger especially when new shoots are emerging from the ground.

## DODECATHEON
Primulaceae
*shooting stars, prairie pointers*

Dodecatheons grow in almost every state of the United States and the flower is the logo for NARGS. In the same family as cyclamen, it has a very similar flower with five backward pointing petals in shades of magenta, rose, lilac, or white. At the tip of each dodecatheon flower, however, a conelike stamen tube juts out giving the flower an illusion of speed. This feature gives it the common name of shooting star. When in bloom the flower stems curve so that the flowers nod, but once pollinated and the fruits start to ripen, the flower stems straighten so that when the seed is ripe the stems are erect. The seed capsule is barrel shaped and contains a great number of tiny seeds.

The specific name dodecatheon comes from the Greek, meaning twelve gods or a plant that is protected by the Greek gods. If you find a dodecatheon in your travels, take a while to examine the flower closely to appreciate its intricate beauty.

*Dodecatheon alpinum* grows in mountain meadows and along mountain streams to 3500 m (11,375 ft.) in eastern Oregon, California, Arizona, and Utah. It has basal linear leaves 3.1–10 cm (1¼–4 in.) long. Magenta to lavender four-petalled flowers in June through August are 2–2.5 cm (¾–1 in.) long, have a yellow base, and are in 1–10 umbels on stems 10–30 cm (4–12 in.) tall.

*Dodecatheon clevelandii* grows from California's Coast Ranges to Baja California, Mexico, on chaparral, grassy slopes and flats, and open woodland. Most varieties have stems 30–60 cm (12–24 in.) tall with umbels of 5–16 pink to magenta flowers (on rare occasions the flowers are white). These early spring flowers can be to 2.5 cm (1 in.) long with white and yellow bands slightly above the dark maroon anther tubes.

Variety *insulare* grows in moist Californian clays that dry out by summer. Leaves 5–20 cm (2–8 in.) long are gray-green and wavy at the margins, and stems 30–45 cm (12–18 in.) tall have umbels of 16–18 lavender-pink flowers with yellow and black anther tubes in February to March. Variety *patulum* occurs in California's shaded, moist, bare granitic banks. The smallest in the species, it grows 5–20 cm (2–8 in.) tall with leaves 2.5–5 cm (1–2 in.) long. In spring, red-violet to rose-purple or rarely white flowers with yellow or white bands bloom in one to six umbels.

Variety *sanctarum* is a vigorous and very early blooming variety that is in growth by January in California at about 1185 m (3860 ft.). Leaves are 5–10 cm (2–4 in.) long. The stems are 15–30 cm (6–12 in.) tall with umbels of three to seven lavender flowers in January to March that can be to 2.5 cm (1 in.) long with a yellow base to each petal. The anther tube is dark purple. Most varieties are reputed to be a little tender, but var. *sanctarum* has survived frost and snow in my garden for many years, though the leaves droop during very cold weather.

*Dodecatheon alpinum.*

*Dodecatheon clevelandii* var. *sanctarum.*

*Dodecatheon conjugans* ranges from Washington to California, Montana, and Wyoming. It grows in vernally wet pasture, stony clay soils, and pine forest at 1360–1915 m (4420–6225 ft.) and is similar in appearance to *D. pulchellum*. Prostrate rosettes of thick oblanceolate to ovate or lanceolate leaves are 5–25 cm (2–10 in.) long. Stems are 10–25 cm (4–10 in.) tall with umbels of two to seven bright rose-violet to white flowers in April through June. At the base of the petals are bands of white and yellow with wavy red markings at the bottom of the maroon stamen tube.

*Dodecatheon dentatum*, the white shoot-ing star, ranges from British Columbia to northern Oregon, Idaho, and Utah, where it grows in moist soil and woodland, often near streams, waterfalls, and wet cliffs. The stalked, ovate to oblong-lanceolate leaves are 3.1–10 cm (1¼–4 in.) long and toothed at the edges. Stems are 10–40 cm (4–15¾ in.) tall and carry umbels of up to seven flowers in May through July. The flowers look like straight, plain white darts and are to 2.5 cm (1 in.) long with a yellow tube and a purple ring at the center. The stamens are deep reddish purple.

Variety *utahense*, first described by Neil Holmgren (1994), grows only in Big Cot-tonwood Canyon in the central Wasatch Range, Utah, in wet, shaded rock crevices in waterfalls, seeps, or near streams. This attractive variety has twisted petals that are suffused with pink. Stems grow 10–30 cm (4–12 in.) tall.

*Dodecatheon frigidum* grows in wet alpine meadows and tundra throughout most of Alaska except the south-eastern and south-central coastal areas. It has petiolate, spade-shaped, slightly dentate leaves 2.5–6.3 cm (1–2½ in.) long and stems to 25 cm (10 in.) tall. Magenta flowers in June through mid-July are in umbels of two to five and have a white base adjoining the stamen tube.

*Dodecatheon hansenii* grows in the lower western foothills of the Sierra Nevada. The stem is 10–25 cm (4–10 in.) tall with maroon flowers in April through May that have a yellow band.

*Dodecatheon hendersonii* ranges from Vancouver Island to California in woodland to around 1250 m (4060 ft.) where the soil dries out in summer. Rosettes of prostrate leaves are ovate to spatulate, toothed, and to 15 cm (6 in.) long. This is a robust species with stems that grow to 45 cm (18 in.) or more with umbels of 4–17 white or magenta to lavender flowers in spring to summer.

*Dodecatheon frigidum*, Denali National Park, Alaska. Photo Verna Pratt.

*Dodecatheon jeffreyi* (synonyms *D. lancifolium*, *D. tetrandrum*, *D. viviparum*) is a majestic plant that grows from Alaska to California in wet and boggy habitats. The leaves are oblanceolate and to 30 cm (12 in.) or more in length. Stems 30–60 cm (12–24 in.) tall carry umbels of up to 18 magenta, lavender, or pink 2.5-cm (1-in.) long violet flowers in May through August. The anther tube is maroon and yellow.

Like other delegates to the NARGS conference in Eugene, Oregon, in 1998, I was thrilled at the wonderful sight of hundreds of thousands of *Dodecatheon jeffreyi* growing in the boggy conditions at Hemlock Butte. This species is named for John Jeffrey who, in 1850, was sent to California by a group of Scottish horticulturalists to collect seed. He discovered this species and also the Jeffrey pine (*Pinus jeffreyi*) that grows in the eastern Sierra Nevada.

*Dodecatheon meadia* (synonyms *D. hugeri*, *D. pauciflorum*). I include this plant for discussion primarily because it is a popular garden plant, although it is an eastern species. It inhabits dry prairies, open woods, and rocky hillsides, blooming in April through June. The basal leaves are ovate to spatulate and 15–30 cm (6–12 in.)

long. Stems 15–50 cm (6–20 in.) tall have 20–50 umbels of five-petalled flowers to 2.5 cm (1 in.) long that are rose, white, lilac, or pink in color.

Early settlers gave this species the common name of prairie pointer, and the flowers were used to make makeup and as beauty accessories. The plant was much more abundant then than it is now.

*Dodecatheon poeticum* is a relatively rare endemic in meadows and open, vernally moist woodlands from the Columbia River Gorge of Oregon to Yakima county, Washington. The gray-green leaves are ovate-lanceolate, 10–12.5 cm (4–5 in.) long, and lightly toothed. Stems are to 15–25 cm (6–10 in.) tall with umbels of 4–10 vivid lavender to rose-purple flowers to 2.5 cm (1 in.) long in March through April. At the base of the petals is a white edging that is separated from a yellow edging by a thin, wavy, purple line. A fine, rough pubescence covers the entire plant.

*Dodecatheon pulchellum* (synonyms *D. amethystinum*, *D. pauciflorum*, *D. puberulum*, *D. radicatum*) is a common, widespread species growing throughout the West in damp, midelevation grassland, mountain meadows, and streamsides to above the timberline. The basal leaves are 5–40 cm

*Dodecatheon jeffreyi*, Hemlock Butte, Oregon.

*Dodecatheon meadia.*

(2–15 ¾ in.) long, oblanceolate to spatulate, and entire (occasionally they have small teeth). Scapes are 10–60 cm (4–24 in.) tall with one to several flowers 2–2.5 cm (¾–1 in.) long. Flowers in umbels of 3–25 bloom in early April to May at low elevation through June to July above the timberline. The petals are pink to deep magenta, occasionally white, and the stamen tube in the flower's center is yellow or yellow and maroon.

Subspecies *alaskanum* grows in saline coastal meadows in south-eastern and south-central Alaska. The short scapes are about as long as the leaves, which are ovate. Subspecies *superbum* grows in the same habitat as subsp. *alaskanum* and has thick erect stems with large flowers.

'Red Wings' has deep crimson petals, and 'Sookes Variety' is a selected small form.

***Dodecatheon redolens*** (synonym *D. jeffreyi* var. *redolens*) inhabits damp places in the southern Sierra Nevada, Nevada, and Utah at 2460–3690 m (8000–12,000 ft.). It is very similar to D. jeffreyi but the leaves are shorter and the plant is glandular-pubescent. Stems are 30–60 cm (12–24 in.) tall and have umbels of magenta, lavender, or white flowers in July through August with greenish yellow stamen tubes. The stamens have short, rugose, black filaments.

*Dodecatheon pulchellum* subsp. *alaskanum*. Photo Verna Pratt.

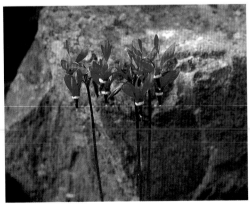

*Dodecatheon pulchellum* 'Red Wings'.

*Dodecatheon pulchellum* subsp. *superbum*. Photo Verna Pratt.

*Dodecatheon subalpinum* (synonym
*D. hendersonii* var. *yosemitanum*), the Sierra
shooting star, grows in moist places from
Yosemite National Park southwards in the
Sierra Nevada at 2155–4000 m
(7000–13,000 ft.). Similar to a dwarf version
of *D. hendersonii*, its leaves are petiolate,
entire, and oblanceolate to spatulate and are
2.5–7.5 cm (1–3 in.) long. Stems 5–15 cm
(2–6 in.) tall have magenta to pink flowers
in May through July with a white base, and
the stamen tube is maroon with a yellow
band. The roots of this species have numerous, tiny bulblets that look like rice grains.

### Propagation

Propagate dodecatheons by seed as soon as
the seed is ripe; late sown seed usually takes
a year to germinate. Let the seedlings grow
on for a couple of years in the pot and do not
prick them out. It is best to plant the complete pot contents out in the garden after
two years and let the seedlings grow into
mature plants. You can divide mature plants
in early spring.

### Cultivation

Grow dodecatheons in a humus-rich soil in
a sunny or shady spot where the roots can
remain cool. Some species require a dry
summer dormancy. They make excellent pot
plants for the alpine house.

Aphids can distort the leaves and stems.
In the open garden slugs eat new growth.

## DOUGLASIA
Primulaceae
*dwarf-primroses*

*Douglasia*—or should it be *Androsace*? The
Alpine Garden Society's (1993) *Encyclopaedia of Alpines* and Smith and Lowe (1997)

have recognized *Douglasia* as being a subdi-
vision of *Androsace* and given it its own subsection in the *Androsace* section. However,
growers still refer to these plants as douglasias and not androsaces, which I think is
correct. I admit that the tight cushions on
douglasias make it easy to understand why
some taxonomists want them to be included
in the genus *Androsace*. Early botanists did
not separate the North American douglasias
or the European Alp species (now called
vitaliana) from the broader grouping of
androsace, but molecular, reproductive, and
anatomical studies in later years showed that
there are very different groups that should
be treated at the generic level as *Androsace*,
*Douglasia*, and *Vitaliana*. I discuss the nine
douglasias that are native to the United
States, five of which grow in Alaska.

Douglasias are a great addition to the
trough or small rock garden, making either
tight mounds or loose mats of deep green
rosettes. They flower from spring into
summer with pale to deep pink blooms that
are stemless in some species. They also make
excellent pot plants for anyone aspiring to
exhibit at shows.

*Douglasia alaskana* (synonym *Androsace
alaskana*) grows at high elevations on sandy
soil or on the scree slopes of the coastal or
interior mountains of Alaska or southwestern Yukon. Likely a short-lived perennial,
this weedy species makes flat, single rosettes
of sessile, wedge-shaped leaves that grow to
1.2 cm (½ in.) long. The tiny flowers are
stemless when they start to bloom and are
purple-violet when young. As the stems
elongate with age (to about 10 cm [4 in.]
tall), the flowers turn white.

*Douglasia arctica* (synonym *Androsace
americana*) has a scattered distribution in

Alaska and can be found on the arctic shore between the Mackenzie and Coppermine Rivers, in the Yukon River valley, and in the Fort Yukon region. This species is very similar to *D. gormanii* but the upper surface of the leaf is hairless and ciliate on the margins with simple hairs. I have never seen it in cultivation.

*Douglasia beringensis*, originally thought to grow only on limestone near the coast on the Seward Peninsula of western Alaska, has since been found in several other locations on the west coast, even as far south as the Alaska Range. First described in 1994, this species is very close to *D. arctica* and *D. gormanii*, differing only in the shape

of the hairs and in having densely pubescent calyx and bracts. Like *D. arctica* it is probably not in cultivation, although the University of Alaska at Fairbanks has been growing it purely for generic work on the leaves. Even so, because these plants have been grown indoors they do not flower; consequently, they cannot be considered to be in cultivation.

*Douglasia gormanii* (synonym *Androsace constancei*) is among the more common douglasias in the interior of Alaska and the western Yukon, but as it grows in areas that are very difficult to reach, seed is not commonly collected. It therefore remains an extremely rare plant. Rick Lupp collected seed during July 1996 just northeast of McKinley Park boundary at approximately 1080 m (3510 ft.). There, in widely scattered colonies of 20–30 plants, most forms were found to be making mats, although a few formed tight little domes. They grew in an area of exposed loose rock and silicate soil with a mainly eastern exposure. Most seed capsules were empty, and judging by the number of capsules on the plants at that time, blooming had been very sparse. Until the limited number of plants in cultivation flower, it is not possible to know if this sparsity is normal.

*Douglasia alaskana*, Alaska Range. Photo Carolyn Parker.

*Douglasia beringensis*, Nulato Hills, northwest Alaska. Photo Carolyn Parker.

Although the mean annual temperature of the area ranges from −6°C to −2°C (21°F to 28°F) the temperature extremes range from as high as 35°C (95°F) in summer to −63°C (−81°F) in winter with only 40 to 60 frost-free days per year and almost constant, sometimes severe wind. Total mean precipitation is approximately 41 cm (16¼ in.), only 15 cm (6 in.) of which occurs during the growing season, which is only 120–140 days long. How on earth can we gardeners imitate such conditions? Although Rick Lupp and other members of the Androsace Society have grown plants of *Douglasia gormanii* 10–12.5 cm (4–5 in.) across quite easily, lack of flowering has been the problem. This lack of flowering is most probably due to the habitat and climatic conditions that exist where the plants grow naturally. This species requires bright light over a long period, and it will be some time before it is cultivated widely enough for growers to fully understand its flowering requirements in cultivation.

I, like others who received seed from Rick, have grown a plant from his July 1996 collection. The cushion is the tightest I have seen on a douglasia after two years of growth—it is 7 cm (2¾ in.) across and 2 cm (¾ in.) high—but it has shown no sign of blooming. Verna Pratt has told me that even in Alaska it takes several years from seed to bloom properly. Flowers of *Douglasia gormanii* in the wild are bright pink during the first couple of days of blooming, and they fade to pale pink with age.

Some interesting plants that grow in the screes with *Douglasia gormanii* include *Saxifraga eschscholtzii*, which makes lovely pulvinate mounds, *Androsace chamaejasme* subsp. *lehmanniana*, which forms mats to 45 cm (18 in.) across, and *Dryas octopetala* var. *octopetala*, which also forms mats.

*Douglasia gormanii*, Ogilvie Mountains, Alaska. Photo Carolyn Parker.

*Douglasia gormanii*. Photo Verna Pratt.

*Douglasia gormanii* is recorded by Smith and Lowe (1997) under the name *Androsace constancei*, an old synonym not recognized by North American botanists.

*Douglasia idahoensis* was first described in 1981. It is endemic to granitic, gravel soils of the open, subalpine ridges, summits, and upper slopes in the mountains of central Idaho, where it grows at 2215–2740 m (7200–8900 ft.). Ground coverage by this plant is usually extensive, and most populations occur on north-facing slopes indicating that the species requires moist, cool conditions. Some populations are restricted to the lee side of ridges where windblown snow accumulates and snowmelt lasts later into summer than in adjacent areas. This species is among the earliest to commence flowering in the subalpine communities, usually in late June or early July. It makes mats or low spreading cushions with small, succulent, bright green leaves. Short stems are terminated by clusters of three to five relatively large pink to magenta blooms. Soon after flowering the leaves turn red and the whole plant becomes a distinctive dark red-green.

Although they make tight mats or cushions in the wild, plants in cultivation form only loose mats if grown in an alpine house.

When grown outside and in partial shade, however, they tighten up like other cushion plants. It is still a rarity in cultivation although it is fairly amiable and grows quite quickly. The Idaho Conservation Data Center reports that plants excluded from insect visitors failed to set seed, which indicates that plants in cultivation should be hand pollinated.

*Douglasia laevigata* ranges from west of the Cascades in Washington to northwest Oregon on rocky alpine slopes.

Variety *laevigata* occurs around Mount Hood and in the Columbia River Gorge, where it creeps over rocky alpine ledges and coastal bluffs (hence the common name cliff

*Douglasia idahoensis*, Salmon River Mountains, west-central Idaho. Photo Jay Lunn.

*Douglasia idahoensis* in habitat, Salmon River Mountains, west-central Idaho. Photo Jay Lunn.

douglasia). Small, tight rosettes can form either a good, dense, mounded mat to 7–8 cm (2¾–3 in.) high and 30 cm (12 in.) across or a mat that is quite lax. It is an easy-going species in cultivation and has very attractive flowers in spring through summer that are a pale to deep pink in large umbels held just above the foliage. Newcomers to douglasias find that this variety is an easy one with which to start. It is also a good trough companion for saxifrages.

Variety *ciliolata* is larger in all its parts. The mounds are more lax than the type, and large, rounded pink flowers grow on stems 7–8 cm (2¾–3 in.) tall. The leaves are ciliate and often toothed.

Two cultivars are worth noting. 'Gothenburg' was introduced after that well-known exhibitor Geoff Rollinson cultivated it from seed he received from the Gothenburg Botanic Gardens in 1986. Much more compact than the type and with slower growth, it has large rosettes and large, deep pink flowers with broad petals. Plants grown from the seed of this non-sterile cultivar exhibit the same large rosettes and flowers. It is well suited to the alpine house.

'Packwood' originated from near Packwood in the southern Cascades. This selection by Rick Lupp makes a really dense globose dome just like the best androsace, though I find it easier than androsaces to grow into a reasonably large dome. Large

*Douglasia laevigata*, Mount Townsend, Washington.

*Douglasia laevigata* var. *ciliolata*. Photo Jay Lunn.

*Douglasia laevigata* var. *laevigata*, light pink form. Columbia River Gorge. Photo David Hale.

*Douglasia laevigata* 'Gothenburg' in cultivation.

flowers on 5-cm (2-in.) stems help make this cultivar among the best.

*Douglasia montana* occurs in the Rocky Mountains of Montana, Idaho, and Wyoming, inhabiting open ridges and scree slopes. This is another easy-going and vigorous species that can be very floriferous. The mounds and mats are variable, from the loose to the very tight, but all have rich pink to rose-purple flowers on very short stems. Blooming is in May but at higher elevation it blooms during July. I have grown many plants of *D. montana* from seed but none better than those from the limestone screes of the Big Belt Mountains of Montana, where it grows with *Draba oligosperma* and

*Phlox albomarginata*. This form makes an extremely impenetrable tight mound that from April is covered with deep pink flowers on 2.5-cm (1-in.) stems.

Another exciting introduction from Mt. Tahoma nursery is a form of *Douglasia montana* that also comes from Montana. It has tiny needlelike foliage and makes a lovely tight mat that is covered with rose-colored flowers during spring with a lighter blooming in autumn. The mat is particularly tight in a trough.

*Douglasia nivalis* grows on scree slopes and alpine rocky ridges from the south Washington Cascades to the Wenatchee Mountains and the Rockies of British

Limestone scree in the Big Belt Mountains, Montana. Site of *Douglasia montana*, *Draba oligosperma*, and *Phlox albomarginata*. Photo Ev Whittemore.

*Douglasia montana*, Medicine Wheel, Wyoming. Photo Peter Downe.

*Douglasia montana* in cultivation.

*Douglasia montana*, Hunt Mountain, Big Horn Mountains, Wyoming. Photo Chris Norton.

Columbia and Alberta. It has lovely silver-gray foliage with 5-cm (2-in.) stems and striking androsace-like blooms that vary from an intense, rich-colored wine-red to violet-purple. This species is quite variable because although it forms a mat, it can be untidy. The untidiness is annoying if you grow the plant in a pot as the mat flops to one side, but the plant more than compensates for this with silver foliage and beautiful flowers. A form from British Columbia I am growing is completely different with a low, tight dome and stemless pink flowers.

Variety *dentata*, found only in Washington, varies only in that it has several marked dentations near the leaf tip instead of entire margins.

*Douglasia ochotensis* (synonym *Androsace ochotensis*) is the fifth of the

*Douglasia nivalis*, Wenatchee Mountains, Washington. Photo Tony Barber.

*Douglasia nivalis*, south Washington Cascades. Photo David Hale.

Alaskan douglasias and grows on the north slopes of the Brooks Range. It makes cushions to 5 cm (2 in.) high, and although the 1.2-cm (½-in.) stems bear only one pink to purple flower, the green cushion can completely disappear beneath the blooms at flowering time in March. A plant of this species was exhibited for the first time at an Alpine Garden Society show in 2001.

**Propagation**
Seed of *Douglasia laevigata*, *D. montana*, *D. nivalis*, *D nivalis* var. *dentata*, and occasionally *D. idahoensis* has been available in the society seed exchanges and commercial lists since 1990. Seed sown in the autumn usually germinates in the following spring, although sometimes it waits another year. Spring-sown seed does not usually germinate until the following year, although there may occasionally be sporadic germination in the first year. Germination is nowhere near 100 percent, even with freshly collected seed. Although cultivars such as *D. laevigata* 'Packwood' and 'Gothenburg' have set seed, the germination rate has been just as poor as the species. Normally many plants can be produced from seed but because of the

*Douglasia nivalis* in cultivation.

irregular germination in douglasias, it may be better to resort to cuttings. Of course, if you want to duplicate any of the cultivars you will have to propagate them vegetatively anyway.

With the exception of *Douglasia idahoensis*, you should take douglasia cuttings after flowering, usually in June. Cut off a rosette with a piece of stem attached and insert it into sand in a closed cutting frame. Rooting usually takes place by early autumn when the small plants can be potted up and kept in a cold frame over winter. Cuttings can be taken later but they do not usually root until the following spring.

Douglasia rosettes vary in size. *Douglasia laevigata* 'Packwood', for example, has very small rosettes, and because of the tightness of the cushion, cuttings around the edge of the plant are easiest to come by. *Douglasia nivalis*, *D. nivalis* var. *dentata*, and the more usual forms of *D. laevigata*, including the cultivar *D. laevigata* 'Gothenburg', have fairly large rosettes, so you can take cuttings from wherever you wish. As *D. montana* varies in habit, those with tight cushions have to be dealt with by taking cuttings from the edge as with *D. laevigata* 'Packwood'. Those making a looser cushion can be treated like the other douglasias. *Douglasia gormanii* cuttings, taken in June, normally root within four weeks.

Cuttings from *Douglasia idahoensis* are best taken in the autumn since they root over winter. Make sure the cuttings have a fairly long stem, and remove leaves to allow at least 2 cm (¾ in.) of bare stem to be inserted into the cutting medium. Leaves that are not removed curl back after a while and push the cutting out of the medium.

## Cultivation

All douglasias make excellent pot plants; they appear on the show bench without fail during the Alpine Garden Society spring shows. The most widely grown species is probably *Douglasia laevigata*, which is an easy plant for a scree.

To ensure a good compact form, grow douglasias from seed and select the best. Plants in pots do much better if you grow them outside for the majority of the year and bring them into the alpine house or frame only to overwinter. *Douglasia idahoensis* becomes very loose if you grow it under cover all the time.

Wherever you position your douglasias, make sure they are not in full sun all day especially during summer. In the growing season douglasias need plenty of moisture, and even during winter they prefer some occasional water. Those in troughs do well when left outside all year round. None of the species I grow needs lime in the soil or soil mix, although plenty of grit for drainage is a necessity.

Most douglasias suffer dieback at some time during the year, which is occasionally caused by aphids. Dieback usually occurs during winter but the dead foliage can be cut off in spring. Aphids, mainly whiteflies, can cause a plant in the alpine house to collapse at any time. These pests exist under the foliage and sometimes grow into a big infestation before any sign of them is evident. You should regularly lift the foliage to examine the pot edges for the sooty, sticky substance that indicates aphid infestation, as it is not always obvious. A systemic insecticide spray or weak drench normally gets rid of these pests, and root aphids can also be destroyed with a systemic drench. Birds occasionally pull the rosettes apart especially if you grow douglasias in tufa outside.

## DRABA
Cruciferae, or Brassicaceae

Around 300 species of *Draba* grow throughout the world. Many can only be distinguished by very small and technical features such as differences in their fruit, their hairiness, or their leaves, and these differences are often only visible with the use of a hand lens. The North American drabas are no exception, and although a number of those I describe are clearly identifiable, many others require very close examination to be identified. Drabas grow all over the West, and a great many inhabit the Rocky Mountain fell-fields. One reference suggests that it is easy to differentiate them from other plants since any small, tufted alpine plant with short, flat, or swollen pods is likely to be a draba. A distinguishing feature is the white or yellow flowers that are cruciform or crosslike with four sepals and, more often than not, four petals. Many make tight, compact mounds, cushions, or mats with short-stemmed or even stemless flowers. Most of the popular species are excellent for planting in troughs.

*Draba alpina* grows in rocky or gravel areas in the Alaska and Brooks Ranges of Alaska. It is mat or clump forming with oblong to lanceolate, densely hairy leaves. Bright yellow flowers in June are in racemes 5–10 cm (2–4 in.) tall. This species hybridizes with *D. macrocarpa*.

*Draba asprella* var. *zionensis* grows in the southwest corner of Utah and into Arizona inhabiting mixed desert shrub and ponderosa pine and manzanita communities at 1050–2600 m (3410–8450 ft.). This caespitose species has stems growing to 14 cm (5½ in.) tall and racemes of 10–30 yellow to yellow-orange flowers.

*Draba aureola* is quite rare and grows above the timberline along the crests of the Cascades from Mount Rainier in Washington into California as far as Lassen Peak, sprawling out of the volcanic rock. The

*Draba* species, Mount Evans, Colorado.

Alpine fell-fields in Rocky Mountain National Park, Colorado.

*Draba asprella* var. *zionensis*, Kolob Canyons, Zion National Park. Photo Chris Norton.

decumbent branches are very pubescent and grow to 20 cm (8 in.) long, and the white hairs give them a silvery sheen. The stems are leafy with yellow flowers in July through August, and the flattened, oblong seedpods, which are also pubescent, are about 1.2 cm (½ in.) long.

*Draba breweri* grows in California from the Sierra Nevada to Mount Shasta in alpine meadows and rocky places at 2615–4000 m (8500–13,000 ft.). It has small tufts of one to four gray-green oblanceolate leaves. White flowers bloom July through August on a 5–10-cm (2–4-in.) tall branching stem. The seedpods are oblong, twisted, and hairy. This species is named after William Brewer (1828–1910), who led a team that explored, surveyed, and mapped California for the first time from 1860 to 1864.

*Draba corrugata* var. *corrugata* grows in California at around 2985 m (9700 ft.) in pockets of fine, silty soil among quartzite boulders. It has a buried caudex similar to that of *D. aureola* with several rosettes of many small, hairy, densely overlapping, and spatulate leaves that make tight mounds of foliage. The tiny yellow flowers form a dense pyramid to 5 cm (2 in.) tall and 10 cm (4 in.) across. Hundreds of tiny, twisted, shiny septums make a showy display after the seed has dispersed.

*Draba crassa* grows on ridges, talus slopes, and alpine tundra in southern Montana, western Wyoming, northern Utah, and Colorado at 3355–3965 m (10,905–12,885 ft.). It has a dense basal rosette of long, fleshy, glabrous leaves and stems that grow 8–18 cm (3–7 in.) tall with yellow flowers.

*Draba cruciata* can be found in the southern Sierra Nevada, where it grows in rocky places at 2770–3845 m (9000–12,500 ft.). It forms a cushion with many prostrate stems and yellow flowers in July through August. The leaves have stiff, forked hairs on their faces and stalked, star-branched hairs on their margins.

*Draba densifolia* is widespread in scattered locations from the Alaska Range to California, Nevada, and Utah. It grows at alpine levels in crevices and rocky gravel ridges. The small, very tight cushions of tiny, gray-green rosettes have linear leaves with prominent hairs along the margins. The dense cluster of yellow flowers in mid-June through August are on stems 3–15 cm (1¼–6 in.) tall, depending on geographical habitat. Some forms bloom so well that the flowers appear to be stemless.

Variety *apiculata* (synonyms *Draba apiculata*, *D. apiculata* var. *daviesiae*) grows in the Uinta Mountains of Utah and in western Wyoming, the Bitterroot Mountains of Montana, and central Idaho. Minute differences from the type include hairs on the leaves, rounded leaf tips, and shorter stiles.

*Draba howellii* is endemic to a few counties in southern Oregon and northern California, where it grows on the high, rocky summits of the Siskiyou Mountains. The

*Draba densifolia*, Yukon-Tanana Uplands, Alaska. Photo Carolyn Parker.

dense basal clumps have tiny spatulate leaves with entire margins, and both surfaces of the leaves are covered with fine hairs. Stems grow to 6 cm (2¼ in.) long with six to eight yellow flowers in June through August.

*Draba incerta* ranges from Alaska to Washington, Utah, and Wyoming, growing on ridge crests in subalpine and alpine habitats at 2980–3050 m (9685–9915 ft.). The loose, gray-green cushions have relatively large hairy leaves, and the many large, light yellow flowers in racemes grow on leafless stems 2–20 cm (¾–8 in.) tall. Some dwarf forms resemble *D. densifolia* but with slightly larger leaves.

*Draba lanceolata* (synonym *D. cana*) ranges from Alaska to Nevada and central Colorado in dry, open meadows and in rock crevices in Utah's mountains at 3200–3910 (10,400–12,710 ft.). It is not a very showy species with a basal rosette of gray-green velvety leaves and small white flowers in May through August in open racemes on stems 5–25 cm (2–10 in.) tall.

*Draba lemmonii* grows on gravel ridges and rocky alpine slopes at 2615–4000 m (8500–13,000 ft.) throughout the Sierra Nevada, particularly in Yosemite Park on the Mount Dana Plateau and around Mount Lyell. It was there in 1878 that John Lemmon (1832–1908), after whom this species is named, first collected it. Dense basal tufts of spatulate leaves make a mat or a flattened cushion that spreads out along the ground. Leafless stems 2–30 cm (1–12 in.) tall are very hairy with yellow flowers in July through August. The seedpods are flat and twisted.

*Draba macrocarpa* is very similar to *D. alpina* and grows in the same habitat. The stems can be glabrous or slightly hairy, and there may be hairs on the seed capsules. This species hybridizes easily with *D. alpina*.

*Draba oligosperma* is a variable species and is widespread across the western United States, where it grows on open slopes, ridges, and limestone outcrops from the foothills to alpine fell-fields. The dense mat of tufted gray-green leaves are covered with microscopic hairs in the shape of a comb, which gives it the common name of comb draba. The yellow flowers are on stems 1–10 cm (½–4 in.) tall and they bloom May through August. Some references liken it to a condensed form of *D. incerta*. Like others in this genus, the rosettes become lax if grown in the alpine house but form a firm mat if grown outside in a sunny, gritty situation. This reliable bloomer is among the best western drabas.

*Draba oligosperma*, Hunt Mountain, Big Horn Mountains, Wyoming. Photo Chris Norton.

*Draba oligosperma*, Mount Evans, Colorado.

Variety *juniperina* has whitish flowers and is endemic to the Uinta Mountains and Bridger Basin of Wyoming at 1920–3200 m (6240–10,400 ft.). Variety *subsessillis* has very short stems and smaller flowers. Ron Ratko of Northwest Native Seeds queries this varietal name as the plant seems to be simply a dwarf form of the species, and I am inclined to endorse his observation.

*Draba paysonii* ranges from British Columbia to California and east to the Rockies, growing on rocky ridges in subalpine and alpine habitats. The hairy leaves make dense cushions, and the whitish yellow flowers are in racemes on stems to 5 cm (2 in.) tall.

*Draba paysonii* var. *treleasei*, Burnt Mountain, eastern Cascades, Washington.

Variety *treleasei* grows in a similar habitat of exposed alpine ridges on volcanic outcrops but makes a much tighter cushion with shorter stems. Ron Ratko has described a form of this variety growing at 1755–2245 m (5705–7300 ft.) in Washington as being the tightest and most dwarf of the Pacific Northwest drabas. The extremely dense, silver-gray cushion is covered with stemless flowers in July through August.

*Draba sierrae*, the Sierra draba, is endemic to Mono and Inyo counties, California, in dry screes and rock crevices at 3385–4000 m (11,000–13,000 ft.). This tiny, cushionlike species has gray leaves that are densely overlapping, leafless stems to 2.5 cm (1 in.) tall, and yellow flowers in July through August. The hairs on the leaves' margins are branched like a comb. The flowers are followed by twisted seedpods.

*Draba sphaerocarpa* is like many western drabas except that the inflorescence is extremely globe shaped. It is a nice plant with yellow blooms that comes from the Sawtooth Mountains of Idaho.

*Draba sphaeroides* grows in Nevada and Oregon at about 3325 m (10,800 ft.). Stems are 1.2–15 cm (½–6 in.) tall and bear yellow flowers in July through August.

Variety *cusickii* is a rarity that grows mainly in the Steens Mountains of southeast Oregon but also ranges south to northern Nevada. It inhabits screes and rocky outcrops at about 2000 m (6500 ft.). Basal tufts of small obovate leaves are covered with whitish forked hairs, and the stems grow to 15 cm (6 in.).

*Draba stenopetala* grows on loose, fine gravel slopes and rocky areas and is limited to a few locations in the Alaska Range, the Chugach Mountains, and St. Lawrence Island. It is a small mat-forming species with a long taproot. The very small, spatulate, hairy leaves make dense rosettes with tiny yellow flowers from late May through early June. The narrow petals make this a distinctive species, but because it is such a tiny plant it is difficult to see when not in bloom.

*Draba subalpina* is endemic to southern Utah, where it grows on pink and white silty limestone in very dry areas at 2130–3355 m (6920–10,905 ft.). Small compact cushions to 5 cm (2 in.) across of dark green rosettes are slightly larger than those of *D. densifolia*. Stems 2.5–5 cm (1–2 in.) tall have relatively large white flowers.

*Draba ventosa* has a limited distribution from the Beartooth Range in Wyoming to northeastern Utah, growing in alpine tundra and talus at 3050–3800 m (9915–12,350 ft.). This cushion-forming species is not as compact as *D. paysonii* but it has similarly dense and hairy leaves. The leafless stems are 2–6 cm (¾–2¼ in.) high with racemes of yellowish flowers.

## Propagation

Most drabas set copious seed enabling many species to be offered in seed lists. To collect seed, cut off the stems as soon as the seed is ripe and put stems and pods upside down in an envelope. Once it has dried, most of the seed falls out. It is very awkward to collect seed from pods on the plant; often the pod splits and the seed falls out everywhere.

Propagation by cuttings of single rosettes is fairly straightforward with the cushion- or mat-forming species. Take cuttings in spring to summer and root them in the cutting frame.

## Cultivation

Many drabas are excellent plants for cultivation in troughs, and the cushion- or mat-forming species stay in character when they grow in full sun in gritty soil. The drabas with soft, hairy rosettes or woolly leaves are at risk of damping off if exposed to wet conditions, especially in winter. Bring these into the alpine house during the wet season or at least offer some protection such as from a pane of glass.

Red spider mite and aphids, especially whiteflies, can cause problems in the alpine house. Slugs eat the centers of rosettes in the garden unless some form of slug bait is used.

## DRYAS
Rosaceae
*mountain avens*

*Dryas* is made up of two, possibly three, species of evergreen prostrate shrubs that are as attractive in seed as in flower. The leaves are similar in shape to the oak leaf and are shiny above and downy white below. *Dryas octopetala* is fairly easy to grow in the rock garden.

*Dryas drummondii*, a North American boreal species, grows above the timberline in cirques, on rocky ridges, on talus slopes, and

*Draba stenopetala*, Alaska Range. Photo Carolyn Parker.

occasionally on lower elevations along streams in Alaska, Washington, northeastern Oregon, and Montana. Prostrate mats to 50 cm (20 in.) across have dark green, shiny, elliptical leaves with rounded lobelike teeth. The leaves are downy white on the underside. Stems 5–20 cm (2–8 in.) tall have solitary pale to deep yellow cup-shaped flowers that grow to 2.5 cm (1 in.) across and in most forms do not open properly.

Two varieties of *Dryas drummondii* that have also been described are var. *eglandulosa* and var. *tomentosa*.

One reference suggests that *Dryas drummondii* 'Grandiflora' is a free-flowering cultivar that should be grown whenever possible but I am sure what is meant is *Dryas octopetala* 'Grandiflora'. Rick Lupp considers those plants of *D. drummondii* 'Grandiflora' that he has seen in cultivation and grown himself to be a form of *D.* × *suendermannii*, and Jerry Flintoff, a botanist and plantsman from Washington, agrees. As Rick explains, " The fact that every one of the thousands of plants of this species that I have seen in the wild in Alaska, Canada, and the United States failed to open in bloom only goes to reinforce my opinion."

*Dryas integrifolia*, though normally associated with Labrador and Greenland, can be found in the Rockies of northwest Montana, where it differs by having entire leaves that are not glandular on the lower surface. This species is very similar to *D. octopetala* and is often included in that species. Rick Lupp has found that *D. integrifolia* in Alaska is very distinct from *D. octopetala*, and he agrees with the late Eric Hultén that the plant deserves species status. Hultén, who was the world's preeminent authority on Arctic floras and director emeritus of the botanical department of the State Museum of Natural History in Stockholm for many years, was the author of numerous works on the flora of the Arctic.

Before he died in 1981, Hultén described two subspecies, subsp. *integrifolia* and subsp. *sylvatica*, and he admitted seeing many hybrids between these two subspecies and between the subspecies and *Dryas octopetala*. More work still has to be carried out to clarify this situation.

*Dryas octopetala* is circumboreal, ranging from the Arctic to the northern temperate zone in mountains, open woodland, and rocky slopes. In North America it grows on exposed ridges and rocky places

*Dryas drummondii*, Denali National Park, Alaska. Photo Verna Pratt.

*Dryas octopetala*, Loveland Pass, Colorado.

from middle elevations to fell-fields from Alaska to Washington, northeastern Oregon, central Idaho, and Colorado. Large prostrate mats have woody stems that root as they spread. The basal lanceolate leaves are a dark, shiny green and grow to 3.2 cm (1¼ in.) with rounded teeth along the edges. The leaf underside is white and hairy. Stems 5–25 cm (2–10 in.) tall have white to cream solitary flowers 2.5 cm (1 in.) across, and each flower has 8–10 petals. This species is also very attractive in fruit with long white plumes packed together in a tight feathery head. It is variable and has a number of subspecies, varieties, and cultivars.

Subspecies *alaskensis* from Alaska has deeply toothed, narrowly ovate leaves. The glands on the middle vein of the leaf's underside are stalked.

Variety *argentea* grows in Alaska and is widespread in Europe. The leaves are downy on both surfaces; variety *argentea* 'Minor' is small, neat, and free-flowering.

'Grandiflora' is a free-flowering cultivar with blooms to 5 cm (2 in.) across.

*Dryas* × *suendermannii* is a hybrid between *D. drummondii* and *D. octopetala*. It resembles the latter parent but with yellowish buds that open to nodding, creamy yellow flowers. This attractive hybrid is easy to cultivate.

**Propagation**

Propagation is by seed, but check the seed before sowing it especially if you have paid for it. On many occasions I have noticed that a lot of seed from my own plants had no embryo and was useless. Dryas seed is not long-lived and you should sow it as soon as it is ripe and then place the pot outside. If you keep the seed until the following spring it is likely to be past the "sell by" date. If you collect your own seed do not be too impatient; leave it on the plant for as long as possible to ensure that most of it will be ripe when you collect it.

Another problem with propagation has been the damping off of many seedlings once they germinated, but I believe this problem resulted from me bringing the germinating seedlings into the alpine house too early. Dryas seed is slow growing, and when I left the later sowings to overwinter outdoors where there is more air movement, the problem solved itself.

Dryas also layer themselves as the mat grows outwards, so it is easy to remove the rooted stems and pot them up in spring.

**Cultivation**

The *Dryas* species do not need specific soil conditions. They do, however, require some sun. The ideal position is a moist gravel spot in full sun, but they will also grow well in a deep sand bed. No dryas plants are suited to an alpine house as they do not grow well under glass, flowering very infrequently if at all.

Other than the problem of the damping off of seedlings, this plant is trouble free.

*Dryas octopetala*, Alaska Range. Photo Carolyn Parker.

# E

## EPILOBIUM
Onagraceae
*fireweeds, rosebay willowherbs, wickups*

Like a great number of people I always thought epilobiums with their tiny pink flowers were weeds. The fireweed or rosebay willowherb that appears in my garden is a menace. It grows to 90 cm (36 in.) long and germinates in every nook and cranny the wind can blow seed into. However, after reading an article by the respected seed collector John Andrews (1990), in which he described three epilobium species, and seeing a beautiful close-up photograph of *Epilobium obcordatum*, I changed my mind and became determined to grow them.

Epilobiums have a wide distribution throughout the West, and although 25 species occur in the Rockies, few can be classed as alpines. They grow on waste or disturbed ground, stony slopes, and moist gravel soils, and the genus is usually among the first to invade areas destroyed by disasters such as forest fires or volcanic eruptions such as that of Mount St. Helens. Although the seed is small, each is tufted with silky hairs that imitate parachutes and help to distribute the seed over a wide area. If you collect your own seed, catch it as the pods are splitting; if you wait another day the seeds will have floated away.

*Epilobium alpinum* is usually found in forest seeps and wet meadows, but it also inhabits snowmelt runoff areas in the western Cascades. A matted species that grows from spreading rhizomes, it grows to 30 cm (12 in.) tall with ovate-lanceolate leaves and terminal, erect, white or pink flowers with notched petals in June through August. The herbage is glabrous except for lines of hairs on the stems. I was delighted to see this species at the edge of the trail on the Burroughs Mountain hike during my visit to the Sunrise area of Mount Rainier in 1998.

*Epilobium glaberrimum* is a widespread and highly variable species that ranges from British Columbia to southern California, Montana, Idaho, and Utah. It is tufted to mat-forming with stems 10–90 cm (4–36 in.) long, and the pink to rose-red or white flowers in June through August are 1.5–2 cm (⅗–¾ in.) long. The opposite paired leaves are 2.5–5 cm (1–2 in.) long and the glaucous foliage is a distinct blue-green.

Burroughs Mountain trail, Mount Rainier, Washington.

*Epilobium alpinum*, Burroughs Mountain, Mount Rainier, Washington.

It grows in xeric meadows to alpine or sub-alpine talus, ridges, and stream courses to around 2745 m (8920 ft.).

Variety *fastigiatum* is smaller with crowded and overlapping leaves.

'Sulphureum' has pale yellow flowers.

*Epilobium glandulosum* is another wide-spread species ranging from the Sierra Nevada to Washington. It inhabits moist areas, grows 30–90 cm (12–36 in.) in height, and has small, pale pink to deep rose flowers in June through August. An unusual feature of this species is that it has tiny bulblike swellings called *turions* at the base of the stem or on the rhizomes.

*Epilobium latifolium* is common throughout the northern temperate zone in Alaska, Washington, Oregon, Idaho, Montana, and Colorado, growing on stream banks, moist meadows, and rocky slopes in alpine and subalpine zones. The decumbent stems are 30–60 cm (12–24 in.) long and can be a little too sprawling in cultivation. It is clump forming and spreads quickly by rhizomes. The pink to purple flowers are 2.5 cm (1 in.) in diameter. Try growing this species in the alpine bed but be wary of its spreading qualities.

*Epilobium obcordatum* grows in alpine and subalpine habitats in California, Oregon, Nevada, and Idaho and is a superb, mat-forming species that grows to 10 cm (4 in.) tall. Beautiful soft to bright pink, 2.5-cm (1-in.) wide flowers cover the gray-green

*Epilobium latifolium*, Alaska Range. Photo Carolyn Parker.

Close-up of *Epilobium obcordatum* flowers in cultivation.

*Epilobium obcordatum*, Carson Pass, California. Photo Chris Norton.

foliage. Jim Archibald (1989–1990) quotes Reginald Farrer (1913) who said, "the rock garden establishes its claim to one species especially, and this is the really beautiful and gorgeous little *E. obcordatum* . . . a mass of leafy shoots . . . ending in clusters of very large and very brilliant full-petalled flowers of glowing rosy pink . . . a rare choice treasure." It is exceptional as an exhibition plant.

Variety *siskyouense* grows on exposed stony slopes at an altitude of 2100–2600 m (6825–8450 ft.) on and near Mount Eddy in northern California, where it forms more of a clump than *Epilobium obcordatum*.

*Epilobium rigidum* is quite a rare species from Oregon and endemic to serpentine soils of the Siskiyou Mountains. It grows at a much lower elevation than *E. obcordatum*—460–720 m (1495–2340 ft.)—and is considered by many to be the finest in the genus. Phyllis Gustafson of Rogue House Seeds describes it in her list as "the most beautiful offering from Rogue House," and I agree. It is more upright than *E. obcordatum*, to 40 cm (15¾ in.). The plants in my Timsbury nursery, which are grown from Rogue House seed collected in Josephine county, Oregon, at 460 m (1495 ft.), are 15 cm (6 in.) tall with racemes of deep pink blooms 4 cm (1½ in.) across. One of my plants won an Alpine Garden Society

*Epilobium rigidum* in cultivation.

Certificate of Merit in July 2000, proving what a fine plant it is.

Phyllis has also told me that the stems are rigid and upright early in the season; the young plants do not lay the stems out until late in the season. By the time the plant blooms in late August and sets seed, it is so dry that she believes the lack of moisture is what makes the stems lax. The plant gets very hot on the rocks where it grows but does not bloom well in the shade even though a lot of plants can be found under the pines and oaks. Seed has been collected as late as November. I grew a plant in a scree bed but it did not survive the wet winter; Phyllis recommends trying a trough.

## Propagation

Propagation of this genus is mainly by seed, and if you already have plants of *Epilobium rigidum* and *E. obcordatum* you will find that viable seed is usually set. The three species I grew have all set seed, and when I sowed them in autumn they germinated well the following year. Owing to the long flowering period of both *E. obcordatum* and *E. rigidum*, it is possible to collect ripe seed from plants still in flower well into October.

Cuttings taken of *Epilobium obcordatum* from spring to summer have rooted fairly quickly from nodes above the surface of the rooting medium (like *Ourisia microphylla*) as well as below the surface. *Epilobium rigidum* rarely has enough cutting material as practically all the stems have flowers, but the amount of seed that is set more than makes up for this.

## Cultivation

Although you can grow both *Epilobium obcordatum* and *E. rigidum* in a trough or well-drained scree bed without much trouble (provided they stay dry over winter), I prefer to cultivate them as pot plants in an alpine house. A gritty soil mixture with added peat is suitable. Since *E. obcordatum* comes from an exposed alpine habitat, take care not to overwater it. They both make excellent exhibition plants and should be cut back in spring to remove the previous year's growth and encourage new growth.

While *Epilobium glaberrimum* would be best in a scree bed, *E. latifolium* is more suitable for a rock garden. Be careful, however, where you site it because of its spreading habit.

The plants are affected by winter dieback and the blackened leaves become brittle. Remove these in spring when you cut back the stems. In plants where dieback is severe, fresh growth is usually sent up from below ground in spring.

Aphids occasionally attack the leaves especially on plants in the alpine house. Powdery mildew affects the leaves if the location becomes too damp.

## ERIGERON
### Compositae, or Asteraceae
*fleabanes*

There are about 200 species within *Erigeron* and all have daisylike flowers of white, pink, lavender, purple, blue, or yellow. Such is the resemblance of many species to one another that there is often confusion over identification. Rick Lupp and I found at least five variations of *Erigeron flettii* while hiking on Mount Townsend, Washington, although leaf shape and size, flower size, and stem height were all different. Some have even mistaken this species for a lawn daisy.

Adding to the confusion in identifying plants in this genus is the fact that erigerons

are also somewhat difficult to distinguish from asters. However, if you closely inspect both asters and erigerons you will notice that erigerons have relatively long and narrow involucral bracts that are more or less equal in length and many, narrow ray flowers. In contrast, the involucral bracts in asters are fairly broad and usually unequal in length and the rays are broad and few in number. Many species of *Erigeron* are very attractive and easy to identify, and the distinctions I mention should help you identify plants in the wild.

Some erigerons can become a pest in cultivation as they sow themselves like weeds. Other species are very difficult to grow and require alpine house treatment especially in wet areas. Still others make excellent exhibition plants, and several dwarf forms are ideal for troughs. Many in the genus are also very short-lived and in cultivation must be propagated each year. All require excellent drainage and a place in full sun where they usually commence flowering in spring and can continue blooming through summer and into autumn. For this reason alone there should be at least one species in every garden and several more if you have a trough.

*Erigeron aureus*, a variable species that offers some good compact forms, grows on alpine rocky ridges in the Washington Cascades. Stems are 8–13 cm (3–5 in.) tall, and the bright yellow flowers in July through August are to 2.5 cm (1 in.) across.

'Canary Bird' is a selected cultivar popular among exhibitors that the well-known nurseryman Jack Drake raised. It is quite compact at just 10 cm (4 in.) high and has creamy yellow blooms to 4 cm (½ in.) across. When grown outside it dies back in winter and commences growing again in early spring.

*Erigeron chrysopsidis* grows from California to Nevada and Washington in dry, open places and makes a tufted clump to 15 cm (6 in.) high with solitary yellow flower heads 2.5–5 cm (1–2 in.) across.

'Grand Ridge' was originally discovered by Phil Pearson and Steve Doonan, proprietors of Grand Ridge Nursery in Issaquah, Washington, during a trip to Ice Lake in the Wallowa Mountains in 1981. Although cuttings from about 30 plants in the wild showed potential as good introductions, Phil and Steve discarded them all in 1986 except the one named 'Grand Ridge'. A much more compact and floriferous cultivar, it has bright yellow blooms of many petals that make it look like a double. It flowers over a long period from spring to autumn, and in the unusually mild winter of 1998 and 1999, my large plant was still in flower in December. Although it grows fairly quickly from a rooted cutting and can make a large plant within two to three years, it is prone to sudden collapse (my large plants have never lasted more than three to four years). Despite this drawback, its ease of propagation and free-blooming nature make it a favorite on the show bench.

*Erigeron compactus* var. *consimilis* grows among salt desert shrub and pinyon and juniper communities in sandy limestone soils at 2075 m (6745 ft.) in eastern Utah and Arizona. Short, linear, grayish green leaves form dense, caespitose mounds with 2–3-cm (¾–1¼-in.) wide white flowers that have lavender tips on short stems. This is a choice erigeron for the alpine house in areas of medium to high annual rainfall and probably the biggest challenge of all the species since the watering it receives must be carefully controlled.

*Erigeron compositus* is wide-ranging across the West in sandy or rocky places, and although not a particularly spectacular species, some have nice compact forms. Among the easier species in cultivation, it seeds itself in the alpine bed. Seedlings in a sand bed can become a little invasive. It grows 5–20 cm (2–8 in) tall and has white, bluish, lavender, or pink flowers 1.5–2 cm (⅗–¾ in.) across.

Variety *glabratus* grows on the moraine ridges of Mount Adams, Washington, at 2340 m (7600 ft.). Hairy cushions are small and dense, and the white flowers are 2.5 cm (1 in.) across. A slightly larger form grows in Colorado at 2955 m (9600 ft.) and makes a

*Erigeron aureus* in cultivation.

*Erigeron compositus*, Craters of the Moon, Idaho. Photo David Hale.

cushion 2.5 cm (1 in.) high with stems 5–7 cm (2–2¾ in.) tall and violet flowers.

Originally grown from seed collected at 3300 m (10,725 ft.) in Colorado and introduced under the number JCA 8911, one lovely erigeron was first thought to be *Erigeron vagus*. It has rich lavender-blue flowers on 15-cm (6-in.) stems growing from pads of dissected gray leaves, but it now appears to be a form of *E. compositus*.

There are two cultivars worth considering. 'Mt. Adams Dwarf' (found and introduced by Mt. Tahoma Nursery) grows at 2310 m (7500 ft.) on the north face of Mount Adams, Washington. The mats of tiny silver-gray leaves have small white flowers on 2.5-cm (1-in.) stems. 'Pink Forms' was found in the Cascades and introduced into cultivation by Rick Lupp. This good scree plant has finely cut, hairy, gray-green foliage with 2.5-cm (1-in.) wide pink flowers on 7-cm (2-¾ in.) stems.

*Erigeron eriocephalus* grows in dry areas in the Brooks and Alaska Ranges of Alaska. Although similar to *E. humilis*, it spreads a lot more and forms a small mat. It has narrower leaves, and the flowers are usually white.

*Erigeron flagellaris* is widespread throughout the West from the plains to subalpine zones in meadows and near streams. It is unusual in that it has creeping, procumbent, leafy stolons that send up stems 10–25 cm (4–10 in.) tall with white to light purple flowers. Although a short-lived species, it has provided a great display of summer color in my alpine bed for two years, dying down in winter and sending up more flowering stems the following year.

*Erigeron flettii* grows in the dryer parts of the Olympics. The elliptic gray-green leaves and white flowers are 2.5 cm (1 in.) in diameter on stems of 7–15 cm (2¾–6 in.). Although in some ways similar to a lawn daisy (*Bellis perennis*), it is far superior to that common plant. In association with *E. aureus* at Will Ingwersen's Birch Farm Nursery, it produced a natural hybrid with cream flowers named *Erigeron* 'Birch Hybrid'.

*Erigeron humilis* grows in snowbeds throughout the mountains of Alaska. It makes loose rosettes of long stemmed, spatulate, hairy leaves one to two per flowering stem. Stems grow 5–7.5 cm (2–3 in.) tall and are hairy with solitary white flowers in late June through early August that become purplish with age.

*Erigeron hyperboreus* grows mostly in rocky, gravel areas in the Brooks Range of Alaska. It is also scattered in the Alaska Range, though it is quite rare in Denali National Park. It grows 7.5–12.5 cm (3–5 in.) tall with narrow spatulate, hairy leaves, and the 2–2.5-cm (¾–1-in.) wide bluish lavender flowers in late June through July fade to pink or white with age.

*Erigeron leiomerus* grows at an altitude of 2950–3750 m (9590–12,190 ft.) in Utah and in alpine tundra communities in Nevada, Idaho, Wyoming, Colorado, and New Mexico. This is a mat-forming species

*Erigeron flettii*, Mount Townsend, Washington.

with spatulate green leaves and deep blue to lavender-blue, occasionally white, flowers on very short stems. As it is often found on moist gravel soils, it will likely survive a little more moisture in cultivation than most.

*Erigeron linearis* grows in Oregon and Washington at 1045–2000 m (3400–6500 ft.) on exposed, rocky, subalpine ridges and in basalt scablands. The numerous tufts of linear gray leaves make cushions or compact domes that have 3–15-cm (1¼–6-in.) high stems. It is very free-flowering, and the best forms can be entirely covered with many petalled, bright yellow flowers. A good exhibition plant, this species also grows well in a trough. However, having grown it quite

satisfactorily in a pot, I realized that I still had a lot to learn when I saw the nice compact mounds growing on Burnt Mountain in the eastern Cascades. *Erigeron linearis* is quite hardy to cold wet winters and humid summers, and it grows well in a scree.

*Erigeron montanensis* from eastern Montana is a nice compact species with beautiful tight foliage and small white blooms on 5-cm (2-in.) stems. This is a good trough plant that does not appear to mind a lot of wet weather.

*Erigeron poliospermus* grows in rocky clay soils in basalt scablands of Washington at around 1140 m (3705 ft.). The lovely compact tufts of hairy linear leaves grow from a branching woody base. The 5-cm (2-in.) wide lavender-blue flowers with

*Erigeron hyperboreus*, Yukon-Tanana Uplands, Alaska. Photo Carolyn Parker.

*Erigeron linearis*, Burnt Mountain, eastern Cascades, Washington.

*Erigeron purpuratus*, Alaska Range. Photo Carolyn Parker.

orange discs on thin, 5–10-cm (2–4-in.) stems make this erigeron among the most attractive of all the species. It is also a real challenge in cultivation because the hairy leaves attract botrytis very easily, which is a problem during winter cultivation in moister areas. It is well worth trying in an alpine house.

*Erigeron purpuratus* in the Brooks and Alaska Ranges and the Wrangell–St. Elias Mountains is similar to *E. humilis* but with narrow leaves. The white flowers turn purplish as they age, and the calyx has purplish hairs.

*Erigeron rydbergii* is restricted to southwest Montana and northwest Wyoming, especially the fell-fields and dry alpine

*Erigeron rydbergii*, Beartooth Highway, Wyoming. Photo Chris Norton.

*Erigeron scopulinus* in cultivation. Photo Ev Whittemore.

meadows of Yellowstone National Park. It makes a compact clump of entire, finely haired leaves with stems to 15 cm (6 in.) tall and solitary, violet-lavender to white flowers.

*Erigeron scopulinus* is a lovely plant with a tight mat of slightly glossy, tiny leaves with almost stemless white to pinkish flowers. Sonia Lowzow (Collins) wrote to me in December 1991 describing this species' habitat as moist, shaded rocks near a waterfall in Cochise county in the Chiricahua Mountains of Arizona at about 2615 m (8500 ft.). Sonia said it was the best plant of *Erigeron* she had ever seen. The plant is very rare in the wild and grows in one or two additional stations in the Chiricahuas and in the Black Range in New Mexico. The species was first discovered and described botanically in 1981.

*Erigeron simplex* grows in Utah among the alpine meadows and tundra communities at a similar altitude to *E. leiomerus*. This species also has a wide range from Oregon to Montana, Nevada, Arizona, and New Mexico. Stems vary in height from 2.5 to 15 cm (1 to 6 in.) and the flowers range from blue-purple or pink to white.

*Erigeron uncialis* var. *conjugans* grows on Mount Charleston in Clark county, Nevada, at about 3500 m (11,375 ft.). In

*Erigeron uncialis* var. *conjugans* in cultivation.

1992 John Andrews collected seed for this variety from that site, and he considers it the smallest erigeron of all, which I cannot dispute. Quite different from the other species, it grows as a tiny clump of spoon-shaped leaves with stems 2–3 cm (¾–1¼ in.) tall that are topped with white flowers. It is worth collecting this very dwarf plant, which is known as the inch high fleabane.

*Erigeron vagus* grows in the scree areas and fell-fields of the White Mountains in California as well as in Nevada, Utah, and Colorado at 3300–4250 m (10,725–13,810 ft.). It makes small mounds of hairy, gray, dissected leaves with purple, rose, or white flowers on stems 2–5 cm (¾–2 in.) tall. It is very similar to *E. compositus* var. *glabratus* in appearance and is a very good trough plant.

*Erigeron* 'Chameleon' is closely related to *E. chrysopsidis* 'Grand Ridge' and shows some potential to emulate that cultivar. It was introduced in approximately 1998 so there has not been enough time for a full evaluation. It appeared as a chance seedling beside a plant of *E. chrysopsidis* 'Grand Ridge' in the Portland, Oregon, garden of David Hale. Somewhat larger than 'Grand Ridge', it has the same constant blooming habit. The flowers differ in that they start out yellow, turn to white, and age to pink. It seems to do better than 'Grand Ridge' in the open garden especially in areas of wet winters, but only time will tell.

*Erigeron* 'Goat Rocks', a natural hybrid between *E. aureus* and *E. compositus*, was found by Rick Lupp in Washington's Goat Rocks area. It makes tufts of hairy, silver-gray foliage with bright lemon yellow flowers on stems 7–8 cm (2¾–3 in.) tall throughout the summer. It is a great plant in a sand bed.

There are several unidentified noninvasive dwarf erigerons in the trade. One that is grown from seed collected in the Big Horn Mountains is a wonderful trough plant because apart from being small, it also survives wet weather. It is densely tufted with dissected dark green leaves and stems 5–7 cm (2–2¾ in.) tall with pale mauve flowers. My customers and I have grown another species from seed collected by Sonia Lowzow in White Cloud Mountains, Idaho. Although it has similar foliage to the unidentified Big Horn Mountains species, it is much smaller with stems 2.5–5 cm (1–2 in.) tall and white to pale purple flowers. It is also more tricky to grow and is inclined to rot off if too damp.

*Erigeron* 'Chameleon' in cultivation. Photo Rick Lupp.

*Erigeron* 'Goat Rocks' in cultivation.

## Propagation

Growing erigerons from wild-collected seed is an easy way to start a collection. Seed is the usual method of propagation for the many species within this genus as most set seed easily. Many can be propagated vegetatively, though, and where cultivars exist this is of course the only available method. Some species are stoloniferous and can be lifted and divided in spring.

The tufted- and clump-forming species are propagated by cuttings taken from around the basal rosette in spring and by what is called the "the carrot shoot trick," a useful method when propagating *Erigeron aureus* 'Canary Bird', for example, or other species that do not easily produce propagating material. In early spring when growth is starting, take a sharp knife and cut straight across the top of the caudex. Be ruthless—but try it on a carrot first. After a few weeks new growth starts from the edge of the caudex, and many more shoots than were previously growing will appear. When they are long enough, they can be used for cuttings.

## Cultivation

Although some erigerons I mention tolerate wet conditions, it is much better to give them the conditions they really desire, which is a well-drained, warm, even hot position, and usually poor soil. I grow many in south-facing alpine beds, and except for the short-lived species, winter wet has killed the plants. Nevertheless, I continue to grow them because of the summer color they bring to the garden, and those that tolerate damp conditions continue to thrive year after year. Several species require acid conditions, *Erigeron aureus* being among them. Most erigerons revel in sand beds and I fully

recommend growing them that way, even if you have to fit some form of cover over them during winter.

One quite different species is *Erigeron scopulinus*, and to quote from Sonia Lowzow's letter again, "We grow it in full sun, but only about 1.2 cm (½ in.) above the edge of one of our shady bogs. The less moisture, the more shade it needs." It makes a good exhibition plant and several have been on the show bench in the last few years.

Those species that require alpine house treatment are among the most choice and desirable within the genus. Use this method of cultivation to prevent excessive moisture from killing the plants as they are more susceptible to damping off than the rest of the species. You can also grow erigerons in tufa, where the more compact species form lovely neat plants.

Very little affects this genus, slugs being the biggest pests of garden-grown plants. In the alpine house, greenfly, whitefly, and red spider mite can cause problems.

## ERIOGONUM
Polygonaceae
*wild buckwheats*

The genus *Eriogonum* contains a very large number of species. In California and Nevada alone there are almost 200 species, and it is impossible—and impractical—for me to discuss and describe all of them. I describe those I have grown and that are the most widespread, those that have been available from seed since approximately 1988, and some of those not yet in cultivation but worth a second glance in the wild.

Newcomers to this genus may wonder what all the fuss is about when they listen to enthusiasts discussing the plants' garden worthiness or hear of plant hunters seeking out eriogonums in barren areas of the West. Once you have seen several of the species yourself, however, you begin to understand. Not only is there the variation in flower color from white to red, orange, and yellow, but also the size of the flower. Some species have beautiful silver leaves while others have extremely small silver leaves that make the plant look like a silver ball. Some species form flat mats or have a natural cushion shape. Many others have woolly leaves, while still others have lovely autumn colors that add an extra dimension to their flowering. The foliage on most eriogonums dies back in autumn and the plants appear almost dead. Most species are summer flowering.

Although most buckwheats grow in dry soil, I have been surprised at the number of species that grow uncovered all the year round in my garden. I have had to accommodate their need for good drainage, but it has been well worth the effort.

There are still many species offered as seed in commercial lists that I have yet to grow, though some are more desirable than others. Some seed is offered for species that are relatively easy to grow and for species that are almost impossible; either way, the seed collections nowadays make it possible to grow many species that were practically unknown in the early 1990s, and these species all pose a challenge to the most experienced growers.

*Eriogonum acaule* is a cold-desert plant from Wyoming. This is the tiniest buckwheat and makes rounded buns of gray-green leaves 2 cm (¾ in.) high and 25 cm (10 in.) or more across. The practically

stemless flowers of burnished gold, orange, and red appear in June.

*Eriogonum argophyllum* grows at the base of Ruby Mountains, Nevada, in a habitat where one would think they could not grow. Although the soil there contains a large quantity of unusual chemicals, the plant thrives. However, it is so rare it is now a protected plant. This mat-forming species has silver foliage with yellow balls 2.5 cm (1 in.) in diameter on short stems.

In approximately 1996 I potted up one small plant in the usual neutral, soil-based compost, but as it was impossible to replicate the unusual soil structure of its native habitat, I did not expect it to live for very long. Much to my surprise it has grown well ever since and I have exhibited it three times in an 18-cm (7-in.) pot, once winning an award. I am always amazed that plants can come from a great variety of habitats and soil makeup, yet still flourish in cultivation. I have not noticed seed on my specimen, and I therefore have to sow all the crushed and dried flower heads. Germination has been spasmodic but each year there have been some seedlings. I have grown many of the resultant plants to maturity, and while most had silver leaves, some had green leaves.

*Eriogonum bicolor* comes from Utah, where it grows on fragmented sandstone

*Eriogonum argophyllum* in cultivation.

ledges in very dense, silty soils at 1340–1985 m (4355–6450 ft.). This superb miniature shrub is 10–15 cm (4–6 in.) tall with pink and white powder-puff flowers and twiggy gray leaves. The branching, woody stems become grayish black and gnarled with age. It is similar to *E. thymoides* but with longer leaves and a less dense habit.

*Eriogonum breedlovei* var. *breedlovei* grows at approximately 2700 m (8775 ft.) on metamorphic limestone in California, particularly on Mount Pinos, and varies between a tight mat and a mound. It has short stems with little elliptic leaves that are topped with large white flowers (some of which have pinkish to yellow tints) that are covered with small black dots. The surface of the leaves is green-gray above and woolly white below, making it a very striking plant. Seed of this species was introduced into cultivation in 1993 by John Andrews. In spite of being neglected at times regarding watering, it has always recovered with new growth covering up all the dead leaves. Based on this experience I would say it is among the easier eriogonums, and if you grow it as a show plant, you will be rewarded.

*Eriogonum brevicaule* grows in Nevada, Wyoming, and Utah. A very variable species depending on the habitat, it is late flowering with bright yellow, white, or pink-tinged white blooms. The narrow leafed stems are 5–40 cm (2–15¾ in.) tall, and the best plants are mat forming.

Variety *laxifolium* (synonym *Eriogonum kingii* var. *laxifolium*) grows in a harsh habitat of limestone crevices on exposed ridge tops at around 3445 m (11,200 ft.) in Utah and Nevada. The mats of woolly, gray-green leaves grow in small tufts, and the small yellow flowers with reddish tints are on short stems. Variety *nanum* from Utah is a shorter, more alpine version of *E. brevicaule* var. *laxifolium* with a mixture of yellow, red, and bronze flowers.

*Eriogonum caespitosum* ranges from California to Idaho, Montana, and Colorado, where its habitat is open stony, limestone slopes and sagebrush scrub and pine woodland at 1550–3170 m (5040–10,300 ft.). Among the most desirable dwarf species, it has compact mats of small, spatulate, white felty leaves and clustered, yellow flowers flushing to red that often open almost stemless on the cushion. As the plant matures the stems elongate to 5 cm (2 in.). This species is regularly exhibited on the show bench in pots 25 cm (10 in.) in diameter. The plants should be kept out of doors most of the year if they are to remain in

*Eriogonum breedlovei* var. *breedlovei* in cultivation.

*Eriogonum brevicaule* var. *laxifolium*, Ruby Mountains, Nevada. Photo David Hale.

character. It grows well in a raised bed, where it forms a tight, compact mound and flowers better than if grown in a pot.

*Eriogonum chrysocephalum* occurs in Idaho at 1540 m (5000 ft.) and makes mats of silver, spatulate leaves with bright yellow pom-pom flowers on 10-cm (4-in.) stems all summer.

*Eriogonum compositum* grows on the dry rocky slopes and gravel clay of California, Washington, Oregon, and Idaho at about 60–1570 m (196–5100 ft.). This woody-based perennial usually has flat mats of loose basal rosettes that have large deltoid leaves. Stout stems 15–50 cm (6–20 in.) tall carry umbels of large yellow to greenish white flowers that mature to rose.

Variety *lancifolium* grows in Washington on south-facing, dry gravel slopes at approximately 370 m (1200 ft.). The leaves are narrower and the inflorescence is greenish white. Variety *leianthum* grows in rocky scabland openings in Washington's subalpine forest at 1710 m (5550 ft.). A dwarf variety, it has smaller, rough, gray leaves in a loose broad mat. The 8–15-cm (3–6-in.) wide cream or yellow flowers are on stems 15–25 cm (6–10 in.) tall.

*Eriogonum caespitosum* in cultivation in a raised bed.

*Eriogonum diclinum* grows on very high outcrops in the Siskiyou Mountains at around 2155 m (7000 ft.). Its tight mats of small leaves are covered with white wool. This dioecious species has deep yellow and orange flowers, which makes it look like two separate plants.

*Eriogonum douglasii* grows from Washington to California and Nevada at 1110–2450 m (3610–7965 ft.) on dry, rocky slopes. Some plants in the wild are reminiscent of silver-gray balls and others form white mats about 30 cm (12 in.) across. The yellow heads of 3-cm (1¼-in.) wide flowers, some of which are flushed red, are on stems 5–10 cm (2–4 in.) tall. Since these plants made such an impression on me when I first saw them in the wild I thought they would make a terrific show plant, but unfortunately they have failed to grow as well in a pot. Although my plants (which were all grown from wild-collected seed) have been slightly different in form from those seen in the wild, they have all sent out the same short stems with a small leafy rosette on each end but have never flowered.

*Eriogonum ericifolium* var. *pulchrum* is unlike any eriogonum I know. It grows in Arizona like a bonsai shrub. It is 12.5–20 cm (5–8 in.) tall with tiny gray-green leaves, and tufts of white or red flowers appear on top of each twiglike stem in July through October. As the plant ages, the bark on the main stem begins to peel making it a very attractive plant. It is so different from other eriogonums that when it was first exhibited in 1993 the judges could not initially decide whether or not it was an eriogonum. In 1991 Sonia Lowzow, who at the time lived in Lakeside, Arizona, sent me seed that she had collected in the wild from white- and pink-flowered plants. I have grown both in a pot and I find the pink flowering forms far superior. They both grew much better in the scree bed than in a pot, flowering well and growing like real bonsai for several years.

*Eriogonum fasciculatum* **var.** *foliolosum* is a shrubby eriogonum that is widespread on the dry chaparral slopes of California at 800 m (2600 ft.). The dark green, linear leaves are tightly revolute in clusters along the stem, and the small, pinkish white flower heads are very showy when seen all together. Although an interesting variety (it is widely used for honey production), this eriogonum is not very choice and could be tender in cultivation.

*Eriogonum flavum* is a variable species from the exposed grassland of the Rockies. It is a neat plant with bright yellow heads that flush orange where they emerge from the tidy mats.

Variety *piperi*, a very compact form from Idaho at about 2985 m (9700 ft.), has large green-gray leaves and makes thicker mats than *Eriogonum flavum*. Large flowers are on 5–10-cm (2–4-in.) stems, and the leaves remain green all winter and turn reddish maroon with age. It grows well outside. Variety *xanthum* is endemic to the high tundra around the Continental Divide in Colorado, where it grows on exposed stony slopes. It is a good alpine house plant that forms mats of silver leaves and short-stemmed flower heads that fade to red.

*Eriogonum gracilipes* is endemic to the White Mountains of California, growing on exposed stony slopes and alpine limestone fell-fields at approximately 3600 m (11,700 ft.). It forms pads of gray, felty rosettes with short-stemmed heads of pink flowers that mature through rose and raspberry shades and finally rust-red tones. Although a lovely alpine house plant, it does not like to be contained in a small pot for long. You should cut back the old growth in spring.

*Eriogonum heracleoides* grows in the Rockies from Wyoming to British Columbia and forms a dense mat or mound to 25 cm (10 in.) high with cream flowers aging to pink on stems 30–50 cm (12–20 in.) tall. This is an easy species for the garden.

Variety *angustifolium* grows in Washington on north-facing sagebrush slopes and in gravel soils at 985 m (3200 ft.). Spreading tufts of narrow leaves form a low, wide mound, and several white balls are clustered on 25–30-cm (10–12-in.) stems. Variety *minus* grows on rocky, gravel, subalpine

*Eriogonum gracilipes* in flower, White Mountains, California. Photo Chris Norton.

*Eriogonum gracilipes* showing foliage, White Mountains, California.

ridges in Washington at around 2100 m (6825 ft.). The most dwarf variety, it makes broad mats of narrow, soft, gray leaves in loose rosettes only 5–10 cm (2–4 in.) high. Large, pale cream inflorescences are on stems 5–10 cm (2–4 in.) tall. This variety tends to remain small in cultivation.

*Eriogonum holmgrenii* grows at 3385–4155 m (11,000–13,500 ft.) on Mount Washington in White Pine county, Nevada, where its habitat is the limestone fell-fields and talus of the Snake Range. Among the most rare dwarf species, it is endemic to this area where it grows with *Aquilegia scopulorum* and *Primula nevadensis* well above the bristlecone pines. It forms a silver-leafed mat with small white pom-poms that turn raspberry-pink with age

*Eriogonum holmgrenii*, Mount Washington, Nevada. Photo David Hale.

on stems 2–3 cm (¾–1¼ in.) tall. This species was introduced into cultivation in 1996 as the result of a seed collection by John Andrews. This close relative of *E. gracilipes* is a delightful species for a pot in spite of the slightly longer stems—5 cm (2 in.)—in cultivation.

*Eriogonum incanum* is endemic to the Sierra Nevada, where it grows on gravel slopes at about 3140 m (10,200 ft.). It forms mats of dense, woolly, gray leaves to 30 cm (12 in.) across with flower stems to 15 cm (6 in.) tall that carry umbellate heads of pale yellow flowers. This species is unusual because it is dioecious with male flowers in a smaller, tighter, brighter yellow umbel than the female.

*Eriogonum jamesii* grows in the central Rockies at 1000–2830 m (3250–9200 ft.) and forms a dense mat to 50 cm (20 in.) across with broadly elliptic leaves that are green above and white tomentose below. It has white to cream or yellow flowers on short stems in June through September.

Variety *flavescens* grows in Wyoming at approximately 2145 m (6970 ft.). Lovely yellow-red or yellow-orange flowers appear on stems 25–30 cm (10–12 in.) tall over a

Young flowers of *Eriogonum holmgrenii* in cultivation.

Mature flowers of *Eriogonum holmgrenii* in cultivation.

cushion formed by tightly overlapping, gray leaves.

Variety *wootonii* is narrowly endemic to the Sacramento and White Mountains of south-central New Mexico. It grows on mountain slopes and small openings in lower and upper montane coniferous forests at 1800–3500 m (5850–11,375 ft.). The leaves are broader than in other varieties, and the yellow flowers are on inflorescences 20–50 cm (8–20 in.) tall that are branched three to five times.

Variety *xanthum* grows in Colorado at 2830 m (9200 ft.). Mounded buns of short, pilose leaves have capitate flower clusters of bright yellow on 15-cm (6-in.) stems.

*Eriogonum kelloggii*, an extremely rare endemic to Red Mountain, California, grows on rocky to scree areas at around 1200 m (3900 ft.). It makes large, dense, woolly mats or cushions with 5-cm (2-in.) stems and heads of pink flowers flushing to orange. This slow growing species is a much sought after rarity and a dwarf species to drool over.

*Eriogonum kennedyi* grows in California at 1200–3000 m (3900–9750 ft.) and was at one time thought the most compact. It forms wide, hard, silvery white mats of tiny leaves. Stems are to 15 cm (6 in.) long and bear pinkish flowers that mature to rust-red.

Variety *alpigenum* grows on limestone and granite ridges in California at 2525–2710 m (8200–8800 ft.) and is by far the superior variety. Tiny rosettes have elliptical leaves and stemless red and white flowers. It makes a very choice trough or exhibition plant. Variety *austromontanum* has a larger branching inflorescence and small capitate heads at the nodes that terminate the stems. The mats are not as hard, and the slightly larger leaves are pointed.

*Eriogonum libertini* grows in California on southeast-facing serpentine slopes of fine mineral soil at about 1570 m (5100 ft.). In its natural habitat it makes large compact mats to 152 cm (60 in.) across. Tiny elliptical leaves, which look like rosettes, are clustered on very short shoots and are whitish blue-green on top and white tomentose on the underside. As the leaves mature they turn rosy pink to maroon, and the pale, translucent yellow, 2.5 cm (1 in.) ball-shaped flowers age to pink and then red when the seed matures.

*Eriogonum lobbii* grows in loose talus on steep slopes and in the alpine fell-fields of California and Nevada at 1530–3600 m (4975–11,700 ft.). This very unusual species makes flat rosettes of rounded, gray, fairly large leaves that are almost 5 cm (2 in.) wide and sends out one or two prostrate stems to 15 cm (6 in.) long. The flowers appear slightly flattened to 5 cm (2 in.) wide and they range from cream to pink and green-yellow, maturing to rose and apricot shades. This species does better in the rock garden than a pot, although the sprawling stems tend to elongate at low altitudes, making it untidy. Unlike some, I am unimpressed with this plant.

Variety *robustum* grows in Nevada at 1800 m (5850 ft.) on southwest-facing slopes in loose gravel soil derived from altered volcanic soils. Thick, white felty leaves grow in huge rosettes, and flat-topped white to primrose-yellow umbels grow to 10 cm (4 in.) across on stems that are barely higher than the rosettes. Four to six umbels completely hide the foliage, and the inflorescences mature to an unattractive beige-tan.

*Eriogonum mancum* is from the Birch Creek area in Idaho, where it grows at

1800 m (5850 ft.). A 1991 introduction by Rocky Mountain Rare Plants, it remains a rarity in cultivation even in 2001. Tight silver mounds of foliage with fragrant 1.2 cm (1/2 in.) white or pinkish lavender to dark purple balls of flowers bloom on stems 7–12 cm (2¾–4¾ in.) tall. It makes a fine plant for the alpine house.

*Eriogonum marifolium* grows on rocky slopes and disturbed roadsides in Nevada, California, and Oregon at 1050–3300 m (3410–10,725 ft.). It makes loose mats of small rosettes with olive-green leaves that lose their cobweblike covering as the season progresses. The small yellow umbels are often tinged red and are on branching prostrate stems to 20 cm (8 in.). Like *E. incanum*, this species is dioecious.

*Eriogonum nervulosum*, from California's north-facing, serpentine screes, is like a red-flowered version of *E. ovalifolium* with mats of round leaves that are densely tomentose on the underside. The red flowers are on 5-cm (2-in.) stems.

*Eriogonum niveum* occurs in dry, open areas in Washington, Oregon, California, and Idaho at 65–1850 m (210–6010 ft.). A shrubby perennial with stiff stems to 80 cm (32 in.) high and leaves that are tomentose

*Eriogonum mancum* in cultivation.

on both surfaces, it grows to 76 cm (30 in.) across. The shimmering white cloud of bloom in late summer (which gives rise to the common name of snow buckwheat) ages to a rusty strawberry color.

Variety *dichotomum* grows in Idaho and California at around 1690 m (5500 ft.). A perfect combination of the best in *Eriogonum strictum* and *E. niveum*, it has attractive mounds of white, felty, orbicular leaves on 35-cm (14-in.) high stems. Clouds of white balls in late summer turn a warm pink with age.

*Eriogonum nudum* is very common in California and Oregon on cliffs and coastal sandstone bluffs to 2700 m (8775 ft.). This species owes its attractiveness more to the foliage than the flowers. White tomentose leaves are clustered on short prostrate shoots forming large, loose mats. Branching umbels of white to rose heads are prostrate as they spread over and out from the mats on leafless stems of 15–76 cm (6–30 in.). They flower well into autumn.

Variety *oblongifolium* grows on dry rocky banks in California at about 1720 m (5590 ft.) and makes tufts of oblong, gray and white felty leaves in large mounds of foliage with branching stems to 60–90 cm (24–36 in.) tall. The flowers are bright yellow. Variety *scapigerum* grows on bare dry slopes in pure granite grit at around 2955 m (9600 ft.) in California. The compact mounds are of long lanceolate leaves with yellowish white flowers on bare stems 15–22 cm (6–8¾ in.) tall. The flowers are the largest at 7–8 cm (2¾–3 in.) in diameter. In late summer the leaves turn a startling translucent scarlet.

*Eriogonum ochrocephalum* grows on volcanic gravel soils in California and Nevada at 1200–3000 m (3900–9750 ft.). It makes mats of grayish, tomentose, lanceolate leaves. Stems 5–15 cm (2–6 in.) tall are topped with dense yellow balls.

*Eriogonum ovalifolium* is variable in the wild with a number of varieties and subspecies growing throughout the West in stony soil in Washington, Oregon, California, Idaho, Nevada, Utah, and Wyoming at 2030–3600 m (6600–11,700 ft.). It makes a mat of densely woolly leaves. The lovely pom-pom flowers in July through August are either yellow or white on 10–20-cm (4–8-in.) stems that turn a nice buff color as they age. A plant I grew in a raised bed (it is uncovered throughout the year) eventually made a flat mat 30 cm (12 in.) across with more than 50 flowers.

As an exhibition plant, *Eriogonum ovalifolium* usually forms a tight silver-gray dome and can fill a 15-cm (6-in.) pot in three years from seed. Many consider this species the easiest to grow and yet also among the most rewarding.

Several varieties are worth noting. Variety *depressum* grows in Idaho and Oregon at 2740–2985 m (8900–9700 ft.). Although similar to var. *nivale*, it makes a more rounded mat. The foliage is especially desirable during autumn as the silver leaves take on rusty tints.

Variety *eximium* grows in California's stony, silty soils alongside sagebrush at approximately 2630 m (8550 ft.). It has distinctive brown-margined, whitish gray

*Eriogonum ovalifolium*, White Mountains, California. Photo Chris Norton.

*Eriogonum ovalifolium* and driftwood, Burnt Mountain, eastern Cascades, Washington.

*Eriogonum ovalifolium* in seed, White Mountains, California.

*Eriogonum ovalifolium* in cultivation in a raised bed.

leaves. Although larger than var. *nivale*, the short-stemmed, pinkish white umbels are an improvement over the type in that they are more compact.

Variety *nivale* grows in the Sierra Nevada on ridges and fell-fields at 3000–3600 m (9750–11,700 ft.) and in Oregon and Washington. The stems are shorter at 1.2–5 cm (½–2 in.), and its dense mat and smaller, white, felty leaves are preferred by many exhibitors.

*Eriogonum panguicense* **var.** *alpestre* grows in Utah at 3260–3325 m (10,600–10,805 ft.) in silty limestone clay on barren, subalpine slopes. It makes a small cushion with a congested woody base from which 1.2-cm (½-in.) shoots emerge. The tiny, linear, pale green leaves are clustered at the stem ends and are covered with fine, cobweblike hairs on the upper leaf surface and dense white hairs on the underside. The flowers, pink in bud, open to white with red tints in small heads on short, prostrate stems. It is a beautiful variety.

*Eriogonum parvifolium* grows at a low elevation on the coastal cliffs and dunes in California, where there is fog, mild temperatures, and cool moist winters. It makes mats of 100 cm (39 in.) or more. This prostrate shrub has large rosettes of thick triangular leaves that are dark green on the surface and covered with thick, white felt on the underside. The large, whitish green umbels are densely packed with small flowers that strongly contrast with the foliage. This species could be tender in cultivation and is best grown in an alpine house in cold areas.

*Eriogonum pauciflorum* **var.** *nebraskense* from Colorado has lovely, gray, fuzzy foliage and forms a mat to 60 cm (24 in.) wide with 1.2-cm (½-in.) balls of cream flowers that turn rust red with age. The stems are 5 cm (2 in.) tall.

*Eriogonum rosense*, although very tender looking, grows on harsh, bare, stony exposures of Nevada and California at 2985–3275 m (9700–10,640 ft.). A very striking plant, the large, ever-blooming, yellow pom-pom flowers fade to a rose color, and silver-gray downy leaves form low mats. The 10-cm (4-in.) tall stems turn brown as they die back in autumn, and the plant appears dead over winter. Having grown plants from a John Andrews seed collection, I find it best to cut back these stems in spring so that new growth emerges quickly from the shortened stems to form a nice compact plant. If you do not cut the stems back, the fresh spring leaves and flowers sit on top of a dead-looking stalk. This is a choice species.

*Eriogonum saxatile* grows on gritty serpentine or granitic banks in California at 1200–3300 m (3900–10,725 ft.). A very unusual species, the few rosettes are loosely packed and the inflorescences are on branching stems 15–30 cm (6–12 in.) tall. The dangling flowers range from a pale translucent yellow to pale pink, aging to maroon. Plants from higher elevations tend to be much more compact and almost matlike with the flowers held just above the rosettes. It is usually grown as a foliage plant in cultivation, the large silver leaves shimmering in bright light.

*Eriogonum shockleyi* inhabits the dry, barren limestone areas and exposed sandstone ridges of Utah, Nevada, and Arizona at 1700–1900 m (5525–6175 ft.). A pulvinate-caespitose species, it is similar in many ways to *E. rosense* in forming dense cushions of silvery foliage, although the stems are shorter. The yellow or orange-red flowers mature to apricot and rust shades. One plant I grew from seed collected by John Andrews survived in my scree bed for four years and eventually formed a 15-cm (6-in.) wide flat, silver mat. It flowered profusely each year in spite of the downy silver foliage having to endure wet, cold winters. This species is well suited to a trough or alpine house.

*Eriogonum siskiyouense* grows in California at 900–2700 m (2925–8775 ft.) on south-facing, serpentine, talus slopes. Its tight, woody-based mats of woolly-backed leaves often have red edges. Bright yellow pom-poms on stems 5–10 cm (2–4 in.) tall age to orange-red. It is similar to a compressed version of *E. umbellatum*. Although it appears to be very tough in the alpine bed, it has not flowered in three years.

*Eriogonum soredium* grows at around 2030–2710 m (6600–8800 ft.) in Utah on limestone slopes. Among my favorite eriogonums, it is densely pulvinate with firm, woolly, gray-white mounds to 50 cm (20 in.) across and 12.5–15 cm (5–6 in.) high. The white, sometimes pink-flushed, flower heads are almost stemless and sit just on top of the cushion.

Ron Ratko described it beautifully as the West's version of *Raoulia eximia*, the famous "vegetable sheep" from New

*Eriogonum shockleyi* in cultivation.

Zealand. I cannot imagine it surviving even a single heavy downpour but it is an exceptional alpine house plant and a real challenge to grow.

*Eriogonum sphaerocephalum* grows in dry, rocky areas at 900–2250 m (2925–7310 ft.) in northern California, Oregon, Washington, Idaho, and Nevada. A neat evergreen shrub, it makes loose mats with decumbent stems 5–12.5 cm (2–5 in.) long. Flowering stems are 5–15 cm (2–6 in.) tall and have vivid cream to yellow balls of summer bloom and white tomentose leaves.

Variety *halimioides* grows in Oregon at approximately 1140 m (3705 ft.) on rocky areas in sagebrush. It makes mounds 15–20 cm (6–8 in.) high of linear, whorled, gray-green leaves with numerous large cream balls on stems 5–10 cm (2–4 in.) tall.

*Eriogonum strictum* grows from Washington to California, Nevada, and Montana in ponderosa pine forest and dry, open places. It forms tufts or small mats with gray-white hairy leaves on stems to 10 cm (4 in.) tall that are topped with cream, yellow, or white flowers.

Subspecies *proliferum* grows on rocky slopes in Oregon at 1500–2500 m (4875–8125 ft.). The small mats are of silver-gray spatulate leaves and the creamy white flowers grow on stems 15–20 cm (6–8 in.) tall.

Subspecies *proliferum* var. *anserinum* grows in stony soils on dry sagebrush slopes in Washington and Nevada at around 1770 m (5752 ft.). It is more compact than subspecies *proliferum* and has bright yellow perianths.

Subspecies *proliferum* var. *greenei* occurs in crevices and on ledges in serpentine outcrops at about 2230 m (7245 ft.) in California. It is very dense with woolly, white mats.

The inflorescence is a combination of cymes and dense umbels with rose-violet buds opening to white with rose tints on stems 2.5–7.5 cm (1–3 in.) tall.

*Eriogonum thymoides* is different from the other species and comes from Washington, Oregon, and Idaho, where it grows at fairly low altitudes. This slow growing, deep-rooted, dwarf shrub is just 7.5–15 cm (3–6 in.) tall with short, needlelike leaves terminally congested on the stems. The short-stemmed, bright lemon-yellow inflorescence matures to orange, rusty red, dark red, and maroon. A population of older, gnarly-stemmed plants clothed in these various colors is a spectacular sight. In its natural habitat of rocky basalt scablands, a hot, dry environment ensures this species has extremely slow growth. This plant is not only a gem for a trough, but also an excellent exhibition plant, although from autumn to spring it looks nearly dead. It takes about three years to flower from seed

*Eriogonum tumulosum* is from Colorado and Utah, where it grows on shaley clay soils in juniper and pinyon-pine woodland from 1500 to 2200 m (4875 to 7150 ft.). The fantastically tight cushions with almost stemless flowers on the bun have olive-gray foliage with small white-pink umbels nestled among the tiny leaves. Although an ideal trough plant, it ranks among the best and most challenging to grow.

*Eriogonum umbellatum* has much the same wide range as *E. ovalifolium* with habitats varying from deserts to alpine ridges at 1815–4000 m (5900–13,000 ft.). It has an even greater number of variations, and most are well worth the effort. Although the plant is mat forming, the stems can be 7.5–30 cm (3–12 in.) high at flowering time with blooms that in most varieties range from bright yellow to cream. If you cultivate this species, grow it in a scree bed outside, where it is easier to grow than in an alpine house.

There are several varieties to consider. Variety *bahiiforme* occurs in California at around 2075 m (6745 ft.) and is a small, spreading shrub that is lovely in a scree garden, growing to 15 cm (6 in.) tall. It has finely tomentose leaves and bright yellow flowers that age to coppery red. Variety *glaberrimum* (synonym *Eriogonum torreyanum*) is both easy to grow and long lasting in an alpine bed. It has yellow flowers that are sometimes tinted red on 7.5–15-cm (3–6-in.) stems.

Variety *hausknechtii* grows in Washington and Oregon at 2000–3000 m

*Eriogonum thymoides* in cultivation.

*Eriogonum umbellatum*, Mount Evans, Colorado.

(6500–9750 ft.). It makes dense, flat mats to 60 cm (24 in.) across with small, grayish, blue-green leaves that have wisps of long white hairs. The leaf undersides are thick with white felt, and many leaves age to maroon. The 5-cm (2-in.) wide cream to pale yellow inflorescences are on stems 2.5–7.5 cm (1–3 in.) tall. Its tidy habit makes it one of the best varieties.

Variety *humistratum* grows in California at approximately 2500 m (8125 ft.) on west-facing, serpentine, and talus slopes. Dense, tight mats are of silvery gray rosettes. The large umbels vary from greenish yellow to bright yellow upon opening and then transform into innumerable degrees of red, bronze, orange, and maroon.

Variety *hypoleium* is from Washington's Wenatchee Mountains and Oregon, usually on steep, east-facing slopes and dry gravel openings in subalpine forests at around 1815 m (5900 ft.). Small rosettes of 1.2-cm (½-in.) wide, dark green oval leaves turn purple and dark red in the winter. The small mats have 5-cm (2-in.) long, bright sulfur-yellow perianths on 5–10-cm (2–4-in.) stems.

Variety *minus* grows in California at about 3000 m (9750 ft.) on alpine ridge tops of metamorphic talus in compact gravel soils. The dense, silky white mats must be the tightest and most dwarf of any *Eriogonum umbellatum* variety, and the inflorescence color surpasses all others as the pom-pom flowers on stems 2.5–12.5 cm (1–5 in.) tall vary from deep amethyst-red to blackish red.

Variety *nevadense* comes from a habitat similar to var. *minus* and makes a loose mat or a low mounding shrub with greenish leaves clustered at the nodes. Branching umbels of bright yellow mature to brassy gold heads and are on short stems. Variety *polyanthum* resembles the *nevadense* variety in that it makes a loose mat of rosettes. The leaf undersides are densely tomentose and the umbels are greenish yellow.

Variety *porteri* grows in Utah at almost 4000 m (13,000 ft.) on rocky, volcanic slopes and is a beauty for a hot, dry position. The yellow to red pom-poms are virtually stemless over flat mats of foliage that in autumn are colored with red shades.

Variety *subalpinum* is quite variable. One plant I grew from seed collected from a colony growing in dry, grassy meadows on sandy, rocky soil at 1690 m (5500 ft.) in Washington does well in a well-drained, sunny position in my garden. The 2.5–5-cm

*Eriogonum umbellatum*, Wasatch Mountains, Utah. Photo David Hale.

*Eriogonum umbellatum*, Mount Townsend, Olympic Mountains, Washington.

(1–2-in.) leaves are dark green on top and white on the underside, and the 5–7.5-cm (2–3-in.) wide cream to pale yellow inflorescences are on stems 5–15 cm (2–6 in.) tall. Although in the wild it forms tight dense mats more than 60 cm (24 in.) across, my plant has never reached this size. A second plant of var. *subalpinum* was from seed collected from a meadow near a stream in Wyoming, so I grew it in a slightly moister position (it died because the position was too damp). It made a wide mat with stems 20–30 cm (8–12 in.) tall and huge creamy heads that matured to pink and amber.

Variety *versicolor* grows in the desert ranges along the southern border of California and Nevada. A distinct dwarf variety, it has mats of dull gray-green rosettes and flowers that mature to shades of deep rose.

*Eriogonum ursinum* grows on barren, volcanic, talus slopes in California at 460–2300 m (1495–7475 ft.). It makes a dense, wide mat, and the leaves are small and pale olive green with a white felty underside. Stems are 10–20 cm (4–8 in.) tall with heads of pale yellow flowers that are 7 cm (2¾ in.) wide, that open from attractive, reddish yellow buds, and that age to deep yellow and pinkish orange.

Variety *nervulosum* grows on north-facing, serpentine screes in California at around 460 m (1495 ft.). The rhizomatous mats have leaves that are white and densely tomentose on the underside, and the congested umbels of red flowers are on stems only 5 cm (2 in.) tall.

*Eriogonum villiflorum* grows on limestone gravel flats in Utah and Nevada at about 2000 m (6500 ft.). It is another of the pulvinate, caespitose, mound-forming species with small cushions tinged red-purple and white-pink flowers on short stems.

*Eriogonum wrightii* grows in gravel at 1190–3150 m (3870–10,240 ft.) in California, Nevada, Utah, New Mexico, and Arizona. It forms a mat of tiny, silvery, woolly leaves with pink or white flowers in August through October on leafless flowering stems 15–25 cm (6–10 in.) tall. It resembles a miniature *E. niveum*.

Variety *subscaposum* grows on hot, dry, gravel slopes in the Sierra Nevada at 1500–3150 m (4875–10,240 ft.). Small dense mats of gray leaves are in tiny axillary clusters 15–30 cm (6–12 in.) across. Among the latest to bloom—often not until September—the flowers, which are on stems 10–25 cm (4–10 in.) tall, cover the mats.

*Eriogonum wrightii* in a clearing on Mount Pinos, California.

## Propagation

Whether you collect seed from your own plants or those in the wild you will find that the dead heads take time to release the seed. Each seed is shaped like a teardrop, has a very sharp pointed end, and can be fairly large in some species. One way to find the seed is to roll the dead seedheads around between your thumb and forefinger, and when you feel a sharp point stick into your finger, you have found a seed. When I collect smaller seeds that are more difficult to release (for example, seeds of *Eriogonum breedlovei*, *E. shockleyi*, and *E. soredium*), I crumble the dried flower heads between my fingers and thumb and continually drop the resultant chaff onto a piece of white paper. Every now and again I discover a small seed and put it to one side. Patience is a real virtue here; it has taken me up to an hour to obtain 15 seeds from *E. shockleyi*. When I find no seed I sow all the dead heads as a last resort, and each time I have done this a few seedlings have germinated.

Growing this genus from seed is fairly straightforward. Sow the seed in 7-cm (2 ¾-in.) pots on the surface of the soil mix in autumn, cover it all with grit, and place the pot outside. When the seed has germinated bring the pot into the unheated alpine house for the seedlings to grow on. However, you must prick out the seedlings very early just as you would with *Astragalus* or *Oxytropis* seedlings as the taproots grow very quickly and wind around each other, making pricking out extremely difficult. This early pricking out does not cause any problems as long as it is done with great care. Each seedling should be pricked out into a 7-cm (2¾-in.) pot.

Although other nurseries have reported success with cuttings, I have had about a 50 percent success rate. These cuttings are taken in late summer. Although I have tried a number of different species I have had no consistent results with any of them. I therefore prefer to grow from seed, whether it is my own or from the exchanges or commercial lists. I nevertheless feel that propagating by cuttings, especially to increase the stock of a particularly good form, is something I must attempt each year.

## Cultivation

Where to grow these plants, in the garden or in a pot?—that is the question. Eriogonums need a deep root run wherever they are cultivated. They grow best in a hot, xeric garden and sometimes succeed in raised or normal alpine beds. In every instance mix a lot of grit into the top 30 cm (12 in.) of soil leaving the top 15 cm (6 in.) as pure grit. I believe the grit is the main reason my plants have lived through the damp, cold winters. I tried two plants in a spot where I had normal garden soil mixed with a little grit, and although they grew perfectly well in spring and early summer, they died during a spell of really hot weather as the roots had not penetrated deeply enough into the soil to take up moisture. Plenty of grit encourages this penetration action and also allows quick drainage of excessive moisture.

In the United Kingdom plants are more widely grown in pots than anywhere else in the world, and I believe this is the only way to successfully grow the more difficult eriogonums no matter where you live. The soil mixture used for eriogonums contains almost 50 percent grit, so when you grow them in a pot, check the moisture content almost daily during summer. Overwintering in an alpine house enables plants to come into growth much earlier than they would outdoors, and of course they flower earlier. This genus is sun loving, and the pots can be put outdoors from late spring to autumn. Be aware of the likelihood that the pots—and thus the roots—will overheat, and keep the pots plunged in moist sand or at least shaded.

Some species need individual treatment. *Eriogonum breedlovei*, for example, goes completely brown or black during winter and comes into growth so late the following spring that it often causes concern. I know of several growers who have thrown their plant away thinking it was dead. Do not be too hasty to get rid of a plant and do not start ripping off the "dead" leaves and stems before growth has commenced as you are likely to remove lots of living tissue and ruin the plant. I tried growing this species in a piece of tufa outside, and although it survived for three years, the growth rate was practically nil.

*Eriogonum soredium* tends to have dieback in patches during winter and early spring, and just when it appears that new growth in spring has covered up the last patch of dieback, another dead patch appears. A cunning use of scissors and grit enables an exhibitor to disguise these minor disasters. As this species is small leafed and very downy, it is important to get air movement around the mound to prevent a moist atmosphere from causing even more damage.

In the alpine house red spider mite can be a problem, especially on those species with silver foliage. Do not overwater seedlings that have just been potted on or they will damp off.

If possible, grow a range of eriogonums: you will be rewarded with some of the most lovely colors and textures you can find in any plant.

# ERITRICHIUM
## Boraginaceae
*alpine forget-me-nots*

*Eritrichium nanum* has always been among the first plants mentioned whenever discussions turn to classic alpines. Known both in the Old World and the New, this species resides in the arctic and alpine zone. Ingwersen (1978) states that it has been referred to as "the gardeners' classic failure," and Royton Heath (1964) describes it as "a species that must be the despair of all alpine gardeners." If you read Heath's plant descriptions carefully, you will see these comments refer to the European selections, and only Ingwersen refers to the American version, albeit briefly.

For many years I faced a similar block until in 1982 I encountered my first North American eritrichium during a field trip to Mount Evans, Colorado. I gazed with awe at the outstanding *Eritrichium nanum*, particularly since I saw not only the blue flowering form but also the white. Even so, I felt no real inclination to grow the plant, instead believing everything that had been written or said about it, including that the plants and seed were not available. Yet it made such an impression on me the first time I saw it that a photograph of *Eritrichium nanum* I took at Loveland Pass, Colorado, in 1993 holds a place of honor on the wall of my office. This is a plant that, once seen, is never forgotten.

Very little has been written about the three other North American species within this genus (*Eritrichium aretioides*, *Eritrichium chamissonis*, and *Eritrichium howardii*); perhaps they are considered the ugly sisters, but I regard them as classics in their own right.

*Eritrichium aretioides* (synonym *E. nanum* var. *aretioides*) grows in the Brooks and Alaska Ranges and in northwest Alaska, where it inhabits the loose moist screes in the tundra and high alpine zones. Rosettes of hairy, bluish leaves form small cushions or mats. Bright blue flowers with a dark yellow eye bloom in mid-June through early July and grow on short stems that elongate to 7.5 cm (3 in.). I find this species easier to grow than *E. nanum* probably because it comes from a moist area.

*Eritrichium chamissonis* was described by Hultén (1968) as being restricted to Chukotka, western, and northwestern Alaska. In 1872 Herder described *E. aretioides* and *E. chamissonis* as being varieties of *E. nanum*, but such classification will likely be subject to more research. Although similar to *E. aretioides* in appearance, *E. chamissonis* has more congested cushions and stems, and the flowers never rise above the cushion.

*Eritrichium howardii* is a limestone dweller from Montana and Wyoming and inhabits areas of a lower altitude than *E. nanum* from the foothills to alpine level. As its habitat is less harsh, it has looser mounds and longer stems. It forms tufted mounds to 7.5 cm (3 in.) high and 30 cm (12 in.) across with blue flowers that are slightly larger than those of *E. nanum*. Beautiful silky, silver leaves are longer and narrower than those of *E. nanum* plants, and the hairs are shorter.

Loveland Pass, Colorado.

*Eritrichium aretioides*, Yukon-Tanada Uplands, Alaska. Photo Carolyn Parker.

*Eritrichium chamissonis*, St. Paul Island, Bering Strait, Alaska. Photo Carolyn Parker.

In 1989 I drove up the Chief Joseph Highway to Dead Indian Hill Summit in Wyoming, where I expected to easily find *Eritrichium howardii*. After a fruitless hour spent climbing and slipping, I photographed *Clematis columbiana*, *Oxytropis campestris*, and *Townsendia parryi* but found no *E. howardii* plants and returned to the car. My wife, Iris, put down her book and told me to look at the lovely blue forget-me-nots at the top of a nearby embankment. Sure enough a patch of blooming *E. howardii* stretched for about 15 m (50 ft.) in a tufa scree, and although its cushion is taller and more lax than in *E. nanum*, it is still an exciting plant to see in the wild. Sadly that group of *E. howardii* no longer exists because a

road has been built over the pass, but other populations still inhabit the summit area.

*Eritrichium nanum*, the most beautiful, compact, silky cushion, grows in exposed positions in the Rockies. It occurs mainly in granite rubble at 2275–3690 m (7400–12,000 ft.) in Colorado, Montana, and Wyoming, although it is also found in limestone areas. Roy Davidson writes that it also occurs in Alaska's mountains as far east as the Yukon. A disjunct population grows in the Wallowa Mountains of Oregon. Just 5 cm (2 in.) tall and to 25 cm (10 in.) across (and occasionally more), this is, of course, the species everyone knows from the European Alps. Among the first alpines to bloom at this altitude, the small forget-me-not

View from Dead Indian Hill Summit, Wyoming.

Site of *Eritrichium nanum* on Mount Evans, Colorado.

*Eritrichium howardii* at Dead Indian Hill Summit, Wyoming.

*Eritrichium nanum*, Beartooth Pass, Wyoming. Photo Peter Downe.

flowers in June through August are a striking blue (sometimes it is turquoise or aquamarine) with a yellow eye and can cover the cushion. Silky hairs on the tiny leaves capture moisture from the early morning dew and also hold in air that acts as insulation against the hot sun.

*Eritrichium splendens* is exclusive to Alaska, where it grows in dry, sandy areas near the tree line in the Alaska Range and the south side of the Brooks Range. It makes mounds of narrow, hairy, bluish green leaves 2–3.8 cm (¾–1½ in.) long. The clear blue flowers in mid-June through early July have bright yellow eyes and grow on stems to 7.5 cm (3 in.).

## Propagation

Unlike authors of some articles written in the early years of rock gardening, I do not recommend digging up these plants in the wild as they will never survive. Seed is the tried and true method for growing eritrichiums, and seed-raised plants, having naturally selected themselves by germinating, are much easier to grow. Since 1990 I have had access to a great deal of seed from both *Eritrichium nanum* and *E. howardii*, and that has enabled me to learn the cultivation techniques for growing these plants.

I sow the seed in November, December, and January exactly as I do other alpine seed and stand the pots outside. It usually takes three to six weeks to germinate *Eritrichium nanum* whether the weather is wet or freezing, and whether I use fresh or two-year-old seed. *Eritrichium howardii* takes about three months to germinate. Once the seeds have germinated I bring the pots into the alpine house to encourage the seedlings to grow on more quickly. I prick out the seedlings as early as possible—as soon as the first two real leaves are formed—into 7-cm (2¾-in.) pots using a soil mixture that contains plenty of granite grit. *Eritrichium howardii* will grow in a mix containing lime-free grit even though it grows on limestone in nature.

## Cultivation

I often hear comments that the American *Eritrichium nanum* is much easier to grow than the European form. Most of these comments come from those who have not grown the plant. I also hear people say that *Eritrichium howardii* is easier to grow than *E. nanum*, again usually from those who have not grown both species. Like many other plants that have proved difficult in the past (dionysias, for example), the more freely available a plant becomes the more it is

*Eritrichium nanum* in habitat, Duncum Mountain, Big Horn Mountains, Wyoming. Photo Chris Norton.

*Eritrichium nanum*, white form. Mount Evans, Colorado.

understood. Since 1995 I have grown and flowered both species side by side, admittedly in the alpine house, but I now have some experience to pass on to other growers. It may take three or four attempts to grow these gems to a reasonable size but it *can* be done.

I use the same cultivation methods for both *Eritrichium nanum* and *E. howardii*, the only difference being that because *E. nanum* grows mainly in granite areas I use a soil-based mixture with no added lime and I add extra granite grit. Although *E. howardii* grows in limestone areas, I use a neutral, soil-based compost for pot cultivation. If the compost includes chalk, I add granite grit rather than limestone grit since the chalk provides enough lime.

*Eritrichium howardii* is not only less compact than *E. nanum* but also a much faster grower. When both species are seedlings they can take more moisture on their foliage in summer without damping off probably because when they are mature plants there are more rosettes in which moisture can become trapped. During hot days in late spring to summer, I operate the sprayers in my alpine houses twice a week so that the seedlings, some of which double in size at this stage, get 15 minutes of moisture each time. I do not treat my mature plants similarly, however, and carefully examine the foliage on each watering and mop up any excess moisture with a paper towel.

About six months after I prick them out into 7-cm (2¾-in.) pots, the seedlings

*Eritrichium splendens*, Yukon-Tanana Uplands, Alaska. Photo Carolyn Parker.

*Eritrichium splendens*, Alaska Range. Photo Carolyn Parker.

measure around 1.2 cm (½ in.) across and are ready to be potted into larger pots to grow on for another year if they are to be show plants. I do not knock the seedlings out of their pots but instead transfer the entire block of soil mix and root ball to a new pot by cutting downwards along the creases at the four corners and bending the old pot's flaps back. During the spring and summer, growth is quite fast, so during summer they need a fair amount of moisture. Any water that lingers on the cushions of *Eritrichium nanum* seedlings soon evaporates because of the warmth or air movement.

As autumn approaches, I gradually withhold water until I am not giving the plants any water over winter. I either stand the pots on damp grit that I water occasionally or partly plunge them in sand. The plant roots need only a little moisture, but any moisture at the neck of the plant will cause it to rot off in a very short time.

Winter brings the most worry for the gardener. *Eritrichium nanum* stays almost green throughout winter, which means that if it succumbs to an attack of botrytis or dies from overwatering you will immediately notice. *Eritrichium howardii*, however. guarantees worry for the grower until spring. The rosettes on this species turn black with only a faint green tip on each rosette showing that it is alive. Several growers experiencing this plant for the first time have thrown it out when it has taken on that appearance. You must be patient and cultivate *E. howardii* over winter exactly as you would *E. nanum*. As spring approaches and temperatures begin to rise, the plant undergoes an almost miraculous change from dead looking black foliage to a healthy green. This transformation happens over a very short period—usually a week or so—

depending on the weather, and is the period when you will know whether your plant is still alive or not. Unlike *E. nanum* that you can see dying in winter, you do not know whether you have lost *E. howardii* until the spring when the foliage either becomes green or remains black.

If my plants have come through the winter and look healthy, I begin by watering them first around the base of the pot to ensure that the roots have more moisture, and then around the edge of the pot as spring growth becomes more obvious. Many of my plants have flowered in the spring of the second year from sowing. I pot on plants that I grew in a square plastic pot by transferring the complete block of soil mix and roots into another pot, having first made sure that the compost is not dry. If you grow the seedlings in a clay pot you should break the pot in order to keep the soil mixture intact. Once repotted, *Eritrichium nanum* grows slowly. *Eritrichium howardii*, on the other hand, is a very fast grower and can fill a 15-cm ( 6-in.) pot in the third year. Although both my species have flowered and set seed, they have, like a lot of the high alpines, not flowered as freely as in the wild. There is also another slight problem of the flowers being a dull imitation of that piercing blue you see in the wild. I have had this misfortune with both species.

Just because I grow these two gems in an alpine house does not mean that they cannot grow outside. The main problem is winter wet around the neck of the plant and lack of air movement when the plant is in growth. If your garden receives snow cover in winter and affords good air movement in summer, particularly during rainy weather, your chances of growing these plants in the garden are improved. Of course they must have a deep enough root run to allow the roots access to a little moisture in winter and enough moisture in baking hot summers.

I also grew *Eritrichium nanum* in a lump of tufa in a trough outside the alpine house most of the year, bringing the trough inside only for winter protection. Although it had to accept whatever the weather threw at it, the plant did grow, albeit slowly. Its demise had nothing to do with botrytis or overwatering but a ravenous slug.

Perhaps because of its natural habitat of loose moist screes, *Eritrichium aretioides* (which I grow from seed collected in Alaska) has proved a lot easier to grow in cultivation than the other species. The plant I grow can take more moisture than *E. howardii* or *E. nanum*, and the problem of botrytis has not yet arisen.

Botrytis caused by overwatering and a lack of air movement during humid conditions in winter is the plants' biggest killer. Once they start to collapse nothing will bring them back to life. Keep a close watch for aphids, especially whiteflies, under the cushions as they are a menace.

# G

## GENTIANA
Gentianaceae
*gentians*

Although the phrase "gentian blue" is often used to describe a rich blue color, not all gentians are blue; they range from blue to purple, violet, white, and yellow. Their tubular to bell-shaped flowers are usually upright with spreading petal lobes that are linked together by pleats. There are approximately 300 species of gentians throughout

the world and they are among the loveliest of wildflowers. They are an essential addition to the rock garden as apart from their beauty they bloom at a time when the garden is a little lacking in color.

The gentian is named after Gentius, King of Illyria, an ancient country east of the Adriatic Sea, who is reputed to have found that the herb had a healing effect on his malaria-stricken troops in the second century B.C.

The genus has been the focus of great taxonomic activity, and plants once considered gentians, such as the fringed gentian *Gentiana holopetala*, have been moved into new genera such as *Gentianopsis* and *Gentianella*. I consider all of these as a single group.

*Gentiana affinis* (synonym *G. oregana*), the marsh gentian, grows in the West Coast and throughout the Rockies in limestone areas that are vernally marshy, in open places, and among thickets to 3850 m (12,515 ft.) that dry out by late summer. Stems 10–30 cm (4–12 in.) tall typically have rich blue-purple, tubular, 2.5-cm (1-in.) long flowers in July through September that are solitary or in terminal clusters.

Variety *bigelovii* (synonym *Gentiana bigelovii*) ranges from Colorado to Arizona and is more erect. The cylindrical flowers are mauve-blue to purple or occasionally white or greenish with a blue to purple flush.

*Gentiana algida* ranges from Alaska to Montana, Utah, Wyoming, and Colorado at alpine levels in grassland, bogs, and moist tundra. This lovely species grows to 15 cm (6 in.) tall, with smooth, yellowish green opposite leaves. Upright, tubular, flaring flowers in mid-July through mid-August are 3.8–5 cm (1½–2 in.) long and are creamy white with bluish purple streaks. The five petals are fused together and pleated between the petal lobes for most of their length. In some cases seed is hardly set before the first snows arrive.

*Gentiana bisetaea* from the upper Illinois and Chetco drainages in Oregon is considered by some a synonym of *G. setigera*. It is tufted with crowded basal leaves and erect to ascending stems to 35 cm (14 in.) tall. Solitary, erect, funnel-shaped flowers in July through September are 2.5–8 cm (1–3 in.) long and have bright purple-blue lobes with a pale tube that is spotted with green dots inside and greenish on the outside. The flowers are finely toothed between the lobes. An unusual feature of the species is that the five petal lobes are separated by several long, threadlike, pointed appendages.

*Gentiana calycosa*, the bog gentian, ranges from California to Montana and British Columbia, where it grows in wet alpine or subalpine meadows and bogs at around 1940 m (6305 ft.). In late summer, broad mounds of decumbent stems 5–35 cm (2–14 in.) tall bear solitary (occasionally there are clusters of up to six), deep blue tubular flowers to 5 cm (2 in.) long. The petal lobes of the beautiful flower are often covered with tiny yellow dots. Each pleat between the lobes usually ends in two fine, sharply pointed teeth between the petals. When the sun disappears behind a cloud the flowers immediately close.

Variety *asepala* grows in Idaho at about 2340 m (7600 ft.). Upright stems to 30 cm (12 in.) tall have many blue fluted flowers with greenish spots inside.

*Gentiana douglasiana* grows in Alaska's bogs and wet meadows. Angled stems to 15 cm (6 in.) tall grow from a thin root and are mostly branched. The small white flowers are bluish on the outside and closely subtended by ovate bracts.

*Gentiana glauca* ranges from Alaska to Montana inhabiting subalpine and alpine slopes and tundra. It has a creeping

*Gentiana algida*, Denali National Park, Alaska. Photo Verna Pratt.

*Gentiana douglasiana*, Turnagain Pass, Kenai Peninsula, Alaska. Photo Verna Pratt.

rootstock with a tight basal rosette of 2-cm (¾-in.) long leaves. Stems 5–15 cm (2–6 in.) tall have two to four pairs of stem leaves and terminal clusters of three to seven dark blue to bluish green flowers in July through August. The 2-cm (¾-in.) long flowers open with a slight flare in sunshine.

*Gentiana newberryi* grows in Oregon, California, and Nevada in alpine meadows, seeps, and moist fell-fields to 1210–4038 m (3937–13,125 ft.). It makes tufted mats to 7.5 cm (3 in.) across with decumbent stems growing 2.5–12.5 cm (1–5 in.) long. Solitary, broad, funnel-like flowers in July through September have pale blue to deep purple lobes, dark purple bands on the white exterior, and a white to pale blue interior that is spotted with green. *Gentiana*

*newberryi* is host to *Colias behrii*, the Sierra sulphur butterfly, and it was named for John Newberry, a botanist and physician on the Pacific Railway Surveys of the 1850s. Pale and dark blue forms occur at the northernmost limits of the species' range, and there is also a white form.

Variety *tiogana* is native to California's White Mountains at 1515–4038 m (4922–13,124 ft.) but it also occurs just over the border in Nevada. It is more compact with white, dark striped flowers on short stems that radiate from around the crown and appear to sit upright, encircling the prostrate rosettes of fleshy green leaves.

*Gentiana parryi* is common throughout the central and southern Rockies at approximately 3060–3385 m (9945–11,000 ft.) and

*Gentiana glauca*, Chugach Mountains, Alaska. Photo Verna Pratt.

*Gentiana newberryi* var. *tiogana* in cultivation. Photo Harold McBride.

is variable in habitat from moist edges of meadows and forests to moist pockets of gritty soil at the base of boulder slopes. Its habit is also variable with stems that are either erect to 15–23 cm (6–9 in.) or decumbent and matlike. Both kinds of stems have terminal clusters of four to six rich blue, urn-shaped flowers that closely resemble *G. calycosa*, except the pleats between the petals of *G. parryi* usually end in one sharp tooth. These pleats give rise to the common name of pleated gentian. On cloudy days the blooms stay closed.

*Gentiana platypetala* comes from Alaska and is an alpine meadow species growing on grassy slopes to 1000 m (3250 ft.). Stems grow to 15 cm (6 in.) from a long, thick, horizontal to oblique caudex with very large blue flowers in August through September.

*Gentiana prostrata*, the moss gentian, is an annual or short-lived perennial inhabiting wet open ground, scree, and high mountain meadows in Alaska through the Rockies to Colorado, Utah, Nevada, Idaho, and California. A small sprawling species, it has whitish stems to 10 cm (4 in.) tall. Tiny, bright blue flowers in mid-June through August have a white center and open only in bright sunshine. They often close when shaded or touched.

*Gentiana sceptrum* (synonyms *G. menziesii*, *G. orfordii*) ranges from west of the Cascades to the northern Californian coast inhabiting wet meadows and marshes below 1300 m (4225 ft.). It is clump forming with fairly dense, ovate to lanceolate leaves 3.1–6.3 cm (1¼–2½ in.) long. The blue, funnel-shaped, 2.5–3.8-cm (1–1½-in.) long flowers in June through September are in terminal clusters on stems 15–60 cm (6–24 in.) tall. The flowers have a flat, smooth edge between the petal lobes.

*Gentiana setigera* in northwest California and southwest Oregon grows in moist and marshy places to 1900 m (6175 ft.). It is tufted with several erect to ascending stems 20–30 cm (8–12 in.) tall, and solitary or small clusters of large blue, bell-like flowers have many long, hairlike bristles on the folds between the petal lobes.

*Gentiana prostrata*, Denali National Park, Alaska. Photo Verna Pratt.

*Gentiana platypetula*, Chugach Mountains, Alaska. Photo Verna Pratt.

*Gentianella amarella* (synonym *Gentiana amarella*) is a common annual species growing in wet meadows at 1385–3385 m (4500–11,000 ft.) from the Sierra Nevada, north to British Columbia, and as far east as New Mexico. Disjunct populations occur in Vermont and Maine. It has slender stems 5–50 cm (2–20 in.) tall, and tubular, lavender to pink flowers to 2 cm (¾ in.) long cluster along each stem. The flower has a fringe of hairs across the inside of the five petal lobe bases. It blooms June through September, and although among the smaller and less showy species, it often grows in dense, colorful patches.

*Gentianella propinqua* (synonym *Gentiana propinqua*), the four-parted gentian, is an annual in northwest Wyoming, Idaho, Montana, and Alaska, inhabiting meadows, woodlands, and sandy open areas. Closely resembling G. amarella, this spindly, thin-stemmed plant is 10–30 cm (4–12 in.) tall, and the narrow, tubular, four- to five-petalled flowers in midsummer are violet to pink.

*Gentianopsis thermalis* (synonym *Gentiana detonsa*, *Gentianopsis detonsa*), the fringed gentian, is a wide-ranging annual or biennial growing throughout most of the West's mountains in short turf meadows, bogs, and moist ground at elevations of around 1700–3550 m (5525–11,540 ft.). The plants are very compact at higher elevations. Variable both in form and botanical name, it is the official flower of Yellowstone National Park and is named for the hot springs found there. It is indistinguishable from *Gentiana holopetala* or *Gentianopsis holopetala* in the Sierra Nevada, which is known as the tufted gentian. Growing 5–40 cm (2–15¾ in.) tall it has several clumped stems and solitary, intense blue flowers 3.1–5 cm (1¼–2 in.) long with four fringed, rounded lobes.

**Propagation**

Propagate by sowing seed as soon as it is ripe. Late sown seed usually takes a year to germinate. The seed is very fine so do not cover it with too deep a layer of grit as this prevents germination. In spring you should propagate these plants by cuttings or careful division. You can layer plants with prostrate stems during summer.

**Cultivation**

Gentians need a moist, humus-rich soil, and some species may require the protection of an alpine house or frame during winter.

*Gentiana setigera* in cultivation. Photo Rick Lupp.

*Gentianopsis thermalis*, Yellowstone National Park.

Slugs are the worst pests whether the plants are grown in the garden, frame, or alpine house as they eat the newly emerging fresh shoots. Red spider and aphids can be a problem when gentians are cultivated under glass. Also keep your eyes open for gentian rust fungus.

# GILIA
Polemoniaceae
*gily-flowers*

*Gilia* is a genus of approximately 25 species mainly from the drylands of the West to South America. Although *Gilia* has been moved into the genus *Ipomopsis*, I have kept the generic name *Gilia* to help with plant identification, particularly of those species not mentioned in the *Encyclopaedia of Alpine*s.

I started growing gilias when my interest in North American alpines began to broaden but I admit that although the species in this genus were quite pretty, they did not impress me too much. They usually turned out to be monocarpic or not suited to growing in areas of wet winters and humid summers. I tried growing several plants in the alpine house but they did not live for very long. Some very attractive, taller species from the western

United States tempted me but I knew they would not last too long in a perennial border.

In 1991 John Andrews distributed *Gilia caespitosa* seed, and a couple of years later seed of *G. formosa* became available. I grew these two very beautiful but rarely cultivated species and found them admirably suited for pot cultivation; perhaps they would grow well in a xeric garden in a suitable climate. There are still many species with flowers of amazing colors that I want to try cultivating, and I hope seed will become available from these species in the near future.

*Gilia aggregata*, the scarlet gilia, grows throughout the West, both as roadside flower in Colorado and side by side with *Hymenoxys lapidicola* in the sand of Blue Mountain, Utah. It grows 30–60 cm (12–24 in.) in height and has pinnately dissected

Flowers of *Gilia aggregata*. Photo Chris Norton.

*Gilia aggregata* on a roadside, Mount Shasta, California.

leaves. The largest feature is the beautiful scarlet trumpets that hummingbirds love. This plant would likely flower well in a hot, dry spot in summer.

Variety *arizonica* is monocarpic and has a lower habit and shorter trumpets; it is often lightly woolly. Variety *bridgesii* grows in California at around 2585 m (8400 ft.) on the gravel slopes of lodgepole pine forests. This perennial form has a woody crown of rosettes with several stems and brilliant cerise flowers that grow to 5 cm (2 in.) long.

Variety *macrosiphon* grows in Utah at a higher altitude of 2860 m (9300 ft.) in grassy openings of aspen woodland where the soil is sandy. It grows 45–60 cm (18–24 in.) tall with superb, neon violet-pink flowers well over 5 cm (2 in.) long.

*Gilia caespitosa*, probably the very best gilia of all, grows in north-facing fissures on sloping, white Navajo sandstone outcrops at about 2450 m (7965 ft.) in the Boulder Mountains southeast of Teasdale in Wayne county, Utah. Stems grow 8–10 cm (3–4 in.) tall with sticky leaves and 2.5-cm (1-in.) long tubular, bright orange-scarlet flowers that bloom over a long period, from April through August. As an exhibition plant it has been invaluable, appearing in several

shows from May through June. Plants grown from seed have flowers that vary in color from orange-scarlet to a brilliant scarlet.

*Gilia congesta*, the ballhead gilia, has a wide range from eastern Oregon and eastern California to Wyoming, northwest New Mexico, and Utah, growing on dry open slopes at 1540–2985 m (5000–9700 ft.). It has very lacy foliage with stems 15–30 cm (6–12 in.) tall that are branched, woody, and topped with roundish heads of small, white trumpet-shaped flowers in June through September.

Variety *congesta* is the shortest variety at 15 cm (6 in.) tall. One plant I grew from seed collected at 2985 m (9700 ft.) in Wyoming was a poor imitation of the superb congested mat it makes in the wild; as with many plants, it is almost impossible to imitate this variety's natural habitat in cultivation.

Variety *montana* grows in California at approximately 2310 m (7500 ft.) on exposed ridges in stony silty soils. Dense silver-blue cushions of small, trilobed, hairy leaves are on short prostrate stems that have ball-like white flowers with exserted stamens. A good looking plant whether in or out of flower, it

*Gilia caespitosa*, Teasdale, Utah. Photo David Hale.

*Gilia caespitosa* in cultivation, third year from seed.

needs to be grown in full sun with a very gritty mix to keep it in character.

Variety *palmifrons* grows in Nevada at the lower altitude of 1660 m (5400 ft.). A more common variety, it is slightly more robust than the *montana* variety. The leaves have five lobes and the inflorescences are larger on taller and more leafy stems than the type.

*Gilia formosa* grows in New Mexico along ridge tops of eroded alkaline clay hills with *Astragalus* and *Calochortus* at around 1900 m (6175 ft.). This species looks so delicate that you have to wonder how it survives there. Although this woody-based plant flowers in cultivation from seed during the first year, it does not appear very exciting early on with a couple of small and spindly flowers. After two or three years it becomes a good, low, tufted cushion with short wiry stems of about 7 cm (2¾ in.) tall. It survives drought very well, and pink-lavender tubular flowers bloom over a long period (as do flowers of *G. caespitosa*) but are not long lasting. Unlike *G. caespitosa* it sets seed fairly easily. This extremely rare plant deserves to be kept in cultivation.

*Gilia globularis*, the globe gilia, is endemic to the Colorado tundra at about 3690 m (12,000 ft.). A good dwarf species, it forms basal clumps of small, needlelike, succulent leaves, its stems grow to 15 cm (6 in.) tall with clusters of ball-like lavender to white flowers that have turquoise stamens and a fragrance like sweet heliotrope. Weber's field guide describes this species as "One of the most handsome alpine tundra plants, with a heavy fragrance."

*Gilia pinnatifida* grows in Utah and Colorado at 1600–2030 m (5200–6600 ft.), where it grows in desert shrub, sagebrush, and pinyon and juniper communities.

It makes a lovely filigree rosette the first year with a stem 15–25 cm (6–10 in.) tall that sometimes branches near the base. Flowers are lavender-purple tubes.

*Gilia roseata*, another good dwarf form, grows near the Uinta Mountains of Utah and occasionally on the glacial outwash from the major canyons of Uinta at around 1815–2340 m (5900–7600 ft.). Similar to *G. congesta*, it makes a mound of silvery green, finely cut leaves. White balls of flowers on 15-cm (6-in.) stems bloom all summer. I grew this xeric species as a pot plant and it looked lovely during the three years it survived.

*Gilia spicata* grows in Idaho, Montana, Colorado, New Mexico, and Utah among juniper and sagebrush.

Variety *capitata* (synonym *Ipomopsis globularis*) is endemic to the area around Hoosier Pass, Colorado. Narrow pointed leaves with mops of gray flowers grow on stems 30–40 cm (12–15¾ in.) tall.

Variety *orchidacea*, the little gilia, grows in Idaho at approximately 3200 m (10,400 ft.). The pink stems are 10–15 cm (4–6 in.) tall and topped with a 2.5–5-cm (1–2-in.) dense cluster of white, woolly, ball-shaped flowers. A lovely little high alpine, it is covered with long, wispy, cobweblike hairs

*Gilia spicata* var. *capitata*, Hoosier Pass, Colorado. Photo David Joyner.

and is ideal for growing in dry, gravel alpine soils.

*Gilia stenothyrsa* is a restricted species growing among desert shrub and sagebrush in the "barrens" around the Uinta Basin at around 1930 m (6270 ft.). Exquisite basal rosettes overlap the beautifully cut, gray, flat, felty leaves. From each rosette rises a cylindrical spike 30 cm (12 in.) tall with white to pale lavender-blue flowers in May through September. I have had only moderate success with this species although it flowered in the alpine house the second year from seed. It appears to be monocarpic or biennial and dies after flowering; nevertheless it is worth trying.

*Gilia subnuda* is a short-lived perennial found in Utah at about 2000 m (6500 ft.) in the fine dense soil derived from lime siltstones. Stems to 60 cm (24 in.) tall grow from a small gray rosette, and the typical tubular flowers are brilliant crimson-carmine.

*Gilia tridactyla* grows in Utah at around 3385 m (11,000 ft.) on limestone gravel slopes. Although very similar to *G. congesta* var. *montana*, the rosettes of dark green, hairless leaves are denser, the stems are taller, and the flowers larger.

## Propagation

Seed is the usual way to start growing gilias but it is not often available in the various societies' seed exchange lists. Seed of some species that does appear often in commercial lists is wild-collected seed. Fresh seed of *Gilia caespitosa* was again offered in commercial lists in 2001, as was *G. formosa* seed.

You should not treat gilia seed any differently from other seed. Sow it as soon as you receive it and stand the pots outside. I sow my own seed of *Gilia formosa* in the autumn. As the majority of the species that grow in the United Kingdom are monocarpic or at least short-lived, I have attempted vegetative propagation only with *G. caespitosa*. Having tried to set seed by all sorts of methods—using a very thin paintbrush and a magnetized needle, then blowing into the flower—I resorted to taking four cuttings just before flowering, three of which rooted. The following year I tried 30 cuttings of which 28 rooted, and most of those I distributed throughout the United Kingdom as strong plants via my trade outlets. During the following two years not one cutting rooted. I have concluded that rosette cuttings have to be taken very early when the plant is in growth but *before* the flowering stems have started to grow. As this plant is an early flowering and quick growing species, you should watch its growth closely to catch the rosettes at just the right time.

## Cultivation

As most species within this genus need free-draining soil, they should be very carefully sited if you grow them outside. Gilias need lots of sun and plenty of quick drainage; do not expect them to survive a wet, humid winter. Many make good alpine house plants even if they are short-lived. A neutral, soil-based compost with added grit is adequate, and the plants, even *Gilia caespitosa* and *G. formosa*, are unaffected by the lime in the mix. Some winter dieback in the rosettes of a large plant of *G. caespitosa* is typical, and you can it cut off once growth has recommenced in the spring. The stems of *G. caespitosa* naturally die off in autumn to winter but do not be tempted to pull these stems out until spring. If you grow these plants in pots they will require some moisture in the winter and must not dry out.

One of my three-year-old plants of *Gilia caespitosa* fills a 15-cm (6-in.) pot with a mound 7 cm (2¾ in.) high that is made up of dozens of tufted rosettes each with a flowering stem. I first sowed seed of this species in December 1990, and it germinated very quickly. Once potted on the seedlings grew well and the plant flowered in May 1992.

Aphids and red spider mite in the alpine house can cause the plants to collapse. In the garden or scree area slugs eat the plants to the ground unless some form of slug bait is used.

# H

## HULSEA
### Compositae, or Asteraceae
### *alpinegolds*

There are seven species of *Hulsea* in the western United States but I discuss only the three that are perennial. Those three are fairly dwarf and clump forming, and they have daisylike flowers. In spite of being quite attractive plants that make good plants for the rock garden or alpine house, they are rarely seen in cultivation. Seed is available fairly regularly in the commercial lists.

*Hulsea algida* is wide-ranging from Idaho and southwestern Montana to Oregon and the Sierra Nevada. It grows on talus and rocky alpine slopes to 5000 m (16,250 ft.) making loose tufted clumps of sticky, linear leaves that grow to 15 cm (6 in.) long and are troughlike with slightly toothed margins. The leafy stems are 15–35 cm (6–14 in.) tall with yellow flower heads to 5 cm (2 in.) across.

*Hulsea nana* grows from northern California to Washington on steep slopes of volcanic soils to 3500 m (11,375 ft.). Similar to but more dwarf than *H. algida*, it is tufted and can make mats to 30 cm (12 in.) across. Stems to 2.5–15 cm (1–6 in.) tall have yellow flowers to 4.25 cm (1⅔ in.) in diameter in July through August. The spatulate leaves are 2.5–7.5 cm (1–3 in.) long and have rounded linear lobes along the margins.

*Hulsea vestita*, the pumice hulsea, inhabits sandy pumice or granitic flats at 1845–3385 m (6000–11,000 ft.) in the southern Sierra Nevada, Nevada, and the San Jacinto Mountains of southern California. Rosettes of spatulate, densely felty leaves are 2.5–5 cm (1–2 in.) long and the leafless flower stems grow to 30 cm (12 in.)

*Hulsea nana*, Mount Shasta, California. Photo John Andrews.

tall. The dense bright yellow flower heads have rays that are tinted red.

## Propagation

The best way to propagate this species is by seed as soon as it is ripe or by careful division of the plant in spring. You can use the basal side shoots as cuttings in spring but this is not always successful.

## Cultivation

If you cultivate hulseas in the rock garden or trough, place them in a warm spot in a free draining soil. They can rot off in a wet and cold winter. They make good pot plants for the alpine house or frame if you can control its growing conditions.

Slugs in the garden eat off new growth, and aphids can be a nuisance on the leaves of plants in the alpine house.

## HYMENOXYS

Compositae, or Asteraceae
*rubberweeds, pingues*

The genus *Hymenoxys* contains enough variation in species to satisfy even the most discerning grower or alpine traveler. They range from a small mounding plant with 2.5-cm (1-in.) stemless flowers to one with huge flowers on 30-cm (12-in.) stems. All have yellow daisylike flowers. I first became excited by these plants while hiking the Mount Goliath Pesman trail in 1982. *Hymenoxys grandiflora* and *H. acaulis* were the first two species I learned to recognize. Since 1982 many have been added to the list including the best of all, *H. lapidicola*.

The common name "rubberweed" derives from the toxic latex produced in varying amounts by the various species; *Hymenoxys richardsonii* was used in the

emergency manufacture of rubber during World War II.

*Hymenoxys acaulis* covers a wide area of the western drylands from central Canada to Texas. Growing at a range of altitudes it is highly variable: on Mount Evans in Colorado it grew in nice healthy tufts but in the red-colored soil of the Pryor Mountains in Montana it was a sorry looking plant. It forms a basal clump of silky gray leaves with stems 7.5–30 cm (3–12 in.) tall. Bright yellow, daisylike flowers from late spring to summer have broad trilobed petals and are to 5 cm (2 in.) across. Although not scene-stealers, plants grown

*Hymenoxys acaulis* var. *acaulis*, Mount Goliath Pesman trail, Mount Evans, Colorado.

*Hymenoxys acaulis* var. *acaulis*, Hoosier Pass, Colorado. Photo Chris Norton.

from seed of the high-altitude dwellers can be very attractive.

Variety *acaulis* plants I grew from seed collected at 1725 m (5600 ft.) in Wyoming had stems 7–8 cm (2¾–3 in.) tall. Variety *caespitosa* grows at 1585–3660 m (5150–11,895 ft.) in Colorado, Utah, Wyoming, and New Mexico. It makes clumps of hairy silver leaf tufts with short-stemmed or stemless flowers 2.5–5 cm (1–2 in.) across that sit on top of the tufts. It is an excellent pot plant for exhibition and a trough if you can keep the slugs at bay. You will have to grow this variety from seed collected from a number of locations because of the variation and then make your selection.

*Hymenoxys acaulis* var. *acaulis* in the parking lot at Big Horn Canyon overlook in Wyoming.

*Hymenoxys acaulis* var. *caespitosa* in cultivation.

Variety *ivesiana* (synonym *Hymenoxys argentea*) grows at 1150–3260 m (3740–10,600 ft.) in Utah, Colorado, Arizona, and New Mexico. Welsh et al. (1987) give this variety the synonym of *H. argentea*, and a plant listed as such that I grew from seed collected in New Mexico certainly lived up to its name with lovely silver-gray, needlelike leaves forming a dense dome 7–10 cm (2¾–4 in.) high. The 5-cm (2-in.) wide flowers are almost stemless.

*Hymenoxys brandegii* from southern Colorado's high altitudes looks like a reduced version of *H. grandiflora* with smaller flowers on stems about 20 cm (8 in.) tall. I have not seen this species in the wild so cannot comment on its suitability for the rock garden.

*Hymenoxys cooperi* comes from Utah, Nevada, California, and Arizona, where it grows at 975–2380 m (3170–7735 ft.). It is a biennial or short-lived perennial that has basal rosettes of silver-green leaves with stems 15–60 cm (6–24 in.) tall and numerous yellow flowers.

*Hymenoxys grandiflora* (synonym *Rydbergia grandiflora*), known as the real old man of the mountains, is a magnificent sunflower that grows at high altitudes in Idaho,

*Hymenoxys brandegii*, south of Pueblo, Colorado. Photo David Hale.

Montana, Utah, Wyoming, and Colorado. Among the easiest plants to identify, its bright yellow heads 5–12.5 cm (2–5 in.) across are on stems 10–30 cm (4–12 in.) tall. Although I have no trouble growing this species, I cannot get it to flower like those I saw at Summit Lake on Mount Evans, Colorado. There is some argument about whether or not it is monocarpic in cultivation; I have found that the seed that was set never germinated. Perhaps I have been unlucky.

*Hymenoxys lapidicola* grows in Weber sandstone crevices on Blue Mountain's cliff faces and edges toward the east of the Uinta Mountains in Utah at an elevation of 1830–2500 m (5950–8125 ft.). Well-known botanist Elizabeth Neese discovered this species and wrote about it in the 1986 edition of *Uinta Basin Flora*. She (1986) describes it in *Rocky Mountain Alpines* as "a crevice plant that forms tight rounded mounds on rock faces, with golden-yellow flower heads scattered starlike across the dark green mounds." The specific name *lapidicola* means "dweller of a place where things have petrified," which led Nicholas Klise to suggest the descriptive name of dinosaur daisy.

After the NARGS 1993 Conference in Vail, Colorado, Ev Whittemore took me up Blue Mountain to find *Hymenoxys lapidicola*. I had grown two plants for nearly three years but they had not flowered so I was extremely anxious to see it in the wild. After an extremely difficult drive and a treacherous hike that involved crashing through masses of *Arctostaphylos patula* (manzanita) and *Artemisia*, stumbling over hidden rocks, and slipping into small ravines, we eventually came across *Hymenoxys lapidicola* in the shade of a group of six ponderosa pines. One *Hymenoxys lapidicola* was in flower and about 15 cm (6 in.) across. Stemless yellow flowers sat on top of the cushion and sticky leaves glistened where sand had stuck to them.

*Hymenoxys grandiflora* at the edge of Summit Lake, Mount Evans in Colorado.

Sandstone slabs, penstemon, *Arctostaphylos patula*, and pines on Blue Mountain, Utah.

All the information I had read said the species grew only sunny cliff edges, but this plant grew in the shade in a crevice facing north about 6 m (20 ft.) from the cliff's edge. Later that day I saw dozens more plants on another cliff edge, some in the crevices of flat sandstone slabs that was reminiscent of a crazy paving, others hanging out of cracks on ridges overlooking the cliff face. Not one was in flower but all were in seed. Cushions varied from the slightly loose to the tightest possible, and the short, dark green leaves glistened like those on the plant we had seen previously.

*Hymenoxys richardsonii*, like *H. acaulis*, covers a very wide range and could possibly come into the category of "just another D.Y.C."(Damned Yellow Composite). From basal clumps grow stems 20–30 cm (8–12 in.) tall with bright yellow daisies one to three per stem. Having photographed this species on Blue Mountain, Utah, very near to *H. lapidicola*, I thought I was looking at just another tall-stemmed yellow flower until I checked my field guide. Growing in between this species and the plants of *H. lapidicola* that were in seed was another hymenoxys species; it remains unidentified at present. Although hybrids likely appear in this area, this unidentified plant is not necessarily one of them.

Close-up of *Hymenoxys lapidicola*, Blue Mountain, Utah.

*Hymenoxys lapidicola* in cultivation grown from seed I collected in 1993.

Sandstone slabs with *Hymenoxys lapidicola* plants in seed, Blue Mountain, Utah.

*Hymenoxys richardsonii*, Blue Mountain, Utah.

*Hymenoxys scaposa* from Utah, Colorado, and Kansas. A good rock garden perennial with grassy foliage and stems 12.5–35 cm (5–14 in.) high, its masses of yellow daisies flower all summer, especially with ongoing deadheading. It thrives in a dry spot.

*Hymenoxys subintegra* grows in a limited area in Utah as well as on the Kaibab Plateau of northern Arizona. I have grown this species (it is one you either love or hate) from seed Sonia Lowzow collected from the Kaibab Plateau. Sonia's advice is to grow several but to let only one bloom since the flower, a typical yellow daisy on 30-cm (12-in.) stems, is not beautiful. The attraction is in the foliage, a very intense gray-silver that shimmers in the sun. Although it is a biennial, it can be kept for several years if you remove the flower stems, preventing it from blooming.

*Hymenoxys torreyana* grows in northeast Utah and Wyoming at 1830–2200 m (5950–7150 ft.) The compact silver cushion grows 5–10 cm (2–4 in.) high with large yellow daisies on short stems. If you protect this plant from excess moisture in winter, you will find it a superb cushion plant to grow outside. I have grown it successfully

*Hymenoxys subintegra* foliage in cultivation.

both as a pot plant in the alpine house and in an alpine bed without overhead protection during the winter. Although it is not as compact in the alpine house as it is outside, it is nevertheless an outstanding hymenoxys blooming during midspring.

While I was collecting seed of *Hymenoxys lapidicola* on Blue Mountain I noticed other hymenoxys plants with the same compact cushions of *H. lapidicola* but with stems that varied from 5 to 10 cm (2 to 4 in.) tall. All plants were in seed so I could not compare its flowers with those of *H. lapidicola*. Seed I collected from several plants have resulted in some very attractive plants with compact basal cushions very similar to those of *H. lapidicola*. Since hybrids often exist where different species grow together, I thought these plants might be natural hybrids of *H. lapidicola* and *H. acaulis*. Stems vary in height from 10 to 15 cm (4 to 6 in.), which is expected in plants that grow at a much lower altitudes and in the alpine house. It will take a few more years before we know if these plants are worthwhile additions to the alpine flora.

**Propagation**

Until 1997 the only way I propagated plants in this genus was by seed but not all seed is viable, and even when the seed is good, its germination is affected by when it is sown. Sow seed as soon after you receive it as possible, preferably in several batches. For example, sow one batch as soon as it is ripe, another in autumn, and a third later on in spring. I have collected seed of *Hymenoxys argentea* and *H. acaulis* var. *caespitosa* from my plants and sown it with varying results.

Once seed has germinated, treat the seedlings like those of most plants and prick them out when they are large enough to handle. Some growers prefer to let seedlings of this genus grow on in the seed pot for a year before pricking out. I do this only with *Hymenoxys lapidicola* because it is so slow growing the first year that it seems almost not to move. From the second year onwards though, the cushion plants start to grow fairly quickly.

Although this species has rosettes, I have very limited success using them as cuttings. I do not know if the percentage of successful cuttings can be increased in future, but I'm certain I will try this method again.

## Cultivation

A warm dry spot in either an alpine bed or trough is suitable for plants in this genus. I grew *Hymenoxys grandiflora* in a pot several times but it always looked very unhappy and never flowered as well as it did in the wild.

Though *Hymenoxys acaulis* var. *ivesiana* is a fine plant for the exhibitor, it is a xeric variety that would not grow well outdoors in areas of high winter rainfall; it may, however, be suited to a trough that can be covered in winter. Even in the alpine house, it is a preferred titbit for slugs.

At first glance *Hymenoxys subintegra* is not among the most likely show plants, but it has nevertheless won several prizes as a foliage plant, the pot being top-dressed with black slate that sets off the silver foliage. To get this plant to a reasonable size without flowering, nip all side shoots out as soon as possible. It grows perfectly well in the warm garden and looks good in a group.

*Hymenoxys lapidicola* is especially suited to a pot, trough, or crevice work. It has a very long taproot so does best in a deep rather than a shallow pot. After the 1993 Vail NARGS conference I visited the garden of Gwen and Panayoti Kelaidis in Denver, where it was growing well in their simulated mountain range. Ev Whittemore of North Carolina also grows and flowers her plants of this species in a similar way.

Plants in this genus do not seem to require a particular soil; they grow in my limey alpine bed, in pots with a neutral, soil-based compost, and in troughs with a very lean mixture. I top-dress one of the specimens of *Hymenoxys lapidicola* I grow as show plants with the actual sandstone from its habitat so that when I water it the moisture that runs over the sandstone pieces carries the chemicals from the sandstone to the plants' roots. Perhaps my attempt to make this plant as floriferous as those on Blue Mountain is nothing more than wishful thinking.

In 1992 I grew two of my plants of *Hymenoxys lapidicola* from seed distributed by John Andrews. They are each in a 15-cm (6-in.) pot and have flowered every year since 1995. Seed I collected in 1993 has resulted in three plants that flowered in 1996.

An aphid attack in the alpine house is the only problem I have noticed.

# I

## IVESIA
Rosaceae
*mousetails*

*Ivesia* is a western North American genus of about 20 species of which approximately half a dozen occur in the Rockies. Although the clumps of yellow or white blooms are quite attractive, it is the foliage that has most appeal. The leaves have few to many leaflets and some form congested silver rosettes. Plants of this genus are summer blooming, and many grow at alpine elevations. At one time *Ivesia* was included in potentilla but *Ivesia* plants have very narrow bipinnate leaves and small flowers in dense clusters. The common name mousetail describes the complicated leaves that on some species look like the tail of a mouse. The genus is named after Dr. Eli Ives (1779–1861), a professor at Yale who lectured in medicine and botany.

*Ivesia argyrocoma* can be found in California at around 2275 m (7400 ft.) growing in dense sandy clay in Jeffrey pine woodland. Beautiful silvery rosettes of tiny, densely overlapping leaflets are obscured by fine wispy hairs. The small, white, potentilla-like flowers are in large clusters on prostrate stems that encircle the rosettes.

*Ivesia baileyi* grows at high elevations in the southeast corner of Oregon and the northwest corner of Nevada on cliff faces. The leaves are pinnately compound and 7.5–10 cm (3–4 in.) long, and each leaflet is indented into several lobes. Small white to yellow saucer-shaped flowers bloom July through August.

*Ivesia gordonii* ranges from Washington to Montana, California, Utah, and Colorado growing in rocky subalpine and alpine meadows, tundra, and talus slopes. A very distinctive plant, it has a basal rosette of bright green, pinnately compound leaves 1.2–25 cm (½–10 in.) long with 10–50 pairs of minute leaflets whorled on the leaf axis. The stems are 5–30 cm (2–12 in.) tall with tight clusters of small yellow flowers in June through August that age to red purple.

*Ivesia kingii* comes from California, Nevada, and Utah, where its habitat is saline meadows, rabbitbrush, and sedge communities at 1460–2380 m (4745–7735 ft.). The basal rosettes of leaves to 12 cm (4¾ in.) long each have 24–60 or more leaflets. Decumbent stems are 5–22 cm (2–8¾ in.) long with cymes of white flowers.

*Ivesia lycopodioides* (synonym *I. gordonii* var. *lycopodioides*) grows in the alpine fell-fields of California and Nevada inhabiting moist gravel. Very similar to *I. gordonii*, it has a tufted clump of basal leaves to 6 cm (2¼ in.) long with many pairs of leaflets. Rosettes are 5–7.5 cm (2–3 in.) wide, and prostrate stems to 10 cm (4 in.) tall encircle the plant and carry dense, headlike cymes of yellow flowers in July through August. Flowers age to red during fall. Cylindrical green leaves have many pairs of tiny leaflets.

Subspecies *scandularis* grows in the White Mountains, California, at about 3630 m (11,800 ft.) in vernally moist alpine drainages. Dense green cushions are of hairy, minutely dissected, wormlike leaves, and small yellow flowers are in headlike cymes on stems 2.5–5 cm (1–2 in.) tall.

*Ivesia muirii* grows on gravel alpine slopes in the Sierra Nevada. It is very similar to I. lycopodiodes but has silver, densely haired leaves with 25–40 pairs of very tiny leaflets. Pale yellow flowers during July through August are in congested clusters on stems 2.5–18 cm (1–7 in.) tall.

*Ivesia pygmaea* (synonym *I. gordonii* var. *pygmaea*) grows in the alpine fell-fields of California at approximately 3510 m (11,400 ft.) in granite, gritty soil. Similar to a compact form of *I. lycopodioides*, it makes little tufts of hairy leaves with 10–20 pairs of tiny leaflets. The 2.5-cm (1-in.) clusters of yellow flowers are on 2.5–15 cm (1–6 in.) prostrate to erect stems that encircle the plant in late summer.

*Ivesia rhypara* is endemic to a very specific area of loose volcanic ash at around 1385 m (4500 ft.) in eastern Malheur county of Oregon and northern Nevada. An extremely rare plant that was only described in 1977, this spreading species has very villous, pinnate leaves. The leaves have up to 15 overlapping pairs of leaflets that are also divided into several segments. Stems grow to 15 cm (6 in.), and flowers in terminal clusters bloom in May through October. Each flower has green woolly sepals, white petals, and a honey-colored center.

*Ivesia sabulosa* typically grows on limestone in sagebrush, pinyon and juniper, and ponderosa pine communities at 1735–2745 m (5640–8920 ft.) in the southwest corner of Utah, the northeast corner of Arizona, and the southeast corner of Nevada. This glabrous to villous species is quite large. Leaves are 3.2–23 cm (1¼–9 in.) long with 30–80 paired leaflets and petioles that are often tinted red-purple. Stems are 10–50 cm (4–20 in.) tall with branched cymes of yellow flowers.

*Ivesia santolinoides* grows in California on subalpine flats, alpine fell-fields, and in ponderosa pine forests on gritty, granitic soil. Compact cushions of pinhead-sized, densely overlapping leaflets are obscured by a dense covering of silvery, silky fine hairs. Creamy white flowers in summer to early autumn are in loose, many flowered cymes on wiry stems that grow 10–40 cm (4–15¾ in.) tall, depending on the altitude.

*Ivesia setosa* grows in the Deep Creek Mountains of Tooele county, Utah, and eastern Nevada inhabiting mountain slopes at 1700–3100 m (5525–10,110 ft.). Basal leaves are 3.2–12 cm (1¼–4¾ in.) long and glandular-pubescent, and they have 10–20 leaflets that are parted to divided. Stems grow 4–25 cm (1½–10 in.) tall with white to cream flowers.

*Ivesia shockleyi* occurs in California, Nevada, and Utah on rocky, quartzitic outcrops among pinyon and juniper and ponderosa pine at 1950–2410 m (6340–7830 ft.). The gray basal leaves are 2–7 cm (¾–2¾ in.) long and densely glandular-pubescent, and leaflets grow in 7–10 crowded pairs. Decumbent to erect stems have open cymes of yellow flowers.

*Ivesia tweedyi* inhabits serpentine gravel ridge tops in the Wenatchee Mountains of Washington at about 2030 m (6600 ft.). Similar to *I. gordonii*, its smooth, gray-green leaves are both larger and divided into linear segments, and the larger and showier flowers also age to red and purple.

*Ivesia utahensis* is endemic to the Wasatch Range in central Utah, where it grows in talus on alpine tundra at 3200–3600 m (10,400–11,700 ft.). The basal leaves 1.2–9 cm (½–3½ in.) long have 30–40 tiny paired leaflets. The short decumbent or ascending stems have congested cymes of white flowers.

### Propagation

Propagation is by seed, which is usually available in commercial lists. You can divide clump-forming plants in spring.

### Cultivation

Ivesias are fairly easy to grow in any alpine bed that has moisture-retaining soil, but I recommend cultivating the high alpine species in troughs. Plants of this genus also make good subjects for exhibition but tend to become drawn if they remain under glass too long.

Pest problems include red spider in the alpine house and slugs that nibble new growth.

# K

## KECKIELLA
Scrophulariaceae
*bush beardtongues*

*Keckiella* is a small genus of shrubs from Mexico, Arizona, California, Nevada, and southern Oregon and is in the same family as penstemons. Keckiellas are so closely related to that genus that they were classed as penstemons until 1967. In cultivation they prefer a habitat of hot, dry summers and cool, moist winters. Most species are fairly tall so I discuss only those species that are useful for the average rock garden.

*Keckiella cordifolia* is an evergreen shrub that grows in southern California to 1211 m (3935 ft.). At low elevation the plants grow to 2.5 m (98 in.) but at higher elevation it becomes shorter, from 60 to 90 cm (24 to 36 in.). Scarlet tubular flowers 5 cm (2 in.) long make this species look like a red-flowered honeysuckle. After the flowers bloom the leaves turn yellow to red and crimson, and because they remain on the plant they provide beautiful, long-lasting, late summer to fall color. The heart-shaped leaves give rise to the common name of heart-leaved penstemon.

*Keckiella corymbosa* comes from northern Californian forests and has stems growing to 60 cm (24 in.) with red, penstemon-like flowers. Ron Ratko has introduced two lovely dwarf forms that would be welcome in any rock garden. One makes a low mound growing to 15 cm (6 in.) and the other grows as a woody mat only 5 cm (2 in.) high. Both forms were found growing at 1725–1815 m (5600–5900 ft.) on volcanic and serpentine outcrops. Their flowers are a brilliant red-carmine to orange-red.

*Keckiella ternata* is similar to *K. cordifolia* and comes from southern California. The species varies in height from 15 to 180 cm (6 to 72 in.), and the shorter forms grow at an elevation of around 1310 m (4250 ft.). The tubular flowers are a brilliant orange-red.

### Propagation
You can easily raise all the species I describe from seed.

### Cultivation
Seedlings are very quick growing and must be potted up as soon as possible to prevent

Compact form of *Keckiella corymbosa* in cultivation.

Close-up of *Keckiella corymbosa* flower.

root damage. *Keckiella corymbosa* dies back in winter and looks like a dead twig. It is very late coming into growth and often shoots from below ground. The plant of *K. corymbosa* I grow has been hardy and wet resistant in a scree bed for several years, and in hot summer conditions it has shed leaves that have not regrown until I have given it plenty of water. I recommend growing the dwarf form of this species as it is much more suited to trough culture than any other.

The higher elevation form of *Keckiella cordifolia* is reported to be more hardy than those growing at a lower elevation.

I know of no pest or disease problems.

## KELSEYA
Rosaceae

*Kelseya uniflora* is a limestone lover from Idaho, Montana, and Wyoming, where it grows on rocks that are almost vertical or on steep sliding screes. (This of course makes seed collecting or photography a very dangerous occupation.) Fine specimens flower in early May on the windswept Hogback in the Big Belt Mountains of Montana at an elevation of 1230–2155 m (4000–7000 ft.). Once the plants have flowered they quickly set seed, usually by mid-June, before the onset of winter when temperatures plummet to well below freezing. By autumn the plants have already turned black in preparation for the long winter rest. Despite these low winter temperatures, temperatures that can reach 27°C (80°F) in the summer, and an annual rainfall of 31 cm (12 in.), some huge plants grow on the Hogback. One measuring approximately 3 m (10 ft.) × 1 m (39 in.) was clinging to a vertical cliff—a truly venerable specimen.

*Kelseya uniflora* is the shrublet to end all shrublets, and, amazingly, it is in the same family as the rose. The only member of the genus *Kelseya*, it forms a wonderful, slow growing, creeping mat of tiny blue-green rosettes with solitary sessile flowers of pinkish white. As it grows it sends out very fine hairs on the underside that make their way into any crack that can supply moisture.

### Propagation
Seed is the best way to propagate this species. Although I have sowed batches of seed at different times from October through December, they all took an average

Masses of *Kelseya uniflora* clinging to vertical rocks, Big Belt Mountains, Montana. Photo Ev Whittemore.

*Kelseya uniflora* in flower, Big Belt Mountains, Montana. Photo Ev Whittemore.

of three months to germinate. The seedlings grow at differing speeds, but after three to four months some are big enough to pot on. Prick out the largest seedlings into 7-cm (2¾-in.) pots even though they may look a bit ridiculous. Be very careful as you do this because the tiny rosettes have a hairlike root that can be easily broken. You can pot up the smaller seedlings in groups and let them grow on for dividing and repotting later in the year, even as late as autumn. Put the pots of seedlings in a frame to grow on. Seedlings pricked out in spring to early summer usually reach 5–7 mm (¼ in.) across by the autumn. As the seedlings grow at different speeds, some putting on more rosettes than others, you may even find that a few of the more rapid growers are about 1.2 cm (½ in.) across by summer, which is the ideal size for tufa planting.

Large, very old specimen of *Kelseya uniflora* in Big Belt Mountains, Montana. Photo Ev Whittemore.

If you have no access to seed but have a reasonably sized plant (or you know someone who is willing to give you one or two rosettes), you will have to take cuttings of individual rosettes in spring. Just as you would when taking dionysia cuttings, use tweezers to put the rosettes into the rooting medium in a closed frame or cutting box. Treat these cuttings like you do any others and keep them in shade until they are rooted, which usually takes 4–12 weeks. Although the rooted cuttings do not grow as fast as seedlings and usually have only a solitary rosette by the time winter arrives (many seedlings, by contrast, form five to six rosettes), they do not need to be treated any differently from seedlings once they are potted up. If you want to use these rooted cuttings for growing in tufa you will have to wait until the following spring when the root system is large enough.

**Cultivation**

Kelseyas are *not* plants to carelessly grow in just any place in the rock garden: do that and their death is guaranteed. *Kelseya uniflora* should occupy a very special place whether in a pot for exhibition or in a piece of tufa in a trough. If you choose a pot use a soil mix that is neutral and soil based and supplement with additional limestone grit. Plants grown from seed or a cutting will grow very slowly in the early years. As the plant gets bigger, though, growth speeds up, the plant's circumference becomes larger, and more rosettes appear at its edge.

If you want to grow this species in a trough ensure that it cannot be overtaken by any neighbors. You would do well to bore a hole in a piece of tufa and carefully insert a very small plant of *Kelseya uniflora* until the roots reach the hole's bottom. Fill the hole with a little soil mix and top it with a tiny piece of tufa. Trough plants obviously grow a lot slower than those in a pot in the alpine house but they will be beautiful and tight.

You can water the plant quite freely in summer but in winter it goes dormant, sometimes turning black. If you grow kelseyas in a pot, carefully control the moisture by watering just enough to keep the plants alive. Do not let the plant dry out; remember that hairlike roots are on the underside and need moisture. Plants you grow in tufa in an outdoor trough will receive adequate moisture from rainfall and the capillary action of the tufa, although in times of drought you can water your plants from a watering can without worry.

*Keseya uniflora* usually takes several years to flower from seed. It normally has to build up a mature cushion first, but I have heard of plants grown from seed that flowered early in life. Whether you grow your kelseya in a pot or trough, you should sit back and admire this fantastic "rose" when at last it blooms.

I have experienced only two pests. The dreaded red spider mite that thrives in dry conditions can attack the rosettes of plants in the alpine house and leave them very mottled. The other pest is the ever-present blackbird that pulls any available cushion plant out of a trough.

# L

## LEPIDIUM
Brassicaceae
*pepperworts*

I first saw a lepidium at an Alpine Garden Society show. The almost rock hard cushion of *Lepidium nanum* was dotted with tiny,

pale yellow flowers, and such was the exhibitors' interest in this plant that I felt had to explore this genus. An ideal show plant if you can grow it really tight, it is also worth trying in a piece of tufa. The two other species in the genus are not as compact and dense as *L. nanum.*

***Lepidium barnebyanum*** grows on fragmented, shale limestone in northwest Utah at around 1970 m (6400 ft.). Listed as endangered by the U.S. Fish and Wildlife Service, it makes a dense mound of congested tufts of dark green linear leaves. Stems 5–10 cm (2–4 in.) tall rise above the foliage and are densely packed with white flowers. Although bearing little physical resemblance to *L. nanum*, this species is still a challenge to grow.

***Lepidium nanum*** grows on the dry, bare hillsides of limestone gravel in Nevada at 1585–2050 m (5150–6660 ft.). The hard dense pancake of tiny spatulate green leaves have minute cream-yellow flowers that can completely cover the cushion. Many consider it the ultimate cushion, although dionysia lovers may not agree. Dwight Ripley (1944) described it as "the draba to end all drabas."

*Lepidium nanum* from central Nevada. Photo David Hale.

*Lepidium ostleri* grows at a slightly higher altitude than *L. barnebyanum* at 2055 m (6680 ft.) in Utah's limestone screes. A lovely aromatic species, it makes a dense cushion that is higher and not as tight as that of *L. nanum*. It has tufts of tiny, incised leaves with racemes of pale cream to pure white that completely cover the cushion.

## Propagation

Seed is the best method of propagation. As is the case with many of the more choice North American alpines, we have to resort to the commercial seed lists to obtain seed of this genus. Seed has been available since 1990.

I have had some success with cuttings of *Lepidium nanum* and also, surprisingly, of *L. ostleri*. I took cuttings of *L. nanum* fairly early in the year, just after it had flowered. I took cuttings of *L. ostleri* in the autumn because I received the plant at that time of the year, and not knowing anything about it, I wanted cuttings as insurance against anything happening to the plant during winter. The cuttings stayed green over winter and rooted in spring, and the mother plant came into flower in the alpine house during February.

## Cultivation

Lepidiums like a dry position and plenty of sun, and *Lepidium nanum* grows best where there is little rain and plenty of scorching sun as in the wild. Where this is impossible I recommend growing all three species I describe in the alpine house, a frame, or in tufa in a trough. Even so, grow them in full sun with plenty of grit to keep them compact.

If you grow these species in a pot, use a standard mix (a neutral, soil-based compost) with added grit. *Lepidium nanum* needs a little help to make a tight, compact cushion, so tuck slate or some other suitable rock around the plant's neck when the plant is small. Rock in this position constricts the neck and enables the plant to grow as it would in the wild. Rocks around the necks of the other two species also help the plants to grow mounds, but they are higher than in *L. nanum*. Remember that even though lepidiums receive very little rain in the wild, you should water those you grow in pots with the same frequency as other pot-cultivated dryland plants.

Slugs attack the young growth of plants cultivated outside and under glass. You must keep spider mite in check or it will ruin the plant.

*Lepidium nanum* in cultivation. Photo Robert Rolfe.

*Lepidium ostleri* in cultivation.

## LEPTODACTYLON
### Polemoniaceae
*prickly phloxes*

The sight and smell of leptodactylons in the wild is something not to be forgotten. Not many shrubs or sub-shrubs in the North American flora make good plants for rock gardens but this genus contains several attractive species that deserve every attempt to cultivate them.

*Leptodactylon caespitosum* is found in Wyoming, Colorado, Nevada, and Utah growing in bare limestone shale soils and often in barrens at about 1675–2350 m (5445–7640 ft.). It is a superb cushion plant with tiny, stiff, three- to five-lobed leaves that densely overlap and completely obscure the short erect stems. The cushions can spread to 50 cm (20 in.) across with the four-petalled, phloxlike, white to cream flowers standing just above the foliage. Such a floriferous and compact species is often mistaken for one of the caespitose phloxes.

*Leptodactylon californicum* grows on dry, rocky ridges, embankments, roadsides, and cliff faces in southern California below 1700 m (5525 ft.) and is among the most common members of the phlox family occurring there. Twiggy stems 30–90 cm (12–36 in.) tall are covered with small prickly leaves that give it the common name of prickly phlox. The plant produces many loose clumps of white, pink, cream, and lavender to pale purple flowers 2.5–4.5 cm (1–1¾ in.) wide that have a narrow tube and an abruptly flared top. Fragrant flowers bloom in March through June. Whenever this species is exhibited it is a showstopper, not only because of the beautiful flowers but also because of the strong sweet fragrance.

Subspecies *glandulosum* is a more compact form growing 15–23 cm (6–9 in.) tall. Closely resembling Leptodactylon pungens, it has rose-purple to purple flowers and the foliage is densely covered with sticky glands.

*Leptodactylon pungens* ranges from Washington to California, Montana, Nevada, New Mexico, and Utah on dry gravel slopes, sometimes with sagebrush and ponderosa pine, at 460–4000 m (1495–13,000 ft.). The intricately branched spreading shrublet is 10–50 cm (4–20 in.) tall with congested whorls of short needle-like leaves. The cream to yellowish, long,

*Leptodactylon californicum*. Photo Chris Norton.

*Leptodactylon pungens*, Squaw Valley, California. Photo Chris Norton.

tubular flowers that often bloom in the afternoon to evening are very fragrant. They are sometimes suffused with purple on the exterior.

Subspecies *pulchriflorum* grows in quick draining volcanic soils and rocky outcrops on exposed alpine ridge crests at around 2710–2890 m (8800–9400 ft.) in the northern Sierra Nevada and San Gabriel Mountains of California. A lovely exhibition plant, this subspecies makes a small compact mound 10–15 cm (4–6 in.) high and to 45 cm (18 in.) across. When the cream to yellow, pink-tinted flowers close, the petals spiral up into closed blooms.

*Leptodactylon watsonii* grows in Idaho, Wyoming, Nevada, and Colorado, and in Utah at 1220–3050 m (3965–9915 ft.) among sagebrush and pinyon and juniper communities. It forms a sprawling cushion with small needlelike leaves and long, tubular, white to cream flowers.

### Propagation

Propagate leptodactylons by seed sown in spring or from cuttings taken in spring or early summer.

### Cultivation

All plants in this genus require a well drained, sunny situation and very little moisture at the neck during winter. *Leptodactylon californicum* may not be hardy in cold areas although the two subspecies are more cold tolerant. The plants are quick growing after germination and need planting out before becoming pot bound. Cut back the stems after flowering, which will induce new growth and keep the plants tidy. As autumn approaches, the tiny leaves turn brown and the plants look as if they are about to die. From that time until the plants begin to grow again in spring, water the plant only enough to keep it alive.

Compact forms such as *Leptodactylon caespitosum* make good pot plants for the alpine house or exhibition. It is best to cultivate plants of these species in large pots or a trough because of the vigorous root growth. Be careful when you handle this genus as the tiny prickly leaves can cause injury.

Aphids, especially whiteflies, can be very active on plants that grow under glass.

## LESQUERELLA
Cruciferae, or Brassicaceae
*bladder pods*

In the spring 2000 issue of the NARGS' *Rock Garden Quarterly*, Panayoti Kelaidis, the curator of the rock garden at Denver Botanic Gardens, observed, "*Lesquerella* is one of the most widespread, numerous and important genera of American plants." Not many would dispute that statement as 83 of the 95 known species of annuals and perennials within this genus occur in North America from Alaska to California and eastwards over the Great Plains. Twenty-three species have been tested as potential oleaginous crops for arid areas in the United States, the most important being *L. fendleri*, which reflects the importance of this genus.

As a group, lesquerellas are easy to recognize since they are all rosette forming. Stellate or star-shaped hairs cover the plant, which makes it look silver-gray and downy. Small, mainly yellow, four-petalled flowers are in racemes that look very similar to an arabis. The small, generally ovoid seedpods give rise to the common name of bladder pod.

Lesquerellas have not been very popular in cultivation in the past perhaps because there are many more attractive plants in the West. However, the growing of lesquerellas is becoming more widespread, probably because of the increase in the number of species offered in seed lists.

*Lesquerella alpina* is wide-ranging from British Columbia to Idaho, Colorado, and Utah growing in fragmented, shaley limestone on very hot and dry ridges at 1540–3050 m (5000–9915 ft.). Dense tufts of linear leaves have clusters of yellow flowers on stems that grow to 10 cm (4 in.). Flowers are followed by tiny round seedpods.

Variety *condensata* comes from Wyoming and a small area in the north of Utah's Daggett and Uinta counties. This tiny tufted plant has stems that barely exsert beyond the leaves. Variety *parvula* grows in pinyon and juniper and Douglas fir communities at 1830–2960 m (5950–9620 ft.) in Utah, Colorado, and Wyoming. The leaves are uniformly narrow, linear, or linear to spatulate.

*Lesquerella arctica* is wide-ranging from Greenland and the Canada arctic and subarctic to the Seward Peninsula of Alaska and British Columbia. It grows in alpine and lower elevations on rocky, barren sites or disturbed areas such as gravel pits, and

although rarely common it is abundant when found. A densely pubescent plant, the basal leaves are to 5 cm (2 in.) long, rosulate, obovate to oblanceolate, and entire. Several erect to spreading or prostrate stems are 5–20-cm (2–8-in.) long and have loose yellow inflorescences.

Subspecies *calderi* (synonym *Lesquerella calderi*) is caespitose with stellate, silver hairs. The few reduced leaves are to 8 cm (3 in.) long, and the inflorescence has 2–14 flowers with slightly longer petals than *L. arctica*.

*Lesquerella arizonica* grows in Kane and Washington counties of Utah and in Arizona on barren outcrops among sagebrush, grassland, and pinyon and juniper at 1280–2750 m (4160–8940 ft.). Among the tiniest mat-forming lesquerellas, this species has oblanceolate to spatulate basal leaves growing to 4 cm (1½ in.) long and stems

*Lesquerella alpina*. Photo Jane Grushow.

*Lesquerella arctica*, Kobuk Sand Dunes in northwest Alaska. Photo Carolyn Parker.

2–10 cm (¾–4 in.) tall. Masses of yellow flowers completely cover the plants and they are followed by ovoid seedpods.

*Lesquerella carinata* is endemic to the limestone mountain ranges of east-central Idaho, southwest Montana, and Teton county in Wyoming. The prostrate stems and comparatively narrow and pointed seedpods with keeled margins help one identify this species. Ovate leaves with long petioles make up gray rosettes.

*Lesquerella douglasii* ranges from British Columbia to Oregon and Idaho among sagebrush and juniper and on the sandy shores of the Columbia River. The 5–8-cm (2–3-in.) long basal leaves are obovate to oblanceolate, and the erect or

decumbent stems are 10–45 cm (4–18 in.) long. Small yellow flowers in May through July are followed by globose, seedpods, which are covered with silvery stellate hairs.

*Lesquerella fendleri* ranges in the southwestern United States to central Colorado, southern Utah, central Arizona, and New Mexico. It grows in rocky or sandy soils, often on limestone, in dry grasslands, juniper communities, or deserts at 600–1800 m (1950–5850 ft.). Low, tightly tufted, silver-gray rosettes consist of occasionally toothed, lanceolate leaves 5–10 cm (2–4 in.) long. Stems 2.5–40 cm (1–15¾ in.) long have small yellow flowers in March through April and occasionally again after the summer rains. It is among the earliest plants to flower in the area. Seedpods are 6–9 mm (¼–⅓ in.) long, smooth, and almost globose. Although *L. fendleri* is perennial it also behaves as a winter annual with seeds that germinate in late summer to early autumn. It shows very little growth during winter, increases its growth in early spring, and flowers and sets seed by late spring.

David A. Dierig (1995), contributor to the *New Crop FactSHEET*, states that *Lesquerella fendleri* is grown commercially as a crop and the seed harvested, as it contains an oil that is rich in hydroxy fatty acids. The oil

*Lesquerella arctica* subsp. *calderi*, Ogilvie Mountains, Alaska. Photo Carolyn Parker.

*Lesquerella douglasii*, Columbia River Gorge. Photo Russ Jolley.

is an important raw material used by industry for making resins, waxes, nylons, plastics, corrosion inhibitors, and cosmetics. Cattle-feeding trials have also shown that the seed meal may be promising as a protein supplement for livestock.

*Lesquerella garrettii* is endemic to Utah's Davis, Salt Lake, Utah, and Wasatch counties. It grows among spruce fir and in alpine tundra areas, often in talus or on rock outcrops at 3050–3660 m (9915–11,895 ft.). The basal leaves are elliptic to obovate and are to 3.5 cm (1⅗ in.) long. Stems 5–15 cm (2–6 in.) long are decumbent to suberect with leaves that are about half the size of those at the base. Yellow flowers are relatively large for the size of the plant at 1.2–2 cm (½–¾ in.) across. This is a variable species according to altitude and habitat; plants in my alpine house I raised from seed collected at alpine level measure 10 cm (4 in.) across. If I had grown these plants outside they would be at least half that size. Seed is very rarely available for this species, which is unfortunate because it could be a beauty in a trough.

*Lesquerella goodingii* grows on rocky slopes in Arizona and New Mexico and is among the larger species in the genus. Obovate basal leaves are silver-gray, and the yellow, 1.2-cm (½-in.) flowers are on 30-cm

*Lesquerella fendleri.* Photo Ed Godleski.

(12-in.) long stems that have oblanceolate, finely toothed leaves.

*Lesquerella hemiphysaria* grows on exposed, flat, rocky ridge tops among sagebrush and pine communities at 2135–3355 m (6940–10,905 ft.) and is endemic to the Wasatch Plateau and the southwestern rim of the Uinta Basin in Utah. The spatulate, silver-gray basal leaves to 5 cm (2 in.) make up small rosettes encircled with yellow flowers on stems 3–10 cm (1¼–4 in.) tall. High altitude plants rarely grow to more than 5 cm (2 in.) across, including the small heart-shaped seedpods.

Variety *lucens* grows at 2700–2800 m (8775–9100 ft.) and is endemic to the West Tavaputs Plateau in Carbon county, Utah. It differs from the type only in the size and shape of the silicles.

*Lesquerella intermedia* (synonym *L. alpina* var. *intermedia*) comes from Utah, Arizona, and New Mexico, where it grows on loose scree slopes of fragmented limestone shales among aspen and ponderosa pine at 1525–2840 m (4955–9230 ft.). Small linear leaves to 5 cm (2 in.) long are crowded onto several short shoots that form silver cushions. Erect or ascending stems are 2–15 cm (¾–6 in.) tall and produce dense racemes of yellow flowers that on the compact forms look like yellow balls dotting the landscape.

*Lesquerella kingii* grows on dry, rocky desert slopes among sagebrush and pinyon and juniper at 1370–3450 m (4450–11,210 ft.) in Oregon, California, Nevada, and Utah. It is caespitose with spatulate to ovate silvery leaves to 5 cm (2 in.) long, and decumbent to suberect stems 5–18 cm (2–7 in.) long radiate from the basal rosette. Yellow flowers bloom from early to mid-summer.

Variety *parvifolia* from Utah is very similar to Lesquerella wardii.

*Lesquerella ludoviciana* (synonym *L. argentea*) can be found in the Great Plains, Utah, and Nevada growing from the plains to submontane levels in sandy and gravel soils. It is loosely caespitose with small silver-white spatulate to oblanceolate leaves making up the rosettes. Ascending to erect stems grow 7–30 cm (2¾–12 in.) tall and have compact inflorescences of yellow flowers in April through August followed by seedpods that are almost globose.

*Lesquerella occidentalis* grows in Oregon, California, Idaho, Nevada, and Utah among sagebrush, pinyon and juniper, and alpine meadow communities, often in shale outcrops on subalpine ridge crests at 1800–2355 m (5850–7655 ft.). A caespitose species, it makes single rosettes of spatulate bluish gray leaves that are pubescent with stellate hairs. Yellow flowers are on 2–20-cm (¾–8-in.) long ascending, decumbent, erect, or prostrate stems. This is a fine trough plant.

*Lesquerella ovalifolia* comes from the Great Plains, where it grows on rocky knolls, limestone outcrops, and rock crevices. The round, silver-gray leaves are reasonably large, and the yellow flowers in April through June are on stems 5–30 cm (2–12 in.) tall.

*Lesquerella paysonii* is endemic to eastern Idaho, western Montana, and western Wyoming, where it grows at 1845–3170 m (6000–10,300 ft.) on rocky, sparsely vegetated slopes that are often calcareous. It is densely pubescent with 5–15-cm (2–6-in.) long decumbent stems, four-petalled yellow flowers, and hairy silver leaves. Although very similar to *L. carinata*, it lacks the keels on the fruit margins.

*Lesquerella rubicundula* is endemic to the pink and white Wasatch limestone of the Paunsagunt Plateau in Utah, where it grows among ponderosa and bristlecone pine communities at 2350–3355 m (7640–10,905 ft.). This dwarf species makes mats of gray-leaved stems that grow to 5 cm (2 in.) with yellow flowers and inflated pods. Leaves are mainly basal to 1.2 cm (½ in.) long and the foliage is pubescent with stellate hairs.

*Lesquerella subumbellata* grows in Colorado and Wyoming as well as in the dry, white, oil shale barrens of Utah's Uinta Basin among sagebrush and pinyon and juniper communities at 1645-2440 m (5346-7930

*Lesquerella occidentalis*. Photo Bruce Barnes.

*Lesquerella paysonii*, Pryor Mountains, Montana.

ft.). This is a very small species with gray obovate-spatulate leaves growing to 3 cm (1¼ in.) long and stems to 10 cm (4 in.) tall. At blooming time the plant becomes almost globose with masses of yellow flowers.

*Lesquerella tumulosa* is endemic to Kane county, Utah, on white, bare shale knolls among juniper at 1500–1800 m (4875–5850 ft.). It must be the most condensed species within this genus being pulvinate-caespitose, and its mounds of tiny silver-white, downy leaves are hard and densely matted. Yellow flowers on stems that are 1–4 cm (½–1½ in.) tall are followed by small round pods tucked into the foliage. This xeric species is a good plant for growing in tufa.

*Lesquerella wardii* is endemic to southern Utah in alpine tundra on volcanic gravel soils at 2255–3475 m (7330–11,300 ft.). Silvery green spatulate leaves are pubescent with stellate hairs and they form a single rosette growing to 7 cm (2¾ in.) across. Relatively large yellow flowers, which are on prostrate stems 2–20 cm (¾–8 in.) long, are followed by small beadlike siliques. This is a choice species for trough culture.

### Propagation
Propagation is best by seed sown in spring. Seed is usually set quite profusely.

*Lesquerella paysonii,* Beartooth Highway, Wyoming. Photo Chris Norton.

### Cultivation
You should *not* grow lesquerellas under glass; if grown in those conditions the stems will elongate so much that the small flowers will appear disproportionately large and the plant will become weak. This is a genus for the trough or, better still, the sand bed. It needs sharply drained conditions in a sunny spot. In the right conditions the best of the species makes compact domes that are covered with flowers. During the fall of 2000 (the wettest on record in the United Kingdom) I left a dozen 7-cm (2¾-in.) pots outside, each of which contained *Lesquerella wardii.* Despite all that moisture—and a cold wet winter—all came through with no sign of rotting off, and in January 2001 the buds were showing color. These lesquerellas were extremely compact, which demonstrates that they should be attempted in the open air.

I have had no problems other than slugs and snails when growing lesquerellas in the garden. Aphids attack plants in the alpine house.

## LEWISIA
### Portulacaceae
*bitterroots*

Few plants epitomize the dryland West as well as those of *Lewisia.* Found nowhere else but west of the Rockies in North America, the plants memorialize the name of the great explorer of the West, Meriwether Lewis.

Among the first plant books I purchased was the *Collins Guide to Alpines and Rock Garden Plants* in the late 1960s, and while reading the book I became aware of the genus *Lewisia.* It described *L. cotyledon* as having a "wonderful color range" and flowers of "mulberry-red and flaming scarlet." This was one of the few Lewisia species that was in cultivation at that time, and before long I fell in love with the genus, a love affair that continues to this day. The majority of the species within this genus are now in cultivation, as are many attractive hybrids between the various species. I discuss some hybrids, but if you want a full list I recommend turning to specialist literature.

Some species are evergreen but the majority are deciduous, meaning that they die down for a rest after flowering. Flower color ranges through the painter's palette, from white to shades of pink, apricot, salmon, yellow, orange, red, and even striped. Several of the species have huge flowers in comparison to the plant size (they look almost like small water lilies) and others have smaller flowers in clusters on a stem. Many species have tall stems while others are practically stemless. It is always a great thrill to see lewisias growing in the wild, and many are popular enough to be in most growers' collections. Nevertheless, at least three species are extremely rare in the wild and are not good candidates for cultivation. I have seen only one of those three in cultivation, *Lewisia kelloggii*, and that is because I grow it myself; the other two, *L. disepela* and *L. maguirei*, are perhaps best seen in their native habitat. Another lewisia, *L. stebbinsii*, is known to only a few ridge tops in a small area but has been in cultivation for at least 20 years.

*Lewisia brachycalyx* grows primarily in Arizona, southwestern Utah, and western New Mexico, but it also occurs in southern California and Baja California, Mexico. A lovely deciduous species, it has short leaves 8–10 cm (3–4 in.) long that are quite glaucous. Growth of this species commences in the autumn usually after rain; in the southwestern United States, the late summer and early autumn "monsoons" trigger growth. In March through May and sometimes June, large white to pink flowers, some of which are white with pink veining, appear on short stems. After flowering and setting of seed, the plant dies down for a relatively dry summer.

For many years the true species was difficult to obtain, primarily because *Lewisia nevadensis* masqueraded as *L. brachycalyx*. Many plants were wrongly identified and were sold, exchanged, or given away. I had to travel to Lakeside, Arizona, to obtain my first true plant from Sonia Lowzow. Although the plants in cultivation at that time were white, and Sonia assured me that although she had never seen a completely deep pink flower, she had seen many that varied from pale to medium pink in the White Mountains of Arizona at an altitude of 2100–2500 m (6825–8125 ft.). From a distance they formed a lovely pink mass.

*Lewisia cantelovii* is endemic to the Plumas and Nevada counties in the Sierra Nevada, where it grows at a relatively low elevation of 700–920 m (2275–2990 ft.) on

*Lewisia brachycalyx* in cultivation.

moist, north-facing, vertical rock outcrops in the Feather and Yuba River Canyons. Although it resembles *L. serrata* in a number of ways—not the least of which are the heavily serrated leaves—the leaf shape is different. There is a suggestion to include *L. serrata* as a variety of *L. cantelovii*, although it grows slightly further north than *L. serrata*. Stems are a little taller than *L. serrata* at 30 cm (12 in.) but the flowers in May through June are similar in size and color. Like L. serrata, this is not among the most attractive species.

*Lewisia columbiana* grows in Oregon, Idaho, Washington, and British Columbia on rocky slopes of granite and serpentine at an altitude of 510–2290 m (1660–7440 ft.). It is evergreen and has small compact rosettes of dull green leaves. Stems to 30 cm (12 in.) carry panicles of small flowers in colors varying from off-white with pinkish veins to pink and magenta. All *L. columbiana* varieties flower May through August and are perfect for outside cultivation as they are reliable bloomers and resistant to winter wet. Some experienced growers dismiss these varieties as not being worth cultivating because of their diminutive size. However, these are gardenworthy plants especially if you grow them in a trough.

Variety *columbiana* grows mainly in the Cascades of Washington, Oregon, and southern British Columbia. The most robust variety with stems to 30 cm (12 in.), it has white to mid-pink flowers with magenta veins.

Variety *rupicola* (synonym *Lewisia columbiana* 'Rosea') is a real beauty from northwest Oregon and the Olympics and western Cascades of Washington. It has the smallest leaves and rosettes of all the varieties with extremely attractive flowers in rose or deep magenta on stems 5–15 cm (2–6 in.) tall.

Variety *wallowensis* grows in the Wallowa Mountains of northeastern Oregon and in Idaho. White flowers with pink veins grow on stems as high as *Lewisia columbiana* var. *rupicola*.

*Lewisia congdonii* grows in wet conditions often in moss on steep shale screes on the north and west slopes of the Sierra Nevada at 500–2100 m (1625–6825 ft.), where it can be dripping wet through winter. It ranks with *L. triphylla* in horticultural value and is among those lewisias cultivated only by "the collector." Stems grow to 60 cm (24 in.) tall, and the small, pale pink flowers with darker veins are in loose panicles. Normal flowering season is from April through June, but in cultivation it may bloom in the autumn, though that has not yet happened with my plants. Having been soaked through after December rains on one occasion, they came into growth very early in January.

*Lewisia cotyledon* is a highly variable species that grows mainly in the Siskiyou Mountains and in the Trinity River area of

*Lewisia columbiana* var. *columbiana*, Wenatchee Mountains, Washington. Photo Tony Barber.

California. The most common species in cultivation, it is also among the easiest. Although a good species with which to start your collection, it hybridizes readily, and plants grown from garden-collected seed may seldom come true to color.

Variety *cotyledon* grows in the rock crevices and nonlimestone formations of the Siskiyou Mountains of northwest California and southwest Oregon at 150–2300 m (490–7475 ft.). Flowers vary from pink with darker pink to purple stripes to white or cream with stripes of orange or yellow and are 2.5–5 cm (1–2 in.) in diameter in dense panicles from May through July. An evergreen species, it has a basal rosette of deep green glaucous leaves and stems to 30 cm ( 12 in.). Rosettes that form at the edge of the original plant as it ages can be used to make cuttings. Variety *cotyledon* f. *alba* is a white form in cultivation that originated from the Siskiyou Mountains. Cultivated plants have gone through so much hybridizing and color selection, the original colors have been lost.

Variety *heckneri* grows in the canyons of eastern Trinity county, California. It has leaves with fleshy teeth. Variety *howellii* grows in wooded areas over a broad range of southern Oregon and northern California and has crimped leaf margins.

*Lewisia disepela*, an extremely rare plant in the wild, grows only in gravel and rocky granite places at 1950–2600 m (6350–8450 ft.) near the snow line in and around Yosemite National Park, California. (Remember that plants you find in Yosemite are protected so do not collect them or their seeds!) *Lewisia disepala* is a dwarf species not more than 5 cm (2 in.) in height, and the pale to rose-pink flowers are quite large for such a dwarf—2–3 cm (¾–1¼ in.) across—and are solitary on very short scapes.

The complete cycle of growing, flowering, setting seed, and dying back takes no more than 10 weeks. Flowering commences in February and can go on until June. Like *Lewisia rediviva* and *L. maguirei*, the leaves of *L. disepala* disappear at flowering time. The seed dispersal method is the same for all three. It is unfortunate that few of us have had the chance to cultivate this very attractive species, especially since it might not be any more difficult to cultivate than *L. rediviva*.

*Lewisia kelloggii*, another rarity, occurs near the snow line in gritty, granitic sand at an altitude of 1370–2360 m (4450–7670 ft.) in the northern Sierra Nevada, on the edge of and in Yosemite Park, and in the mountains of central Idaho. Plants in these

*Lewisia cotyledon* in cultivation.

*Lewisia cotyledon* hybrid.

habitats receive a lot of moisture in spring from the snowmelt, but they also have enough sharp drainage to grow and flower well in May through July. Stemless, beautiful flowers are white or pink, about 3 cm (1¼ in.) in diameter, and cone shaped. The plant is 3–4 cm (1¼–1½ in.) tall.

Sean Hogan (1990) has noted that "*Lewisia kelloggii* plants often emerge downhill from snowbanks and sit in running water for most of their growth period." Plants die down soon after flowering, as do *L. brachycalyx* and *L. rediviva*, although unlike those two species, *L. kelloggii* seed is difficult to find. You will have to scratch the soil at the base of the plant, and if seed has been set you will find the pods just below the surface. Be careful, though, because this seed is very precious. Once the plant has died down it is almost impossible to find in order to collect the seed, hence its rarity in cultivation. I grew this species for two years, and although I had no problems collecting the seed it never germinated.

*Lewisia leeana* grows on north-facing screes in the Siskiyou Mountains of northern California and Oregon at an altitude of 1350–3350 m (4390–10,890 ft.). An evergreen species, the leaves are like no other in the genus. When you look at them in cross section you will see that they are almost cylindrical. Stems vary in height from 10 to 20 cm (4 to 8 in.) with many-flowered panicles. Flowers in June through August are usually magenta with occasional veining. White flowering forms crop up in cultivation and appear in the trade as *L. leeana* 'Alba'. This is another species I do not consider attractive.

*Lewisia longipetala* has a very limited distribution in the northern Sierra Nevada at about 2600 m (8450 ft.). It generally comes into growth later than all the other species, flowering in June through July. Flowers on stems 8–10 cm (3–4 in.) tall are a very attractive pink growing to 4 cm (1½ in.) across; they look like tiny water lilies. This species flowers throughout summer as long as moisture is available, and although deciduous, it has tiny tufts of leaves that are visible during winter if grown in the alpine house. Although I have grown it successfully outdoors it has not been long-lived, rotting off over winter. If you plant in the right situation, namely a rock crevice with lots of drainage, I believe it could do well. It makes a good pot plant and appears on the show bench fairly regularly.

*Lewisia maguirei,* the third rare species, occurs in the Quinn Canyon Range,

*Lewisia cotyledon* var. *howellii*, Oregon. Photo Neal Maillet.

*Lewisia kelloggii* in cultivation.

Nevada, where it inhabits open, south-facing slopes of clay soil among limestone rocks at approximately 2286 m (7430 ft.). During the growing season that starts in spring, the soil is wet until flowering in June through July. The plant forms a loose tuft of basal leaves 1.2–2.5 cm (½–1 in.) long, and the flowers are usually in cymes of two to three that are white with a pink flush and 2–3 cm (¾–1¼ in.) in diameter. The soil dries out in late summer and the plant dies down. This species is similar to *L. rediviva* in that when it is in bud the leaves wither and almost disappear. When in seed the entire flower cluster, including the upper bracts, becomes like dried paper and detaches. Seedpods are then blown around, which disperses the seed.

*Lewisia nevadensis* in southern California to Washington and east to Nevada and Montana grows in moist gritty soils that are dry in summer. It is a short-stemmed deciduous species with white flowers, is slightly smaller than *L. brachycalyx*, and bears petals that appear misshapen. Although more widespread than *L. brachycalyx*, it has a similar growth pattern, but because of its range shows a greater variation in the wild. It grows well in the garden for a couple of years and sets a lot of seed; many seedlings always crop up around a cultivated plant.

(Under suitable conditions it can become invasive.) One drawback of the species is that although the flowers in May through August open fully in the bright sun, they remain closed on dull days. In contrast, the flowers of *L. brachycalyx*, although closed in the evening, open during the day regardless.

'Rosea' appeared as a chance seedling in a Swedish garden, and although much different in appearance, it does seem to be of this species. The stems are longer—to 15 cm (6 in.)—and bear clusters of smaller pink flowers. It is a shame this cultivar is not often offered in catalogues as it is a much more desirable form and makes a lovely pot plant.

*Lewisia oppositifolia* is restricted to the Siskiyou Mountains of northern California and southern Oregon. Among the less appealing lewisias (it is rarely cultivated), the ungainly stems to 25 cm (10 in.) have loose panicles of up to five white flowers in March through May before the moist soil has begun to dry out. This is an unusual species in that the root stock grows well below ground level; consequently, a length of stem that bears leaves is also underground. Much more attractive is a dwarf form *L. oppositifolia* 'Richeyi' that has shorter

*Lewisia nevadensis* 'Rosea' in cultivation.

*Lewisia oppositifolia*, Oregon. Photo Neal Maillet.

stems and distinct rosettes that make the flowers appear larger.

*Lewisia pygmaea* is widely distributed in most western states including Alaska. Much discussion in the past centered on identifying this plant, and even now the variations in the wild can cause identification problems. There is now general agreement that the plant presently being cultivated as *L. pygmaea* is the correct one. It grows in pastures and short turf, gravel, or rocky places that are usually moist at flowering time. In 1990 Sonia Lowzow took me to a vast grassy area at 3000 m (9750 ft.) near Crescent Lake in the White Mountains of Arizona, where thousands upon thousands of *L. pygmaea*

were flowering shortly after snowmelt. They were much smaller than the form currently being cultivated but the habitat was probably the reason for the difference. A few years later I was on a field trip to Ute Pass near Vail, Colorado, when I spotted a small group of *L. pygmaea* at the bottom of a snowmelt runoff. These plants are larger than those in Arizona, although the flowers look similar. These two observations highlight the variations not only in the species' appearance but also in its distribution. *Lewisia pygmaea* is nowhere near as showy as *L. longipetala* but it survives the wet winters much better.

In late spring, the linear leaves spread outwards to 10 cm (4 in.) long from an

*Lewisia pygmaea* pale pink form, Cody, Wyoming. Photo Tony Barber.

*Lewisia pygmaea* carmine form, Big Horn Mountains, Wyoming.

*Lewisia pygmaea* dark pink form, White Mountains, Nevada. Photo Chris Norton.

*Lewisia pygmaea* pink and white forms, Wyoming. Photo Tony Barber.

underground resting taproot. Stems of about the same length also spread out, terminating in scapes of as many as seven flowers on each. White or pink to magenta flowers to 2.5 cm (1 in.) across sometimes lie on the ground.

*Lewisia rediviva* has a very large distribution, ranging south from British Columbia into most of the West. This species is the famous bitterroot that is the state flower of Montana. Captain Meriwether Lewis tasted this lewisia's root in August 1805 when he discovered that the Indians used the roots as food, and a year later the first of several botanical specimens was collected. The specific name *rediviva* refers to the plant's

*Lewisia rediviva*, Table Top Mountain, California. Photo Chris Norton.

Habitat of *Lewisia rediviva* on Burnt Mountain, eastern Cascades, Washington.

ability to grow again after being preserved as a dried specimen for over two years. I have seen *L. rediviva* in full bloom during mid-July on Burnt Mountain in the eastern Cascades, and anyone who has not seen it flower (usually in May through July) will be excited when they see it for the first time. Just as *L. tweedyi* is the showiest among the evergreen group, *L. rediviva* is its counterpart in the deciduous group; many think it the most beautiful of all lewisias.

Jerry DeSanto (1993) stated that no *Lewisia rediviva* occurs in the wet coastal parts of California, Oregon, and Washington, and Rick Lupp has found them growing in all sorts of habitat in eastern Washington from the high volcanic screes to much heavier soils among the sagebrush. The only common thread is low rainfall. Rick notes with pleasure that the bloom season can last for months if you visit the right spots.

*Lewisia rediviva* has huge flowers, one per stem, that are 5–7 cm (2–2¾ in.) across. They range from pale pink to deep pink or rose-red. Some plants have white or ivory flowers but only var. *minor* has separate taxonomic status. Wayne Roderick introduced 'Jolon', a cultivar with large reddish flowers,

*Lewisia rediviva*, Burnt Mountain, eastern Cascades, Washington.

that he found growing in Jolon, California, but it is very rarely seen now. Unfortunately plants grown from seed do not always come true to color so you will have to propagate them vegetatively.

Variety *minor* has a smaller distribution in southern California, southern and western Nevada, and Utah. It comes true from seed, flowering white true to the parent, and its flowers are smaller. In May 1999 I was accompanied by Wayne Roderick and Janet Haden along the Fire Interpretive trail in Mount Diablo State Park (only 45 km [28 miles] from San Francisco in the eastern San Francisco Bay Area at 1185 m [3860 ft.]), where I was impressed by a large colony blooming on a small ridge. Clumps of that colony varied in size, and some had 8–10 flowers that stood out from the red-brown shale, reminding me of the species' Burnt Mountain habitat in the eastern Cascades.

Beginning in May, *Lewisia rediviva* is a regular feature at the Alpine Garden Society shows. Exhibitors freely admit, however, that it is not the easiest plant to have in full flower on the show bench during early morning because the flowers are light and heat sensitive and the buds are reluctant to open during dull, sunless mornings.

*Lewisia serrata* grows only in the counties of El Dorado and Placer in eastern California at an altitude of 900–1300 m (2925–4225 ft.). It inhabits north-facing shady cliffs in steep gorges that are often moss covered. A distinctive evergreen species with heavily serrated leaves, the thin stems to 20 cm (8 in.) carry many small white to pale pink flowers in May through July that have darker pink veins. Although not a particularly outstanding or attractive species, it is still useful for a trough.

*Lewisia sierrae* has a very limited distribution in the central Sierra Nevada growing

Habitat view of *Lewisia rediviva* var. *minor*, Mount Diablo, California.

*Lewisia rediviva* var. *minor*, Bristlecone Pines Road, California. Photo Chris Norton.

*Lewisia rediviva* var. *minor*, Mount Diablo, California.

at an altitude of 2370–4100 m (7700–13,325 ft.) in open sandy and gravel places or in short turf that is moist during flowering time during late June through August. The smallest of all the species both in growth and flower size, its leaf tufts to 5–6 cm (2–2¼ in.) grow from a tiny carrot-like root. Very short, thin, procumbent stems have two to three flowers approximately 1.2 cm (½ in.) wide that are white to pink, usually with a dark pink-carmine stripe. A tiny form from Mount Yosemite that was exhibited in 2000 at an Alpine Garden Society show is compact with minute white flowers. Lewisia sierrae is by no means showy but rather one for the collectors of this genus.

*Lewisia stebbinsii* grows at an altitude of 1920 m (6240 ft.) on south-facing gravel slopes and flowers June through July, though in cultivation it begins flowering in May. A recent addition to the genus, it was discovered in 1967 by Roman Gankin and W. Richard Hildreth in the Mendocino National Forest in the north Coast Ranges of California. It grows to about 5 cm (2 in.) high with procumbent stems to 15 cm (6 in.) and panicles of 3–11 flowers with deep pink petals that are white at the base and that have darker pink veins. The flowers are quite large for the size of the plant, to 2.5 cm (1 in.) diameter. A really attractive species that is worth searching for in specialist nurseries and seed lists, it is sometimes confused with *L. pygmaea* because the flower, though smaller, is a similar color. *Lewisia stebbinsii* takes a long time to grow to flowering size from seed, usually four to five years. With such a restricted distribution and its slow growing habit, *L. stebbinsii* is rarely seen in cultivation and only occasionally appears on the show bench.

*Lewisia triphylla* has a widespread distribution from British Columbia in Canada through the Cascades and to the Sierra Nevada, Montana, and Colorado at altitudes that vary from 1500 to 3270 m (4875 to 10,625 ft.). During the growing period its

*Lewisia stebbinsii* in cultivation.

*Lewisia sierrae* in cultivation.

*Lewisia triphylla*, Siskiyou Mountains, Oregon.

habitat is quite wet, often near melting snow, although it has a relatively dry period in summer. Slender stems 2.5–25 cm (1–10 in.) tall bear groups of small white to pink flowers May through August. After seeing the smaller form in the Siskiyou Mountains, I agree that *L. triphylla* is of no great horticultural value; only a fervent lewisia collector would want to cultivate it.

*Lewisia tweedyi* (synonym *Cistanthe tweedyi*) has a limited distribution in the Wenatchee Mountains of Washington and Manning Park in British Columbia. It grows in acid conditions in a sharply draining mixture of granite rocks and pine duff. The plant survives in this habitat because the long fleshy roots reach down for moisture in the hot summer.

Considered the aristocrat of the evergreen species, *Lewisia tweedyi* is named after Frank Tweedy, a keen amateur botanist and topographic engineer who worked on the United States Geological Survey. With leaves so much larger and much more succulent than all other lewisias, plants of this species have been described as "cabbages." The leaves often have an attractive purplish tinge to them, although I have noticed that leaves on cultivated plants occasionally distort where this purple color appears. The flowers are outstanding and can be to 5 cm (2 in.) across in beautiful pinks and apricots to orange and yellow on stems 10–20 cm (4–8 in.) tall. If you want to grow something that is outstanding and showy then grow this species. Although a little tricky, it is a firm favorite with exhibitors, and when grown well in a large pot can be absolutely stunning.

The cultivar 'Alba' has clear white flowers that are almost crystalline in appearance. Two additional lovely cultivars include Jack Drake's 'Inshriach Strain', which has flowers in a rich rose-red, and 'Rosea', which has salmon-pink flowers.

*Lewisia tweedyi* 'Rosea' in cultivation.

*Lewisia tweedyi*, Wenatchee Mountains, Washington. Photo Ev Whittemore.

The flower of *Lewisia tweedyi* 'Alba' in cultivation.

*Lewisia brachycalyx* has been used to produce some good hybrids. In 1998 Ashwood Nurseries produced a lovely deep magenta hybrid from *L. brachycalyx* and Lewisia magenta strain. It was named 'Magenta Magic'. Two of the more well-known and older hybrids from *L. brachycalyx* × *L. cotyledon* are 'Phyllellia', a dwarf form having pink flowers with darker stripes, and 'Brachyheck' (*L. brachycalyx* × *L. cotyledon* var. *heckneri*). Among the best crosses made since 1986 or 1987 is 'Patricia Forrest'. It is evergreen with large flowers of a clear pink graduating to yellow orange at the center. There are three flowers to a stem, and the long flowering period is from May through September or October.

*Lewisia columbiana* has featured as a seed parent to a number of choice hybrids, and all withstand the winter rains just as well as the species. *Lewisia* 'George Henley' a magenta, and *Lewisia* 'Trevosia', an orange-pink, are two lovely cultivars from a *L. columbiana* × *L. cotyledon* cross.

Rick Lupp bred *Lewisia* 'Norma Jean', a *L. columbiana* 'Alba' × *L. cotyledon* var. *heckneri* cross, and named it for his wife. A large specimen survives well in an alpine bed, the many rosettes covering the plant with hundreds of soft pastel-pink flowers with darker veins. It blooms twice a year, in spring and in autumn.

As a result of deliberate hybridizing, a range of color selections has been made from *Lewisia cotyledon*. Some examples of these hybrids are 'Ashwood Strain', which is a clear yellow, and 'Birch Hybrids', which has rose-pink shades. 'Sunset Strain', a yellow to dark orange-red, was raised by Jack Drake of Inshriach Nursery. *Lewisia* 'Rose Splendour', a well-known selection of *L. cotyledon* var. *howellii*, is a clear, strong rose. A large number of hybrids with other species have also been produced using the pollen of *L. cotyledon*.

There are many attractive hybrids of *Lewisia longipetala* × *L. cotyledon*. *Lewisia* 'Pinkie' is a soft rose-pink that grows well outside, *L.* 'Matthew' is a soft orange, *L.* 'Ashwood Pearl' is a pearly white, and *L.* 'Oxstalls Lane' has dark red stamens and is similar to 'Pinkie' although smaller and not as good a plant. *Lewisia longipetala* × *L. rediviva* also produces good plants with larger but deeper pink flowers and shorter stems. One such hybrid is *L.* 'Roy Elliott'. There are also records of white-flowered hybrids.

There are also many excellent hybrids of *Lewisia rediviva*. One such cross,

*Lewisia* 'Magenta Magic' in cultivation.

*Lewisia* 'Pinkie' in cultivation.

*L. rediviva* × *L. longipetala,* has flowers slightly smaller than *L. rediviva,* but because its flowers stay open, it makes a great show plant. *Lewisia cotyledon* × *L. rediviva,* a readily available hybrid from many specialist nurseries, is easy to grow and has produced plants with very large and vividly colored flowers.

## Propagation

The most obvious and easiest way to start with lewisias is to grow them from seed. Seed from the majority of the species is freely available from all the seed exchanges and various commercial lists. If you sow seed in autumn it will usually germinate the following spring, and you can prick out the seedlings when they are large enough to handle. Some books recommend that you leave seedlings from the deciduous group for a year, but I have found that it is better to treat them all the same. If you are careful with *Lewisia rediviva* seedlings you can grow them to flowering size a year earlier than if you left them in the seed pot until the following spring. When starting a collection of lewisias, buy *L. cotyledon* in flower because unless it has been propagated by cuttings its color is not guaranteed. Although most *Lewisia* species readily hybridize, *L. cotyledon* is more wayward than most, and seed-grown plants produce a wide range of colors.

If you want to increase your lewisia stocks a little more quickly or duplicate one of your favorite color forms, use vegetative propagation. Any plants that make side shoots or rosettes can be increased by using these as cuttings. Occasionally a hybrid sends a flower stem from every rosette leaving none for propagation, but if you remove the flower stem, the rosette will grow on so that you can then use it for

cutting material. Cuttings I take in mid- to late June root within four to five weeks, much quicker than they do if I take them in spring. Cut the offsets off close to the caudex or with a piece of the caudex attached and insert them in your normal cutting mix in a frame that has some air movement. If the cover of the frame is too close the cuttings tend to rot off.

Lewisias such as *Lewisia rediviva,* *L. brachycalyx,* or *L. stebbinsii* do not make side rosettes; instead they gradually send out more shoots from the caudex. I have propagated these species by slicing down the caudex lengthways with a very sharp knife, ensuring that each piece has a growing point or shoot. I then dust these pieces with a hormone-rooting compound and treat them as cuttings. Once they are rooted I pot them up in the normal way.

If your plants are reluctant to make even side growth, then more drastic measures are called for. When plants start to grow more quickly in early spring, cut out the growing point and make a few notches in the caudex. New shoots emerge, and when you see they are growing well you can apply the "slicing" method to the caudex I described. Growth time does vary from species to species, and you may have to wait until the following spring after notching the caudex to begin slicing. Be patient knowing that you will have the extra shoots that you need.

## Cultivation

Lewisias prefer to be damp throughout their growing season and do not do well if they dry out between watering periods. As the season progresses and it becomes warmer, dormancy in the deciduous species is induced. You should cease their regular watering at this time. The more vigorous evergreen species such as *Lewisia columbiana*, *L. cotyledon*, *L. leeana*, and *L. serrata* can still receive copious amounts of water, but I find that even *L. cotyledon* and its hybrids go into a dormant state during hot weather if they become overheated in an alpine house. If a period of very hot weather is forecast you should temporarily move the plants in pots to a shady spot especially if you require side rosettes for cuttings. Once the plants have stopped growing you simply have to wait for cooler conditions and nature to take its course for them to start growing again. Give only a little moisture during this period or else the plants rot off.

When you grow lewisias from seed, prick out the seedlings into 7-cm (2¾ in.) pots using a neutral, soil-based compost. Seedlings of most species grow on fast and probably need repotting at least a couple more times in the first year. Exceptions include *Lewisia rediviva* and *L. stebbinsii*, which can be left to grow on after pricking out into their individual pots. *Lewisia stebbinsii* is very slow growing and usually stays in the same pot for at least two years after pricking out. Potted plants in the alpine house do well in a neutral, soil-based compost with about 25 percent extra grit, preferably lime free. As lewisias tend to be hungry plants, give them occasional liquid feeds throughout the year.

Lewisias require repotting every year, and although you can do this in autumn through to winter, I prefer to repot in early spring when growth becomes obvious. During this time you can also remove the old withered leaves from the previous year's growth.

Many lewisia species grow outdoors perfectly well either in an alpine bed or in a trough. I do not have any special formula for their soil; I just mix in some extra grit to provide adequate drainage.

*Lewisia pygmaea* and *L. nevadensis* grow well outside and can receive moisture all year round. *Lewisia pygmaea* goes dormant in summer if subjected to hot and dry conditions but as soon as there are a few days of rain, growth and even flowering recommences. Both species set ample seed, and where they are doing especially well, they will seed themselves around; *L. nevadensis* can even become a menace. I have not grown *L. nevadensis* 'Rosea' outside, but have heard that it does very well in a trough. It does set seed but its germination rate is poor, although subsequent plants do come true to color and flower within two years.

*Lewisia serrata* has lasted three years in my garden when I grow it outside in an alpine bed. In a trough, where it is more suited, it has lasted longer. Strangely, it was drought that killed it and not overwatering. It is easy to grow from seed so keeping a supply of plants going is straightforward. Even when not in flower, the plant's highly serrated leaves make it a nice foliage plant.

*Lewisia rediviva* has a reputation for being difficult to cultivate but it is really quite easy once you understand the growth cycle. If you live anywhere that has rain from May through September, you must cultivate this species under cover during that time. During September in cultivation and usually October in the wild, small tufts of green shoots appear above ground and grow on slowly through the winter. This growth happens initially without the plant receiving any moisture. At high elevations growth commences below ground and shoots do not surface until the spring. Your plant in the alpine house needs very small amounts of water during its growth through winter and more as it comes into full growth in spring. Buds appear from the base of the tuft during May, and as the stems elongate the leaves start to wither once again and the cycle is complete. Suddenly—usually on a bright sunny day in May—the buds open to reveal the huge flowers that will amaze and delight you. Seed is not always set but if it is you will see that each seed is quite large and varies in color from shiny black to muddy brown.

I tried growing *Lewisia brachycalyx* in a raised bed a couple of times, and although it grew well there, the beautiful flowers were destroyed by a mixture of rain, wind, and slugs. I now cultivate it only as a pot plant in the alpine house, where it is quite superb. This species dies down fairly quickly after flowering, all the leaves curling up and becoming a squishy mass. Take care when you are looking for seed as the short stems die back into the rosette—it is so easy to nudge a seedpod and lose the seed into the gritty top dressing. Although plants of this species rest during the summer they do need a slight amount of moisture. It is easy to water a plant that has been plunged, and if you stand the pot on grit then water it occasionally around its base. Growth commences below ground in autumn and leaves appear in winter to very early spring depending on the temperature. As temperatures rise in spring the plants grow more vigorously until lovely huge flowers finally appear in May. This species is excellent for showing and also does well in a trough if you can shelter it from the summer rains.

*Lewisia stebbinsii* requires similar cultivation to *L. brachycalyx*, meaning it should be slightly damp during the dormancy period. Top growth is not evident as early as *L. brachycalyx*, however, but once it is growing, cultivate it the same way. *Lewisia*

*stebbinsii* is a good show plant that is seldom seen as there are not too many true plants around. I have not had seed set with only one plant. *Lewisia triphylla* has similar requirements to *L. brachycalyx* regarding moisture but does not come into growth as soon.

*Lewisia kelloggii* should be cultivated in much the same way as *L. brachycalyx* and *L. stebbinsii*. I potted up a plant of *L. kelloggii* I received in the autumn of 1995 in my normal soil mix that was slightly damp, and although it came into growth in very early spring of the following year it did not flower. After it died down I left it to have a rest and did not water it at all. When I saw no growth in the spring of 1997 I was a little worried, but once I watered it, it commenced growing again, albeit very slowly, and grew on through the summer. Although extra side shoots had grown it still did not flower and started to die back once again. In November of that year when growth was still evident I carefully watered it, and both the mild winter weather and moist soil mix helped it start growing once more. It bloomed in late spring to early summer of 1998 with an upward-facing, stemless, white trumpetlike flower similar in shape to a very small *Narcissus bulbocodium*. Seed was set, though had I not done some research on lewisias in the wild, I would not have known to scratch around at the base of the stem as the plant died back to find just two pods with ripe seed. This seed, though sown, never germinated.

*Lewisia tweedyi* is fairly difficult to grow outside where there is excessive winter wet, although I have heard of some success in Scotland. Sean Hogan (1990) suggests that the conditions of central Washington are probably the key. The various types of soil there, although well drained, often retain moisture just below the surface, so moisture is available to the plant all the time during the dry summer. Masses of *L. tweedyi* I saw in June or July that were planted out like bedding plants in a shady border around a garage in central Washington were huge— as large as cabbages—and obviously thriving in the moist situation. Sean also suggests that plants prefer damp but not saturated conditions in winter.

Cultivating *Lewisia cotyledon* in a pot is straightforward, and each year huge specimens turn up on the show bench. The species remains a slight enigma, however, when cultivated outdoors. We all see those huge flowering plants in garden centers each spring and are enticed to buy these "easy" lewisias for the garden, and yet it is practically guaranteed that most will be dead and rotted off by the following year if grown anywhere outside the western United States. I have, like you, read all the advice in other books that advise planting them on their sides or covering them with a sheet of glass in winter, but I have killed dozens of this species no matter what advice I follow. It is best that you grow a lot of plants from seed and try them in different locations around your garden. If you find the right situation and can keep the caudex reasonably dry over winter, *L. cotyledon* will flower well for you.

I have only grown *Lewisia cantelovii* and *L. leeana* as pot plants but they appear to be happy with the same cultivation technique as *L. cotyledon*. I have grown *L. congdonii* only in a pot, but as it likes autumn and winter moisture and comes into active growth during winter in the alpine house, it should be alright in a trough.

*Lewisia longipetala* grows equally well outside as it does in a pot for showing, although the flowers are much less damaged when they bloom in the alpine house. The hybrid *Lewisia* 'Pinkie' is excellent outdoors and has been grown both as a show plant in a pot and in an uncovered raised bed. While the pot plant has flowered reasonably well, the outdoor plant has put on a fantastic display for the last three years with more than 50 flowers in bloom for weeks on end. It has also stayed compact. I have not yet tried other hybrids of *L. longipetala* outdoors.

I have successfully grown *Lewisia oppositifolia* outside as its native Oregon habitat receives about the same amount of annual rainfall as in Timsbury, approximately 90 cm (36 in.). I normally grow it as a pot plant, though, under similar conditions to other deciduous species.

*Lewisia sierrae* is usually grown only by those keen "want to grow all the species" types, so you rarely see it. Although not a showy species it is diminutive, and even though the flowers could be called cute, they are not very long lasting. It is also a deciduous plant, so it does not have too much going for it. Seed germinates well, but it takes longer than average to grow a plant to any reasonable flowering size. It is easy to grow, requiring a dryish summer rest. If you want to grow this species you will have to go to the specialist nurseries and seed catalogs or exchanges.

*Lewisia tweedyi* is excellent as a pot plant but appears to require slightly different growing conditions from most other evergreen species. Kath Dryden (1989) in *The Genus Lewisia* states that, "Strictly no water should be applied directly to the pots after seed has been set until midautumn and also no water during the winter months." These conditions contrast those that Sean Hogan suggests the species in the wild prefers, and those of you who have grown *L. tweedyi* in a pot have probably noticed the leaves wizen in summer because of a dry soil mixture. This dry soil mixture has sent the plant into premature dormancy, and if you subsequently water it to try revive it, the caudex will likely rot off.

In view of these differing opinions on growing *Lewisia tweedyi*, I suggest that you plunge the pot to ensure that there is adequate moisture throughout the summer. However, if you stand the pot on damp grit or sand, ensure that the pot is shaded and apply water around the edge of the pot during summer. Although in the wild the soil appears to be dry, the roots and the succulent leaves are storing moisture. Roots in a pot are slightly different because they have not had a chance to go deep down to the cooler soil. Give the plant a little more moisture during autumn and keep the soil mixture slightly moist throughout winter. Growth is slowly going on below ground during this time. Many old, dry leaves will still be around the edge of the green growth left from the previous year. Do not remove these leaves until the plant has returned to full growth in spring otherwise you will allow disease to enter the caudex. As *L. tweedyi* comes from a granite area with acid conditions you will need to make some alterations to the soil mixture. A lime-free and neutral, soil-based compost with extra grit added is suitable.

I have never grown either of the two rarities, *Lewisia disepala* and *L. maguirei*, and do not know anyone who has. However, as they are related to *L. rediviva*, you will likely be successful if you grow them the same way but with a neutral soil mixture, even though *L. disepala* grows in a granite

area and *L. maguirei* in limestone. Unfortunately the chance of putting this theory to the test is virtually nil.

There are many more hybrids and cultivars in cultivation than I have mentioned, and they are well worth hunting down. Often you can find them on the plant sale table at group or chapter meetings or at the various shows.

Not too many things affect lewisias. Some species suffer neck rot when they grow outside in damp conditions. Slugs are also partial to lewisias so be prepared for your plants to be eaten. Aphids can be problematic in the alpine house or frames. Like *Silene hookeri*, *Lewisia rediviva* is among the first plants in the alpine house to be attacked. Aphids can cause major damage to leaves, making them curl and twist so that previously healthy plants will look decidedly sick.

## LUPINUS
### Fabaceae
### *lupines*

Throughout my travels in the West I have never failed to see lupines in all shades of blue, purple, or white. A 1993 field trip to the wonderful Colorado lupine fields, the mighty Rockies in the background, stands out in my memory to this day. Trying to identify all these lupines, however, is another matter. Craighead et al. (1963) (known as Peterson's Guide) state that "of approximately 200 known lupines about 50 species occur in the Rocky Mountains." Wilson et al. (1987) observe, "Lupines comprise of one of the largest and most confusing genera in California." It comes as no surprise, therefore, to find that California has more than 80 species. That lupines also hybridize extensively makes me wonder if it makes sense to consider them gardenworthy. There are a number of lupines, however, that can be identified and that also stand out as great plants, not only for the flowers but also the superb silver-gray foliage. I have grown some lupines, and although short-lived or even monocarpic, they set abundant seed and can be kept growing in succession.

*Lupinus arcticus* occurs on the dry slopes, fields, and roadsides throughout most of Alaska except the southern coastal areas. It grows 25–40 cm (10–15¾ in.) tall with many large, flower-filled stalks and palmate leaves with long stems. Showy blue to dark blue flowers open June through July, and when in bud cause the flower stalks to look quite woolly as a result of their hairy calyx lobes.

*Lupinus argenteus*, the silvery lupine, grows throughout the West in low elevation prairies to alpine levels and is highly variable. It has several stems that grow 15–60 cm (6–24 in.) tall with palmately compound leaves, usually with six to nine narrow leaflets, that are silky haired on the underside. The deep blue to white flowers have white or reddish centers on the banner petals and are in terminal racemes.

Variety *depressus* grows in Idaho, Montana, and Wyoming. Shorter than the

Colorado lupine fields with the Rockies in the background.

*Lupinus arcticus*, Yukon-Tanana Uplands, Alaska. Photo Carolyn Parker.

*Lupinus argenteus*, Albion Basin in Wasatch Mountains, Utah. Photo Jane Grushow.

type at 15–25 cm (6–10 in.), it blooms with deep blue or violet flowers in the subalpine and alpine zones during July.

*Lupinus breweri* occurs not only on Mount Rose in California but also along the Sierra Nevada and in southern Oregon at an altitude of 1300–3700 m (4225–12,025 ft.). That well-known plantsman Jim Archibald once described it as "the plant that wove together Mount Rose." It certainly appeared to do that when I hiked up that mountain and saw large mats of *L. breweri* at the side of the trail turning the sandy soil a deep blue. Although not as widespread as on Mount Rose, it grows on Mount Whitney in what appear to be sand dunes. This superb dwarf species makes prostrate mats of dense woolly foliage with racemes 3–15 cm (1¼–6 in.) tall and flowers of violet-blue with white or yellow markings in June through August.

*Lupinus latifolius* var. *subalpinus* grows on open subalpine slopes in Washington at around 1985 m (6450 ft.). A very floriferous, mounding species, it is 22–30 cm (8¾–12 in.) tall with lavender-blue flowers with white markings.

*Lupinus lepidus* (synonyms *L. aridus*, *L. caespitosus*, *L. confertus*) ranges through-out the West and is probably among the most well-known caespitose species. Stems grow to 40 cm (15¾ in.) and the flowers are violet to blue.

Variety *lobbii* (synonyms *Lupinus danaus*, *L. fruticulosus*, *L. lyallii*, *L. perditorum*) usually grows in rocky gravel soils at a moderate elevation throughout the Rockies. It makes a prostrate mat with stems 10–20 cm (4–8 in.) tall and varies in color from a dull faded blue to a deep rich blue. Closely packed racemes to 5 cm (2 in.) long appear to start flowering at ground level.

Variety *utahensis* (synonym *Lupinus lepidus* subsp. *caespitosus*) grows in Utah, Idaho, Montana, Wyoming, California, Nevada, and Colorado in meadows, open

Mount Whitney California. Photo Tony Barber.

*Lupinus argenteus* var. *depressus*, Idaho. Photo Peter Downe.

*Lupinus breweri*, Mount Whitney, California.

deciduous woodland, and mixed conifer at 2130–3350 m (6920–10,890 ft.). Although a dwarf form at 2.5–12.5 cm (1–5 in.), the plant I grew for a year was a little taller at 15 cm (6 in.). The specimen I photographed at Dead Indian Hill Summit, Wyoming, is the most compact lupine I have seen with the flowers starting at ground level.

*Lupinus nootkatensi*s grows in southeastern and south-central Alaska and the Aleutian Islands. It is similar to *L. arcticus* but grows 40–90 cm (15¾–36 in.) tall and has shorter leaf stems, blunt leaves, and numerous flower stalks. Pea-shaped seedpods are covered with small hairs.

### Propagation

Seed that you sow outdoors germinates very quickly, usually in 7–10 days during wet conditions. Seedlings do not like very cold weather, however, and those early seedlings grown from seed that you sow in the autumn are likely to die off in a severe frost. Once the seedlings germinate the stem reaches 2–3 cm (¾–1¼ in.) tall before the true leaves appear: this is when the cold can kill them. Seedlings will also damp off if you do not give them overhead protection soon after they germinate. Autumn sowing is obviously preferable if your area has no winter frost or if you can protect them when a severe frost is forecast as they will then get off to a great start the following spring. Seed is usually set quite freely.

### Cultivation

As with all the peas, you should prick them out early to prevent root damage. (Lupines also dislike root disturbance.) Let them grow on until they look like miniature lupines, which is usually in late spring with an autumn sowing. As soon as they have reached this stage you can plant them out in

*Lupinus lepidus*, Mount Hood, Oregon. Photo David Hale.

*Lupinus lepidus* var. *lobbii*, Mount Townsend, Washington.

*Lupinus lepidus* var. *lobbii*, Mount Rainier National Park, Washington. Photo Jane Grushow.

the small alpine bed, trough, or pot where they will grow to maturity. Lupines have a long taproot so if you grow them in a pot ensure that it is a deep one. The lupines I describe are usually short-lived so collect seed to keep them going; those I grew flowered the first year before dying so they may be monocarpic. A gritty, well-drained, warm position suits these plants well.

Seedlings and young plants damp off if you water them too much. Slugs love lupines and can reduce them to short stems in no time. In the alpine house aphids and red spider mite are the worst pests, but snails take over where slugs leave off.

# M

## MONARDELLA
### Labiatae, or Lamiaceae
### *mountain balms*

The flowers of *Monardella* are more unusual than beautiful. They are made up of clusters of small, tubular, two-lipped flowers that are usually surrounded by colored leaflike bracts. Also in the genus are some aromatic plants, which in addition to being welcome in the trough or scented garden, are useful for the medicinal properties they contain.

*Lupinus lepidus* var. *lobbii,* white form. Photo Rick Lupp.

*Lupinus nootkatensis*, St. Paul Island, Bering Sea. Photo Carolyn Parker.

*Lupinus lepidus* var. *utahensis*, Dead Indian Hill Summit, Wyoming.

*Lupinus nootkatensis* white form, St. Paul Island, Bering Sea. Photo Carolyn Parker.

The essential oil thymol is one of several present in the volatile oils. While hiking the Illinois River trail in Oregon a few years ago I unknowingly stepped on several monardella plants, and instantly a pleasant mintlike smell drifted toward me. If you grow monardella plants in the alpine house you only have to stroke a potful to benefit from the fragrance.

A number of species are worth growing in the trough or alpine garden, and although they are fairly short-lived—three to four years—I recommend that you try them.

*Monardella cinerea* is a high alpine from California growing at an altitude of 2890 m (9400 ft.) that could be mistaken for a mint-scented thyme. Tight hairy mats of silver-gray, thymelike leaves grow to 2 cm (¾ in.) high as it creeps across the ground. At 2.5 cm (1 in.) across, the pale lavender, stemless flowers are unbelievably large for such a tiny plant. Since this species is smaller than all the others in the genus, the tubular flowers make it look like a pin cushion. It is not as delicate as it looks and is well suited to a trough.

*Monardella macrantha* grows in California on dry gravel slopes and ridges at 760–1820 m (2470–5915 ft.). The most

spectacular species of the genus, brilliant scarlet funnel-shaped flowers 3–4 cm (1 ¼–1½ in.) across explode from open mats of dark green leaves on short stems.

*Monardella nana* subsp. *tenuiflora* grows in California in gritty granitic soil at about 2155 m (7000 ft.). It makes prostrate mats of dark green leaves. Although the short brittle stems are quite thick and woody it is still a very attractive species with large, pale yellow, feathery flowers and pale green and purple bracts. It needs a little more humus in the soil than others in the genus.

*Monardella odoratissima* grows on gravel slopes or dry rocky subalpine ridges at 1980–2150 m (6435–6990 ft.) in Idaho, eastern Washington, Wyoming, New Mexico, Utah, and southern California. It makes a small mound of blue-gray leaves 10–20 cm (4–8 in.) high that is attractive even out of flower. Stems are 10–45 cm (4–18 in.) tall with heads of pink to purple or sometimes white tubular, feathery flowers 3 cm (1¼ in.) long and purplish bracts.

*Monardella nana* subsp. *tenuiflora*.

*Monardella macrantha*.

Subspecies *glauca* is less robust and has purple to bright rose-violet flowers. Subspecies *pallida* grows to 30 cm (12 in.) with pale blue-lavender and occasionally white flowers.

*Monardella palmeri* grows in California at approximately 770 m (2500 ft.). A mat-forming species growing to 5 cm (2 in.) tall it spreads by underground rhizomes to a square meter (10.76 sq. ft.) or more. The flowers are rose-purple and tone well with the purplish green leaves. Owing to its spreading nature I recommend that unless you have a large rock garden you should give this species a miss.

*Monardella villosa* subsp. *globosa* is found at a very low altitude in California— just 170 m (550 ft.). This spreading form grows 30–60 cm (12–24 in.) high, which is a little tall for the average rock garden. The light purple flowers are 7 cm (2¾ in.) across and very feathery.

*Monardella villosa* subsp. *obispoensis* grows in California in dry serpentine soils at around 660 m (2150 ft.). More compact than subsp. *globosa*, it makes loose mats of gray foliage. Stems are 22–30 cm (8¾–12 in.) tall with pale lavender flowers. One attraction of this subspecies is the spicy peppermint scent.

**Propagation**
Seed is being collected regularly and is available from several commercial lists. It germinates well if you sow it in the autumn. Although seed of attractive Monardella species other than those I discuss has become available, the plants may be too large for the typical rock garden.

Propagation from cuttings or rooted side shoots is also easy. Cuttings root quickly whatever time of year you take them; those I took in the autumn rooted within three weeks in sand. You can pot up the rooted side shoots immediately.

**Cultivation**
The plants are very quick growing and the seedlings, once potted on, soon become large enough to be planted out in the rock garden in a sunny spot. There are no special cultivation methods for this genus as all the species are easy to grow; many flower in the same year they are pricked out. They do resemble dead twigs during winter, however, so do not be too impatient but give them a chance to come back to life in spring before pulling them up and throwing them away. New growth usually commences low to the ground at the base of the stem or even below ground.

None of the species does well in a pot but if you find it impossible to grow them in the garden then try the plants in a larger than normal pot in the alpine house.

Aphids in the alpine house can be a menace.

# O

## OXYTROPIS
Leguminosae, or Fabaceae
*locoweeds*

*Oxytropis* is closely related to the genus *Astragalus* but the keel (or lower petals) of oxytropis is contracted into a distinct beak whereas the keel of astragalus flowers is quite blunt. *Oxytropis* is similar to *Astragalus*, albeit in a more limited way, in its range of species, from those that grow to 60 cm (24 in.) to the superb, low growing and compact plants we all love and want to cultivate. Flower color of *Oxytropis* varies from the deepest purple to rich pink, lavender, pale yellow, and cream, but in cultivation the blooms do not appear to last as long as those of *Astragalus*. Not only do oxytropis flowers have vivid colors when in bloom from spring to summer, but the leaves are also very attractive as some are silky and others silvery. Some species also have large and beautiful seedpods. *Oxytropis* shares the common name locoweed with *Astragalus* and has the same poisonous characteristics. Both genera are similar in that they grow best in sunny, dry places and are well worth attempting in sand beds.

*Oxytropis campestris* ranges from Oregon to Montana, Utah, and Colorado growing at varying elevations. It is not long lasting in areas of winter damp but will grow at the front of a rock garden for a couple of years if needed. Although the species attains the same height—10–20 cm (4–8 in.)— in both North America and Europe, the North American species is much more desirable as plants at high elevation grow to only 2.5–8 cm (1–3 in.) high. White to yellowish flowers grow in erect clumps with hairy, grayish leaves. Although not an outstanding species (many people in Europe consider it a weed), it is attractive when in large clumps.

Variety *cusickii* is a beautiful dwarf variety that grows on high montane to open alpine slopes northwards from Colorado and Utah. Variety *gracilis* has light yellow to cream clusters of flowers and pretty, silver pinnate foliage. It makes a reasonable plant for the small rock garden.

*Oxytropis deflexa* grows throughout the Rockies from arctic Canada to Utah and Colorado in alpine and subalpine meadows and other moist areas at 2750–3350 m (8940–10,890 ft.). This species is unusual in that the purple flowers, though erect when in bud, are pendent by blooming time. The pods are also pendulous, and the specific name *deflexa* reflects this pendulous nature of both flowers and pods. It varies in height from 8 to 45 cm (3 to 18 in.) and can take more moisture during winter than many others in the genus. The shorter form is very good for trough culture.

*Oxytropis lagopus* grows in Montana, Wyoming, and Idaho in sagebrush plains to lower mountain slopes. It is a lovely dwarf species that makes a low and densely caespitose mat 2.5–5 cm (1–2 in.) high with rose

*Oxytropis campestris*, Dead Indian Hill Summit, Wyoming.

Colony of *Oxytropis lambertii* near Thermopolis, Wyoming.

to deep purple flowers. Leaves and stems have long, silvery, spreading hairs with several crowns clustered on the summit of a simple or forking taproot. This species is a challenge in cultivation.

*Oxytropis lambertii*, the purple locoweed, grows across the prairies and mountain meadows of the western states, coloring the ground purple-red to light purple and white during summer and occasionally into fall. It is not compact at 10–40 cm (4–15 3/4 in.) tall, but *O. lambertii* is nevertheless an extremely attractive plant. A word of warning though: this species is classed among the most dangerously poisonous plants on the western ranges and is highly toxic, even lethal, to many kinds of livestock.

*Oxytropis maydelliana* is found on stony slopes and tundra throughout the mountains of Alaska, where it flowers June through early July. It forms a clump of hairy, pinnately divided leaves, and the old stipules around the base of the plant are a reddish brown. The flowers are several in terminal clusters on stems 10–12.5 cm (4–5 in.) tall. Seedpods are elliptical with a long bent beak.

*Oxytropis mertensiana* grows in gravel areas in the Brooks Range, the Nome area of the Seward Peninsula, and northeastern Alaska. It also makes a fleeting appearance in the mountains of Denali National Park. A sprawling plant, its leaves with one to three, occasionally five, pointed leaflets are mostly glabrous with hairs around the edge. The one to three purplish, sometimes white, flowers in late June through mid-July are on stems 5–7.5 cm (2–3 in.) tall.

*Oxytropis multiceps* ranges from Utah to Colorado and Wyoming at 1830–2270 m (5950–7375 ft.) and is an early bloomer. A superb caespitose species with gray, woolly foliage, it has short stems with two to three, or occasionally more, bright pink to purple flowers. The flowers are followed by red calyxes that inflate as the seed develops and becomes as furry as every other part of the plant.

*Oxytropis nana* grows from the plains of eastern Wyoming to that state's mountains at around 2275 m (7400 ft.). Its shaggy, silver-gray mats consist of feathery leaves, and clusters of large, light lavender to hot pink or purple flowers bloom in spring to summer. Anne Spiegel comments that it grows well in her lime bed and the large flowers last a long time. Among the easier species to grow, it is a lovely exhibition plant.

*Oxytropis nigrescens* is found in Denali National Park, Alaska, where it grows on rocky alpine ridges and open exposed areas on alpine tundra. It is mat forming with

*Oxytropis lambertii*, Thermopolis, Wyoming.

*Oxytropis multiceps* in cultivation.

short leaves that have many small hairy leaflets. The June flowers are purple to blue, occasionally white, and there are usually two per stem. Seedpods grow to 4 cm (1½ in.) long, lay flat on the ground, and have a short beak and gray-black hairs.

Subspecies *bryophila* grows on Mount Healy, Alaska, and makes tight, furry mats with amethyst flowers and hairy seedpods. Although cultivating this species is straightforward, the problem lies in the flowering because it requires intense light for long periods. Subspecies *pygmaea* grows in northwest Nome, Alaska. It has the smallest foliage and makes tiny tight mats with large purple flowers that lay flat on the foliage. The plant I grew from seed flowered in 2001

*Oxytropis nana* in cultivation.

Close-up of *Oxtropis nana* flower in cultivation.

from June through July, indicating that perhaps it has adjusted well to the climate.

*Oxytropis oreophila* grows in alpine tundra and ridge tops in California, Utah, Nevada, and Arizona at 2255–3785 m (7330–12,300 ft.). Small pinkish mauve flowers grow on 15-cm (6-in.) stems that rise from a tight tuft of green leaves. Although a neat plant, it is not outstanding, and the seedpods are very small. There is very little difference between the type and var. *jonesii* but both are better to add to a collection than to admire as individual plants. If you are an *Oxytropis* enthusiast then this species is another dwarf to try.

*Oxytropis parryi* is more or less a smaller version of *O. oreophila* and occurs in similar habitat.

*Oxytropis podocarpa* is wide-ranging from alpine conditions in Colorado and north to Canada, where it can be subalpine. When the satinlike purple flowers on short ferny pads are over, the bubblelike seedpods that are colored almost mahogany when they are ripe provide a stunning contrast with the ferny pads. *Oxytropis podocarpa* flowers April through May, and Anne Spiegel confirms that it is usually a very early bloomer in the wild above the Colorado tree line. She notes that by early July,

*Oxytropis nigrescens*, Denali National Park, Alaska. Photo Verna Pratt.

the peak flowering time for other plants, *O. podocarpa* is already in pod with only a few flowers left. It is a late snowmelt season, she says, when much of it is in bloom. Anne has also seen a white form. It keeps a dwarf aspect in cultivation if you grow it hard in full sun using a gritty mix.

*Oxytropis scammaniana* grows at about 1230 m (4000 ft.) in the Alaska and Brooks Ranges and the Wrangell–St. Elias Mountains of Alaska. Only 3.8 cm (1½ in.) tall, it has up to three blue-purple flowers on upright stems and short, thick pods. Like *O. nigrescens*, this species needs long daylight hours and intense light for it to flower.

*Oxytropis sericea*, like *O. lambertii*, also inhabits prairies and subalpine meadows in the West, and although not quite so wide-ranging, it is just as poisonous. It grows a little taller than *O. lambertii*—to 50 cm (20 in.)—but is very similar in many respects with many racemes of white to pale yellow and lavender to purple flowers. You will occasionally see large colonies of hybrids between *O. sericea* and *O. lambertii* with flowers ranging from white to pale yellow or purple.

Variety *spicata* grows in British Columbia to Idaho and Wyoming and has flowers of lemon to sulfur yellow.

*Oxytropis splendens* inhabits the open areas of road and river banks and meadows from Alaska to New Mexico to an altitude of 3650 m (11,860 ft.). Among the showiest of all species, it grows 15–25 cm (6–10 in.) tall and is covered with silky white hairs that contrast wonderfully with the bright, deep pink to blue-lavender flowers. No wonder one common name is the showy loco. Leaflets do not lie flat but rather whorl around the stem. According to Weber (1987), it has "leaves with some leaflets in whorls or more than one at a node." This gives rise to another common name, whorled-leaf loco, and makes the species fairly easy to identify.

*Oxytropis viscida* grows at a similar altitude to *O. splendens* in subalpine and alpine meadows, gravel soils, and alpine limestone slopes and screes to 4100 m (13,325 ft.) in California, north to Canada, Nevada, Utah, and Colorado. It is not as tall as *O. splendens* at 10–20 cm (4–8 in.), and cream, blue-violet, or reddish purple flowers bloom in June through August. The dark green, hairy leaves are very sticky, hence the specific name *viscida*, meaning glutinous.

**Propagation**

Seed is the accepted propagation method with *Oxytropis* and, as with *Astragalus*,

*Oxytropis sericea*, Meadow Creek, Colorado.

*Oxytropis sericea*, Dead Indian Hill Summit, Wyoming.

appears to germinate better during cold weather. I have not had to scarify the seed to make it germinate but when I do, more seed germinates. I therefore recommend you scarify the seed of the more rare species. *Oxytropis* seed is generally smaller than *Astragalus* seed so take care.

## Cultivation

All peas have to be pricked out early to avoid root disturbance. If you resist doing this very few seedlings will survive. Once pricked out into individual pots, the seedlings grow on as normal, and you can grow them like this for the first year after germination. During the winter rest period you will see only a tuft of gray-green but it is essential that you give them some moisture during this period or

else they will not survive. As soon as spring arrives and they start into growth you can either pot the plants on if you need them for pot culture or you can plant them out in a trough or gritty alpine bed in a warm site. This is yet another genus that does well in a sand bed.

Unless you take your normal anti-slug precautions, slugs will likely eat much of the plant if it is anywhere outdoors, leaving you with only a small tuft. Aphids can be a problem in the alpine house, but more lethal are red spider mites, which can turn the lovely silver-gray foliage into a horrible, mottled imitation. A systemic insecticide is a must.

# P

## PARONYCHIA
Caryophyllaceae
*nailworts*

Like many growers looking through a seed list I always select a few packets of seed that I have never tried before and that sound unusual. During the winter of 1991 I received seed of *Paronychia pulvinata* from Rocky Mountain Rare Plants. Four plants

*Oxytropis splendens* showing buds. Photo Peter Downe.

*Oxytropis splendens* showing flowers. Photo Peter Downe.

*Oxytropis viscida*, Mount Sherman, Colorado. Photo Jane Grushow.

survived after germination and flowered the following year with strange, yellow-green stemless flowers on a small cushion. Not knowing quite where to plant them I left them in the 7-cm (2¾-in.) pots until they eventually died of neglect. Two years later on a field trip to Loveland Pass in Colorado I renewed my acquaintance with this unusual plant. I happened to glance down and see, tucked up against a rock, a superb cushion plant covered with small yellow-green flowers. I bent down to press it—rock hard! Instantly I recognized *Paronychia pulvinata*. If you love cushion plants or are near Loveland Pass at the end of June, search out this treasure.

*Paronychia pulvinata* (synonym *P. sessiliflora* subsp. *pulvinata*) comes from high altitude to 3690 m (12,000 ft.), and although my seed came from plants growing on Horseshoe Mountain, Colorado, it can also be found on Loveland Pass, Colorado, the Laramie Plains of Wyoming, and on the summits of the northern Big Horn Mountains. It makes a dense cushion of prickle-tipped leaves only 5 cm (2 in.) high and can be smothered with tiny yellow-green flowers when growing well.

**Propagation**
Having only once grown this plant I have had no chance to examine the possibility of

vegetative propagation. Seed, if you can obtain it, is the most obvious way of starting this plant.

**Cultivation**
What can I say, having killed the only plants I ever had? Having looked at its wild habitat, where it is well covered with snow in winter, I can only think that it must be an alpine house plant or at least need complete cover from winter damp. I would recommend growing the plant in a very gritty and spartan soil mixture in full sun to prevent it losing its tight growth. In the wild it appears to be growing in both limestone and granite areas and so you should not worry much about the makeup of the soil or soil mixture. We need more opportunities to grow this gem.

Aphids and red spider mite are problems for plants growing in the alpine house.

# PENSTEMON
Scrophulariaceae
*beardtongues*

Penstemons are wonderful plants whether in their native habitat or in the garden. Like lewisias, penstemons are signature plants of the West, though some species do grow in

Loveland Pass, Colorado.

*Paronychia pulvinata*, Loveland Pass, Colorado.

eastern climes and as far south as Mexico. We must all grow them in one form or another, from the brightly colored hybrids that light up perennial borders in the summer to the smallest alpine species that creep along and hug the ground. With more species and cultivars in the genus than I can possibly discuss (there are nearly 300 species alone), I focus on those I have grown or on those generally classed as alpines. Most can be grown reasonably successfully, including those "special" plants that are prizewinners.

I prefer growing most penstemons in a trough unless otherwise stated.

*Penstemon acaulis* is a dryland plant that comes from localized areas in Utah, Colorado, and Wyoming, where it grows on dry ridge tops at 1500–2200 m (4875–7150 ft.). A tiny species that makes a tufted, almost grasslike mound, it has virtually stemless blue flowers in May through June that nestle in the tufts of leaves. It is certainly the best penstemon I have ever grown, and it does as well in the trough as the alpine house. The one seedling that survived from seed collected in Utah and sown in the autumn of 1991 grew to 12 cm (4¾ in.) across with 25 flowers. It gained an Alpine Garden Society

Certificate of Merit in 1996. In spite of the heavy flowering no seed was set until 1998 after it was hand pollinated. As the seedpods nestle down in the tufts of leaves, you must take great care to extract the seed with tweezers before the seed disappears into the plant. The tufted stems root as they spread, which can be useful when you propagate this species.

Subspecies *yampaensis* comes from Utah and Colorado at 1780–2120 m (5785–6890 ft.), and although the leaves are slightly larger at the eastern end of its distribution, it is the smallest plant in the genus with tiny tufts 2.5–5 cm (1–2 in.) high. The flowers are blue to pink, and it grows well in both trough and alpine house.

*Penstemon alamosensis* in cultivation.

*Penstemon acaulis*, north-central Utah. Photo David Hale.

*Penstemon alamosensis* comes from the rocky limestone ridges in the mountains of New Mexico and Texas and has a long flowering season. A beautiful species that grows to 70 cm (28 in.) tall with lovely red tubular flowers, it prefers the rock garden.

*Penstemon aridus* comes from the dry, open, rocky hills and slopes of Wyoming at 2090–3500 m (6800–11,375 ft.), and from southwest Montana and southeast Idaho. Variable in height—5–20 cm (2–8 in.)—this species is easy to grow, the spires of bright blue that rise from a basal rosette lasting well in the wet weather.

*Penstemon barbatus* grows over a wide area from southern Utah and Colorado to northern Mexico, from the rim of the Grand Canyon to the roadsides among grass and scrub. It is variable in height from 30 cm

*Penstemon barbatus.*

(12 in.) at 3075 m (10,000 ft.) in the mountains of New Mexico to around 90 cm (36 in.) on the roadsides at lower elevation. Although not a compact penstemon, it does have attractive blooms of long red tubes and yellow hairs in the throat. It makes a very good addition to the rear of a large hot rock garden or a perennial border. A species that has been used to great effect in hybridization, it produces among others the unusual 'Schooley's Yellow', a lemon-yellow flowering form.

*Penstemon caespitosus* grows among sagebrush in Arizona, Colorado, Wyoming, and Utah. Once when I was driving north through Wyoming I saw a stretch of about 300 m (975 ft.) of disturbed soil at the edge of a new road that was blue with large mats of this species. (I do not know if it was an intentional planting by the authorities or natural colonization.) Flat mats can spread to 60–90 cm (24–36 in.) across, rooting from the nodes as it grows, and deep blue 1-cm (½-in.) wide flowers that are white inside can cover the mat. It is an easy species for a trough, though you may need to make judicious use of the scissors to keep it under control.

Variety *desertipicti* from Utah and Arizona is a really choice variation with a

Close-up of *Penstemon barbatus.*

*Penstemon caespitosus* in roadside habitat, Wyoming.

small mat of woody stems that are covered with tiny gray-green leaves and 1-cm (½-in.) wide clear blue flowers. A dryland plant, it is more challenging than the type but well worth the effort in both a trough or alpine house. *Penstemon caespitosus* 'Albus' has smaller leaves and is more difficult to flower.

*Penstemon californicus* inhabits the mountains of San Diego county in California. This beautiful but rare species has small gray-green oblanceolate leaves that are almost hebelike. The stems grow to 15 cm (6 in.) and spread to 20 cm (8 in.). Small blue-purple flowers bloom May through July, and although it tends to collapse without warning, it is well worth trying in a trough.

*Penstemon cardwellii* grows on open or wooded summits and slopes in southwest Oregon and into the western Cascades and Coast Range. This shrubby species grows to 60 cm (24 in.) with thick leathery leaves and bright purple to blue violet flowers. I remember seeing thousands of these beautiful penstemons recolonizing the barren pumice of Windy Ridge on Mount St. Helens, Washington, the seed either having been blown there or dropped by birds. This species does best in a rock garden.

'Floyd McMullen' is a lovely dwarf cultivar growing just 7 cm (2¾ in.) tall with small, dark green leaves and purple flowers; I cannot keep it alive for more than two years as it rots off so easily during the wet winter.

'Roseus' is a superb dwarf cultivar that grows well in partial shade in a rock garden or trough and has bright pink flowers; it comes through year after year in spite of the winter wet.

*Penstemon caespitosus*, Wyoming.

*Penstemon caespitosus* var. *desertipicti* in cultivation.

*Penstemon cardwellii* recolonizing Mount St. Helens, Washington.

Close-up of *Penstemon cardwellii*, Mount St. Helens, Washington.

*Penstemon centranthifolius* from the foothills of southern California attracts hummingbirds to the huge red tubular flowers on stems 152 cm (60 in.) tall. Although quite tall it is spectacular enough to include in a rock garden. It needs a sunny, well-drained spot and protection for the basal rosette during winter.

*Penstemon confertus* grows in open grassy meadows or along streams in Montana, Oregon, and the Wenatchee Mountains of Washington where it is fairly moist. Yellow flowers make a pleasant change from the usual blues, purples, and pinks. Although it can grow to 50 cm (24 in.), seed in the commercial lists is usually from shorter forms that grow 20–30 cm (8–12 in.) tall from a basal

clump of leaves. Similar in habit to *P. procerus*, it has been fairly amenable in my rock garden and has lasted for several years.

*Penstemon crandallii* is a xeric species from Colorado, Utah, and New Mexico growing at 1800–3000 m (5850–9750 ft.). It probably survives in my rock garden because it grows in a sunny spot on a raised bed that has deep drainage. A large flowering species, it sprawls over the edge of the bed, which makes a spectacular sight in summer. Woody stems grow to 20 cm (8 in.) tall with gray-green glabrous leaves and large bright blue or light blue flowers.

Subspecies *glabrescens* grows to 30 cm (12 in.) and has more linear leaves. It also does well in the rock garden.

*Penstemon davidsonii* grows in the Sierra Nevada and north to Oregon and Washington at high elevations. It makes mats with the flowering stems growing to 15 cm (6 in.), has tiny leaves, and flowers that are large for the size of the plant.

Variety *davidsonii* makes dense mats of creeping stems that root as they grow and have small leaves. Blue-lavender to purple-violet flowers, which bloom in June through August, are 2.5–3.5 cm (1–1⅗ in.) long. I have seen it on the rim drive of Crater Lake in Oregon, where it flowers much better

*Penstemon centranthifolius*, Cottonwood Canyon, California. Photo Chris Norton.

*Penstemon confertus* in cultivation.

than it does for me though I still consider it one of my favorite trough plants.

Variety *davidsonii* 'Mt. Adams Dwarf' is a Mt. Tahoma Nursery introduction. Flat, congested mats are only 2.5 cm (1 in.) high with tiny round foliage and 1.2-cm (½-in.) long lavender flowers on very short stems.

Variety *menziesii* grows northwards from Mount Rainier, is smaller than the type, and has toothed leaves; variety *menziesii* 'Microphyllus' is an older but still worthy horticultural selection; variety *menziesii* 'Pink' from the Cascades grows to 5 cm (2 in.) and has huge, soft pink flowers; variety *menziesii* 'Rampart White', also from the Cascades, is a very choice, white-flowering selection by Carla Lankow of Renton, Washington; variety *menziesii* 'Serpyllifolius'

is also an older cultivar but worth growing; and variety *menziesii* 'Tolmiei Peak', an excellent introduction by Don King of Seattle, is 5 cm (2 in.) tall with lavender flowers.

Variety *praeteritus* is a beautiful variety from the Steens Mountains of Oregon. It grows to 15 cm (6 in.) high with huge lavender flowers and tiny leaves that make it look like a dwarf hebe. If you grow it from seed the height will vary so you will have to select the true dwarf specimens.

***Penstemon duchesnensis*** is endemic to Duchesne county, Utah, at 1640–2090 m (5330–6800 ft.). It is quite dwarf with stems 10 cm (4 in.) tall and blue-violet flowers. Although in the wild it grows under extreme conditions in barren, shaley limestone

Crater Lake, Oregon.

*Penstemon davidsonii* var. *menziesii*, Olympic National Park, Washington. Photo David Hale.

*Penstemon davidsonii* var. *davidsonii* at the edge of Crater Lake, Oregon.

*Penstemon davidsonii* var. *praeteritus* in cultivation.

ridges, it makes a lovely pot plant for exhibition if you grow it with care in the alpine house. It also grows well in a trough. This xeric species is not very well known but look out for it in seed lists.

*Penstemon eatonii* has a range similar to *P. barbatus* but it also extends into Nevada and California. A striking species, it can rival *P. barbatus* for its deep red tubular flowers on stems 35–100 cm (14–39 in.) tall that rise from rosettes of green leaves 8 cm (3 in.) long. It seems to like dryer conditions than most penstemons and does well in a rock garden, although it is probably short-lived.

*Penstemon eriantherus* grows from North Dakota to Colorado, British Columbia, Washington, Idaho, Montana, and Oregon in dry open spaces on plains, valleys, and steppes, though it occasionally ascends to moderate elevations. Typical subspecies have stems 15–30 cm (6–12 in.) tall that bear leaves 6–7 cm (2¼–2¾ in.) long, and large lavender to blue flowers with densely bearded throats. The hairy anthers live up to the specific name, *eriantherus*, which means woolly anthered. The stems and leaves are also extremely hairy. One specimen I grew had smooth blue-green leaves and smaller flowers, but the leaves were continually marked with tiny brown blotches that spoiled the plant. The plant I now grow has hairy leaves and makes a good exhibition plant. Be aware that the fine hairs on the leaves tend to catch tiny flies so cleaning up the leaves in preparation for a show can be time consuming.

Subspecies *whitedii* comes from Washington and has striking violet-purple

*Penstemon duchesnensis* in cultivation.

*Penstemon eriantherus* in cultivation.

Close-up of *Penstemon eriantherus* flowers.

2.5–5-cm (1–2-in.) long flowers with densely bearded yellow throats. Flowers are in whorls that are closely spaced into a 10–15-cm (4–6-in.) inflorescence on stems 22–30 cm (8¾–12 in.) tall. A showy penstemon, it too grows well in a xeric garden, trough, and alpine house.

*Penstemon fremontii* is a fairly local plant restricted to the Uinta Plains of Utah, southwest Wyoming, and northwest Colorado. It is beautiful for the glistening hairy stems alone, but the light to deep blue or pink to rich purple spires of bloom on stems 10–30 cm (4–12 in.) tall make it outstanding.

*Penstemon fruticosus* is an easy subshrub from Montana, Wyoming, Idaho, Washington, and Oregon with 30–40-cm (12–15¾-in.) tall stems and blue-lavender to light purple flowers. Anyone new to penstemons and unsure of which species to grow can do no better than to start with *P. fruticosus* or one of its varieties, all of which grow well in a rock garden.

Variety *scouleri* from Washington and northern Idaho is the variety usually seen in cultivation with its toothed leaves and large 5-cm (2-in.) flowers; variety *scouleri* 'Albus' or 'Alba' has white flowers of similar size to var. scouleri and can withstand all winter conditions in Timsbury.

Variety *serratus* from Washington is attractive with serrate or dentate leaves; 'Holly' is a fine cultivar of this variety, making lovely evergreen mounds with bright flowers.

*Penstemon gairdneri* thrives in its natural habit at 1000–1600 m (3250–5200 ft.) on dry open rocky slopes in Oregon, Idaho, and Washington. It makes loose mats of linear, ash-textured leaves on stems 10–40 cm (4–15¾ in.) tall. The early summer flowers are blue-purple or lavender to rose-purple in dense racemes. Among the more challenging species, it nevertheless grows quite well in pots in the alpine house, probably because watering can be controlled. When it is dormant it looks dead

*Penstemon fruticosus* var. *scouleri* 'Albus' in cultivation.

*Penstemon grahamii* in cultivation.

and needs very little water. Depending on the climate, *P. gairdneri* will do well in the xeric garden.

*Penstemon grahamii* grows only in the oil-bearing shales of the Green River Formation of the Uinta Basin, Utah, at 1400–2060 m (4550–6700 ft.). This beautiful species has stems 5–20 cm (2–8 in.) tall and large upward-facing flowers of pale to deep lavender-pink. Densely bearded staminodes are colored old gold and curled downwards at the tip. The upward facing flower reminds one of fledglings opening their mouths for food. Although the Alpine Garden Society (1993) notes that this species grows on "oil shale deposits that sometimes ooze petroleum around the plants," it is not impossible to grow *P. grahamii* away from its habitat as it does

exceedingly well as a trough or an alpine house plant.

This species is among the stars of my penstemon collection and I have to thank the botanist Edward Graham for discovering the species. *Penstemon grahamii* not only adorns the cover of the *Uinta Basin Flora* (1986) but is also the logo of my nursery.

*Penstemon hallii*, despite coming from an alpine habitat of 3500–4500 m (11,375–14,625 ft.) in Colorado, grows equally well in the rock garden, trough, or alpine house. It forms mats with stems to 15 cm (6 in.) tall that, together with the large violet-blue trumpets in early summer, place it among the classics in the penstemon world. During winter dormancy it looks dead and is very late coming into growth the following spring. You can best admire those beautiful early summer blooms in the alpine house, where they are untouched by rain and wind. Seed is set freely and germinates well.

*Penstemon heterodoxus* grows in the alpine fell-fields of California at 2200–3815 m (7150–12,400 ft.), often around melting snowbanks. Its mats compare with the best attributes of the compact mats of *P. procerus* var. *tolmiei*, and the large, dark blue-purple flowers in dense whorls are like those of *P. rydbergii*. This variable species has stems 5–20 cm (2–8 in.) tall but plants I have

Flower stem of *Penstemon grahamii* in cultivation.

*Penstemon hallii* in cultivation.

grown from seed collected at higher elevations remain more compact.

*Penstemon heterophyllus* grows on rocky slopes at about 1650 m (5365 ft.) from the Sierra Nevada to the Siskiyou Mountains of Oregon. Clusters of stems grow 20–120 cm (8–48 in.) tall from a woody base, and striking yellow buds open to blooms of soft lavender blue, dark blue-purple, or red-violet. Jim Archibald (1989–1990) quotes Reginald Farrer as rating it "one of the loveliest of all penstemons."

'Blue Bedder', 'Heavenly Blue', and 'True Blue' are three lovely cultivars selected from this species that grow 20–40 cm (8–15¾ in.) tall. Like *Penstemon heterophyllus*, they grow well in the rock garden.

*Penstemon humilis* grows in dry, rocky places from the plains to high elevations on the Cascade–Sierra Crest and the Intermountain region. A variable species, it reaches 10–60 cm (4–24 in.) tall, and hairy, blue-purple flowers bloom in May through August. Among the most beautiful miniature penstemons with deep blue flowers almost 2 cm (¾ in.) long, it is both a rock garden and trough plant in its dwarf form.

Subspecies *brevifolius* is endemic to the Wasatch Range of Utah at 1765–3390 m (5735–11,020 ft.). It reaches 10 cm (4 in.) in height and has azure-blue flowers. Subspecies *obtusifolius* grows at 1580–2450 m (5135–7965 ft.) in the southeast corner of Utah.

*Penstemon jamesii* occurs in southeast Colorado and New Mexico at approximately 1990 m (6470 ft.) and is a xeric species that does well in the rock garden and trough. It grows 10–45 cm (4–18 in.) tall and has plump lilac to pink flowers. Gwen Kelaidis (1993) described it best: a "super giant flowered penstemon with a gaping mouth and lolling tongue."

*Penstemon janishiae* is a dryland species from California, Idaho, Nevada, and Oregon, where it grows at an altitude of 1300–2250 m (4225–7310 ft.). It looks like a smaller version of *P. grahamii* with a large gaping mouth, lavender-pink flowers in May through June, and fuzzy yellow tongues. Stems 8–20 cm (3–8 in.) tall grow from a basal rosette, and seed germinates quite freely. It is a good exhibition plant for the alpine house and grows well in the trough or xeric garden.

*Penstemon kunthii* originates from the State of Durango in Mexico, where it grows at 2,000–2770 m (6500–9000 ft.). Sally Walker of Southwestern Native Seeds introduced this worthy species into cultivation in

*Penstemon heterodoxus*, Winnemucca Lake, California. Photo Chris Norton.

*Penstemon janishiae* in cultivation.

1992. Stems of 20–40 cm (8–15¾ in.) grow from a central rootstock with 2.5-cm (1-in.) long scarlet flowers that are an unusual funnel shape, reminding me of a larger *Gilia caespitosa*. Although plants in my rock garden last only two years (other nurseries assure me that it is more hardy and long-lasting than that), they do set plenty of seed, and since seedlings grow quickly there are always more plants available. One reference I consulted gives the maximum height of this species as 120 cm (48 in.), but none of the plants I have grown from seed have reached that height.

*Penstemon laricifolius* is from Wyoming and Montana at an altitude of 1845–2155 m (6000–7000 ft.) in rocky hills and sandstone ridges. It has tufted, grasslike foliage with stems 15–20 cm (6–8 in.) tall and delicate, almost crystalline, pink or purple flowers, making it suitable for the front of a xeric alpine bed. While hiking in the Pryor Mountains of Montana some years ago I saw this species for the first time and was smitten by its beauty.

Subspecies *exilifolius* grows also in Colorado at the same altitude and in the same habitat, but its flowers in May through July are white.

*Penstemon leiophyllus* grows at 2970–3400 m (9650–11,050 ft.) in southwest Utah and Nevada, where it inhabits south-facing gravel slopes. This species is remarkably tolerant in my scree garden and has several 45–60-cm (18–24-in.) stems and dense, one-sided racemes of dark blue flowers with a paler throat. The plants grow quite fast from seed once they are planted out.

Variety *francisci-pennellii* grows on open stony slopes at 3400 m (11,050 ft.) in the Snake Range of Nevada, yet it does well in my garden. Often listed as *Penstemon francisci-pennellii*, it is much smaller than the type, making it more suitable for trough work. Huge, 5-cm (2-in.) long trumpets on stems just 5 cm (2 in.) tall bloom in June through August. It looks a bit sick in winter but growth starts again in spring, and as the stems layer themselves, the plant is fairly easy to propagate vegetatively.

*Penstemon leiophyllus.*

*Penstemon laricifolius*, Pryor Mountains, Montana.

*Penstemon leiophyllus* var. *francisci-pennellii* in cultivation.

*Penstemon linarioides* is a small sub-shrub that grows on the plateaus of Utah, Nevada, Arizona, Colorado, and New Mexico. It is quite variable in height—10–50 cm (4–20 in.)—and has linear bluish leaves with blue to violet-blue flowers. The specimens grown from most commercial seed usually stay under 30 cm (12 in.) and do well in the rock garden or trough.

Subspecies *coloradoensis* grows on the plains and foothills of Colorado and northwest New Mexico. At 10–16 cm (4–6¼ in.) tall with blue glaucous foliage and lavender flowers, it is much more desirable. It requires xeric conditions so is well suited to a scree bed or trough. Subspecies *compactifolius* from Arizona makes green-gray mats to 10 cm (4 in.) high. Subspecies *sileri* from Utah, Nevada, and Arizona grows to 30 cm (12 in.); it has very silvery leaves.

*Penstemon nanus* is an extremely rare species and endemic to southwest Utah, where its habitat is limestone gravel at 1580–2140 m (5135–6955 ft.). It grows 2.5–15 cm (1–6 in.) high with gray, felty stems and leaves. Although the usual flower color is blue-violet, white and pink forms have been reported growing there. It does best in the trough or alpine house.

*Penstemon newberryi* fills California's cracks and crevices at an altitude of 2000–3500 m (6500–11,375 ft.). It is a wonderful sight in Yosemite National Park on the road to Olmsted Point and throughout the high Sierra, where it lines the sides of the road, adding vivid color to the rocks. It also grows on the acid screes of Mount Shasta, California, and the Carson Range of Nevada. A sub-shrub that forms clumps 15–60 cm (6–24 in.) tall, it has spectacular tubular flowers of rose-red to rose-purple almost 3 cm (1¼ in.) long. If you are looking for a quieter color, however, go for the white form 'Albus'. Occasionally a commercial seed list offers seed of a very compact form that is 10 cm (4 in.) high with intense rose-red to deep rose-violet flowers.

Variety *berryi* from the Trinity Alps and the Siskiyou Mountains in California is magenta-flowered and grows to 15 cm (6 in.). It prefers the rock garden. Variety *sonomensis* inhabits exposed, rocky ridge tops of California's Coast Ranges and is worth obtaining from a seed list as it is the most compact variety. A hardy plant that grows well in the rock garden, it has small, glaucous, blue-green leaves and deep carmine-pink flowers.

Olmsted Point, Yosemite National Park, California.

*Penstemon newberryi*, Yosemite National Park, California.

The cultivar 'Red Lassen' has cherry-red flowers and also does well in the rock garden.

*Penstemon nitidus* comes from open grassy hillsides and plains of Montana, Idaho, Wyoming, and North Dakota. It grows to 15–20 cm (6–8 in.) tall and blooms in March through April with spikes of brilliant aquamarine blue. The earliest species to flower, it may bloom even earlier than March if you have favorable weather as it did once in my garden. It also makes a superb pot plant but does not like a lot of moisture whether as a trough plant or in the alpine house. If you are looking for a penstemon for the early shows, this is it.

*Penstemon ophianthus* grows in Colorado, New Mexico, Arizona, and Utah at 1500–2250 m (4875–7310 ft.). Stems 15–30 cm (6–12 in.) tall have sticky, narrow basal leaves with hairy, bulging, pale lavender to violet or blue-violet flowers that are 2.5 cm (1 in.) long. Although seldom seen, it is a good dryland species that is worth trying in the xeric bed or rock garden.

*Penstemon ovatus* grows in the open woods of Washington and Oregon at an elevation to 1500 m (4875 ft.). A fairly easy species for the rock garden, it can grow to 30–100 cm (12–39 in.). Flowers are blue

*Penstemon ophianthus.*

and quite large at over 2 cm (¾ in.) long. There are dwarf forms with deep blue flowers that are perfect for a trough.

*Penstemon parvulus* from Oregon and the mountains of California makes a creeping, woody mat with stems 20–60 cm (8–24 in.) tall. Azure-blue flowers 2–3 cm (¾–1¼ in.) long grow in dense racemes during June through August. This species does not do well in a pot so grow it instead in a trough or rock garden.

*Penstemon paysoniorum* is endemic to Wyoming, where it grows on alkaline shale bluffs, desert plains, and dry sagebrush hills at 2000–2300 m (6500–7475 ft.). An attractive, shrubby penstemon with shiny green foliage, the stems are 10–15 cm (4–6 in.) tall and topped with dark blue to blue-purple flowers. Although it is another species for the xeric rock garden, it grows equally well in a trough.

*Penstemon petiolatus* is from the arid limestone ranges of Utah and Nevada at 1000–1700 m (3250–5525 ft.). It forms a small shrub 10–20 cm (4–8 in.) tall and to 50 cm (20 in.) across. Violet to deep pink flowers grow in panicles. Whether it is cultivated in the trough or alpine house it can worry the grower because it looks like a bunch of dead twigs during winter. If you can grow this delightful species then you deserve all the pleasure you get from it.

*Penstemon pinifolius* grows in New Mexico and Arizona from where Dr. Worth first collected seed, and plants that Mrs. Cicely Crewdson grew from that seed in the early 1950s were the first to be cultivated in Britain. Now a very popular penstemon, it is always available at garden centers. A many-stemmed evergreen shrub 15–40 cm (6–15¾ in.) high, it has bright green needle-like leaves and red-orange flowers

3–4 cm (1¼–1½ in.) long from early summer into autumn. Even out of flower it is still attractive, making excellent ground cover in a rock garden.

'Mersea Yellow' is an outstanding cultivar that is as easy to grow as the type. In approximately 1979–80, Mr. J. Jowers of West Mersea in the United Kingdom noticed a sporting shoot on his type plant that had yellow flowers on an otherwise normal red-flowered plant. After he propagated it and grew it on successfully, the plant was increased commercially and given the cultivar name 'Mersea Yellow'. In June 1987 it received the Alpine Garden Society Award of Merit. Although it sets viable seed I have not heard of yellow plants being raised from it, though of course they may have been.

*Penstemon pinifolius* of either red or yellow is a showy specimen for the rock garden that you can plant and forget; even in wet cold winters and very humid summers this species is almost impossible to kill, which is surprising given its native habitat.

*Penstemon procerus* is wide-ranging throughout the West but most of those growing in rock gardens are on the short side and are usually varieties. An extremely variable species with fairly small flowers and stems 5–40 cm (2–15¾ in.) tall, it can also be grown in the trough. A very easy species to grow, I think that of all the penstemons growing in my garden, varieties of *P. procerus* crop up more than any other.

Variety *brachyanthus* grows in the Cascades from northern California to Washington. Stems to 30 cm (12 in.) tall have well-developed basal leaves and blue-purple flowers. Variety *formosus* from the mountains of Oregon, California, and Nevada is among the most popular dwarf varieties growing 5–12.5 cm (2–5 in.) tall. At its best the dwarf mat has densely packed leaves and small, dark blue flowers. It is an ideal variety for the beginner as it grows in any type of soil.

Variety *tolmiei* from the Olympics and Cascades of Washington grows 5–15 cm (2–6 in.) tall with flowers that vary in color from blue to violet, yellow, and yellow-purple depending on habitat; variety *tolmiei* 'Alba' is 9 cm (3 1/2 in.) tall and has fragrant white flowers with a slight yellow tinge; variety *tolmiei* 'Hawkeye' comes from the Goat Rocks area of Washington at 2245 m (7300 ft.) and was introduced into cultivation in 1995 by Rick Lupp; growing to

*Penstemon pinifolius* 'Mersea Yellow' in cultivation.

*Penstemon procerus*, Mount St. Helens, Washington.

10 cm (4 in.) tall, it has creamy white flowers infused with violet and a very sweet fragrance. Bob Nold (1999) lists it as *Penstemon procerus* var. *tolmiei* 'Alpenglow', which was the original name before it was discovered that the cultivar name 'Alpenglow' was already in use.

'Roy Davidson' is surely the most popular garden cultivar of this species. Stems grow to 15 cm (6 in.) tall from very neat mats, and buds with a reddish tinge open to a soft pink with a white interior.

*Penstemon procumbens* from Colorado is a mat-forming species to 2 cm (¾ in.) with purple-blue flowers. It quickly forms a mat to 90 cm (36 in.) across or trails over the side of a trough, the stems rooting as they go. *Penstemon procumbens* 'Claude Barr', a good cultivar (it was originally named *P. caespitosus* 'Claude Barr'), has larger flowers.

*Penstemon pruinosus* is a lovely species from the eastern section of the Cascades. Plants on the dry rocky slopes of central Washington at the lower elevations of 600–650 m (1950–2110 ft.) are suitable for the rock garden with stems 30–45 cm (12–18 in.) tall and dark blue flowers. Those growing in colonies among the scree slopes at around 1950 m (6340 ft.) have stems only 15 cm (6 in.) tall and flowers from a deep bright blue to electric and powder blue. This summer-flowering dwarf form is excellent

*Penstemon procerus* var. *brachyanthus*, Bohemia Mountain, Oregon.

*Penstemon procerus* var. *tolmiei*, Burnt Mountain, eastern Cascades, Washington.

*Penstemon procerus* var. *formosus* in cultivation.

*Penstemon procerus* var. *tolmiei* 'Alba' in cultivation.

for a trough, and seed has been available from commercial lists for several years now.

*Penstemon purpusii* grows on the dry stony slopes of California's Coast Ranges at 1750–2650 m (5690–8610 ft.) but is surprisingly adaptable to garden cultivation. Although compact and mat forming, it tends to be too robust for troughs but does well in a rock garden. The flowers are probably the deepest purple of all penstemons. The woody stems have finely haired, ash-gray leaves that are edged with purple and 2.5-cm (1-in.) long, deep purple flowers. If you grow this species from seed you may be able to select forms that are not so vigorous.

*Penstemon richardsonii* grows in cliff crevices in Oregon and Washington. At

A dead pine at the summit of Bohemia Mountain, Oregon.

20–80 cm (8–32 in.) tall, the 2.5-cm (1-in.) long, bright red-violet flowers cheer up any dull spot in the rock garden throughout the summer and early autumn. An easy species for the garden, the taller forms will lean out from the pockets of soil when you plant them on ledges that imitate their native habitat. It looks dead in winter but grows again from the basal root stock in spring. Take care in choosing a planting location as the tall stems are quite brittle and tend to break off in high winds.

*Penstemon rupicola* grows from Washington to northern California on cliffs and rocky ledges. A sub-shrub, it makes dense clumps with stems to 10 cm (4 in.) tall and flowers that range in color from pink to pink-lavender, rose-purple, and near red. Those I saw growing on Bohemia Mountain, Oregon, in 1998, particularly the plants on the plateau alongside choice specimens such as *Calochortus subalpinus*, *Saxifraga bronchialis* var. *vespertina*, and *Silene campanulata*, took my breath away. *Penstemon rupicola* grew there in profusion, and a hybrid *P. rupicola* × *P. cardwellii* was hanging from a crack in the rocks.

If you can find a cool crevice in your rock garden for this species you are likely to succeed with it, but be warned that many

*Penstemon rupicola* at the top of Bohemia Mountain, Oregon.

plans in cultivation purporting to be *P. rupi-cola* do not have the vibrant colors that they should. Try to buy it in flower if possible or from a reputable nurseryman.

Four cultivars are noteworthy. 'Alba' from the Goat Rocks area in Washington forms mats to 12.5 cm (5 in.) tall and white flowers bloom during spring and summer. I have grown this cultivar in the alpine garden in full sun, and although it flowers well, there is always a great deal of dieback in autumn. It is best suited to the rock garden or trough.

'Diamond Lake' is robust with 3.8-cm (1½-in.) long pink flowers. 'Myrtle Hebert', a beautiful little penstemon that produces dark pink blooms and suffers practically no winter dieback, grows to only 5 cm (2 in.). 'Pink Dragon' has salmon-pink flowers and grows to 20 cm (8 in.).

***Penstemon rydbergii*** grows from Montana and Wyoming to New Mexico, Utah, California, and Washington. It is ubiquitous during summer in the West; I have seen it in meadows, moist open slopes, and occasionally in drier areas. As variable in height (from 20 to 70 cm [8 to 28 in.]) as it is in range, this species has blue-purple flowers in several dense clusters. It grows easily in a rock garden.

***Penstemon secundiflorus*** ranges from southern Wyoming to northern New Mexico and Arizona on gravel or rocky slopes to wooded areas at 1750–3300 m (5690–10,725 ft.). Glabrous stems grow 10–40 cm (4–15¾ in.) tall and have reddish purple to lavender-pink flowers. It grows best in a xeric garden. A dwarf form with red-violet flowers occurs in South Park, Colorado.

***Penstemon serrulatus*** comes from Oregon and Washington. Its habitat includes moist, wet areas and roadside gravel soils, making it easy to grow in the rock garden. Like *P. rydbergii*, it is variable in height—20–70 cm (8–28 in.)—and the reddish violet to deep blue flowers in June

*Penstemon secundiflorus*, Jacob Lake, Arizona. Photo Chris Norton.

*Penstemon rupicola*, Bohemia Mountain, Oregon.

through July are in terminal clusters. This species does not mind some shade.

*Penstemon speciosus* grows in dry, open, sometimes partially wooded slopes at 1200–3300 m (3900–10,725 ft.) in Washington, Oregon, California, Nevada, Utah, and southern Idaho. An attractive species for the rock garden, its bright blue flowers bloom in May through July on stems 20–90 cm (8–36 in.) tall.

Subspecies *kennedyi* has a much smaller range, growing at 3130–3600 m (10,175–11,700 ft.) in the Sierra Nevada and White Mountains of California on rocky volcanic slopes and open summit ridges of gritty granitic soils. Its name is one commonly given to dwarf specimens, and

although not all references recognize it as a separate subspecies, perhaps they should since it remains dwarf in cultivation. It grows to 12.5 cm (5 in.) with a basal cluster of leaves and decumbent racemes of large, deep blue flowers and it prefers the alpine house or trough.

*Penstemon teucrioides* grows in Colorado at 2500–3500 m (8125–11,375 ft.) on dry clay, rocky, or sandy loam soils. Although it has a central woody rootstock, some stems creep out to form a gray-green mat of linear leaves 5 cm (2 in.) high. Bright blue to blue-purple trumpetlike flowers bloom in July. Some forms have smaller flowers and finer, silver leaves.

*Penstemon thompsoniae* comes from the hot drylands of the Mojave Desert in Nevada, Utah, and Arizona, where it grows at 1500–2000 m (4875–6500 ft.). A tufted, shrubby, mat-forming species, it grows to 10 cm (4 in.) with racemes of blue to blue-purple or violet flowers from early summer. Although I recommend growing this species in the trough and alpine house, you could also grow it in the xeric garden.

*Penstemon tracyi* in northwest California at about 2090 m (6800 ft.) is a rare shrubby species with leathery leaves that grows to 12.5 cm (5 in.) with several

Close-up of *Penstemon secundiflorus*. Photo Chris Norton.

*Penstemon speciosus* subsp. *kennedyi*, White Mountains, California.

racemes of tiny pink tubular flowers. Jim Archibald (1989–1990) described it as "An extremely narrow endemic, unlike anything else in the genus, stranded on one or two mountains in the Trinity Alps of northwest California at about 2090 m (6800 ft.)." The plants I grew from seed took three years to flower, needed more moisture than any other penstemon I grow, and preferred partial shade. I was greatly disappointed when it bloomed; the large leaves dwarfed the small flowers, and the color was very wishy-washy. It does best in a scree or rock garden.

*Penstemon uintahensis* is a lovely little endemic from the Uinta Mountains of Utah, where it grows on rocky ridges at an elevation of 3000–3700 m (9750–12,025 ft.). Several slender, erect stems rise 10–15 cm (4–6 in.) from a clump of basal leaves and bear short, stubby, racemelike clusters of violet to sky blue flowers 2.5 cm (1 in.) long. Although this species is rarely seen, it is worth growing in a trough or alpine house if you can obtain the seed. It makes a nice exhibition plant blooming April through May in cultivation and later in the wild.

*Penstemon utahensis* grows in the dryland of California's Mojave Desert, Nevada, Utah, and Arizona at an elevation of 1200–2000 m (3900–6500 ft.). It grows 15–60 cm (6–24 in.) tall, and like *P. eatonii* has quite large red to crimson flowers in April through June. Often confused with the similar sounding *P. uintahensis*, the wrongly named photograph of *P. utahensis* that appears as plate 28 in *A Century of Alpines* (1991) has confused the issue even more. This species has no real similarity with *P. uintahensis* apart from its name. *Penstemon utahensis* is a fine species for the xeric rock garden.

*Penstemon venustus* is from the rocky slopes and foothills of Idaho, Oregon, and Washington. Large, showy, lavender to purple flowers in terminal panicles on stems 30–80 cm (12–32 in.) tall grow from a woody base. It flowers late—in July through

*Penstemon utahensis*, north of Moab, Utah. Photo Chris Norton.

*Penstemon uintahensis* in cultivation.

October—and brightens up the rear of any alpine bed or rock garden.

*Penstemon virens* is from the rocky slopes of granite grit at 1850–3500 m (6010–11,375 ft.) in Colorado and Wyoming. From glossy evergreen mats grow several stiff stems 15–25 cm (6–10 in.) tall with flowers of deep to pale blue-violet in June through August. Although it may grow in xeric conditions in the wild it does not require this culture in the rock garden and makes the transition from the wild with ease. A useful plant for any position, it is among the easiest of all penstemons to grow, and you will usually find it on plant-sales tables priced very cheaply.

*Penstemon washingtonensis* grows in the dry gravel slopes and flats of the Chelan Mountains in Washington. Very similar in appearance to *P. procerus*, it has shiny green leaves 5 cm (2 in.) long growing in rosettes that form loose mats. Stems 10–25 cm (4–10 in.) tall have deep blue flowers in May through July in dense whorls. This species has been described as rare and unknown in cultivation, but once you acquire the seed (it is offered fairly regularly) you will never be without it. As well as growing in the rock garden or trough, it seeds itself around and, in my case, pops up in other pots.

*Penstemon whippleanus* is widespread throughout the West in dry meadows and open rocky slopes, sometimes to timberline. It grows to 60 cm (24 in.) with elliptic to ovate leaves and beautiful flowers that range from cream to violet to dark purple or plum

*Penstemon virens*, Colorado.

Flower of *Penstemon whippleanus*. Photo Chris Norton.

*Penstemon whippleanus*, San Juan Mountains, Colorado. Photo Chris Norton.

colored. It is an easy species for the rock garden.

*Penstemon* 'Six Hills Hybrid', a cross between *P. davidsonii* and *P. eriantherus*, is a rock garden hybrid that originated in Six Hills Nursery. Among the best dwarf selections, this easygoing sub-shrub grows to 15 cm (6 in.) tall with pale mauve, two-lipped flowers.

## Propagation

Without a doubt the best and most common method of propagation is by seed, especially with the upright-growing species such as *Penstemon eriantherus*, *P. grahamii*, or *P. janishiae*. Since penstemons hybridize quite freely, especially with others in the same section or subsection, do not be surprised if something unusual crops up after you sow your own garden-collected seed. You should be able to depend on commercial seed though, especially if it is wild collected, as the owners of that seed have a reputation to preserve.

If you are collecting your own seed for the first time you may be surprised to find that it is not like the regular round or flat seed of other genera. The American Penstemon Society's *Penstemon Field Identifier* has described penstemon seed rather exotically with words such as a "blackberry in a bottle," "helmet," "marble in a net bag," or "banana." The word I would use is "irregular," and it is this idiosyncrasy that makes it slightly more difficult to identify the seed if you also have a lot of dried, blackened seed capsules in your envelope.

Penstemon seed appears to increase in viability with age, so if you have a large amount of seed set one year, you should keep some in case you have a crop failure the following year. In 1994 I was given a large packet of seed of one particular species and every year since I have sown a few; each time germination has been successful.

You should sow seed in autumn and put the seed pots on the staging outside to take whatever the weather throws at them, which gives the seeds time to stratify. Germination usually takes place in spring, but if you fail to sow the seed before the end of January, do not be surprised if germination is delayed a year. Germination is usually spasmodic anyway, so prick out seedlings with care and do not be in a hurry to throw the contents of the pot away. In her germination studies of penstemon, Dr. Susan Meyer of the Forest Service Shrub Research Laboratory in Provo, Utah, has found that the higher the elevation at which a particular species grows in its native environment, the longer the cold stratification period should be. High elevation species may require 90 days or more, whereas those of low elevation usually require much less. In other words, if in doubt, sow early.

You can undertake vegetative propagation in several ways: by taking cuttings from semimature shoots in late summer to autumn (after the first flush of flowering), by taking easy cuttings from stems you remove that have their roots attached, and by division. Insert the cuttings you take from the semimature shoots (some of which may even have embryo roots showing) into your normal cutting medium.

Easy cuttings are available from most shrubby penstemons throughout the year since they tend to layer themselves. Stems sprawling on the surface of the soil put down roots, and you can detach them, pot them up, and keep them out of the sun for a few weeks until growth is obvious. Many penstemons can also be divided. Once you have dug up or knocked the plant out of the pot, you should sever the rooted stems and then replant them. This excellent method of propagation enables you to have a number of mature specimens potted up in the same year that you took the cuttings, especially if you have taken them in the spring. Dig around at the edge of the plant and you will be surprised by what you find—rooted stems. I have successfully propagated the easiest species using this method, such as *Penstemon pinifolius*, as well as the more choice, such as *P. acaulis* or *P. leiophyllus* subsp. *francisci-pennellii*.

## Cultivation

Plants that grow easily in my rock garden or alpine beds need no special treatment other than extra grit in the soil and a warm spot. The lime soil and year-round rainfall of a cool-temperate zone have no apparent adverse effect on those plants I recommend for a rock garden; perhaps that is because many of those species originate from the moister conditions of the Pacific Northwest.

I recommend growing certain *Penstemon* species in a trough for two reasons, their size and the natural habitat. Though some dwarf penstemons may also grow well at the front of a small rock garden, they are best seen in a trough, where they will not be swamped by more vigorous alpines. Although a few species inhabit moist places you must remember that most are xeric, meaning they come from the drylands of hot open screes, deserts, or prairies. Where climatic conditions permit, these penstemons will do well in alpine or rock gardens, but in more hostile conditions you should grow them where you can simulate their appropriate habitat (a trough is ideal for this),

providing temporary overhead protection whenever required.

Some pestemons, particularly the more choice species and especially those lovely dwarf forms that naturally grow in xeric conditions can only be grown in the alpine house or frame. You can grow these specimens in pots either for exhibition or your own pleasure, treating them as individual plants and making careful note of each of their requirements. However, if you live in an area of the world that has suitable conditions, by all means grow them in the garden and enjoy.

First and foremost, I recommend you grow your penstemons in a warm place. If you plant them in the garden, choose a sunny, well-drained scree (though many penstemons need only the normal gritty alpine bed). Species from xeric areas will die if they have too much moisture around the neck and roots during a cold winter. They grow well in sand beds with an annual application of a slow release fertilizer. If you grow penstemons in a trough then use an appropriate soil mixture that is gritty and fairly rich in nutrients.

Penstemons grown in pots should have plenty of water during the growing season with a weak, liquid feed about once a month. They also require just enough moisture during winter to keep them growing, but be careful not to overwater or they will collapse in a few days. Repotting should take place each spring. Stem dieback is a big problem; sometimes the whole plant is attacked until it is dead. In general, however, regrowth in spring from the apparently dead stems enables the plant to recover (you can cut away any dead portions at that time). Even so, you should regularly propagate the plant as insurance against its death.

I have not noticed many pests on the penstemons I grow outside; scale insects are the most prevalent. In the alpine or greenhouse by contrast, whitefly and the dreaded red spider mite can cause chaos. To prevent any real harm being done kill off whitefly with a systemic spray or drench plants as soon as you see the pest. Red spider can kill off many choice exhibition penstemons if you do not immediately stop it. The leaves become gray, mottled, and rough to the touch, the plant looks very lackluster, and in spite of the insecticide will take weeks to grow fresh leaves again as the affected ones drop off. You should inspect penstemon leaves in the alpine house almost daily, especially during hot, dry weather. Prevention here is definitely better than cure.

## PETROPHYTUM
Rosaceae
*rockmats*

Like *Kelseya*, the genus *Petrophytum* is a member of the rose family. (You might also see it spelled "*Petrophyton*," which is how it was first published.) Although the three species in this genus are faster growing than those in *Kelseya*, they grow on rocks in the same way by covering them completely. I find them easier to cultivate than *Kelseya*, two of the three species having grown quite well in my rock garden for three years with no protection. It is only when you see a plant in the wild do you appreciate that their habit is not quite the same as it is in cultivation. While in the parking lot of the Devil Canyon overlook in Wyoming's Bighorn Canyon, I happened to glance down and see *P. caespitosum* on the canyon side of the protective fence. It was almost 30 cm (12 in.) across with a nice tight mound and slightly fading, bottlebrush flowers. The specimen in my alpine bed looks much more lax.

*Petrophytum caespitosum* ranges from Oregon to California and the Dakotas and is also variable in altitude to 3000 m (9750 ft.). This mat-forming species grows to 80 cm (32 in.) across in the wild, but in cultivation it is usually less than half that size. Small, blue-green, spatulate leaves form almost stemless rosettes that turn a deep purple over winter. These rosettes make up the mat as it creeps around following the contours of nearby rocks. White to pale cream flowers on 2–4-cm (¾–1½-in.) spikes look like small bottlebrushes. It is a good plant for a sunny scree.

Devil Canyon overlook, Bighorn Canyon, Wyoming.

*Petrophytum caespitosum* on the edge of Devil Canyon overlook, Bighorn Canyon, Wyoming.

*Petrophytum cinerascens* grows in Washington on basalt cliffs. Similar to *P. caespitosum*, it differs only in leaf veining, color, and flowers that have more stamens. On occasion the racemes can be shortly branched.

*Petrophytum hendersonii* comes from the Olympics of western Washington, where its habitat is cliffs and steep rocky slopes. Unlike *P. caespitosum* and *P. cinerascens*, it forms hummocks in cultivation with rosettes on longer stems. It grows to 10 cm (4 in.) high, and the creamy white bottlebrush flowers that cover the stems are almost double the length of the stems of *P. caespitosum* and *P. cinerascens*. This longer covering gives a foaming effect down the stems, making it the more beautiful species. Scree conditions are suitable for cultivating this plant but it also makes an excellent pot plant.

## Propagation

Seed that you sow in the autumn usually germinates in spring. However, it is very fine, especially that of *Petrophytum caespitosum*, so it is best to sow it on the surface of the grit that covers the soil mixture in the seed pot. If the pot rests in a saucer of water after sowing, the seed is drawn into the grit by capillary action. I collect seed from *P. caespitosum* as soon as the small flowers go brown. The best collection method is to cut the stems off at the base and put both stems and flowers upside down in a seed packet. If you leave the flowers to dry off, seed falls from the dead flowers to the bottom of the packet. As a final touch, lightly crush the dead flowers so that any remaining seed will fall out.

Although my own seed of *Petrophytum caespitosum* germinates well, I have never had success with seed of *P. hendersonii*, either my own or that I buy from commercial lists. I therefore propagate *P. hendersonii* by cuttings after flowering has finished. I also remove rooted offsets in spring and pot them up.

## Cultivation

Scree conditions suit plants of this genus perfectly. However, they do not like full sun all day so will appreciate partial shade that keeps the roots cool. Try planting specimens so the roots are tucked under a rock. Some growers recommend acid soil but both *Petrophytum caespitosum* and *P. hendersonii* grow well in lime soil. I grow *P. hendersonii* in a pot with my usual neutral, soil-based compost and some extra grit.

*Petrophytum caespitosum*, Ten Sleep Canyon, Wyoming. Photo Chris Norton.

*Petrophytum caespitosum* in cultivation in the alpine house. Wisley Gardens, United Kingdom.

I have not noticed any problems with pests on plants I grow outside. However, red spider mite and aphids affect the plants growing under glass.

## PHACELIA
Hydrophyllaceae
*scorpion-weeds*

*Phacelia* is a wide-ranging genus of herbs of about 150 or so species, the majority of which are annuals. Most species are hairy, with purple, lilac, or white flowers that often have protruding stamens. Stems vary in height, and the flowers are in terminal, sometimes dense, cymes. Phacelias inhabit areas of sharp drainage and plenty of sun, and 22 species occur in the Rockies. They are a challenge to cultivate successfully as they require sharp drainage and plenty of sun; they are usually short-lived. Some of those suitable for alpine gardening purposes are very rare and could well be classified as endangered in the future. However, seed for several of the more widespread species has been available for a number of years from commercial seed lists.

*Phacelia argentea* inhabits coastal sandy bluffs and dunes in southwest Oregon and northern California. A species that is more rare than attractive, its stems grow to 50 cm (20 in.) and are ascending or decumbent. Whitish hairs give a silvery sheen to the foliage, and small white flowers appear in globose heads during May through August.

*Phacelia bolanderi* grows in the north Coast Ranges of California at about 525 m (1700 ft.). It forms a low mound of decumbent branching stems, and the large, lavender-blue, bell-shaped flowers are in terminal clusters that cover the plant in late spring.

This is a low elevation phacelia that grows in the partial shade of redwood forests.

*Phacelia corymbosa* grows only on the serpentine soils in the southwest corner of Oregon and northern California and is probably the rarest species in the genus. Stems grow to 40 cm (15¾ in.) and are topped with dense globose heads of white flowers in May through August.

*Phacelia hastata* ranges from Washington to northern California and eastwards to Utah, Idaho, Montana, Nevada, Colorado, and southwest North Dakota inhabiting dry rocky places in sagebrush and conifer forests. It grows 20–50 cm (8–20 in.) high with small white to pale purple flowers in May through July. Features that distinguish it from other phacelias are the almost parallel veins of the leaves and the dense, silvery hairs that lie flat on the leaves.

Variety *alpina* is the high elevation variety growing at 1845–3510 m (6000–11,410 ft.) in dry rock ledges and loose, unstable areas. Many prostrate stems form a compact mound with short clusters of small lavender-violet flowers in midsummer. Large gray-green leaves are elliptical and covered with fine silvery hairs.

*Phacelia heterophylla* grows in Washington, Oregon, and northern California below 2155 m (7000 ft.). It occurs almost everywhere in the western Cascades, from xeric areas to rocky outcrops, the height varying from 30 to 90 cm (12 to 36 in.) depending on the habitat. The entire plant is covered with stiff, short hairs, and small white-purple flowers in May through July bloom on a single, erect stem.

*Phacelia lutea* **var.** *mackenzieorum* is a narrow endemic found only on pumice hills in eastern Malheur county, Oregon. It grows 20–25 cm (8–10 in.) in height, and whitish hairs cover almost the whole plant. Yellow flowers in April through May are bell shaped in terminal clusters.

*Phacelia lyallii* inhabits high alpine screes and talus areas in Montana and Idaho. It is similar to *P. sericea* but the terminal clusters of purple flowers are shorter and the pinnately lobed leaves are dark green.

*Phacelia sericea* ranges from Alaska to Colorado, Utah, and New Mexico on rocky gravel soils from around 1845 m (6000 ft.) to well above timberline. It has from one to several unbranched stems and grows 5–45 cm (2–18 in.) high. This is the more commonly grown species, and with deeply dissected basal and stem leaves and silky, silvery hair that thoroughly covers the plant, it is outstanding. Its hairs are what distinguish it from other species and give it the common

name of silky phacelia. The lavender to purple or blue flowers in June through August have long stamens and look like feathery spikes. From a distance it is easy to mistake this species for lupines or monardellas. I remember a hike on Burnt Mountain in the eastern Cascades where a large scree area dotted with *P. sericea* looked like a shimmering silver blanket and made a lovely contrast to the brown rock of the scree.

Variety *ciliosa* grows in the less harsh environment of grassy slopes in the Steens Mountains of Oregon at around 2740 m (8900 ft.). Mats with tufts of gray-green leaves are covered with fine hairs and purple spikes of flowers 15–20 cm (6–8 in.) tall.

*Phacelia verna* is found in the Umpqua River valley of Oregon, where it grows in moist crevices in basaltic rock. It grows to

Scree area, Burnt Mountain, eastern Cascades, Washington.

*Phacelia sericea*, Mount Townsend, Olympic Mountains, Washington.

*Phacelia sericea*, Burnt Mountain, eastern Cascades, Washington.

*Phacelia sericea*, Glacier National Park, Montana. Photo Peter Downe.

25 cm (10 in.) with terminal racemes of bell-shaped, white to pale blue flowers in April through June.

## Propagation

Propagate these species by seed sown in autumn.

## Cultivation

In my experience, *Phacelia sericea* is easier to grow outside in a scree than as an alpine house plant, although it will be short-lived in areas of winter wet. As a result of its fairly precise moisture requirement, growing it as a pot plant leaves very little room for maneuver; it is likely to collapse at any time from drought or overwatering. Grow *P. sericea* in an acid, gritty soil mixture and repot it into larger pots on a regular basis because it grows so quickly. (Repotting also keeps the soil mixture open, which helps ensure quick drainage.) In spite of the difficulty of growing this species there have been several outstanding exhibits at Alpine Garden Society shows. Seed of *P. bolanderi*, *P. hastata* var. *alpina*, and *P. sericea* var. *ciliosa* has been available since 1995, and plants grown from this seed should be suitable for the sunny scree bed, outdoor sand bed, and the alpine house.

*Phacelia sericea* in cultivation.

Slugs love the plants growing outdoors, and aphids love those in the alpine house. Watch the undersides of the silver leaves where aphids congregate, and check for spider mite, which causes severe mottling.

## PHLOX
Polemoniaceae

*Phlox is* another genus known only in the New World. Though some of the approximately 70 species grow in the central and eastern United States and Canada, the genus is certainly at its best and most diverse in the mountains and drylands of the West.

Most alpine garden enthusiasts grow phloxes, usually the eastern phloxes like *Phlox bifida*, *P. subulata*, or their hybrids, all of which do well in almost any rock garden. The western phloxes are quite different: their colors are perhaps not as vivid, they are more difficult to propagate, and they are more difficult to grow. Then why grow them? I admit I enjoy the challenge but it is more than that. Look at the tiny leaves of the cushion-type phloxes—some are quite needlelike. Admire the tight compact cushions. And notice the delicate shades of flower color from white to various shades of pink, lavender, and blue, many of which are highly scented. No wonder the western phloxes are such a temptation to grow! There are also the more leggy or shrubby types that, while not as cute, display lovely pastel colors and seem slightly easier to cultivate. All western phloxes are wonderful, and every time mine bloom I get a tremendous thrill.

*Phlox aculeata* comes from Idaho on the Columbia Plateau. It forms attractive hummocks to 10 cm (4 in.) high with pink to purple flowers 1.2 cm (½ in.) wide. Although *P. aculeata* is compact, it is more or less a condensed form of P. viridis, one of the more shrubby phloxes.

*Phlox adsurgens* comes from northwest California and western Oregon. Known as the woodland phlox, it is a relation of the eastern *P. stolonifera*. This beautiful phlox grows in coniferous forest openings on slopes to 2000 m (6500 ft.). It has broad oval leaves on stems that creep or grow erect to 30 cm (12 in.) high. Pink, deep rose, lilac, or purple flowers in late spring to summer are few in number and to 2.5 cm (1 in.) across. Although I grow this species in the garden it does not last more than a couple of years. It needs continual propagation, which, thankfully, is fairly easy.

There are some worthy cultivars that appear to be more free-flowering than *Phlox adsurgens*, including 'Wagon Wheel' and 'Red Buttes', both discovered by Lawrence Crocker and Boyd Kline. 'Mary Ellen' makes a dense mound of rounded foliage 5 cm (2 in.) high that in early summer is covered with blooms of rich pink. A white form of *P. adsurgens* has been recorded in cultivation.

*Phlox alaskensis* (synonym *P. richardsonii* subsp. *alaskensis*) grows on stony slopes at 300-950 m (975-3090 ft.) in northwest Alaska. It is cushion forming to 10 cm (4 in.) high and 30 cm (12 in.) wide with pink, lavender, lilac, or white flowers to 2.5 cm (1 in.) across.

*Phlox albomarginata* grows at about 2400 m (7800 ft.) at the top of the Hogback in the Big Belt Mountains of Montana (where there are some wonderful limestone screes), which is one of the most inhospitable habitats you can imagine. It grows in the company of *Douglasia montana* and among grasses. The extreme climatic conditions—high summer temperatures and very low winter temperatures—encourage this phlox to form tight mounds or mats that rival the best androsaces and saxifrages. White to pink flowers cover the plants, and the tiny pointed leaves are edged in what looks like white frosting, a feature that makes it impossible to mistake the species for any other phlox. It is an excellent species either for exhibition or in a scree. Even if you only have one plant, it will still set seed. Ev Whittemore found the Hogback colony by sheer luck during her travels in the West, and her seed collection has enabled me to reintroduce *P. albomarginata* into cultivation in the United Kingdom.

*Phlox alaskensis*, Waring Mountains, northwest Alaska. Photo Carolyn Parker.

*Phlox albomarginata* habitat showing limestone scree and bleached tree trunks. Photo Ev Whittemore.

*Phlox alyssifolia* grows throughout the Great Plains at about 1170 m (3800 ft.) in the lime, sandy, and gravel soils in full sun. Low mats of hard foliage are to 10 cm (4 in.) high. The leaves are similar in appearance to *P. albomarginata* but they are larger, and the short stems have a fibrous, peeling bark. The 2.5-cm (1-in.) wide flowers in late spring to summer are rose-pink or white and are quite showy. Being rhizomatous, this species quickly spreads to make a large patch.

Variety *abdita* is taller and fuller with large, very fragrant flowers. Variety *collina* is smaller and more compact and has flowers that are purple, lavender, or pink. Some clones are sweetly scented.

*Phlox amabilis* comes from the dry stony slopes in the Colorado Plateau. This tufted phlox grows 10–20 cm (4–8 in.) tall with leaves almost 5 cm (2 in.) long. Fragrant flowers with deeply notched petals are purple to deep pink and appear in late spring. If seed were available I would recommend growing this plant in the alpine house.

*Phlox andicola*, the plains phlox, grows in the dry sandy soil of the open prairie. Its habit is similar to *P. alyssifolia* and it also spreads quickly. The leaves are different, however, in that they are needlelike, and the stems are upright. White flowers appear from May through July.

Subspecies *parvula* is smaller with lightly scented, pale lavender to white flowers. Claude Barr found an especially fine specimen of this subspecies south of the Black Hills of Dakota that flowered with wide, overlapping petals. He named it 'Dr. Wherry' in honor of Dr. Edgar Wherry, who did so much to bring phloxes to the attention of gardeners.

*Phlox austromontana* (synonym *P. densa*) grows in the pinyon and juniper woodlands of Nevada, California, Arizona, and the Canyonlands in Utah at 1525–3050 m (4955–9915 ft.). The loose hummocks grow to 15 cm (6 in.) high. The small but slightly fragrant flowers are white, pink, blue, or lavender.

Variety *jonesii* has bright pink flowers and is endemic to southern Utah at 1435–2600 m (4665–8450 ft.), especially in Zion Canyon. Variety *lutescens* is also endemic to one small area in southern Utah but the flowers are pale yellow.

*Phlox borealis* grows in Alaska. Similar to *P. subulata* in appearance, it forms loose cushions to 10 cm (4 in.) high with foliage of linear leaves and flowers of white, lilac,

Mounds of *Phlox albomarginata* in a scree on the Hogback, Montana. Photo Ev Whittemore.

*Phlox albomarginata* in a wooded area of the Hogback, Montana. Photo Ev Whittemore.

lavender, or bright pink in May through June. It inhabits humus-rich gravel soil, and in the right position in the garden grows fairly easy.

*Phlox bryoides* comes from the Great Plains and ranges westwards into Idaho, Nevada, and Utah (it has often been confused with *P. hoodii* and *P. muscoides*, which is why its range is sometimes extended to Oregon and Washington), where it grows at 1400–3265 m (4550–10,610 ft.). Like *P. hoodii* and *P. muscoides*, the foliage is congested, but it is a more upright species—to 5 cm (2 in.). Tiny leaves covered with white wool and white to pale lavender flowers combine to give it the appearance of a cassiope or even a miniature whipcord hebe. Although it has fragrant flowers, the fragrance varies in strength from colony to colony. Thousands of these plants spread across the plains looking like masses of small white balls.

*Phlox caespitosa* grows on open rocky slopes at 1300–4000 m (4225–13,000 ft.) in the southern Rockies and the Great Basin. Cushions to 10 cm (4 in.) high have long narrow leaves, and the lavender to white flowers in spring to early summer are fragrant. Seed of the species and subspecies is periodically available in both the commercial lists and the regular exchange lists.

Subspecies *condensata* (synonym *Phlox condensata*) is even more condensed than subsp. *pulvinata*. It makes dense, flat mats of small narrow leaves just 2–4 cm (¾–1½ in.) high and blooms from spring into early summer with white to pale pink fragrant flowers. I first saw subsp. *condensata* on the

*Phlox caespitosa* subsp. *condensata*, Mount Goliath Pesman trail, Colorado.

*Phlox caespitosa* subsp. *pulvinata*, Loveland Pass, Colorado.

*Phlox caespitosa* subsp. *condensata*, White Mountains, Nevada. Photo Chris Norton.

*Phlox caespitosa* subsp. *pulvinata*, Duncum Mountain, Wyoming. Photo Chris Norton.

Mount Goliath Pesman trail on Mount Evans in Colorado in 1982, where one plant's large mat, about 60 cm (24 in.) in diameter, grew from a crack in the rocks anchored by a taproot. It was covered in flowers and took my breath away. When I grew this plant in a pot, it sent up shoots around the edge despite the taproot. These shoots have roots at the base that, if carefully detached, will propagate the plant.

Subspecies *pulvinata* (synonym *Phlox pulvinata*) has much pricklier foliage, makes lower cushions and tight buns to 5 cm (2 in.) high, and has larger, white to ice-blue flowers.

*Phlox caryophylla*, though closely related to *P. longifolia*, grows only in northern New Mexico and Colorado. Mats are 12–20 cm (4¾–8 in.) high, and pink or purple flowers look and smell like dianthus.

*Phlox covillei* grows in Nevada and California on the Sierra Crest and its eastern slopes at moderate to high altitudes. Some references recognize it as a synonym for *P. caespitosa* subsp. *condensata*. It forms a good, tight cushion to 7.5 cm (3 in.) high with tiny leaves and smallish white to lavender flowers. Although it does well as a pot plant, it needs to be grown hard for it to form the tight cushion it has in the wild.

*Phlox diffusa* is a widespread montane species that grows from Washington to Oregon, southern California, and east to Montana and Wyoming. The specimen I found on the edge of the snowmelt at Crater Lake National Park, Oregon, in July 1996 was growing alongside *Pulsatilla occidentalis* and had deep pink flowers. Further north on Washington's Mount Townsend I saw this species again, this time carpeting the scree

*Phlox covillei*, California. Photo Chris Norton.

Habitat of *Phlox diffusa*, Crater Lake, Oregon.

Close-up of *Phlox diffusa*, Crater Lake, Oregon.

Close-up of *Phlox diffusa*, Mount Townsend, Olympic Mountains, Washington.

areas with mats over 30 cm (12 in.) across that consisted of needlelike leaves and white to lavender and deep pink blooms. *Phlox diffusa* is a valuable addition to the scree garden as it slowly spreads to form a mound, blooming May through August and occasionally into September.

*Phlox dolichantha* is endemic to the San Bernardino National Forest, California, where it is found at 2000–2600 m (6500–8450 ft.) alongside *Calochortus nuttallii* and *Iris missouriensis*. This tufted phlox grows to 30 cm (12 in.) and has flowers of bright pink to 2.5 cm (1 in.) across from a tube almost 5 cm (2 in.) long. It blooms late spring to summer in the forest clearings.

*Phlox douglasii* grows in Montana and in the limestone rock ledges and gravel slopes of California to Washington at high altitudes. It forms mats to 10 cm (4 in.) high with very fragrant flowers of white, pink, or lavender. It is easy to grow in the garden so has been used to produce many quality cultivars of rich colors.

*Phlox gladiformis* is from Utah and Nevada, where it grows in semidesert conditions at 1100–2300 m (3575–7475 ft.). The prickly cushion to 15 cm (6 in.) high is usually covered with white or lilac to lavender flowers in early summer.

*Phlox grayi* grows in California, Nevada, Utah, Arizona, and New Mexico. Rough, furry leaves grow to 15 cm (6 in.) long, and the rhizomatous stems gradually increase the spread of the plant. In Arizona where it is much smaller with soft pink to salmon-pink blooms it grows with *P. austromontana*. *Phlox grayi* is similar to a

*Phlox grayi* in cultivation.

*Phlox hendersonii* and *Phlox diffusa*, Mount Townsend, Olympic Mountains, Washington.

*Phlox hendersonii*, Mount Townsend, Olympic Mountains, Washington.

*Phlox hendersonii*, Mount Hood, Oregon. Photo David Hale.

reduced version of *P. speciosa* and is a good species for alpine house culture.

*Phlox griseola* grows in Utah and Nevada at 1525–2000 m (4955–6500 ft.) and is mat forming. Listed by Welsh et al. (1987) as a distinct species, the similarly colored flowers are larger than *P. tumulosa*, a species with which it is allied.

*Phlox hendersonii* (synonym *P. condensata* var. *hendersonii*) grows in Washington on Mount Townsend and Mount Adams, where it inhabits moraine ridges at 2470 m (8027 ft.). Similar to *P. condensata*, it has densely crowded, needlelike leaves that form hard, flat cushions to 5 cm (2 in.) high and 30 cm (12 in.) across. The 1.2-cm (½-in.) wide white flowers are deeply imbedded in the foliage. I photographed *P. hendersonii* growing alongside *P. diffusa* on Mount Townsend and was surprised not to see any hybrids. This is a challenging species in cultivation.

*Phlox hirsuta* is endemic to Siskiyou county in California, where it grows on dry slopes in fine, gritty soils derived from serpentine. A very close relative of *P. stansburyi*, the small compact mounds look like a condensed version of *P. longifolia*. The dark green, hairy leaves are very stiff, to 3 cm (1¼ in.) long, and congested on the 5–10-cm (2–4-in.) high stems that grow from the crown up. It flowers in spring with large blooms in all shades of pink; Ron Ratko describes it as "one of the loveliest phloxes in flower and habit." In cultivation it has given me similar problems to *P. stansburyi* as it does not do well with a lack of moisture at the roots, despite its dry, wild habitat. I cannot confirm reports that it does not last long in cultivation. The U.S. Fish and Wildlife Service has proposed listing *P. hirsuta* as a threatened species.

*Phlox hoodii* comes from the Great Plains westwards to Oregon and Washington growing at 1400–3265 m (4550–10,610 ft.). It forms a compact cushion in the wild although some specimens have upright stems similar to *P. bryoides*. This phlox is drought resistant as the deep root system allows it to grow where other plants cannot. White to light pink or pale blue flowers can be found in the wild only if the sheep, for whom they are a delicacy, have not got to them first.

Variety *canescens* grows in Washington at around 1000 m (3250 ft.). It forms compact, woolly domes and has very short, stiff, needlelike leaves that are partly obscured by tufts of fine, cobweblike hairs. The flowers that appear in early spring are white and stemless, making you think there are white balls dotted all over the landscape.

*Phlox kelseyi* grows in Montana, Colorado, Idaho, and Wyoming at moderate elevations in a variety of habitats from marshes to alkaline grasslands. Mat forming to 5 cm (2 in.), the leaves are fleshier than most other western phloxes. It is free-flowering and blooms for a long period, from late spring into summer. Although the plant I grow has white flowers, others produce pale

*Phlox kelseyi* var. *kelseyi* 'Lemhi Purple' from one of the cuttings taken at the original site, now in cultivation. Photo Robert Rolfe.

pink, lavender, purple, and deep blue flowers.

Betty Lowry found a colony of *Phlox kelseyi* var. *kelseyi* in 1983 at about 2000 m (6500 ft.) in the high rolling plains of upper Birch Creek Valley in Idaho's southern Lemhi county. The site was a shallow alkaline depression containing plants in a wide variety of colors. A large expanse of var. *kelseyi* with an excellent color range also grows near Birch Creek itself.

A purple form from the colony Betty found was given the cultivar name 'Lemhi Purple' by Panayoti and Gwen Kelaidis, which refers to Lemhi county where it was found. A very vigorous grower in normal, neutral potting mix with leaves about 30 percent larger than the type, it is great for pot work, a trough, or the rock garden if it stays moist in summer. It is among the best introductions of mat-forming western phloxes in recent years, and I am proud to have helped propagate and distribute it in Britain.

Three other varieties are worth noting. Variety *glandulosa* grows in alkaline marshy conditions. Variety *missoulensis* (synonym *Phlox missoulensis*) from the dry prairies of the northern Rockies is remarkably well adapted to cultivation. The leaves of this

beautiful specimen are quite long—to 2.5 cm (1 in.)—and needlelike (it hurts if you catch your hand on one). In exhibition it makes a cushion of exhibition quality with fragrant white, lavender, pink, and occasionally ice-blue flowers. Variety *salina* grows in saline marshlands.

*Phlox lanata* occurs in the Steens Mountains of eastern Oregon in red screes and dry stony slopes at 2460–2770 m (8000–9000 ft.) and in the drier parts of the Cascades and Sierra Nevada from northern California into Oregon. There is doubt about it being a true species, and yet the range of *P. lanata* is far more limited than *P. bryoides* and *P. hoodii*, both of which are considered species. My plants came from seed collected in Steens Mountain, and the small upright growth of tiny, woolly-haired leaves and smallish white flowers vary in size

*Phlox lanata* in cultivation.

Site of *Phlox kelseyi* var. *kelseyi* 'Lemhi Purple' in Birch Creek Valley. Photo Ned Lowry.

*Phlox longifolia* with *Eriogonum gracilipes*. White Mountains, California.

from plant to plant, as do most plants grown from wild-collected seed. Even though it is quite rare in the wild, this plant grows well in cultivation; it seems not to suffer from receiving too much moisture despite its dry natural habitat.

*Phlox longifolia* ranges from the Great Plains to Washington at an of altitude 900–3000 m (2925–9750 ft.) in dry to moist conditions. Stems grow 5–40 cm (2–15¾ in.) tall and bear linear leaves 4–8 cm (1½–3 in.) long. Small white, pink, or lavender to purple flowers appear in spring to early summer. Although it is pretty I do not think it compares with the lovely *P. stansburyi* or *P. speciosa*.

*Phlox mollis* (synonym *P. kelseyi* var. *ciliata*) grows in eastern Washington and Idaho to the Columbia Plateau and adjacent Rockies on dry stony slopes. It is tufted and woody with stems 5–15 cm (2–6 in.) tall. The leaves are very narrow and to 3 cm (1¼ in.) long, and purple to pink, slightly fragrant flowers bloom in spring.

*Phlox multiflora* grows in the southern and middle Rockies at 2200–3265 m (7150–10,610 ft.) and forms cushions or mats to 15 cm (6 in.) high. The foliage is very different from most western phloxes;

the growth is greener and more lax, and leaves are almost 5 cm (2 in.) long. Fragrant, white to deep pink flowers appear in spring to early summer. A lovely species that can easily be mistaken for an eastern phlox, it contrasts well with other western species in the rock garden.

Variety *depressa* grows at a higher altitude and is more compact, forming low cushions of needlelike foliage to 8 cm (3 in.) high. The flowers are slightly smaller, very fragrant, and, like many higher elevation phloxes, can thoroughly cover the plant.

*Phlox muscoides* comes from the Great Plains and ranges to Oregon and Washington, where it grows at 1400–3265 m (4550–10,610 ft.). It makes a handsome mat of tiny woolly leaves, and in April small white, pink, blue, or lavender flowers tumble

*Phlox muscoides*, Albion Basin, Utah. Photo Peter Downe.

*Phlox muscoides* in cultivation.

*Phlox longifolia*, Lemhi Pass, Idaho. Photo Peter Downe.

down over the limestone rock like a waterfall. The flowers are very fragrant. The Great Plains Flora Association (1986) describes *P. muscoides* as a synonym of *P. hoodii* subsp. *muscoides.* However, Welsh et al. (1987) describe *P. hoodii* and *P. muscoides* as separate species, albeit very close ones. Claude Barr also separates them into two species. I grow both of these beautiful phloxes, and as they definitely look different I side with Claude Barr. Nevertheless, more work is clearly needed in correctly identifying this species.

*Phlox peckii* has been found in only one site in southern Oregon. Similar to a condensed version of *P. diffusa*, it has pink flowers with yellow eyes.

*Phlox pungens* is endemic to the Wind River Basin of central Wyoming, where it grows on limestone cliffs and sparsely

vegetated sandstone, siltstone, or limestone slopes at 1845–2275 m (6000–7400 ft.). The mats are tightly congested, the leaves are short, narrow, and very prickly (similar to those of *P. kelseyi* var. *missoulensis*), and the flowers are white, pink, or blue.

*Phlox richardsonii* comes from Alaska's peaty, gravel slopes close to the sea or near streams. Cushions are to 12.5 cm (5 in.) high with highly scented, bright lilac flowers in spring. Perhaps seed collecting trips to Alaska will make this species available in the near future.

*Phlox sibirica* is a high arctic species growing mostly in the Brooks Range of Alaska and possibly in the Alaska Range. This woody-based, tufted plant grows in lime soil and has linear, pointed leaves to 6 cm (2¼ in.) long. The lavender-lilac flowers in spring through summer are usually in clusters of three to six on stems 8–15 cm (3–6 in.) tall.

*Phlox speciosa* ranges from the northern half of California to Oregon, Washington, British Columbia, and Montana, where it grows in woods and on gravel slopes. It forms a clump to 25 cm (10 in.) high but can be much taller with age and it has a woody base from which grow several decumbent to

Site of *Phlox speciosa* along the Illinois River trail, Oregon.

Close-up of *Phlox speciosa* along the Illinois River trail, Oregon.

erect shoots. White, pink, or purple flowers in clumps of up to 15 are wide petalled—2.5 cm (1 in.) across. A lovely population grows alongside the Illinois River in Oregon.

The subspecies I describe are rarely seen though all are worth noting. Subspecies *lanceolata* is similar to subspecies *nitida* but with thicker and wider leaves; the notches in the petals are much reduced. Subspecies *lignosa* has rose-pink flowers that are so deeply notched you would be forgiven for thinking it was a specimen of *Phlox bifida*. Subspecies *nitida* is more shrubby—to 40 cm (15¼ in.) tall—and the petals are nowhere near as notched; it has glabrous herbage. Subspecies *occidentalis* is puberulent and more sprawling; it has larger clusters of flowers with prominently notched petals.

Subspecies *woodhousei* is a beautiful subspecies from Arizona at about 2200 m (7150 ft.). It grows 10–15 cm (4–6 in.) tall with rose-pink flowers that are almost 2.5 cm (1 in.) across with a white center, an orange eye, and deeply notched petals. A plant I grew from seed that I received from Sonia Lowzow is well suited to wet winters and humid summers as the region in which

it grows in Arizona suffers summer monsoons. In cultivation it blooms from March through December (it was once in flower on Christmas day).

*Phlox stansburyi* grows at approximately 2300 m (7475 ft.) in California and has as many as 20, 2.5-cm (1-in.) wide pink, white, or purple flowers in clusters on a 10–20-cm (4–8-in.) stem. I have grown several *P. stansburyi* plants from seed that had smaller clusters of pink flowers with a dark eye. This species is difficult to cultivate in a pot as it resents dryness at the roots. If deprived of moisture the stems go brown as if ripening off and more moisture is required to get it growing again.

*Phlox superba* is similar to *P. stansburyi* but with leaves only to 6.3 cm (2½ in.) long and flowers that are slightly smaller but with

*Phlox speciosa* subsp. *woodhousei* in cultivation, April. Photo Jo Walker.

*Phlox speciosa*, Yreka, California. Photo Chris Norton.

*Phlox speciosa* subsp. *woodhousei* in cultivation, November.

longer tubes. It comes from central Nevada and adjacent California on dry stony slopes and flats.

*Phlox tenuifolia* can only be described as a "straggling shrublet" at 25–76 cm (10–30 in.) high. It grows only in southwest Arizona on dry stony slopes at an altitude of 500–1500 m (1625–4875 ft.). Smallish, white to cream, flowers appear in spring and occasionally in the autumn.

*Phlox tumulosa* (synonym *P. griseola* subsp. *tumulosa*) has the tiniest gray-green leaves and the most congested cushion I have ever seen in a phlox and makes dense, caespitose cushions with small white to pink or lavender flowers in May through June dotted about the foliage. It grows in Utah and Nevada among sagebrush and juniper at 1675–2345 m (5445–7620 ft.). Panayoti Kelaidis (1991) commented in *A Century of Alpines* that it is a "... dominant groundcover over six or seven ranges of mountains on the borders of Utah and Nevada." This plant has been variously described as a synonym for or subspecies of *Pholx griseola*, although my collections bear little resemblance to plants pictured as *P. griseola*. Welsh et al. (1987)

*Phlox tumulosa*, western Utah. Photo David Hale.

suggest that *P. tumulosa* is probably intermediate between *P. griseola* and *P. muscoides*.

It remains the most compact and also the most frustrating of all the western phloxes that I grow. Although a superb alpine house plant, I would like to try it in a scree bed in a hot, dry spot. However, even after seven years its propagation still baffles me.

*Phlox variabilis* grows at high altitudes in Montana, Utah, Colorado, and Wyoming and is similar to P. borealis making small tufted mats of linear leaves to 10 cm (4 in.) high. The pink or white flowers, 1.2 cm (½ in.) across, appear in spring to summer.

*Phlox viridis* (synonym *P. longifolia* subsp. viridis) grows in Washington to Montana and Nevada on dry stony slopes at a fairly high altitude. Most subspecies are woody based with stems to 20 cm (8 in.) high, and the lilac to pink, slightly fragrant flowers appear in spring.

Subspecies *compacta* has the same distribution as subsp. *longipes* but usually grows at higher elevations to around 2800 m (9100 ft.). Usually under 10 cm (4 in.) tall, it has leaves that are nevertheless fairly long at 3–4 cm (1¼–1½ in.). The 2-cm (¾-in.) wide flowers are purple, pink, or white.

Subspecies *longipes* extends its range to New Mexico. It is much taller than the type—to 40 cm (15¾ in.)—which reflects

*Phlox tumulosa* in cultivation.

in the larger flowers and much longer leaves at 5–10 cm (2–4 in.).

*Phlox viscida* grows at 800–2000 m (2600–6500 ft.) in open woodland and on stony slopes in Washington, Idaho, and northeast Oregon, and then very sparsely until reaching Arizona, where several larger colonies can be found. A woody-based and tufted species, it reaches 20 cm (8 in.) tall with linear leaves nearly 5 cm (2 in.) long. Purple, pink, and white flowers in spring to summer are to 2 cm (¾ in.) across, sometimes have a pale eye, and grow in fairly compact clusters of 3–15.

*Phlox* 'Sunrise' (*P. adsurgens* × *P. nivalis*) is an attractive hybrid that grows to 15 cm (6 in.) and has needlelike foliage and peach-pink flowers.

Although a number of phloxes are named *Phlox douglasii*, some are of hybrid origin with *P. subulata* and other species, especially those with rich-colored flowers. 'Crackerjack' and 'Red Admiral', wrongly attributed to *P. douglasii*, are instead the result of the hybridization of *P. douglasii* with *P. subulata* or other species.

Three hybrids became available in approximately 1994 from a Dutch nursery, all of which make deep green mats and are free-flowering. Although also wrongly attributed to *Phlox douglasii*, they are the result of hybridizing *P. douglasii* with other species. 'Boranovice' has deep carmine flowers, 'Karkukula' is smothered with smaller white flowers, and 'Slate' has slate-gray flowers.

## Propagation

The majority of the western phloxes used to be unavailable in the trade and plants were thus difficult to come by, but seed of many species is now available in commercial lists, and most nurseries are now able to stock these phloxes. There is, however, some variation among the plants, especially if the seed has been wild collected. Even the choicest of the cushion phloxes, such as *Phlox bryoides* and *P. tumulosa*, are listed. These western phloxes have become more popular, finding their way into the nursery catalogues or even onto the plant sales tables. Occasionally seed can be obtained from the various society seed lists. Do not expect many seeds for your money if you purchase them from a commercial list; between $4 and $5 for eight seeds is not unusual since demand usually exceeds supply, and if you have ever tried to collect seed in the wild you will understand the reason for the cost. (Anne Spiegel received bruised fingers and very few seeds while looking for seed of *P. condensata* in spite of the plant having bloomed profusely.) Nevertheless, seed of many phloxes I describe is not available and will not become so while there are only a few intrepid collectors.

With few exceptions, the leggy forms appear to be straightforward to propagate by cuttings. Some cushion-type phloxes, however, are almost impossible to propagate this way. Some mat-forming species may root from the prostrate stems as penstemons do, and you can pot up these "easy cuttings" right away. In spite of the difficulty in rooting cushion phloxes, I also take cuttings out of season as I believe that as long as cuttings stay green they will eventually root. You can prepare the cuttings the same way you do most other plants, and I describe some methods you may like to try.

Take cuttings of *Phlox adsurgens* after flowering, usually in May through June, perhaps even into early autumn. They root quite easily. *Phlox alyssifolia* and *P. andicola* spread by rhizomes that can be separated from the main plant and potted on. *Phlox douglasia* cuttings, which I take after flowering, take several months to root. *Phlox grayi* cuttings root in about six to eight weeks if taken just after flowering. It is best to propagate *P. hendersonii* by layered stems or divisions in spring. *Phlox kelseyi* roots quickly from cuttings taken after flowering. *Phlox lanata* cuttings taken after flowering are slow to root and slow to grow on the first year; layering also works with this species. I propagate *P. muscoides* the same way I do *P. lanata*.

I have had almost 100 percent success with cuttings of *Phlox diffusa*. In addition, my pot-grown plants sent up shoots around the edge of the pot, and when I removed the plant, most shoots had roots attached and I was able to pot up the shoots to grow on.

*Phlox kelseyi* var. *kelseyi* 'Lemhi Purple' sets seed quite freely in cultivation even if only one plant is growing. The resultant seedlings are very different from each other—some make tiny, congested mounds while others have long stems lying on the ground—but all the seedlings that flowered in my garden have the same purple blooms. This plant is vigorous in growth, and a two-year-old plant can supply a lot of cutting material. Cuttings of new growth after flowering are usually all successful after six weeks in the cutting frame. Once potted up they are slow to grow but usually put on plenty of growth the following year. This cultivar also layers itself, and if you have a large plant, you can cut off and pot up mature pieces with roots. I once rooted a bunch of stems two months after I cut them off and buried them to half their length in a pot of compost.

For many years I have had a very generous seed supplier for *Phlox albomarginata*.

Although I sell most plants resulting from this seed through my nursery, I grow several in pots for exhibition. These individuals have also set seed, so enabling me to grow plants on from my own stock. The cuttings I take of new growth after flowering are slow to root.

I take cuttings of *Phlox borealis* after flowering, as I do with eastern phloxes. Prostrate stems, which also root, can be separated from the main plant and potted up. I discovered a very unusual propagation method on *P. borealis* when I received a plant in the mail in late summer. The roots and most of the green growth were tightly covered in plastic wrap, and when I removed the plastic wrap I found that almost all the stems had roots growing from the leaf axils. The lack of light and the moisture generated by the whole plant being covered with the plastic wrap had obviously caused roots to form. After cutting the stems into 18 pieces (each of which had roots), I put them into a cutting frame for four to five weeks and then potted them up. This method could work with other species.

Both *Phlox bryoides* and *P. tumulosa* are very difficult to root and I have been successful with the traditional method of cuttings on only two occasions. Like *P. kelseyi* var. *missoulensis*, cuttings die off as they root. To prevent the cuttings from rotting off, you could put the cuttings into a plastic bag with a little fungicide powder, shake the bag so that all the cuttings are covered with fungicide, and then insert the cuttings into the cutting medium. I have had some success with a layering method that Rick Lupp uses with the difficult phloxes, which is to repot the plant lower than it originally was and then work soil mix and grit in around the stems. Rooting takes place after a few months along the stems, and these pieces can be cut off and potted up.

I recommend taking *Phlox kelseyi* var. *missoulensis* cuttings from new growth immediately after flowering, but do not expect more than 50 percent success. Like *P. bryoides*, they die off almost at the same time they make roots.

*Phlox speciosa* subsp. *woodhousei* sets small amounts of seed in cultivation but the seedlings I grow have yet to flower so I cannot compare them with the parent plant. Cuttings of fresh growth early in spring were successful, and when this species is occasionally stoloniferous, I remove and pot up the rooted shoots growing at the side of the plant.

Experiment with methods of propagating the western phloxes as I do. As more of these phloxes become available I hope that those of you who succeed in increasing your stocks will spread your knowledge.

## Cultivation

Although the eastern phloxes give me no trouble whatsoever in the garden, I grow most of my western phloxes in pots in the alpine house. This is not to say that they are all for exhibition or that they stay in the alpine house all year round; rather it is the damp, humid, winter conditions outside that would kill them if I did not treat them this way. Without snow cover keeping them dry during their resting period, and with continual cold moisture at their necks and roots for about four months, the plants have no chance of drying out. Most western phloxes need sun, and those I grow outside are either in troughs (I then move them under cover during winter) or in a raised bed with at least 15 cm (6 in.) of grit or sand at their necks. You might want to emulate Anne Spiegel,

who grows *Phlox hoodii*, *P. kelseyi*, and *P. multiflora* in a sand bed in New York. *Phlox diffusa* is in a scree and the others are mostly in troughs where she can keep an eye on them.

I try to move plants that are in the alpine house outdoors from late spring onwards. It is a lot warmer by then, and as the plants are in full growth, the rain does not appear to have a detrimental effect. Another reason for growing western phloxes in the alpine house—and a very important one—is that in my capacity as a nurseryman I am under pressure to continually propagate the choice phlox species. I grow *Phlox subulata* in the garden and they are easy to propagate, but the westerns are completely different.

*Phlox albomarginata* is an attractive little trough plant that prefers a lime soil. In its hot, windswept habitat among the limestone scree it makes mounds similar to those of the best androsace, but in cultivation it is looser, making a good flat mat instead. It stays almost green over winter in the alpine house and commences growth early in spring. In the open garden it appears almost dead during winter and is very late coming into growth.

Among the easiest western phloxes to grow is *Phlox alyssifolia* as it comes from the lower alpine areas. However, it tends to run a bit wild in a scree. *Phlox andicola* has this same tendency so be careful where you plant these two species.

I keep both *Phlox bryoides* and *P. tumulosa* in pots in the alpine house even though they have flowered with only the odd bloom in the last few years. I have yet to learn how to propagate them, and although I am told that *P. bryoides* grows well in a trough, until I have some excess plants with which to experiment, I have to look after my solitary plant very carefully. Although *P. bryoides* appears on the show bench fairly regularly, *P. tumulosa* is virtually unknown to most growers, and I am being continually asked if I have any.

My plants of *Phlox caespitosa* flower very well in an alpine bed. They do not seem to last very long in cultivation but form a good cushion to 10 cm (4 in.) high. I grew *P. caespitosa* subsp. *condensata* in the raised bed for four years, and after it flowered well in the second year it gradually became less vigorous until it rotted off in a damp and humid autumn. I will try this phlox again in a similar situation but with much more drainage. I have great hopes for *P. diffusa*, which is growing well in the same bed. *Phlox caespitosa* subsp. *pulvinata* has been in a pot for about 10 years and has flowered extremely well despite being pot-bound during later years and receiving a lot of moisture during the summer. It looks lifeless during winter.

*Phlox douglasii*, its hybrids, and *P. borealis* grow outside in a sunny place and are not put off by the wet weather. I can treat them almost like an eastern phlox. *Phlox hendersonii* makes a worthy exhibition plant as it is covered with white flowers in June through July. A gritty soil mixture and plenty of water during the growing season suits it best.

When I first tried growing *Phlox hoodii* it did not do well in a pot so I planted it out in the alpine bed. The plant came through several wet winters before rotting off, although it never flowered. Plants I potted on from a batch of seed sent to me by a friend in Oregon grew quickly and flowered a pretty blue in their first year. Some growers cultivate this species in a deep sand bed, where it seems at home.

*Phlox kelseyi* and *P. kelseyi* var. *kelseyi* 'Lemhi Purple' require more moisture than most other cushion-type phloxes in their native habitat and they grow perfectly well in a sunny trough. In addition, because their natural habitat is saline or alkaline soils, they like lime conditions. Most of the green growth on *P. kelseyi* turns brown in winter, and although there is some dying off of the previous year's growth, simply use scissors to tidy up the plant if you are growing it for exhibition. A lot of new growth commences after flowering, which is when you should begin to propagate it. Plants I grew from this cultivar's seed have all flowered a deep purple, but their size varies from a very small congested form to the normal vigorous mat-forming type. I plan to keep a close watch on the small forms for future introductions.

*Phlox kelseyi* var. *missoulensis* grown in the alpine house also makes a lovely pot plant that is perfect for exhibition. It flowers quite freely but in winter the spiky leaves go brown. *Phlox lanata* and *P. muscoides* are slow growing and look completely lifeless in winter.

*Phlox speciosa* and *P. speciosa* subsp. *woodhousei* grow well in a sunny alpine bed but after they flower in spring or summer I must cut the stems back to instigate new growth ready for the autumn flowers. Since this species flowers on new growth twice a year, it needs to be trimmed a little or else it presents the dismal sight of a brown stem with small green growth and flowers at the top. Perhaps in nature wild animals trim the plants as a matter of course.

*Phlox adsurgens* requires a habitat different from all the other phloxes. It likes nothing better than a shady, woodland area with soil rich in humus and a cool root run. In cultivation, though, it does not have a very good reputation for longevity. My advice is to start your own insurance scheme by propagating your phloxes whenever possible.

When I grow western phloxes in pots I use deep pots since the roots grow deeply into moisture-retaining soil mixture during the growing season. I use the usual neutral, soil-based compost with plenty of added grit—sometimes as much as 50 percent—in order to obtain a free-draining mix. I also apply at least 2.5 cm (1 in.) of gritty top dressing for drainage at the plant's neck. As you do with all plants in pots, pay close attention to watering, as although they grow naturally in dry areas, they do require water all year round. Phloxes usually suffer some dieback of foliage, and I remove it once the plant shows signs of spring growth. Most western phloxes enjoy a hot, sunny aspect and rocky and dry gravel slopes in nature, so if you ever acquire any of these rare and unusual cushion phloxes, I can only suggest that you provide these same conditions even if you have to grow them in pots for a while.

Slugs eat new growth of plants growing in the open garden or in the frame, and you should take appropriate action. Aphids, especially whiteflies, and wood lice thrive under the leafy mats of foliage so keep lifting them to check for these pests. Aphids are also a problem in the alpine house, as is red spider. Since red spider thrives in hot dry conditions, keep the atmosphere moist during hot weather by spraying water.

## PHYSARIA
Cruciferae, or Brassicaceae
*twinpods*

Physarias grow throughout the Rocky Mountain and Intermountain regions but they are often easily dismissed as weeds. Even the Alpine Garden Society (1993) describes them as "a largely neglected genus of second rate plants but not without some charm." Others comment they are like echevarias or ice plants. Next time you see one while hiking around, have a close look: not only are the leaves fleshy but the rosettes are also different from species to species. Leaves are powdery, silver, or gray, and the margins may be smooth or toothed. The long flowering season of physarias extends from early February through to summer, and the four-petalled flowers that range from white to pale or bright yellow are followed by seedpods in a variety of shapes and sizes. There are, however, many others in this genus that require a botanist's trained eye to tell them apart, but most species I discuss are not among those.

*Physaria acutifolia* (synonym *P. australis*) occurs in Colorado, Wyoming, and Utah at 1130–2870 m (3675–9330 ft.) in silty gravel soil among sagebrush, pinyon and juniper, and spruce fir. Rosettes of spatulate, silky, silver-green leaves are 5–20 cm (2–8 in.) across. This very floriferous species has dense clusters of medium to large

*Physaria acutifolia*, Medicine Wheel, Wyoming. Photo Fermi de Sousa.

lemon-yellow flowers on 3–25 cm
(1¼–10 in.) decumbent to ascending or
erect stems that completely hide the foliage
in early spring. Inflated, light brown pods to
1.5 cm (⅗ in.) long with reddish tints follow
the flowers.

Variety *purpurea* is endemic to the
mideastern counties of Utah growing at
2135–2870 m (6940–9330 ft.). The flowers
are yellow and sometimes purple on the
outside. Variety *stylosa* is endemic to Utah's
northwest Duchesne and nearby Wasatch
counties, where it grows among spruce and
fir communities and on alpine tundra at
2955–3450 m (9600–11,210 ft.). The
narrow leaves are not more than 1.2 cm
(½ in.) wide.

*Physaria alpestris* grows on the eastern
side of the Cascades of Washington at
around 710 m (2300 ft.) but occasionally
appears on the west side. It also occurs on
the eastern side of the Wenatchee Mountains, where it grows to alpine elevations.
The habitat ranges from cliffs to talus slopes
and dry, exposed alpine ridges. It makes
fleshy rosettes to 8 cm (3 in.) long of silver-
gray oblanceolate leaves. The 10–15-cm
(4–6-in.) long prostrate stems have crowded
racemes of yellow flowers in late spring to
summer followed by large inflated seedpods.

*Physaria alpina* is endemic to the alpine
screes and dry, rocky meadows of Gunnison
Basin and Mosquito Range of central Colorado at about 3770 m (12,250 ft.). Large
single rosettes of many silver-gray, hairy
leaves in an attractive spiral pattern grow to
15 cm (6 in.) across. The prostrate stems
carry large clumps of orange to yellow
flowers in April through May followed by
inflated pods like small grapes. Panayoti
Kelaidis (1990) has described this species on
Colorado's Mount Bross as "painting aston-
ishing canvases of orange mingling with the
deep purple of *Oxytropis podocarpa* under
the ancient bristlecone pines." Surely the

Flower of *Physaria alpestris*. Photo Ed
Godleski.

*Physaria alpina*, Front Range of the Rockies,
Colorado. Photo David Hale.

*Physaria alpina*, Mount Sherman, Colorado.
Photo Jane Grushow.

best in the genus, this species is a must for the trough gardener.

*Physaria bellii* is endemic to the foothills of the northern Front Range in Colorado on the dry, loose, gray-black shale and limestone slopes of the Niobrara formation at 1600–1785 m (5200–5800 ft.). The large multirosettes to 20 cm (8 in.) across are of silver-gray oblanceolate to ovoid leaves. Many ascending to erect stems to 10 cm (4 in.) are topped with clumps of yellow flowers so profuse that the plants are practically covered during March through May. Unusual chunky pods that are tinted purple and red follow the flowers.

*Physaria chambersii* grows among sagebrush and pinyon and juniper on gritty limestone talus slopes at 820–3420 m (2665–11,115 ft.) in Oregon, California, Utah, and Arizona. The rosettes of broad spatulate leaves to 7.5 cm (3 in.) long and 3.8 cm (1½ in.) wide are covered with fine white hairs. Stems 2.5–25 cm (1–10 in.) long are decumbent to ascending or erect with clusters of yellow flowers in May through June followed by large tan-colored pods.

Variety *membranacea* is endemic to Kane and Garfield counties in Utah, where it grows among pinyon and juniper and mountain brush at 1525–2440 m (4955–7930 ft.). Variety *sobolifera* is endemic to Garfield county, Utah, growing among ponderosa and bristlecone pine at 2135–2900 m (6940–9425 ft.).

*Physaria condensata* is endemic to southwestern Wyoming, in particular Lincoln, Sublette, and Uinta counties, where it grows on shale slopes and ridges at 2000–2155 m (6500–7000 ft.). Ovoid, silvery, pubescent basal leaves have a pointed tip and make tight, densely tufted, flattened rosettes. Stems to 8 cm (3 in.) tall have yellow flowers in May through June that smother the plant. They are followed by inflated, deeply lobed pods to 1.2 cm (½ in.) wide.

*Physaria didymocarpa* occurs in British Columbia, Washington, Montana, Idaho,

*Physaria didymocarpa.* Photo Ed Godleski.

*Physaria chambersii* in pod, Butch Cassidy Draw, Utah. Photo Chris Norton.

*Physaria dornii.* Photo Ed Godleski.

and Wyoming on dry rocky or gravel places from the foothills to alpine levels. The basal rosette is made up of silver-gray leaves 2–7.5 cm (¾–3 in.) long. Prostrate stems to 15 cm (6 in.) long have dense racemes of showy, pale lemon to yellow flowers to 1.2 cm (½ in.) wide. These unusually large blooms are followed by even larger seedpods.

*Physaria dornii* is endemic to Rock Creek Ridge in Wyoming, where it inhabits limestone-shale soils on slopes and ridges among *Chrysothamnus nauseosus,* the common rabbitbrush, and *Cercocarpus montanus,* the mountain mahogany, at an elevation of 2000–2215 m (6500–7200 ft.). Tufts 10 cm (4 in.) high are of silver-gray oblanceolate to ovoid leaves with pointed tips. Decumbent stems barely exceed the rosette and they bear yellow flowers during May through July followed by inflated brown pods to 1.2 cm (½in.) across. It was described as a new species in 1983.

*Physaria eburniflora* is endemic to Carbon, Fremont, and Natrona counties in central Wyoming at 1875–2985 m (6100–9700 ft.) and has a mixed habitat of calcareous ridges, crumbly sandstone, or soil crevices in granite outcrops among other cushion plants. The flattened rosettes of entire, ovoid leaves grow to 5–12 cm (2–4¾ in.) across. Prostrate stems 5–8 cm (2–3 in.) long have clusters of cream flowers in March through June depending on altitude. Inflated pods to 1.2 cm (½ in.) follow the flowers.

*Physaria integrifolia* var. *monticola* is found in west-central Wyoming and eastern Idaho at an altitude of 2000–2645 m (6500–8600 ft.) on barren, rocky, limestone hills and slopes. Rosettes of silver-gray, oblanceolate to ovoid leaves grow to 2.5 cm (1 in.) long with erect flowering stems that

exceed the height of the rosette by 5 cm (2 in.) or more. Yellow flowers in June through July are followed by inflated pods to 2.5 cm (1 in.) across.

*Physaria newberryi* grows in southern Utah, Arizona, and New Mexico among salt desert shrub and pinyon and juniper at 885–2350 m (2875–7640 ft.). Basal leaves grow to 7.5 cm (3 in.) long and to 4 cm (1½ in.) wide. The stems are decumbent to ascending or erect and grow 3.8–23 cm (1½–9 in.) long with mid-yellow flowers. Huge angled pods that are among the largest in the genus are striking.

*Physaria obcordata,* a species discovered in the early 1980s, grows in the Piceance Basin in Rio Blanco county of northwest Colorado. It grows at an altitude of 1815–2310 m (5900–7500 ft.) on the barren white outcrops and steep slopes that have been exposed as water from the creeks cuts into the oil-bearing shale that forms part of the Green River formation. Ascending to erect stems have clumps of small flowers in May through June. The U.S. Fish and Wildlife Service lists this species as threatened.

*Physaria obcordata* in northwest Colorado. Photo Bruce Barnes.

*Physaria oregana* is a low elevation species that grows in dry areas of Washington, Oregon, and Idaho. Silver-gray basal leaves are elongated to 5 cm (2 in.) long and have several large square-shaped margin lobes. Stems are 5–20 cm (2–8 in.) tall with pale yellow flowers in April through June, and the seedpods are flattened and heart shaped.

*Physaria saximontana* var. *saximontana* is endemic to Fremont and Hot Spring counties in the Wind River and Bighorn Basins of central Wyoming, where it grows on rocky, sparsely vegetated slopes of limestone, sandstone, or clay at 1725–2555 m (5600–8300 ft.). Small rosettes are of silver-gray spatulate leaves with prostrate to decumbent stems 2.5–10 cm (1–4 in.) long. Relatively large yellow flowers in May through June are followed by hairy gray pods that are notched only at the top and become large enough to almost dwarf the rosettes.

*Physaria vitulifera* is a fairly common species in the foothills of Colorado's Front Range and to the subalpine level among scrub and ponderosa pine on hot, south-facing slopes at 1540–2770 m (5000–9000 ft.). The single rosette of silver-gray leaves has ascending to erect stems 10–20 cm (4–8 in.) tall with pale yellow flowers in April through June. The blue-tinted pods are spherical in shape.

**Propagation**

Propagate plants of these species by seed only. The seed exchanges or commercial lists often offer physaria seed, which germinates very quickly. The plants are fast growing.

**Cultivation**

I recommend you cultivate physarias as you would lesquerellas, which is not under cover. (You may think that is the best way to grow physarias as they come from dry habitats, but it is not.) When I grew these plants under cover they were overinflated, long-stemmed monstrosities that lasted only a season. A sunny trough culture is the place to start growing plants of this genus, after which you should quickly move them onto sand beds that are also in the sun, where they can live for three to four years unless they succumb to winter wet first.

Slugs love physarias so you should take appropriate care.

## POLEMONIUM
Polemoniaceae
*Jacob's-ladders*

Although most people grow polemoniums in the perennial border, there are many lovely, compact, delicate species for alpine enthusiasts that flower on stems 5–30 cm (2–12 in.) tall. Flowers are funnel- to bell-shaped, and in some species are arranged in crowded heads that from a distance look like small balls. Flower color varies from pale to deep blue, purple, and white, and the stamens sometimes protrude beyond the petals. The leaves are usually sticky, and this

Polemoniums typically grow in alpine fell-fields.

stickiness can be transferred to your fingers together with its unpleasant smell. Even when in seed, the capsules are very sticky, which makes seed collection a difficult pastime. The densely packed leaves in some species are also dissected and whorled— a very attractive feature of the plant.

*Polemonium boreale* subsp. *villosissimum* grows on the steep scree slopes of the Alaska Range, particularly in the backcountry, the Eielson-Polychrome area of Denali National Park, and the Brooks Range, Alaska. The whole plant is densely hairy and grows to 12 cm (4¾ in.) tall. Lavender to white flowers bloom in July through August.

*Polemonium brandegei* ranges from Wyoming to Colorado, Utah, and New Mexico. It is occasionally mistaken for *P. viscosum,* although it has longer, more upward-facing blooms. Flower color varies from white to straw- or golden-yellow. Jim Archibald found a lovely, snowy white form in the Laramie Mountains of Wyoming as well as a colony with golden-yellow flowers near Albuquerque, New Mexico. Although this species makes a lovely alpine house specimen, it can be short-lived. It is not grown very often, probably because seed is difficult to obtain.

*Polemonium chartaceum* flower.

*Polemonium californicum* grows in the Sierra Nevada at 1925–2615 m (6260–8500 ft.). It is similar to *P. pulcherrimum* but larger, and the rich blue, bell-shaped flowers, although also similar, are wider. It spreads quickly by rhizomes.

*Polemonium chartaceum* grows in the Siskiyou Mountains of northern California to the alpine fell-fields. A lovely dwarf species, it looks like a condensed version of *P. viscosum.* Beautiful tufts of dissected leaves grow to 5–8 cm (2–3 in.) tall. In March through June deep blue flowers form balls 5 cm (2 in.) in diameter just above the foliage. I grew this species in the alpine house for a couple of years and found it easier to grow than *P. viscosum.* A plant outside in a scree bed, however, did not make it through the first winter.

*Polemonium elegans* comes from Washington at 2060–2370 m (6700–7700 ft.) and has deep blue to lavender flowers on stems 5–10 cm (2–4 in.) tall. Mounds of sticky leaves make mats 30 cm (12 in.) wide.

*Polemonium eximium* grows in the Sierra Nevada on dry rocky slopes and alpine fell-fields at 3075–4310 m (10,000–14,000 ft.). Mounds form from dense tufts of leaves that have numerous leaflets, and it is taller than *P. elegans* at 10–30 cm (4–12 in.). The 5-cm (2-in.) large heads of deep blue-violet flowers in July through August appear in terminal cymes. Ron Ratko likens the habit of this species to *P. chartaceum.*

*Polemonium pauciflorum* occurs in damp areas of Arizona and New Mexico. The stems grow 15–30 cm (6–12 in.) tall and are occasionally branched. The lovely tubular flowers are horizontal to semipendent, and unlike others in this genus, are a soft yellow with red tints. It is a suitable species for the alpine bed, and although perennial, is short-lived. As it sets plenty of seed and occasionally seeds itself, you should never be without it. Plants I grow in the alpine house purely for propagation purposes have seeded themselves into neighboring pots. This species is noticeably less sticky than the others in the genus.

*Polemonium pulcherrimum* grows in Alaska and is common throughout the West. Variable in altitude (it is subalpine to alpine), it is also variable in height, growing to 8–20 cm (3–8 in.). It makes clumps quite quickly of very sticky, pinnate leaves. Although ideally suited to a trough since it is more amiable to winter moisture than the true alpine species, it is not long lasting in cultivation. Shallow-cupped flowers in May through August are pale blue to purple with a white or yellow throat, and white stamens protrude beyond the petals. Even though individual flowers in cultivation do not last long, there are always plenty more to follow.

'Album', a white flowering form that grows to 15 cm (6 in.), makes an excellent pot plant and looks good in a trough. Although the short-lived flowers are smaller than those of the blue form, there are many more of them and the plant is in bloom for several months. Be prepared to remove the dead blooms from the sticky foliage even on the morning of a show.

*Polemonium viscosum*, the sky pilot, has a large range from eastern Washington to Arizona and New Mexico growing on rocky slopes and alpine ridges at an altitude of 3000–4000 m (9750–13,000 ft.). The tufted, whorled leaves are lovely, and the

*Polemonium pulcherrimum*, St. Paul Island in the Bering Sea. Photo Carolyn Parker.

*Polemonium viscosum* grows prolifically on the Mount Goliath Pesman trail in Colorado.

*Polemonium pulcherrimum* 'Album' in cultivation. Photo Rick Lupp.

*Polemonium viscosum*, Mount Goliath Pesman trail, Colorado.

orange or yellow stamens contrast the sky blue petals beautifully. Large flower heads in June through July grow on stems to 15 cm (6 in.) tall.

When I made my first trip to the West in 1982, I did not notice the pungent odor of the flowering *Polemonium viscosum* that dotted the tundra landscape. Perhaps I was too excited, or perhaps the odor of plants growing outdoors was less concentrated. Craighead et al. (1963) offers this warning: "The hiker who inadvertently steps on the sky pilot is trailed by a powerful skunk odor that keeps pace with him as he climbs, lingers unpleasantly close at lunch time and will haunt him in his tent or sleeping bag if he fails to place his shoes at a safe distance away." In spite of this bad press the beautiful *P. viscosum* is always welcome in my alpine house.

## Propagation

It is possible to grow all the species I discuss from seed, which is set fairly generously. Collecting seed either in the wild or in cultivation is not straightforward since both leaves and seed capsules are sticky. Although the black seed is large enough to be handled either with tweezers or between the thumb and forefinger, it becomes ripe while the capsule is still green. The green sticky capsule looks easy to open yet it resists all but the most persistent attempts to remove the seed. I have left the capsules on the plant to dry before cutting them off and placing them upside down in a seed packet to allow the seeds to drop out, but even this does not work satisfactorily as the stickiness persists and the tweezer tips become covered with green and brown foliage. *Polemonium pauciflorum*, although sticky, is an exception because the seed capsules give up their bounty fairly easily.

## Cultivation

In areas with fairly dry winters, these alpine species can probably be cultivated in a scree bed that provides perfect drainage. I doubt whether they will be long-lived in areas of winter wet, however, as they have lasted only two years in my scree beds. It seems that the alpine house or cold frame offers the best chance of cultivating polemoniums for any length of time.

Compact form of *Polemonium viscosum*, Medicine Wheel, Wyoming. Photo Peter Downe.

White form of *Polemonium viscosum*, Beartooth Pass, Wyoming. Photo Peter Downe.

When the polemoniums die back down during winter, they are at their most vulnerable, and any excess moisture at the neck causes them to rot off. *Polemonium chartaceum* has proved easier to grow than *P. viscosum*, remaining green for most of the winter, but like *P. viscosum* it is virtually dormant so do not be tempted to water it very much at this time.

Although small green shoots appear at its neck during a mild winter, *Polemonium viscosum* dies back to a mass of brown foliage in winter; even in the alpine house or frame it is dormant. Give only enough moisture to keep it alive during this time.

*Polemonium pauciflorum* is by far the easiest to cultivate (their damp habitat in the wild may help), and many nurseries in the United Kingdom offer plants for sale at the large horticultural shows. Do not expect these plants to be long-lived but keep them going from seed and plant out fresh stock every year.

The biggest pests are aphids, especially whiteflies, and they can cover stems and buds in no time unless you keep a wary eye open and take preventive action. Rotting at the neck or powdery mildew as a result of damp are the only other problems I have encountered.

## PRIMULA
### Primulaceae
*primroses*

The genus *Primula* contains approximately 500 species, most of which grow in the Northern Hemisphere. Out of this number there are only approximately 25 recognized species growing in North America. Since so few are recognized, and since seed or plant material is often hard to come by, the North American species are not particularly well known even in American gardens, and it is the European or Japanese species that are typically cultivated. There are nevertheless some very attractive primulas native to North America that deserve to be appreciated both in the wild and in general cultivation.

Most North American primulas have a summer dormancy period but it is difficult to be definite about its timing. Dormancy often starts early in the growing season (March through July, depending on elevation or latitude), and if the weather stays reasonably cool and moist, plants stay in full growth for as long as they can. In typically hot, dry summer climates (as in Idaho and Oregon, and to a lesser extent in the Great Basin), they become dormant quite early.

Several Alaskan primulas grow in frost boils or open polygonal areas on tundra where frost action disturbs the ground. The soil movement from a freeze followed by a thaw disturbs the soil enough to keep a mat of vegetation from forming, but a few plants are able to grow there since there is relatively little competition. A frost boil can be considered a classic tundra (arctic and alpine) habitat.

Some primrose flowers are heterostylous, meaning they require both pin and

*Primula alcalina* habitat, Birch Creek, Idaho. Photo Jay Lunn.

thrum to produce seed, whereas others are homostylous or self-pollinating.

*Primula alcalina* grows in moist, calcareous meadows of Idaho at elevations of 1800–2100 m (5850–6825 ft.). Originally considered by many as a white form of *P. incana*, this heterostylous species has since been given its own specific name. Flowers are white and smaller than *P. incana*. Although plants of this species were once collected in Montana, none have been found since the original site was eradicated by road construction.

*Primula angustifolia*, the fairy primrose, is a high alpine that grows on the rocky slopes and meadows of Colorado and New Mexico at 3075–4310 m (10,000–14,000 ft.). This heterostylous plant was the first North American primrose species I saw in the wild, a small, delicate plant flowering in

the snowmelt of Mount Evans in Colorado. It flowers in late June through July, although I have read reports of it sometimes blooming in May. It grows in clumps 2–8 cm (¾–3 in.) high with 2-cm (¾-in.) wide, five-petalled flowers that are rose-pink to purple-pink with a central yellow eye that is surrounded by a white ring. (When you get close to the ground to look at how the yellow spreads outwards into the white, you will think you are looking into a kaleidoscope and not mind your wet knees!) Although there is normally only one flower per stem, plants with multiple crowns usually produce more.

*Primula anvilensis*, described by Tass Kelso in 1987, is endemic to the frost boils, damp calcareous slopes, and river banks of the Bering Sea coastal region in Alaska. Its name commemorates Anvil Mountain

*Primula angustifolia*, Pikes Peak, Colorado. Photo Chris Norton.

*Primula alcalina* flowers. Photo Jay Lunn.

*Primula angustifolia*, Loveland Pass, Colorado.

*Primula anvilensis*, Alaska. Photo Sylvia (Tass) Kelso.

in the Nome area where the plant grows abundantly. Although first collected in the early part of the twentieth century, it has often been confused with other taxa and included under descriptions of *P. borealis*, *P. chamissonis*, *P. mistassinica*, *P. parviflora*, and *P. stricta*. This delicate heterostylous plant has efarinose, denticulate leaves and umbels of one to five small white flowers subtended by short, thin bracts on scapes 2–12.5 cm (¾–5 in.) tall.

*Primula borealis* inhabits coastal estuarine marshes from the Bering Sea coast to Cape Bathurst in the territories east of Yukon Territory. The heterostylous plants grow singly or in dense clusters and are farinose when young, becoming more or less efarinose at maturity. The leaves are spatulate, elliptical, or rhombic with crenate to

remotely denticulate margins. Scapes grow 2–10 cm (¾–4 in.) tall with umbels of three to eight lavender, occasionally white, flowers with a yellow throat.

*Primula capillaris* is endemic to one canyon in the Ruby Mountains area of Nevada at 2800–3100 m (9100–10,110 ft.), where it flowers in July. Anyone hoping to see this heterostylous species in flower has to have keen eyesight and be very lucky, hiking in the right area at the right time of year. Plants of this species are so small they can be difficult to see in the short turf in which they grow. Stems 1.2–6 cm (½–2¼ in.) high bear one or two rose-purple to bluish purple flowers with a yellow eye. The leaves are linear and 1.2–6 cm (½–2¼ in.) long.

*Primula cuneifolia* subsp. *cuneifolia* is known to grow only in the Aleutian Islands

*Primula borealis*, Prudhoe Bay, Alaska. Photo Carolyn Parker.

*Primula capillaris* with a dime. Photo Jay Lunn.

*Primula cuneifolia* subsp. *saxifragifolia*. Alaska. Photo Verna Pratt.

of Attu, Agattu, and Adak, where it grows in moist, mixed herb meadows with acidic bedrock. A herbaceous species, the foliage is efarinose and the scapes are usually greater than 5 cm (2 in.) tall with umbels of two to nine deep pink to rose, rarely white flowers with a yellow throat. Leaves are to 6.2 cm (2½ in.) long and have coarsely dentate margins. It is heterostylus.

Subspecies *saxifragifolia* is homostylous, growing in the Aleutian Islands and western and southern coasts of Alaska and Vancouver Island on damp, shaded rocks, wet alpine slopes, and meadows above the tree line. It also ranges inland to the Alaska Range, where it becomes a submaritime plant in wet meadows. Thick, glabrous leaves are broadly wedge-shaped and dentate at the apex. The flowering scapes are 1.2–5 cm (½–2 in.) tall with umbels of one to four flowers with petals that are cleft in two. Flowers are usually deep pink but also often white.

*Primula cusickiana* grows in the Wallowa Mountains in eastern Oregon and western Idaho. It has a variety of habitats from meadows and light woodland to south-facing subalpine rocky slopes at elevations of 1000–2600 m (3250–8450 ft.). Flowering is from late March, and it continues blooming in White Clouds Peaks of Idaho in late June through mid-July. Although some areas can be moist from spring snowmelt, they become very dry during the summer, which is when *P. cusickiana* dramatically disappears underground. This heterostylous species is quite dwarf—

*Primula cuneifolia* subsp. *saxifragifolia* white form. Afognak Island, Alaska. Photo Carolyn Parker.

*Primula cusickiana* showing intermediate color, White Cloud Peaks, Idaho. Photo Jay Lunn.

*Primula cusickiana* showing typical color, White Cloud Peaks, Idaho. Photo Jay Lunn.

The pin-eyed flower of *Primula cusickiana*, Wallowa Mountains, Oregon. Photo Jay Lunn.

to 9 cm (3½ in.) high—but plants growing in more moist sites can be taller. Umbels of one to four flowers vary from blue-violet to deep violet that darkens toward a yellow eye.

*Primula domensis*, the house range primrose, is endemic to the House Range in Millard county, Utah. It grows in partial tree or rock shade on ledges that are on or at the base of north- to east-facing vertical limestone cliffs at 2400–2745 m (7800–8920 ft.). An attractive heterostylous species, it has oblanceolate to spatulate leaves and umbels of up to five rose to lavender flowers on stems 7–15 cm (2¾–6 in.) tall. Flowering is in mid-May through early June. John Andrews's seed collection in August 1990 at 2450 m (7965 ft.) was probably the first collection made as the species had only been discovered in 1981. The Alpine Garden Society (1993) and John Richards (1993) both record *P. domensis* as a subspecies of *P. cusickiana*.

*Primula egaliksensis* grows in wet meadows and along streams in the south-central, interior, and arctic regions of Alaska. It also ranges to the mountains of Colorado and Wyoming in similar moist conditions at 2000–2400 m (6500–7800 ft.). Stems 3–15 cm (1¼–6 in.) high have tiny white or lilac flowers in up to nine umbels. This homostylous species is not attractive; John Richards (1993) states, "This little species has no garden merit," while Jay Lunn (1990) assures, "This plant will never be the belle of the garden." Do not let that put you off searching the lists for seed as the species is still a challenge and should make an interesting species for a trough.

*Primula domensis*, House Range, Utah. Photo Jay Lunn.

*Primula domensis* in cultivation.

*Primula egaliksensis*, Denali National Park, Alaska. Photo Verna Pratt.

*Primula eximia* (synonym *P. tschuktscho-rum* var. *arctica*) grows from sea level to alpine elevations throughout western coastal Alaska, the Aleutian Islands, and in Denali National Park at elevations over 1200 m (3900 ft.). The habitat includes late snowbeds along coastal bluffs and ravines, the mountains on frost-disturbed areas, and streambeds. Similar to *P. tschuktschorum* but taller, it grows to 40 cm (15¾ in.) with larger and broader dentate leaves. A homostylus species, it has 5–20 umbels of rose-magenta flowers. Plants are covered with white farina when young but usually become glabrous with age.

*Primula incana* is wide-ranging from Alaska, where it grows almost at sea level, to streambanks and wet calcareous grass-lands and marshes in Montana, Wyoming, Utah, Idaho, and Colorado at 2000–3000 m (6500–9750 ft.). The mealy scape is extremely variable in height—from 5 to 45 cm (2 to 18 in.) tall—and has umbels of 7–19 lavender-lilac flowers. Similar to *P. stricta*, it is a homostylous species.

*Primula laurentiana* grows in open areas along limestone riverbanks in the Gaspe Peninsula of Quebec. It can also be found in

*Primula eximia,* Ogilvie Mountains, Alaska. Photo Carolyn Parker.

*Primula egaliksensis*, Afognak Island, Alaska. Photo Carolyn Parker.

*Primula incana*, South Park, Colorado. Photo Jay Lunn.

the limestone regions of western Newfoundland and northeastern Maine. It is very similar to *P. incana* but has smaller flowers. The plants are usually heavily farinose and glabrous. Scapes grow 10–30 cm (4–12 in.) tall with umbels of 3–12 lavender flowers with a yellow throat. The oblanceolate to spatulate leaves are 3–10 cm (1¼–4 in.) long, including the petiole, and are rounded or acute at the apex with crenate margins. The leaves are densely farinose on the underside with white or cream-colored farina.

While I accept that this homostylous species is not a western alpine, it does frequent the far north of North America. It is a good garden plant that grows easily in cultivation in Colorado although it is not particularly showy in a dry climate.

*Primula maguirei* is endemic to north-facing limestone rocky slopes, moist ledges, and crevices at 1200–1800 m (3900–5850 ft.) in the Wasatch Mountains of Utah. Closely resembling *P. cusickiana*, it is quite small and similar in form, stature, and flower. Many consider it among the most beautiful of the North American primulas. Umbels of one to three on stems 5–10 cm (2–4 in.) tall grow from rosettes of broad, spatulate leaves, and lavender to rose flowers have a dark ring around a yellow eye. It is unfortunate that seed of such a stunning primula is unavailable, but this heterostylous plant is listed under the Endangered Species Act of 1973, the only primula species on the list.

*Primula mistassinica* is a North American boreal species that occurs in Alaska to

Flower head of *Primula incana*. Photo Jay Lunn.

Close-up of *Primula maguirei*. Photo Jay Lunn.

*Primula maguirei* in habitat, near Logan, Utah. Photo Jay Lunn.

*Primula mistissinica* on a single stem, Ogilvie Mountains, Alaska. Photo Carolyn Parker.

Newfoundland, northern Vermont, New York, Illinois, Michigan, and Minnesota. Its habitat includes open meadows, riverbanks, lakeshores, and around hot springs on calcareous substrates. The heterostylous plants are usually efarinose and glabrous, although there are sometimes traces of farina on the vegetative parts. Leaves are spatulate or elliptical, and the margins are widely denticulate to almost entire. Scapes to 5–15 cm (2–6 in.) tall have umbels of one to five lavender, occasionally white, flowers with a yellow throat.

*Primula nevadensis* grows in the Snake Range of east-central Nevada and in the Grant Range about 160 km (100 miles) southwest from there at an elevation of 3385–3475 m (11,000–11,300 ft.). It grows in north-facing, vertical, limestone cliffs and

under *Pinus longaeva* (the intermountain bristlecone pine) in limestone rubble fell-fields and screes. Stems grow to 9 cm (3½ in.) tall with umbels of two to three large violet-purple flowers in late June through mid-July with a dark purple ring around a yellow eye. A number of my plants have reached maturity from seed John Andrews collected in Nevada during 1995. A beautiful species that sometimes makes large clumps in the wild, it is a fairly rare heterostylous primula in cultivation.

*Primula nutans* (synonym *P. sibirica*) grows primarily in coastal Alaska and in estuarine marshes, although it is occasionally found in the interior of Alaska and the Yukon. The heterostylous plants are slender and efarinose, sometime rhizomatous with ovate to slightly elliptical leaves. Scapes are

*Primula nevadensis* in limestone scree habitat, Great Basin National Park, Nevada. Photo Jay Lunn.

*Primula nutans*, Nome, Alaska. Photo Verna Pratt.

*Primula nevadensis.* Photo Jay Lunn.

5–20 cm (2–8 in.) tall with umbels of two to four violet flowers that have a yellow throat and nodding pedicels.

*Primula parryi* grows in Idaho, Wyoming, Montana, Nevada, Utah, Colorado, New Mexico, and Arizona. It inhabits subalpine meadows, streambanks, marshes, and lake margins at 2600–4000 m (8450–13,000 ft.). The most spectacular and largest primula in the West, it is also the most widespread. Depending on the location it can grow to 60 cm (24 in.) tall with fleshy, deep green leaves and terminal clusters of 3–20 flowers per stalk. Flowers range from deep pink to blood red with yellow centers, and the more acidic the soil conditions the deeper the red. Unfortunately, this heterostylous species has a strong carrion odor that tends to be a bit offensive, but try not to let that put you off.

*Primula rusbyi* (synonym *P. ellisiae*) grows in central and south-central New Mexico, in south-eastern Arizona, and as far south as Mexico. It inhabits shady places on hillsides and cool, moist crevices or screes at elevations of 2460–3385 m (8000–11,000 ft.). Spatulate green-gray leaves have denticulate margins, and the 5–20-cm (2–8-in.) tall stems have umbels of

*Primula parryi*, Hunt Mountain. Photo Peter Downe.

*Primula nutans* in cultivation. Photo Verna Pratt.

Deep red form of *Primula parryi*, Independence Pass, Colorado. Photo Chris Norton.

4–12 magenta, purple, or rose-red flowers with a red-ringed yellow eye. This heterostylous species is in bloom from early summer and is probably among the easiest North American primulas to grow. Although it dies back there are still small green leaves in evidence in cultivation, which means it is not dormant as most other North American alpines are. It makes a good pot plant as it quickly forms large clumps.

Many American botanists include *Primula ellisiae* under *P. rusbyi* since the two differ only in the relative lengths of the calyx and corolla, a relationship that can be influenced by the flower's age. Since both short and long corolla types can be found in a single population, I too place this taxon under *P. rusbyi*.

*Primula specuicola* is an endemic of the Colorado River canyons in Utah and Arizona, where it clings to the wet, vertical, sandstone cliff faces in hanging gardens or grows upside down on the roofs of caves at altitudes of 1125–1680 m (3655–5460 ft.). A particularly good form inhabits the cold desert area slightly west of Moab, Utah, at around 1385 m (4500 ft.). High walls of slickrock sandstone have weathered over the years resulting in numerous cracks that are home to a myriad of plants such as

*Aquilegia micrantha*, *Epipactis gigantea*, and various ferns and mosses. *Primula specuicola* also thrives there in the black, spongy, water-retentive soil in the shallow cracks. Although the desert's summer temperatures may exceed 38°C (100°F) in summer, the soil is almost always damp because of the constant seeping of water from the sandstone.

*Primula specuicola* looks like a larger form of the European *P. farinosa* and is another species with farina coating the leaves. It grows 6–28 cm (2¼–11 in.) tall with umbels of 5–40 flowers in shades of lavender to rose, pink, or white. It is early flowering with buds in January and final blooms by May; its tendency to flower at Easter gives it the common name of easter flower. It also has the common name of cave primrose. This heterostylous species, though spectacular, is unfortunately short-lived in cultivation.

*Primula stricta* grows in moist places, often in saline soil, from the Canadian Arctic Archipelago to Greenland and Scandinavia. The homostylous plants are efarinose or sparingly farinose with obovate-lanceolate leaves in a tight rosette. Scapes are 7.5–15 cm (3–6 in.) tall with umbels of two to nine small lavender to pink flowers that have emarginate lobes.

*Primula rusbyi* in cultivation.

*Primula specuicola* near Moab, Utah. Photo Jay Lunn.

*Primula suffrutescens* is the only primula species to grow in California. It occurs mainly in the Sierra Nevada and Trinity Alps at 2460–4155 m (8000–13,500 ft.), where it grows in crevices under overhanging rocks and in slightly shaded places in rocky ground near cliffs. A mat-forming, evergreen sub-shrub, it has branched, creeping stems 4–15 cm (1½–6 in.) tall with two to nine terminal umbels of 2.5-cm (1-in.) wide magenta to bright red flowers that have a yellow eye and an exotic, far-eastern fragrance. Leaves are a dull green and spoon-shaped. This heterostylous species blooms fairly late—from July through August—in the receding snow banks.

*Primula tschuktchorum* grows from sea level to 500 m (1625 ft.) in western Alaska along the Bering Sea coast, in western Alaska's mountains, and along the Bering Strait region of the Russian Far East. It grows in frost boils and in gravel along small streams where the soil is saturated during most of the growing season. The heterostylous plants are completely efarinose and glabrous. The flowering stem grows to 10 cm (4 in.) tall with oblong to lanceolate, occasionally dentate leaves that are 4 cm (1½ in.) long. Umbels contain one to three rose-magenta flowers and the bracts are acutely lanceolate.

**Propagation**

Seed is the customary method of propagation for these primulas, and you can obtain seed for some species from the society

*Primula stricta*, Yukon Territory, Alaska. Photo Verna Pratt.

*Primula suffrutescens*, Winnemucca Lake, California. Photo Jay Lunn.

A large plant of *Primula suffrutescens*, Winnemucca Lake, California. Photo Jay Lunn.

exchanges and commercial seed lists. If you sow seed and place the pots outside during late autumn and early winter, seed will usually germinate during spring. Seedlings are often slow to grow, and you will do them no harm if you wait an additional year after germination before pricking them out. I have often split the seedlings into small clumps that I then pot up and let grow on. In my experience, however, *Primula parryi* does better when I prick it out earlier as it grows more quickly than the other primulas. Primulas naturally become dormant in summer (except for *P. suffrutescens*), but if you do not let them dry out until the autumn they will become more developed plants the following year. If you already have mature plants with formed clumps, divide them in spring when growth commences. Since *P. suffrutescens* is shrubby you can increase it by cuttings or division.

## Cultivation

The initial reaction for first-time growers of western primulas is one of surprise. Most primulas are summer dormant, and when the first species I grew, *Primula domensis*, died back in summer I thought I would have to discard it. I emptied the pot expecting to find the usual rotted mess of a dead plant but instead found a root system with a little point on the top. I was shocked since I had not read anything that said this may happen. I have kept a close check on my North American primulas since then and found that only *P. suffrutescens* remains completely evergreen. My primulas grow in the alpine house and generally stay moist into autumn, so the green foliage tends to last longer than it would in the wild. If you grow primulas in pots keep them slightly moist over winter and use a fairly rich, gritty soil mix.

North American primulas do not tolerate dry conditions during the growing season and will go into their resting period if they receive no moisture. All primulas except *Primula suffrutescens* are summer dormant. Each primula has slightly different needs, which I list briefly.

*Primula angustifolia* needs plenty of water during growth; *P. capillaris* requires a north-facing position with a slightly acidic soil mixture and small to medium-sized pieces of granite incorporated in the soil mix; and *P. cusickiana* and *P. maguirei* require slightly acid conditions during the growing period. *Primula alcalina*, *P. egaliksensis*, and *P. incana* prefer wet calcareous soil, and *P. rusbyi* needs deep, well-drained soil,

Close-up of a pin-eyed *Primula suffrutescens*. Photo Jay Lunn.

*Primula tschuktchorum*, Alaska. Photo Tass Kelso.

plenty of moisture at the roots in summer, and does well in a rock garden. *Primula suffrutescens* requires some shade and does well if granite chippings are added to the soil mixture.

*Primula domensis* is shade loving but does better when it is also exposed to the sun for two to three hours a day, provided the pot does not become warm. It is early flowering—usually in May—and goes into summer dormancy before the others. However, if it is slightly moist it will stay green well into autumn. My plant, which grows in a pot in the alpine house, took six years to go from seed to flower, although it produced a lot of foliage every year.

It is probably better to plunge the pot of *Primula nevadensis* up to its rim in sand and keep it outside during summer rather than in the alpine house. When it is dormant, ensure that it has cool summer conditions. In the wild this plant tolerates frequent, incredibly violent hailstorms in spring and summer, so perhaps planting it in a trough that can be kept dry in winter will suit this species.

*Primula parryi* requires plenty of moisture during the growing season and does well in an acid scree in partial shade and in the alpine house. Keep it just moist during winter, and if you grow it for exhibition, plant it in a fairly large pot with a peaty soil mix.

Prick out seedlings of *Primula specuicola* as soon as possible as members of the farinosae section resent root disturbance. It does well in an alpine house with no overhead watering, which only encourages botrytis. Although short-lived, it usually flowers the year following germination.

Although I have not grown any Alaskan primulas, I imagine you will meet with success if you can simulate their growing conditions. The biggest problem at present is obtaining seed of the Alaska primula species.

Slugs are a problem on plants growing outside. In the alpine house it is aphids, especially root aphids, that are the worry. Root aphids seem to attack plants that become dry during the growing season, perhaps because they are stressed. Watch carefully that the leaves do not go yellow, especially since spider mite also causes mottling.

## PULSATILLA
Ranunculaceae
*pasque flowers*

There are approximately 30 species within *Pulsatilla*, two of which grow in the United States. They are outstanding plants with beauty throughout each stage of their life, from the unusual buds to the dissected, fernlike leaves, the large, cup-shaped flowers, and the silver, silky, plumelike seeds that blow away and drift in the wind. Both species I discuss are well worth growing in a pot, trough, or very gritty alpine bed

*Pulsatilla occidentalis* buds, Crater Lake, Oregon.

*Pulsatilla occidentalis* (synonym *Anemone occidentalis*), the western pasque flower, is a beautiful high alpine that grows in Washington, Oregon, California, and Nevada on rocky slopes at altitudes to 3000 m (9750 ft.). It rarely occurs below the timberline. Snowmelt triggers the onset of this species' rather unusual growth. When buds first appear they look like gray lollipops with their sticks pushed into the ground. As the stems reach 5–10 cm (2–4 in.), the furry, slate blue buds open to display 5-cm (2-in.) wide white, bowl-shaped flowers with yellow stamens on stems that have pinnate, lacy leaves. The backs of the petals are tinted purple-blue. As the flowers age and seed is set, the stems become taller—to 60 cm (24 in.)—and the clumps of long-tailed seeds resemble mop-heads.

It is worth visiting Crater Lake National Park in Oregon in late June to early July to see this species. On the rim drive of Crater Lake not far from Rim Village is a large, shallow depression filled with snow during winter. As the snow melts, hundreds of clumps of *Pulsatilla occidentalis* bloom in the pumice among *Phlox diffusa*. Also look out for these pulsatillas on the approach to the area around Sunrise on Mount Rainier, where they bloom alongside *Erythronum grandiflorum*. If the winter snowfall has been particularly heavy, *Pulsatilla occidentalis* may not bloom until August. This species is considered the equivalent of the European *P. alpina* (synonym *Anemone alpina*).

*Pulsatilla occidentalis*, Crater Lake, Oregon.

Mount Rainier, Washington, habitat.

*Pulsatilla occidentalis* in seed. Photo Rick Lupp.

*Pulsatilla occidentalis* on the approach to Sunrise, Mount Rainier, Washington.

*Pulsatilla patens* (synonyms *P. nuttaliana*, *P. patens* subsp. *multifida*) has a very wide range throughout the West from the Great Plains to alpine levels at 3700 m (12,025 ft.) in Colorado and the dry, sandy

*Pulsatilla patens*, Medicine Wheel, Wyoming. Photo Peter Downe.

*Pulsatilla patens*, Tanana River, Alaska. Photo Carolyn Parker.

soil of Alaska's interior. Similar to the European *Pulsatilla vulgaris*, it is often called the wild crocus or pasque flower. The 3–10-cm (1¼–4-in.) wide pale lavender to purple flowers in late March have yellow stamens and grow from a gray-green basal tuft of leaves on stems 15–23 cm (6–9 in.) tall. The mops of silky seedheads are almost as attractive as the flowers.

### Propagation

Although it is possible to transplant *Pulsatilla vulgaris*, I do not recommend doing this with the American pulsatillas. Both pulsatillas I describe are much easier to propagate by seed if you sow it when it is fresh and do not keep it until the autumn or spring. Germination is usually in the following spring, though occasionally they germinate in the autumn of the year in which they were sown. Seed of *P. patens* is often offered in seed lists, although it is not always that species.

### Cultivation

*Pulsatilla patens* comes into growth much earlier than *P. occidentalis* but both species require a similar culture. *Pulsatilla occidentalis* likes a fairly dry period over winter and rots off if it receives too much moisture. Although a good plant for a trough, it needs protection from winter damp. If you grow it in a pot, incorporate plenty of grit into the soil mix and give it the minimum amount of water during the winter. Let it come into growth on its own in spring before you increase the watering. It is so easy to overwater this plant before growth commences properly, but if you are patient, *P. occidentalis* will reward you in its own time.

There are no disease or pest problems apart from slugs that eat the fresh growth.

# R

## RANUNCULUS
Ranunculaceae
*buttercups*

I am sure that many of you picked buttercups when you were children and put them under your chin to check the yellow reflection and see if you liked butter. In the United Kingdom it is likely that only *Ranunculus acris*, the meadow buttercup, was picked. In the western United States, though, there are numerous species of buttercups growing at moderate elevations as well as alpine and subalpine zones. Most are yellow flowered and have five petals. The leaves are usually palmate, often lobed or dissected, but occasionally simple. The genus name *Ranunculus* means little frog, which refers to the wet habitat of most species and to the frogs that are usually living in the same habitat. Many species are very difficult to identify in the field and require a specialist reference and probably the services of a botanist. Although birds and small mammals eat some parts of ranunculus, they are poisonous in an uncooked state when eaten by humans. The poison in the leaves becomes harmless if they are dried or boiled, which is what the Indians did.

*Ranunculus adoneus*, the snow or alpine buttercup, grows at high elevations above the timberline in Wyoming, Colorado, Idaho, Utah, and Nevada. It blooms in the snowmelt during late June through August, but you will occasionally see it pushing up through thin patches of snow and ice. It grows 10–30 cm (4–12 in.) tall with bright yellow flowers to 2.5 cm (1 in.) across, one to three per stem. The three main lobes of the basal leaves are divided twice into linear segments. Stems are clustered together with the bases covered by old dead leaves. It is closely related to *R. eschscholtzii*, and some authorities consider it a variety of that species.

Variety *alpinus* (synonym *Ranunculus eschscholtzii* var. *alpinus*) grows in alpine meadows, talus slopes, and wet soils where the type grows. The flowers are larger and there are more dissections on the leaves than *R. eschscholtzii*. Ron Ratko found a population growing at 3310 m (10,750 ft.) in San Pete county, Utah, that contained many plants with 2.5-cm (1-in.) wide semidouble flowers in a habitat of moist, fine, silty limestone soil.

*Ranunculus alismifolius* var. *hartwegii* is widespread in the West and is among the first wildflowers to appear in the gravel alpine meadows after snowmelt when it blooms in May through July. It has 5–12. 5-cm (2–5-in.) wide lanceolate basal leaves and several stems that range from 5 to 80 cm (2 to 32 in.) tall. There are only a few 1.2-cm (½-in.) wide, five-petalled flowers.

Variety *montanus* grows in Utah with flowers of 9–10 petals.

*Ranunculus adoneus*, Loveland Pass, Colorado.

*Ranunculus andersonii* grows in gravel soils in Oregon, California, Idaho, Nevada, Arizona, and Utah among sagebrush, pinyon and juniper, and ponderosa pine at 1095–2800 m (3560–9100 ft.). The 5-cm (2-in.) long glaucous basal leaves are trilobed, and each lobe is again divided two to three times into linear or ovate segments. Stems grow 5–30 cm (2–12 in.) tall with solitary pink, reddish, or purple flowers in spring to summer.

Variety *juniperinus* occurs in the southwestern counties of Utah and has two flowers per stem.

*Ranunculus californicus*, the California buttercup, grows in Oregon, on the Sierra Nevada, and in Baja California, Mexico, below 925 m (3000 ft.). It is tufted to clump forming with hairy basal leaves that are deeply trilobed or divided into three to five

leaflets. Erect stems are 20–70 cm (8–28 in.) tall with rich yellow flowers in February through May that have 9–16 petals to 3 cm (1¼ in.) across.

Variety *austromontanus* grows in California only at 1360–2250 m (4420–7310 ft.) in moist meadows and conifer forests. It has fan-shaped leaves and smaller flowers.

*Ranunculus eschscholtzii* ranges from Alaska to California, Nevada, Colorado, Montana, Utah, and northern New Mexico in the snowmelt of subalpine and alpine meadows. Leafless stems grow 5–25 cm (2–10 in.) tall with one to three yellow flowers per stem, each of which is 2–3.8 cm (¾–1½ in.) across. The trilobed leaves differ from those of *R. adoneus* in that the central segment is three toothed or entire and the lateral segments are either lobed or toothed. This species is named after Dr. J. F. Eschscholtz, a surgeon and naturalist with the Russian expeditions to the Pacific coast of North America in 1816 and 1824.

Variety *oxynotus* is common in the Sierra Nevada on open rocky slopes at 2460–4310 m (8000–14,000 ft.). It is very compact with stems 2.5–5 cm (1–2 in.) tall and it blooms in July through August. Variety *suksdorfii* has more sharply lobed lower leaves. Variety *trisectus* can be found

Habitat of *Ranunculus eschscholtzii* on Hunt Mountain, Wyoming. Photo Chris Norton.

*Ranunculus eschscholtzii*, Hunt Mountain, Wyoming. Photo Chris Norton.

in eastern Oregon, Idaho, and Utah; it has slender and more acute lobes.

*Ranunculus gelidus* has very scattered locations in the Alaska and Brooks Ranges and the Talkeetna Mountains of Alaska but it also occurs in Utah and Colorado. It grows in alpine tundra, wet scree slopes, and talus at 3415–3800 m (11,100–12,350 ft.). The trilobed basal leaves are cleft or parted several times. There are one to three small yellow flowers on stems 2.5–10 cm (1–4 in.) tall that curve either above or below the floral bracts.

*Ranunculus glaberrimus* is widespread, ranging from British Columbia to the Dakotas, the eastern slopes of the Cascades and Sierra Nevada, California, Utah, and New Mexico among sagebrush and in lodgepole pine communities at 1460–3050 m (4745–9915 ft.). This small fleshy plant has glabrous stems 5–20 cm (2–8 in.) tall and the basal leaves to 5 cm (2 in.) long have entire or trilobed blades. Yellow flowers in March through June are to 3 cm (1¼ in.) across.

Variety *ellipticus* has linear, basal leaves.

*Ranunculus hystriculus* can be found in the Sierra Nevada, particularly in Yosemite National Park in California, at 925–1845 m (3000–6000 ft.) on mossy rock ledges and moist areas around waterfalls. The stems grow 15–45 cm (6–18 in.) tall, and the white, cream, or yellow flowers in April through June have 5–12 petals. The shiny leaves have three shallow lobes and look similar to maple leaves.

*Ranunculus macaulayi* grows in the high mountain habitats of Colorado and New Mexico. Unlike other ranunculus the elliptical basal and stem leaves are nearly all entire; in fact the stem leaves are toothed only at the ends. The one to three bright yellow flowers are 2.5 cm (1 in.) across on stems 10–15 cm (4–6 in.) tall. Flowers bloom during midsummer in the snowmelt

*Ranunculus nivalis* grows throughout much of Alaska in late snowbeds and mountain streams. The one to two basal leaves are trilobed with blunt segments and the stem leaves have three to five segments. Stems grow to 12.5 cm (5 in.) tall with solitary yellow flowers and a calyx of five sepals covered with black hairs.

*Ranunculus pedatifidus* is a circumpolar species that is widespread through the western United States in alpine tundra at about 3415 m (11,100 ft.). Erect stems grow 6–30 cm (2¼–12 in.) tall and are covered with long, soft, straight hairs. The 2.5-cm (1-in.) wide yellow flowers are few in number, and the petals are twice as long as

*Ranunculus gelidus*, Alaska Range. Photo Carolyn Parker.

*Ranunculus glaberrimus*. Photo Rick Lupp.

the sepals. The petals and leaves are similar in size to *R. gelidus*, and the narrow leaf segments resemble *R. adoneus*.

*Ranunculus populago* occurs in the grasslands and moist open areas of Washington, Idaho, Montana, and California at 1500–1850 m (4875–6010 ft.). It is tufted to clump forming with long-petioled basal leaves that are narrowly ovate or cordate. Stems grow 10–30 cm (4–12 in.) tall with pale to deep yellow flowers in May through June that grow to 2.5 cm (1 in.) across.

*Ranunculus pygmaeus* ranges from Alaska to Colorado at high elevations in the Rockies. It is a very small species, and the basal leaves, though also small, are broad and have rounded lobes. Ascending to erect stems grow to 5 cm (2 in.) tall and each one has one to two tiny yellow flowers.

*Ranunculus reconditis* (synonym *R. triternatus*) is endemic to the Dalles Mountain in Washington and two sites in Wasco county in Oregon. Known as the Dalles Mountain buttercup, it grows in moist areas among sagebrush and ponderosa pine and open grassland at 923–1230 m (3000–4000 ft.). Stems grow to 15 cm (6 in.) tall with leaves that are triternately divided, a feature that distinguishes it from other *Ranunculus* species. Yellow flowers in March through May are 3.8 cm (1½ in.) wide with a V-shaped yellow gland at the base of each petal.

*Ranunculus verecundus* is common in alpine meadows and talus slopes from Alaska to northeast Oregon, Idaho, and northwest Wyoming. At the ends of the sprawling 7–20-cm (2¾–8-in.) long stems grow one to five small yellow flowers. The sepals, which are about the same length as the petals, are quickly deciduous.

## Propagation

Propagate ranunculus plants by seed as soon as it is ripe. You can also divide the clump-forming species in spring once growth commences.

## Cultivation

Many small and desirable species within this genus do well in cultivation in a sunny but moist and well-drained site. Those from alpine levels are much more difficult to grow and they require special conditions that only the alpine house or cold frame can provide: adequate moisture in spring, sharp drainage, a cool, moist root run, a humus-rich soil mixture, and a dormant summer period. Some species that come from low to medium elevations in the southernmost areas of the genus's range, such as California, need frost protection.

Slugs and snails eat the growing tips in early spring, and aphids in the alpine house distort the leaves.

# S

## SAXIFRAGA
Saxifragaceae
*saxifrages*

Saxifrages are well represented in the West with about 25 growing in the Rockies. Over half this number grow at alpine elevations, and several are circumpolar or circumboreal. Unlike the European saxifrages, most North American species have basal clusters of leaves, fairly tall stems, and small white flowers; they grow in damp, sometimes shady, habitats and very few are garden worthy. A number of cushion- or mat-forming species are, however, worth growing, and three are available commercially. Although the other cushion- or mat-forming species are difficult in cultivation, they are slowly becoming available, and if their requirements are satisfied, they will become valuable additions to the garden.

*Saxifraga adscendens* ranges from the northern Rockies and Cascades to Colorado and Utah. A short-lived species, it grows on rocky slopes, crevices, moraines, and alpine tundra. The 5–10-cm (2–4-in.) tall stems grow from a tight cluster of short leaves and bear small white flowers during midsummer.

*Saxifraga aprica*, the Sierra saxifrage, is common in the moist alpine meadows of the Sierra Nevada and southwest Oregon. It has a basal tuft of purple-green oval leaves and leafless stems that are 2.5–12.5 cm (1–5 in.) tall. The greenish white flowers form small, rounded, terminal clusters in May through August and have round petals.

*Saxifraga bronchialis* is widespread from Alaska to northern Oregon, Idaho, and New Mexico. It inhabits open slopes or rocky crevices that are usually high in the mountains and is a common plant along mountain trails. A mat-forming species, the basal rosettes are often tinged with red and the tiny lanceolate leaves have short bristles

along the margins. Stems grow to 30 cm ( 12 in.) with small white flowers in June through August that have numerous maroon, yellow, or orange spots.

Three subspecies are notable, though Rick Lupp says none blooms as well in cultivation as in the wild. Of the three, subsp. *vespertina* blooms best at his nursery in a sand bed on the north side of a rock.

Subspecies *austromontana* grows on rocky ridge tops and ledges in Washington and northeast Oregon, though it also occurs almost at sea level on some islands in northern Puget Sound in Washington. The most common subspecies, it does not make big mounded plants like subsp. *vespertina* but forms flat mats that at most are about 30 cm (12 in.) across. Flowers on 5–10-cm (2–4-in.) tall stems have truncate petals with

*Saxifrage bronchialis* subsp. *funstonii*, Alaska. Photo Verna Pratt.

Large group of *Saxifraga bronchialis* subsp. *funstonii*, Alaska. Photo Verna Pratt.

*Saxifraga bronchialis* subsp. *vespertina* in a rock crevice on Bohemia Mountain, Oregon.

red-purple spots toward the apex and yellow spots near the base.

Subspecies *funstonii* from Alaska has flowers with clawed petals and that are spotted yellow (sometimes they are yellow with orange spots). A form that was introduced by Mt. Tahoma Nursery from the Talkeetna Mountains grows to 10 cm (4 in.) tall, has attractive low mats of tight, green, needlelike leaves, and produces large, soft yellow flowers that have orange spots. It is easy to grow provided it has ample moisture at the roots.

Subspecies *vespertina* is distinguished from subsp. *austromontana* in that it grows only at alpine elevations and makes very tight mats of much smaller rosettes. I once saw a magnificent 275-cm (108-in.) long

*Saxifraga bronchialis* subsp. *vespertina* cascading down the rock face of Bohemia Mountain, Oregon.

specimen that flowed down a vertical crevice at the edge of the Bohemia Mountain summit plateau at 1840 m (5980 ft.). It is an easy plant in the garden, where it makes large mats. Opinions are divided on whether it is a subspecies of *Saxifraga bronchialis* or a species on its own, but I believe it is an authentic subspecies.

*Saxifraga bryophora* grows in the moist, subalpine, and alpine meadows of the Sierra Nevada at 2155–3385 m (7000–11,000 ft.). The straplike leaves have scattered hairs and are in basal tufts. Slender flowering stems are 5–20 cm (2–8 in.) tall, and white flowers have two yellow spots on each petal. An unusual feature of this species is that the flower is often replaced by a miniature bud or plantlet, hence the common name bud saxifrage. It blooms July through August and is probably an annual.

*Saxifraga caespitosa* grows in British Columbia, Washington, and Oregon, where it inhabits rocky crevices and cliff faces, usually with *S. bronchialis*. Tiny trilobed leaves form a basal tuft from which the stems grow to 30 cm (12 in.) tall. White flowers in June through July are bowl-shaped, and each has five rounded petals.

*Saxifraga caespitosa*, Mount Townsend, Olympic Mountains, Washington.

Variety *emarginata* grows on talus slopes and rocky ledges in Washington at 1785–2340 m (5800–7600 ft.). The basal tufts of leaves are so tight that they form small dense cushions. Small white flowers grow on 2.5–5-cm (1–2-in.) tall stems.

*Saxifraga californica* (synonym *S. virginiensis* var. *californica*) grows on shady banks or in scrub and pine woodland at low elevations in California and Oregon. It has a basal rosette of rectangular leaves 1–5 cm (½–2 in.) long and leafless flower stems that are 10–30 cm (4–12 in.) tall. Small white flowers in February through June are in loose corymbose cymes with five stamens opposite the rounded petals.

*Saxifraga cernua* is a circumpolar species that also ranges from Alaska to the Rockies and New Mexico. Leaves are palmate, rust-colored, and hairy on the undersides. Stems grow 10–15 cm (4–6 in.) tall with solitary, terminal, nodding white flowers—rarely more than three per stem—that are often not developed. Flowers bloom in midsummer and are replaced by red bulblets. It is not a very attractive plant.

*Saxifraga chrysantha* grows in the Rockies of northwest Wyoming, Utah, Colorado, and northern New Mexico, inhabiting open rocky slopes and moraines

*Saxifraga chrysantha*, Mount Evans, Colorado.

at elevations near or above timberline. At high elevation the mats of apple-green fleshy leaves look similar to an androsace, and the 2–5-cm (¾–2-in.) tall stems have one or two round-petalled, golden-yellow flowers in midsummer. This species must be the best in the genus; a friend once described it to me as being "like a pot of gold at the end of the rainbow" since it lights up the ground wherever it grows. During my second trip up Mount Evans in Colorado, I photographed a superb specimen growing between two rocks. Of all the western saxifrages, this is the species that I, like others, would love to grow.

*Saxifraga davurica* grows in moist places in alpine areas throughout Alaska. Basal tufts consist of glabrous, cuneate leaves with five to seven pointed teeth. The 10–15-cm (4–6-in.) tall stems have white to purplish flowers with purplish sepals in July.

*Saxifraga debilis* ranges from Canada to California, Arizona, and New Mexico on damp cliffs and rock crevices that are frequently near snowbanks. Closely related to S. cernua, it is considered by some to be a subspecies of it. The basal leaves are orbicular with three to seven lobes. Stems grow 1–10 cm (½–4 in.) tall with white flowers that have pink veins.

*Saxifraga eschscholtzii* grows in scattered locations throughout Alaska inhabiting rocky outcrops and lichen tundra. A beautiful high alpine, it forms a small rounded cushion from rosettes of very small, light grayish leaves that have hairs along their edges. Tiny yellow flowers in late May through June grow on short stems. Such is the shape of the cushion that Verna and Frank Pratt (1993) have given it the common name of barnacle saxifrage.

*Saxifraga ferruginea* ranges from south coastal Alaska (beginning in the Aleutian Islands southward to southeast Alaska) to northern California. It grows on rock outcrops, wet banks, and along trails and roadsides. The straplike basal leaves have toothed margins and are glandular-pubescent. Stems to 15–60 cm (6–24 in.) tall bear flowers that are unusual in that they have two kinds of petals: three broad petals that each have two yellow-orange spots, and two narrow petals that have no markings. The white flowers are small, on bracted open panicles, and bloom in June through July.

*Saxifraga flagellaris*, the whiplash saxifrage, is a circumboreal species that grows in the Rockies in alpine screes and moist rocks of southern Montana, Wyoming, Colorado, Arizona, and New Mexico. In eastern Utah it occurs among alpine tundra at 3350–3960 m (10,890–12,870 ft.). It forms loose mats of rosettes and red runners, and at the end of the runners are small rosettes by which this species roots and spreads into new plants. Leafy stems 5–10 cm (2–4 in.) tall have loose cymes of one to four yellow flowers in midsummer.

*Saxifraga fragarioides* grows on dry cliffs in the Siskiyou Mountains in Oregon and to the Trinity Mountains of northern

*Saxifraga eschscholtzii*, Kantishna Hills, Alaska. Photo Carolyn Parker.

California. It has a basal rosette of near glabrous, wedge-shaped leaves that are toothed at the furthest edge. The main stems are 25–30 cm (10–12 in.) tall with branching flower stems at regular intervals. The inflorescence in June through July is in a loose panicle. Although many tiny white petals make up the flower, it actually looks yellow because of the bright yellow carpels at the flower's center.

*Saxifraga hirculus* can be found in the wet meadows of the Uinta Mountains of Utah and the alpine bogs of Colorado. A yellow-flowered species that is similar to *S. chrysantha*, it is different in that it has no basal rosette and is larger with stems 6–20 cm (2¼–8 in.) tall.

*Saxifraga hitchcockiana* (synonym *S. occidentalis* var. *latipetiolata*) is endemic to the summits of some of the higher elevations in the north Oregon Coast Range, including Saddle Mountain. The basal rosettes of rounded leaves are covered with glandular yellow hairs. Stems grow 25–30 cm (10–12 in.) tall with heads of small white flowers in June through July.

*Saxifraga integrifolia* grows on the wet, grassy, coastal hillsides of Oregon and Washington to 1000 m (3250 ft.). Similar to *S. rhomboidea*, it has a basal rosette of 5-cm (2-in.) long leaves that generally have entire leaf margins. Stems are 15–30 cm (6–12 in.) tall with a head of white to greenish, occasionally pink-tinged, flowers.

*Saxifraga lyallii* grows in the shade in damp meadows and near streams and ponds in Alaska, the northern Cascades, the Rockies in northern Idaho, and western Montana. It forms basal rosettes of many fan-shaped, toothed leaves with red, leafless stems that grow 8–35 cm (3–14 in.) tall. Several small white flowers in July through

August have two yellow dots on the petals. The flowers age to pink. This species is easily confused with *S. punctata* but the latter grows much taller.

*Saxifraga mertensiana* occurs in Alaska, the mountains of central California, central Idaho, and western Montana, where it grows on wet banks in rocky and forest seeps and along streams. A basal cluster of large shiny, succulent, and rounded leaves grows to 10 cm (4 in.) across. The leaves are edged with toothed lobes. Branched stems grow from 10 to 40 cm (4 to 15¾ in.) tall with tiny white flowers that have narrow petals.

The flowers of variety *bulbifera* that are lower down on the stem are replaced by red bulbils or tiny plantlets that grow into new plants after they drop to the ground.

*Saxifraga occidentalis* is widespread in the western mountains from Canada to Washington, northeast Oregon, Idaho, Montana, Nevada, and Wyoming. It is common on cliff faces, moist slopes, rocky outcrops, and seeps. Basal leaves are ovate and toothed, and they form tight rosettes around the stems. Stems grow 5–30 cm (2–12 in.) tall and bear open inflorescences of many white flowers in April through August. The leaves and stems sometimes have a reddish tinge. This is a variable

species that almost certainly hybridizes with other saxifrages growing nearby.

*Saxifraga odontoloma* (synonym *S. arguta*) is very common in the mountainous regions of the West, where it grows on stream banks, around ponds and lakes, and in wet meadows to alpine areas. The basal leaves are rounded and toothed with leafless flower stems 15–78 cm (6–31 in.) tall. Numerous small white flowers in June through September are in an open inflorescence.

*Saxifraga oppositifolia* is circumpolar, occurring in Alaska, British Columbia, Washington, northeast Oregon, central Idaho, Montana, and northern Wyoming. (It also grows in the United Kingdom.) Its habitat includes talus slopes and rock debris at 2770–3385 m (9000–11,000 ft.). Those plants that grow in the Pacific Northwest usually make very tight domes; the European forms, by contrast, make mats. Both mat-forming and domed forms are sometimes growing together in Alaska, but usually only the mat forms occur in the Rockies. Plants of this species grow to 5 cm (2 in.) tall and to 20 cm (8 in.) across, and the oval leaves are sometimes tinged with maroon. Purple to reddish lavender flowers in June through August are on very short

*Saxifraga oppositifolia*, Alaska Range. Photo Carolyn Parker.

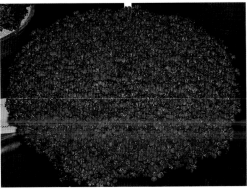

*Saxifraga oppositifolia* 'Theoden' in cultivation.

stems. In cultivation, blooming starts in March.

This species is widely available in the horticultural trade although the cultivars from Europe predominate. Three of the best are 'Wetterhorn', which has large rose-red flowers, 'Ruth Draper', a vigorous and large-flowered form, and 'Theoden', which has large rose-purple flowers. 'Corrie Fee' is a white flowering form.

*Saxifraga oregana* grows in wet meadows in Washington, Oregon, and the Rockies to Colorado at 2000–3000 m (6500–9750 ft.). A large plant, it has a basal rosette of spatulate leaves 2.5–15 cm (1–6 in.) long. The small, delicate, greenish white or occasionally yellowish white flowers have oval petals. These flowers grow in clusters on stems 30–90 cm (12–36 in.) tall in May through August.

*Saxifraga rhomboidea*, the snowball saxifrage, is a fairly common species throughout the Rockies from British Columbia to Utah, Colorado, and New Mexico. It grows in a wide range of habitats from dry to moist regions on sagebrush hills to alpine tundra. The basal cluster has toothed, diamond-shaped leaves that give it the alternative common name of diamond leaf saxifrage. Tight globose heads of many white to cream

*Saxifraga rhomboidea*, Echo Lake, Mount Evans, Colorado.

flowers in late spring to midsummer grow on a single erect stem 5–30 cm (2–12 in.) tall. Duft and Moseley (1989) suggest that in Colorado *S. oregana* hybridizes with *S. rhomboidea*.

The first western saxifrage I saw was *Saxifraga rhomboidea*. It was growing in moist shade among the trees at the edge of Echo Lake rest area at 3075 m (10,000 ft.), about 15 km (14 miles) from Mount Evans Summit in Colorado. It looked different from other saxifrages that I knew and grew at that time, and only after visiting a bookshop did I identify it.

*Saxifraga rivularis* is circumpolar, growing in Alaska and to a lesser degree in the Rockies and Colorado along alpine rivulets and dripping cliff faces. Similar to *S. debilis*, it has spreading, inflorescent branches and very small, toothed, round to kidney-shaped leaves. Its habit is tufted and it spreads by underground stolons. Stems grow 5–15 cm (2–6 in.) tall with one to six very small, loosely clustered, white flowers in June through July.

*Saxifraga serpyllifolia* grows in dry rocky places at high alpine levels throughout Alaska. Tiny tight rosettes of small, shiny, oval leaves grow on stems 5–7.5 cm (2–3 in.) tall. The bright yellow flowers are 1.2 cm (½ in.) across and have orange spots on their petals.

*Saxifraga tolmiei*, the alpine saxifrage, ranges from Alaska to central California, central Idaho, and the Bitterroot Mountains of western Montana. It inhabits moist rocky places, particularly melting snowbanks, at 2615–3690 m (8500–12,000 ft.). Tiny succulent leaves are smooth and densely tufted, forming low mats over 60 cm (24 in.) across. Red leafless stems are 2.5–15 cm (1–6 in.) tall with tiny white or pale yellow flowers in

July through August that have oval petals and white clublike stamens. The plant in some ways resembles a sedum. This species is very difficult in cultivation as it requires a well-drained soil and constant moisture.

*Saxifraga unalaschcensis* (synonym *S. calycina* subsp. *unalaschcensis*) occurs on both coasts of the Bering and Chukchi Seas and on the Aleutian Islands. It grows 5–25 cm (2–10 in.) tall depending on habitat, although the average height is 8–15 cm (3–6 in.).

### Propagation

You can propagate many *Saxifraga* species by removing the tiny plantlets that replace some flowers. *Saxifraga flagellaris* propagates itself with new plants at the end of runners that you can pot up and grow on.

If you want to increase your cushion- or mat-forming saxifrages (such as *Saxifraga oppositifolia* and *S. bronchialis* varieties), propagate those forms by cuttings since they root very easily in sand during most times of the year. Winter, however, is usually the best time to take such cuttings.

Most western saxifrages are not cushion or mat forming, nor do they develop plantlets, so you will need to use seed to propagate them. Unfortunately, very little

*Saxifraga unalaschensis*, St. Paul Island, Bering Sea. Photo Carolyn Parker.

of this seed is ever available, perhaps because most North American saxifrages are not very attractive and therefore not commercially profitable. Since 1999, seed of *Saxifraga bryophora*, *S. caespitosa*, *S. chrysantha*, *S. ferruginea*, *S. odontoloma*, *S. oregana*, and *S. tolmiei* has been available in commercial seed lists. All these species are a challenge to cultivate—even to germinate.

### Cultivation

Considering the native habitats of the saxifrages I describe, most would likely require a gritty and moist soil. For example, *Saxifraga tolmiei* requires a place in the sun and a very gritty, continually moist soil mix throughout the growing season. It must not be allowed to dry out. I succeeded once in germinating *S. tolmiei* and growing it to a reasonable size under these conditions, but it died before flowering. Although I tried twice to germinate seed of *S. chrysantha* I never succeeded.

*Saxifraga oppositifolia* and *S. bronchialis* subsp. *vespertina* grow well in my alpine bed, where they receive shade only in late afternoon. *Saxifraga bronchialis* subsp. *funstonii* grows in a pot in my alpine house because I have not yet propagated enough of this plant to try it outside.

Red spider mite is problematic in the alpine house, and vine weevil grubs attack plants growing in pots outside that contain a peat-based soil mixture.

## SCUTELLARIA
### Labiatae, or Lamiaceae
*skullcaps*

There are approximately 300 species of *Scutellaria* throughout the world, and although many are quite tall, some attractive species in the United States are nevertheless suitable for rock gardens. Scutellarias are square-stemmed herbaceous plants that generally lack any significant aroma or fragrance and are grown primarily for their ornamental flowers, foliage, or calyxes, although several species have recognized medicinal or herbal uses. The flowers are tubular and outwardly flared to form two lips, and the seedpods (which are the calyxes) are shaped like hooded helmets.

*Scutellaria angustifolia* grows in Washington, western Idaho, Oregon, and California at low elevations in open places. Stems grow 10–30 cm (4–12 in.) tall and have long, gray, lanceolate to ovate leaves. Both stems and leaves have upward curving hairs that often have glands at their tips. The long, tubular, deep blue-violet corolla is bent above the calyx, which has an unusual hornlike crest on the topside. It spreads via slender rhizomes and blooms in May through June.

*Scutellaria antirrhinoides* inhabits rocky areas in northern California and southern Oregon. Forms with larger flowers chiefly occur east of the Cascades and in areas of Idaho, Nevada, and also Utah, where it grows at 1500–2000 m (4875–6500 ft.). Stems 15–25 cm (6–10 in.) tall grow from the thick rhizomes that spread in dry, gravel soils. In June through August it has violet blue flowers (there are two lighter blotches on the lower lip) that usually occur in pairs except in the upper axils, where they are singular. Stems and leaves have upward curving hairs and are often gland tipped. Ovate leaves are to 1.2 cm (½ in.) long with crenate to serrate edges and petioles to 2 cm (¾ in.) long.

*Scutellaria austiniae* grows in the San Jacinto and Santa Rosa Mountains of California, the Sierra Nevada, and the northern Coast Range. It occurs in rocky places in yellow pine forests and chaparrals and is a glabrous plant that occasionally has a few hairs on the leaves. Middle leaves may be lanceolate or very narrow—1.2–3 cm (½–1¼ in.) long—and sessile. Stems 10–30 cm (4–12 in.) tall that grow from slender rhizomes bear violet-blue flowers to 3 cm (1¼ in.) long in May through July.

*Scutellaria bolanderi* occurs in California near valley woodlands in sand or gravel stream banks or wet meadows alongside yellow pine, white fir, and Douglas fir. It grows in both sun and shade. Typical stems are 20–40 cm (8–15¾ in.) tall and bear white to near white flowers in July through August that are to 2 cm (¾ in.) long. On each flower's lower lip, which is flecked or tinged with violet, there are fine hairs. The foliage is pubescent and sometimes glandular. Coarsely crenate to serrate leaves are deltoid to narrowly ovate and grow to 2 cm (¾ in.) long on petioles half that length. The seeds are smoke-colored, warty, and ridged.

Other forms (they are possibly variants of *Scutellaria californica*) may appear with ovate, crenate, or dentate leaves similar to those of *S. tuberosa*.

*Scutellaria brittonii* grows in hills and valleys from Wyoming to New Mexico. Stems grow 15–30 cm (6–12 in.) tall from a thick rhizome-forming rootstock. In May through June there are deep violet-blue flowers 3.2 cm (1¼ in.) long with a magenta-pink area on the lower lip. I do not recommend this species for the rock garden as it is potentially very invasive.

*Scutellaria californica* (synonym *S. bolanderi* var. *californica*) ranges from central California to the Siskiyou Mountains in Oregon in dry gravel soils or chalky slopes among thickets. It spreads by thick rhizomes. Stems are 10–30 cm (4–12 in.) tall and often have glands at the tips; like the leaves they have upward curving hairs. The ovate leaves are to 1.2 cm (½ in.) long with crenate to serrate edges and petioles that are to 2 cm (¾ in.) long. White to pale yellow tubular flowers in June through July grow to 2 cm (¾ in.) long and occur in pairs at each pair of opposing leaves. The seeds are ridged.

*Scutellaria nana* occurs in Idaho, western Nevada, central to southern Oregon, and California to 2300 m (7475 ft.), where it grows among sagebrush and pinyon and juniper communities on dry volcanic soils. It is mat forming from tuberous rhizomes. Stems are branched near the base and grow 5–15 cm (2–6 in.) tall. Oblanceolate to oblong-ovate silver-gray leaves are to 2 cm (¾ in.) long. The white, cream, or pale yellow flowers are solitary, usually erect, to 2 cm (¾ in.) long, and similar to snapdragons; they bloom in May through June at lower elevations and in June through August above 1250 m (4060 ft.). Some flowers are tinted with streaks of orange to magenta across the hood of the upper lip as many variant color populations exist. Blue flowers are rare, however. Populations of pure white or cream-colored flowers grow east of Eagle Lake in California and along the Oregon highway between Denio Junction, Nevada, and Frenchglen, Oregon.

*Scutellaria sapphirina* (synonym *S. nana* var. *sapphirina*) is endemic to the Great Basin area of Nye county, Nevada, and southwestern Utah, where it grows on fine, dry, granitic or calcareous scree among artemisia at around 1980 m (6435 ft.). This gem of the genus was discovered by Dwight Ripley and Rupert Barneby and described by Barneby in 1947. Known as the white pine skullcap, the typical skullcap flower is a rich gentian blue. It grows from underground rhizomes and makes little tufts to 5 cm (2 in.) high and to 30 cm (12 in.) wide. The gray-green leaves are tiny, rounded, and felty. I grew this plant for many years in the alpine house, and although the flower color made it worthwhile, the thin stems grew 10–15 cm (4–6 in.) tall and tended to flop over. It is a species that really needs to be cultivated outside to keep it compact but only in areas where it can be kept dry over winter.

*Scutellaria tuberosa* grows in Baja California, Mexico, California, southern Oregon, and the Sierra Nevada primarily on dry slopes. Stems 5–20 cm (2–8 in.) tall grow from creeping tuberous rhizomes and are often sticky, hairy, and branched at the base. Blue flowers to 2 cm (¾ in.) long bloom in April through May and are solitary in the axils. The hairy leaves have ovate blades to 2.5 cm (1 in.) long and are coarsely dentate on short petioles. Seeds are black and coarsely toothed.

## Propagation

Although seed is the usual method of propagation for most scutellarias, you can also propagate them by dividing the rhizomes in autumn or spring. Specialist societies currently supply seed of the more unusual species.

## Cultivation

Any well-drained, gritty soil suits scutellarias but *Scutellaria sapphirina* does better in a frame or alpine house.

Aphids and red spider mite are problems for plants growing under glass.

## SHOSHONEA
### Umbelliferae, or Apiaceae

In 1986 Erwin Evart published details about a new monotypic genus that he had discovered in Wyoming called *Shoshonea*. Almost immediately some growers in the United Kingdom, particularly the exhibitors, began frantically chasing after seed in order to get the plant on the show bench. Sure enough, it was exhibited in the "New or Rare in Cultivation" class a couple of years later, and yet unlike many other choice North American cushions, it has rarely appeared since. I believe this scarcity is due mainly to the plant not being showy enough, especially since seed is often available from commercial lists and the plant is easy to grow. I still

have a plant that has come back to life each spring since 1992 and gradually grown larger, although when I look at it each year I wonder if it is a beauty or just a curiosity.

When describing the plant, Erwin Evart mentioned that although his initial discovery was at 2770 m (9000 ft.) on the top of Rattlesnake Mountain in Wyoming, he was also amazed to find plants growing just 6 m (20 ft.) from the Cody to Yellowstone highway in Shoshone Canyon, Wyoming. I did not have Erwin's luck in finding plants close to the highway so had to climb the steep mountain beginning where the bridge crosses the Shoshone River. After climbing past the cacti and grass that cover the crumbling rock, I reached a large stable rock area where *Shoshonea pulvinata* appears with *Kelseya uniflora*, some penstemons, and a few grasses.

*Shoshonea pulvinata* grows on exposed limestone cliff crevices, ridge tops, and talus slopes at altitudes of 1540–2830 m (5000–9200 ft.). Although initially thought to be restricted to the Shoshone River area in Park county, Wyoming, it has been reported growing in the Absaroka Range and Owl Creek Mountains in Wyoming, and in the Pryor Mountains near the

View of *Shoshonea pulvinata* habitat from Shoshone Bridge. Photo Ev Whittemore.

*Shoshonea pulvinata* with *Kelseya uniflora*. Photo Ev Whittemore.

Montana–Wyoming border. A cushion-forming species that is somewhat woody at the base makes large mounds of highly aromatic, tight pinnate foliage not more than 15 cm (6 in.) high. Small, lemon-yellow flowers with short peduncles appear in June.

**Propagation**

Seed is the usual method of propagation, and you can obtain it from various commercial lists. You may want to try rooting the side rosettes, something I have not yet attempted.

**Cultivation**

Although I grow Shoshonea pulvinata in a pot of neutral soil mix with plenty of grit, I am sure it would do equally well in a trough.

*Shoshonea pulvinata*. Photo Ev Whittemore.

Close-up of *Shoshonea pulvinata* flower.

It grows very slowly and dies back to brown foliage in winter, though it becomes green again in early spring. In spite of neglecting my plant by forgetting to water it or not repotting it, I am pleased to report that it still comes back to life every year. If you have a couple of spare plants I recommend trying one in a trough, though I would probably cover it or move the trough inside over winter.

To date I have found no problems with either pests or diseases.

**SILENE**
Caryophyllaceae
*campions, catchflies*

*Silene* is a remarkable genus of carnation relatives with representatives dispersed from the arctic to tropical regions of Africa and South America. Only a tiny minority of the 500 or so species within this genus grows in the West, and yet this minority contains some of the best species. One I describe is circumpolar and a true alpine cushion with small flowers, whereas most others grow at a lower elevation and have flowers with inflated calyxes and often notched or split, clawed petals. Very large flowers in several species make for ideal exhibition plants.

***Silene acaulis*** is unusual in that it is not just a North America native but is also circumpolar, even growing in Europe's mountains. In the United States it grows at high altitudes in Colorado, the Big Horn Mountains of Wyoming, the Wallowa Mountains of Oregon, the Olympics, the northern Cascades of Washington, and Alaska. A superb alpine cushion, *S. acaulis* makes a dense mosslike mat or low cushion to 30 cm (12 in.) across. Solitary, star-shaped flowers

1.2 cm (½ in.) wide appear just above the foliage in June through August. Flower color usually ranges from pale to deep pink to brilliant rose, but there is also a white form. Where it grows in the tundra areas, a good specimen can look like a pink ball perched between rocks. Like so many other high alpines, *S. acaulis* does not flower well in cultivation despite how easy it is to grow. Seed harvested from free-flowering plants is available nowadays in commercial lists.

Variety *exscapa* has shorter flowering stems, and plants I grew from seed collected in Idaho flowered quite well. Variety *subacaulescens* from the high alpine areas of Wyoming and Colorado has pale pink flowers that flower freely all summer.

*Silene acaulis*, Summit Lake, Mount Evans, Colorado.

*Silene californica*. Photo Tony Barber.

'Alba' is a white flowering cultivar with an obscure origin; there are many clones of this form in cultivation, and some are more free-flowering than others. 'Pink Pearl' is a recent pink cultivar listed by Rick Lupp. 'White Rabbit' is white flowering and also listed by Rick Lupp.

*Silene californica* grows in coarse, gritty soil in the woodlands of southern Oregon and California and is among the more colorful Californian wildflowers, even competing with some castillejas. Although it can start flowering by the end of March at lower elevations, it may still be in bloom in higher places around 1550 m (5040 ft.) in August. Depending on the location, some populations may be to 20 cm (8 in.) tall. Deeply lobed, vivid scarlet flowers 5 cm (2 in.) in diameter are on prostrate stems usually 5–10 cm (2–4 in.) long that grow from rhizomatous mats. The compact form makes a lovely pot plant.

*Silene campanulata* grows in California and southern Oregon on rocky outcrops and along trails among thickets. Stems 10–30 cm (4–12 in.) tall have broad, oval, sticky leaves. Nodding flowers in May through August are bell-like with an inflated calyx, and the petal tips, which are in four sections, are further divided, meaning there are eight

*Silene californica* in cultivation.

linear lobes. A nice plant grows on the summit of Bohemia Mountain in Oregon alongside *Calochortus subalpina*, *Penstemon rupicola*, and *Sedum oregonense*.

*Silene douglasii* is widespread from British Columbia to Montana, Utah, and central California. It grows to 60 cm (24 in.) tall, but plants in Utah at an elevation of 3570–3690 m (11,600–12,000 ft.) are shorter and more compact. Each stem carries two to three white to pinkish flowers in July through August with enlarged calyxes. Not among the most attractive species, it is probably one for the enthusiast rather than the general alpine grower.

*Silene hookeri* subsp. *hookeri* (synonyms *S. hookeri* subsp. *ingramii*, *S. ingramii*) grows in southern Oregon and northwest California in dry soil of open woods and hillsides that dries out even further in summer. Flowers are typically to 3 cm (1¼ in.) across, are deeply cut into linear lobes, and vary in color from pale pink to apricot. The plant formerly distinguished as subsp. *ingramii* is from a population of deep magenta or pink flowers growing near Roseburg, Oregon. The hairy, gray stems are about 5–15 cm (2–6 in.) tall.

There are two subspecies to consider. Subspecies *bolanderi* once grew on serpentine slopes in Josephine county, Oregon, but is now believed to be extinct there. It is still fairly common in dry areas of northern California, however, at around 770 m (2500 ft.). The common name stringflower perfectly describes the beautiful petals that

*Silene campanulata*, Bohemia Mountain, Oregon.

Selected deep pink form of *Silene hookeri* subsp. *hookeri* in cultivation.

*Silene hookeri* subsp. *hookeri*. Roseburg, Oregon. Photo David Hale.

*Silene hookeri* subsp. *bolanderi*, California. Photo David Hale.

are divided into four narrow, stringlike lobes. The whole plant is no taller than 15 cm (6 in.) with decumbent stems 2–15 cm (¾–6 in.) long that grow from a buried rootstock and terminate in huge white flowers to 5 cm (2 in.) across. The more condensed plants grow in full sun, and though blooming in the wild is usually in May through June, it can continue into July in cultivation. It is an excellent exhibition plant.

Subspecies *pulverulenta* is a rare plant that grows in the Siskiyou Mountains of southwest Oregon, although some may also grow in Del Norte county, California. Stems grow to 12 cm (4¾ in.) tall with the lower leaves to 7 cm (2¾ in.) long. Flowers vary from a rich pink to white and have a tubular calyx.

*Silene laciniata* is a xeric species from the White Mountains of New Mexico. Star-shaped, red-orange flowers bloom all summer on stems 30–35 cm (12–14 in.) tall.

*Silene parishii* is a native of California with two varieties in cultivation. Variety *latifolia* is a little known species from California's north-facing granite outcrops at about 2030 m (6600 ft.). It forms a compact mound to 10 cm (4 in.) high that is made up of many sticky stems that grow

Close-up of *Silene hookeri* subsp. *bolanderi* flower. Photo Jane Grushow.

from a woody crown. Twenty or more pale yellow flowers are clustered at the end of the stems.

Variety *viscida* grows at around 2350 m (7640 ft.) in the San Jacinto Mountains. This sticky plant is well branched and quite lax in its habit. It has dark green foliage and pale yellow flowers.

*Silene parryi* grows in the Olympics of Washington, where it inhabits southeast-facing, open, dry slopes at approximately 1800 m (5850 ft.). Stems 22–30 cm (8 ¾–12 in.) tall bear large, white, tattered flowers that fade to pink and lavender. Similar to *S. douglasii* in appearance, it is more robust and has much larger flowers.

*Silene petersonii* is fairly rare and grows in the steep limestone screes of central Utah at 2135–3450 m (6940–11,210 ft.). At 5 cm (2 in.), it has been described as the loveliest intermountain silene; Rebecca Day-Skowron (1996–1997) says it is "Surely one of America's most beautiful little known alpines." The flowers are quite large at 2–3 cm (¾–1¼ in.) across and are a pretty rose-purple to pink with darker veins. I find that plants grow to 15 cm (6 in.) tall and tend to flop over in cultivation. The sticky foliage also attracts and holds aphids.

Variety *minor* grows in red, sun-baked limestone at a lower elevation.

*Silene sargentii* grows at alpine levels in California and Nevada. It is closely related to *S. suksdorfii* and looks similar but is a little larger with flowers that vary from white to pale rose or purple.

*Silene scouleri* is a species from Utah that normally grows to 80 cm (32 in.) tall. At its highest elevation of around 3300 m (10,725 ft.), it can be quite dwarf at 15 cm (6 in.). It has a few narrow leaves, and the pink flowers are very sparse.

*Silene suksdorfii* grows primarily on the alpine talus slopes of the Cascades volcanoes in Washington and Oregon. A little known but very attractive species, it makes hard, compact cushions with upright stems 3–15 cm (1¼–6 in.) tall. The unusual flowers from mid to late summer are just 1 cm (½ in.) across and are similar to smaller versions of *S. hookeri*. They have inflated sticky calyxes and are white, sometimes with lavender or green tints. This extremely uncommon species makes a good exhibition plant in the alpine house or a trough. Plants I grow from seed collected on Mount Adams, Washington, are 5–10 cm (2–4 in.) high.

*Silene wrightii* grows in sandstone crevices at around 2185 m (7100 ft.) and has stems to 18 cm (7 in.) with attractive, frilly white flowers. In spite of being a xeric plant, this species tolerates a wide range of conditions. It is now available through seed lists.

## Propagation

You can most easily propagate *Silene acaulis* from cuttings taken in late summer (of course this is essential if you have a free-flowering clone). The other *Silene* species are all usually grown from seed but you should propagate any really special form you wish to increase by taking cuttings or

*Silene suksdorfii* in cultivation.

making divisions in spring. You can divide *S. suksdorfii* in spring.

I hand pollinate *Silene hookeri* subsp. *bolanderi* with a small paintbrush to ensure seed is set. I sow the seed as soon as it is ripe, and it usually germinates the following spring. If you delay sowing until spring, germination most likely will not occur until the following year. One big advantage of growing this species from seed is that if it germinates in spring and you pot the seedlings up early, they usually flower in the summer of the same year.

## Cultivation

Although *Silene acaulis* is fairly easy to grow, it does not always flower as well as it does in the wild. Since it is a high-altitude species it needs to be grown in a very gritty mix in a relatively sunny but not hot site. It requires more moisture than others in this genus and is well suited to a trough. *Silene acaulis* in all its forms is not completely evergreen and usually has only a little bit of green foliage during winter when, in areas of high rainfall, it sometimes looks like a soggy mess.

Although *Silene californica* stays compact in a sunny scree or trough, it is even lovelier as a pot plant. The bright red blooms glow in the alpine house during summer, and if the autumn to winter period is mild it will not die back completely. As long as you keep it slightly moist, *S. californica* will send out very short green shoots from the base that remain green over winter. During one very mild winter this species was blooming in my alpine house in December.

*Silene douglasii* is too tall for my liking but its habitat is similar to the other *Silene* species in that it likes sun and grows in gritty, dry soils. You should be able to grow *S. douglasii* in any garden location where *S. californica* is able to grow.

*Silene hookeri* dies back over winter to a rootstock that is just below ground level. The series of nodes at the top of the rootstock is next year's growth, and as the plant becomes older, the number of nodes will increase so making a bigger plant. The roots need a little moisture over winter to keep the plant alive. This winter rest has been likened to bulb culture by some growers, but keep a close watch to prevent the plant from rotting off. Sometimes the nodes stay green during the winter period, which makes cultivation a little easier. You can pot on the plant in spring as it commences growing again.

I have grown *Silene hookeri* subsp. *bolanderi* and the deep pink subsp. *hookeri* in a trough and the alpine house. They are particularly well suited to trough culture if you can protect them from excess winter moisture and the ever-present slugs. Most growers consider the alpine house the best place to grow both these subspecies because of their fine exhibition qualities. If you grow them from seed and pot them up, do not be surprised if they flower in the same year since they are so fast growing. I have been able to pot on some of my plants into 15-cm (6-in.) pots before the summer. Both subspecies require the same cultivation and will benefit from a weak feed when buds are showing. After flowering, the stems and seedpods eventually turn brown and fall from the root stock. Gently remove any stems that do not fall off on their own. Remember to collect the seed (if it has been set) before the stems and seedpods fall off. The brittle seedpods will break open between your fingers.

*Silene petersonii* grows well in a sunny scree area but because it emerges in spring later than many other plants after dying down for winter, I tend to wonder if it has died. Seed is set very freely however, making it easy to keep a stock of plants in growth.

*Silene suksdorfii* dies down below the surface during winter leaving behind a mat of dead stems. (Shoots emerge from below the surface in spring.) It is fairly easy to keep going in a scree. The very sticky seedpods make seed collection awkward.

If you grow silenes outside pay careful attention to preventing slug damage. Slugs prefer the buds and will not eat the leaves. Aphids love *Silene hookeri*, and sometimes no amount of spraying with an insecticide will prevent an infestation in the alpine house. I must occasionally resort to soapy water and to removing each insect by hand. Red spider mite can seriously affect plants of this genus that grow in the alpine house. Since prevention is better than cure, spray the plants with water all the time in hot weather. Once your plants are affected, however, you will have to use a systemic spray. The plants will take a very long time to recover.

## SYNTHYRIS
Scrophulariaceae
*coraldrops, mountain kittentails*

*Synthyris* contains many species with attractive leaves and flowers. The terminal racemes (many of which are very dense) of blue-purple flowers often appear early in the year before the toothed leaves have fully matured. Their habitat ranges from the shady, moist, low elevation forests to the alpine tundra. Low elevation forms are easy to grow in the garden whereas the higher elevation species require some protection in winter because the wintering buds easily rot off if they receive excessive moisture. *Synthyris pinnatifida* and its varieties all make good exhibition plants.

*Synthyris borealis* is limited to the Alaska Range and Wrangell–St. Elias Mountains of Alaska, where it grows on the high alpine ridges and tundra areas. It makes small hairy mounds of rounded leaves. Stems grow 10–12.5 cm (4–5 in.) tall and have tight terminal heads of blue flowers.

*Synthyris missurica*, mountain kitten-tails, grows in the coniferous forests and moist, west-facing gravel depressions of Washington, Oregon, Idaho, California, and Montana at 1385–2860 m (4500–9300 ft.). The toothed, orbicular leaves are similar to the eastern *Galax rotundifolia*, and the 5–17-cm (2–7-in.) tall, dense racemes of deep blue flowers in April through June grow on stems 10–40 cm (4–15¾ in.) tall. This species is probably the easiest to grow in the shady rock garden.

'Magna' is a cultivar with bright blue flowers.

*Synthyris pinnatifida* grows in the alpine tundra, subalpine limestone ridges, and meadow communities of Washington, Montana, Idaho, Wyoming, and northern Utah at 2560–3390 m (8320–11,020 ft.). It blooms early with dark blue flowers on stems 8–28 cm (3–11 in.) tall. The basal tufts of pinnate leaves grow to 18 cm (7 in.) long at maturity.

Variety *canescens* grows in southwest Montana and in Idaho's north-facing talus slopes and rock ledges at 3140 m (10,200 ft.). The beautiful, gray, hairy leaves are pinnately dissected and in tight rosettes, and dense purple flower spikes grow to 10 cm (4 in.) and bloom soon after snowmelt.

Variety *laciniata* is endemic to the limestone ridges, moist alpine meadows, and tundra at 2775–3630 m (9020–11,800 ft.) in the Wasatch Range and southern counties of central Utah. The 5-cm (2-in.) tall spikes of dark blue-purple flowers are fully mature when the dense tuft of rounded leaves (which are cut into narrow lobes) fully emerges.

Variety *lanuginosa* from the Olympics of Washington is endemic to the drier pine ridges at 2000–2090 m (6500–6800 ft.). Arguably the best garden plant of all the

*Synthyris borealis*, Ogilvie Mountains, Yukon, Alaska. Photo Carolyn Parker.

*Synthyris pinnatifida* var. *lanuginosa* in cultivation. Photo Rick Lupp.

varieties, it has beautiful ash-gray leaves that are pinnately dissected and covered with fine silver hairs. Stemless spikes of blue-purple flowers appear soon after snowmelt. A superb plant, it does best in an alpine house or frame, at least over winter.

*Synthyris reniformis*, the snow queen, grows at low elevations in moist shady forests in southwestern Washington, Oregon, and central California. Stems to 20 cm (8 in.) tall have short racemes of small blue-purple flowers in terminal clusters in April through June. It is less spectacular than other species. 'Ollalia Violet' has deep violet flowers.

*Synthyris schizantha*, the fringed synthyris, is an extremely rare species growing in the Olympics and Cascades of Washington and in Oregon's north Coast Range. The 7-cm (2 ¾-in.) wide kidney-shaped leaves are purplish green, deeply veined, and toothed. Stems growing to 20 cm (8 in.) have 7-cm (2¾ in.) long terminal racemes of purple flowers in May through June.

*Synthyris stellata* is endemic to the west end of the Columbia River Gorge in Oregon, where it grows on mossy, shady banks of rock at around 310 m (1000 ft.). Shiny, deep green leaves are more sharply toothed than most species. Dense racemes of lavender-blue flowers in April through May are 7–15 cm (2¾–6 in.) long on stems that grow to 30 cm (12 in.). *Synthyris stellata*, which is occasionally referred to as a variety of *S. missurica*, is a beautiful species for a moist spot.

## Propagation

Seed is the usual method of propagating plants in this genus. If your plants are large enough, however, you can also divide them in spring.

## Cultivation

The lower elevation species grow well in a moist, shady garden with humus-rich soil. You can grow *Synthyris pinnatifida* and its varieties in the scree or trough, but *S. pinnatifida* var. *lanuginosa* requires alpine house treatment if you want to protect the beautiful foliage and autumn buds. Any species you cultivate in a pot must have ample moisture during the growing season or their buds will abort. Although some references indicate that buds of *S. pinnatifida* var. *lanuginosa* will be aborted if the winter is not cold enough, I have not found this to be the case as my plants have flowered even after a mild winter.

Slugs are the main pest as they eat the buds during winter. Whiteflies can cause problems in the alpine house.

# T

## TALINUM
### Portulacaceae
### *fameflowers*

*Talinum* does not rank high on the list of popular plants and yet there are several attractive species within the genus. During a trip to Arizona in 1990, Sonia Lowzow and I were discussing *Lewisia brachycalyx* when she introduced me to talinums, one of which was blooming in her trough. From a seedling she gave me, a plant of *T. brevifolium* still grows well in my alpine house and over the years has produced many offspring from seed.

Talinums look completely dead during winter but once spring arrives are galvanized into producing delicate blooms that range from cream to a deep pink. Flowers usually open in sunny weather and quite often only in the afternoon. The relationship between talinums and lewisias is most evident in the succulent leaves and fleshy rootstock.

*Talinum brachypodium* is a New Mexico endemic that grows on bare or shallow, silty or clay calcareous soils that are underlain by calcareous rocks. Larger in all parts than *T. brevifolium*, it is extremely rare and will likely be a protected plant. Unfortunately, we will probably never see this species in cultivation.

*Talinum brevifolium* is widespread in Texas, but I am sure the form I have grows as far west as New Mexico, east-central Utah, and north-central Arizona, where fine, reddish sand forms a shallow overlay on red, iron rich sandstone. A mat-forming species to 2.5 cm (1 in.) high, it has leaves that are cylindrical, gray, and succulent. The pale to deep pink flowers 2–3 cm (¾–1¼ in.) across are its outstanding feature. This superb and rare species grows well in full sun, and even though seed is set profusely, it is rarely seen in cultivation.

*Talinum okanoganense* (synonym *T. sedoides*) grows in eastern Washington in a small border area on rocky, sparsely vegetated hillsides of the Okanogan Highlands.

It is tufted to 2–3 cm (¾–1¼ in.) and makes a small prostrate mat of needlelike, gray-green leaves to 20 cm (8 in.) across. The mat is dotted with small, stemless white flowers with yellow stamens in summer. Although not very spectacular, it is useful in a trough.

*Talinum pulchellum* is a mat-forming species in Texas, New Mexico, and Arizona with a long flowering season of stemless pink flowers.

*Talinum spinescens* grows in central Washington on volcanic scablands and in one small area of Oregon. It is very different from the other species with fleshy stems 10–20 cm (4–8 in.) tall and large pale to deep red flowers during summer. This is the most perennial species in the Talinum genus. George Schenk found a double flowered form many years ago.

*Talinum* 'Zoe', a reputed hybrid between *T. okanoganense* and *T. spinescens*, is probably the best plant within the genus. Somewhat similar to *T. okanoganense*, it is larger in all parts, especially the light pink flowers, and is a much more desirable plant. Ingwersen (1978) wrote that he believed 'Zoe' to have been raised by a Mr. Peacock, a keen member of the Alpine Garden Society, who named it after his wife.

*Talinum brevifolium* in cultivation.

*Talinum* 'Zoe' in cultivation.

## Propagation

Seed is set profusely and germinates well with all the species I mention, although no data is available for *Talinum brachypodium*. Seedlings of species I grow often appear in adjacent pots possibly indicating that seed should be sown as soon as it is ripe. If you collect your own seed, take care not to be rough with the seedpods as they easily break open, scattering the seed everywhere. Hold a seed envelope underneath the pods even before you touch them. You can also propagate talinums by taking cuttings in early summer as soon as the plants put on enough growth. Although cuttings from the mat-forming species are small, they usually root fairly quickly, sometimes within three weeks.

## Cultivation

Talinums are dryland plants that make good trough plants; however, they need protection from too much rain, especially during winter. I grow mine in the alpine house where they can be protected during winter, although I move them outside during summer. All species except *Talinum spinescens* disappear below ground during winter, and none of the species needs any water during this time. The taller growing *T. spinescens*, while it does not die down, nevertheless looks dead. In spring when the weather warms up and new growth is visible, then you can water it again. Talinums grow quite quickly over late spring and early summer and they bloom during the summer season. My talinums grow in a neutral soil mixture in both the pot and trough. Give the plants lots of sun and they will reward you with masses of bloom.

Apart from slugs that treat talinums as their staple diet I have not noticed any other problems with pests.

## TELESONIX
### Saxifragaceae

Species of Telesonix have occasionally been included in the genus *Boykinia* since the sole difference between them is in the number of stamens in the flowers.

*Telesonix jamesii* grows in New Mexico, Colorado, Idaho, Wyoming, Nevada, Utah, and Montana at montane to alpine levels, inhabiting cracks in cliffs and rocky slopes that are large enough for the roots to get a hold. Its membership in the *Saxifrage* family is reflected in the reddish purple to dark pink flowers that are arranged in short dense racemes on stems 8–30 cm (3–12 in.) tall. The flower is truly beautiful and appears to ooze nectar from the center. Flower color varies slightly, and those from Pikes Peak in Colorado are thought to be the deepest red of all. Dark green leaves are kidney-shaped, toothed around the edge, and sometimes tinted bronze with age. It is an excellent species for exhibition; in May 2000 a magnificent plant earned an Alpine Garden Society Farrer Medal for a customer who had purchased it from me three years earlier as a small plant in a 7-cm (2 ¾-in.) pot.

Pikes Peak, Colorado, habitat for *Telesonix jamesii*. Photo Tony Barber.

Subspecies *heucheriformis* grows in Wyoming, Nevada, Utah, Montana, and Idaho at about 3125 m (10,150 ft). It creeps through crevices and over the surface of dolomite outcrops forming mats of deep green, scalloped, kidney-shaped leaves with panicles of purple-maroon calyxes and red-purple petals on short stems.

### Propagation

Like all saxifraga seed, telesonix seed is very fine. To collect seed cut the stems when you think the seed is ready (usually when the seedpods become brown) and put them upside down into a seed envelope. As the stems and seedpods dry, the seed falls out into the bottom of the envelope. Sow the seed as soon as possible after it ripens, lightly covering it with grit. You could also sow it

*Telesonix jamesii* in the rocks of Pikes Peak, Colorado. Photo Tony Barber.

Close-up of *Telesonix jamesii* flower in cultivation.

very thinly on top of the grit in a seed pot and stand the pot in a saucer of water to draw the seed down.

If you already have a really good form and want to propagate it you should carefully divide it in spring when growth starts by removing stems with the roots still attached and potting them up.

### Cultivation

Bearing in mind that *Telesonix jamesii* grows in narrow cracks in its natural habitat, you should simulate those conditions by compressing the roots between the rocks in your rock garden. If you grow it as a pot plant, either place rock in the soil mixture or use a smaller than normal pot so the plant becomes pot-bound quickly, forcing it to flower. You can always repot later into something larger if necessary.

*Telesonix jamesii* is one of those unusual alpines that we are always after. It is a really choice plant that can grow outside, even in wet winter conditions, although admittedly it looks dead at that time. Green shoots emerge in early spring and the plant gradually comes back to life. It does well in sun or partial shade and is easily raised from seed. As an alpine house plant it is stunning.

This species is mostly trouble free, although woodlice may reside under the basal rosette of plants that grow in the garden.

### TOWNSENDIA
Compositae, or Asteraceae
*Easter daisies*

As the common name of Easter daisy implies, all the *Townsendia* species have daisylike flowers and commence blooming around Easter. Panayoti Kelaidis (1998) wrote that "Townsendias occupy practically every sunny ecological niche in the great American West, which is to say, some of the loveliest country in the world." Flower color varies from species to species with the discs being yellow and the rays white, pink, purplish, violet, or blue. Two yellow species have also been recorded. The flower stems also vary in height, some with stems to 30 cm (12 in.) growing from a basal rosette, while others have flowers that are either stemless or on very short stems. The stemless or near stemless species usually form mounds and are excellent for cultivation in a trough or pot. The leaves, which vary from needlelike to spatulate, offer an additional attraction, and they are usually a beautiful silver-gray color.

A commonly held belief is that most townsendias are short-lived or even monocarpic. Based on my own experience, however, and on discussions with other growers, I know that many species have been successfully cultivated for up to five years, sometimes even longer. I would not, then, consider most townsendias as either short-lived or monocarpic.

*Townsendia aprica* is endemic to Emery and Sevier counties of Utah at 1690–2155 m (5500–7000 ft.). In habit it is pulvinate-caespitose and about 2.5 cm (1 in.) high with tiny gray-leaved rosettes and stemless yellow flowers. This species has appeared on the show bench a couple of times and is a little beauty. The U.S. Fish and Wildlife Service has listed this species as threatened, which means that few of us will probably ever see it.

*Townsendia condensata* is widespread in the high alpine screes and sparsely vegetated rocky slopes and ridges of Montana, Wyoming, Utah, and Idaho and in the

limestone alpine fell-fields of the White Mountains of California at 2000–3600 m (6500–11,700 ft.). An attractive dwarf species, it grows just 2.5 cm (1 in.) tall and has lovely, spatulate, woolly leaves. Large stemless flowers in May through July are to 5 cm (2 in.) in diameter and white or sometimes pale lilac to lavender. If moisture gets on the hairy leaves in cultivation it will rot off immediately. I originally thought this species was monocarpic but one plant I grow has flowered and set seed for two years, so it is probably more properly classed as a short-lived perennial. Even though it sometimes does not look at all well or attractive in cultivation, when I have grown it well it is stunning.

*Townsendia eximia* from the mountains of southern Colorado and New Mexico to 3690 m (12,000 ft.) is short-lived and probably a biennial. Leafy stems grow to 30 cm (12 in.) tall, and large bluish to lavender-purple flowers are 10 cm (4 in.) across.

*Townsendia exscapa* (synonym *T. wilcoxiana*) grows on the plains and foothills of Utah, Texas, New Mexico, Montana, Idaho, Nevada, Arizona, Wyoming, and Colorado at altitudes that range from 1692 to 3260 m (5500 to 10,600 ft.). This wide range is reflected in the

*Townsendia condensata*, Tushar Mountains, Utah. Photo Ron Ratko.

variations within the species. Although it also has silvery, linear leaves, at its worst it can be a small plant with equally small, muddy white flowers; at best, it makes a sizeable and vigorous mound with large, brilliant white flowers to 2.5 cm (1 in.) across.

A form growing in Arizona has flowers 5 cm (2 in.) across.

*Townsendia florifer* grows in dry areas of sagebrush in eastern Washington, Idaho, Oregon, Nevada, Montana, Wyoming, and Utah. Hairy stems 5–25 cm (2–10 in.) tall topped with white to bright pink flowers grow from a hairy, gray-green to silver rosette. An extremely variable species, it is also either biennial or monocarpic.

*Townsendia formosa* from New Mexico and Arizona is probably the tallest species in the genus with stems 12.5–30 cm (5–12 in.) tall, occasionally taller, that bear large lavenders flowers. Like other tall species, this one grows easily in the rock garden scree but can be short-lived.

*Townsendia glabella* grows in the four corners where Colorado, New Mexico, Utah, and Arizona meet. Hairy stems to 5 cm (2 in.) tall rise from gray-green to silver mats of grassy foliage. The 2.5-cm (1-in.) wide flowers are white to pale lavender. It looks almost like a green-leaved version

of *T. exscapa* and does best in a well-drained spot.

*Townsendia grandiflora* is widespread from South Dakota to eastern Colorado, Wyoming, and New Mexico at moderate elevation in the plains and low hills. Similar in appearance to *T. eximia*, it has leafy stems to 30 cm (12 in.) tall that are branched at the base. Flowers are white and 5–7 cm (2–2 ¾ in.) across. It tends to be short-lived and is probably a biennial.

*Townsendia hookeri* grows in Idaho, Montana, Wyoming, Utah, and Colorado to about 2730 m (8870 ft.). It makes a mound to 8 cm (3 in.) high of quite large rosettes with hairy, silver-gray, linear leaves to 5 cm (2 in.) long. Nestled in each of these rosettes in April is a stemless white flower 2–3 cm (¾–1¼ in.) in diameter that makes the plant look like a white and silver ball. I rate this species among the best as it is not only an excellent plant for the alpine house but also for the scree. It can also be among the most frustrating, especially if it goes dormant over winter, as it is a townsendia that requires some winter moisture when growing in a pot. My *T. hookeri* grew and subsequently flowered the best when it was quite moist for most of the winter as a result of a leak in my greenhouse.

Large-flowered form of *Townsendia exscapa* from Arizona in cultivation.

*Townsendia hookeri* in cultivation.

*Townsendia incana* occurs in New Mexico, Arizona, Utah, Colorado, Montana, Nevada, and Wyoming in dry, barren, shale-clay areas, sometimes among pinyon-pine and juniper woodland, at 1660–2460 m (5400–8000 ft.). I have seen it growing in Wyoming along the roadside among the magenta flowers of *Oxytropis lambertii*. It is sometimes confused with *T. mensana* because it has two forms. There is a compact form with a slightly domed cushion of silver leaves and almost stemless white flowers, and a less compact form with similar flowers but stems that are 2.5–3 cm (1–1¼ in.) tall. Both forms make good plants in pots or troughs, but the compact form is usually more appealing. Fast growing in cultivation (seed germinates easily and quickly), it is among the best for those who are growing townsendias for the first time. An extremely attractive plant, it has won many prizes on the show bench.

A word of warning however. Since 1990, seed and plants of the compact form of *Townsendia incana* have been mistakenly distributed as *T. mensana* followed by a collector's number. This error happened because one particular compact plant in the wild was mistakenly identified as *T. mensana*. Unfortunately, second and third generation plants whose origin was in this seed are still being circulated under the wrong name.

*Townsendia jonesii* is quite rare and grows in the southwest counties of Utah at 1525–2745 m (4955–8920 ft.) and also in Nevada. The dome is 2–4 cm (1–1½ in.) high and to 10 cm (4 in.) across. Flowers are white to pink or cream. It is very similar to *T. mensana* and was originally thought to be a variety of that species.

Variety *lutea* is endemic to Sevier and Piute counties in Utah and is much rarer than the type. It grows at 1675–1830 m (5445–5950 ft.) in Arapien shale and clays in volcanic rubble. This yellow flowering variety is much sought after by collectors, which has put its survival in jeopardy. Plant hunters who frequent the area believe it is the gypsum in the soil that causes the various shades of yellow in the flowers.

*Townsendia leptotes* grows in alpine regions of California, New Mexico, Nevada, Idaho, Wyoming, and Montana to 3145 m (10,220 ft.). Probably the most compact of all the species, it is very slow growing (it can take several years to make a plant 8 cm [3 in.] diameter). However, it is also very rewarding in cultivation as it makes tight mounds of wiry, grooved, silver-gray leaves

Long stemmed form of *Townsendia incana* at a Wyoming roadside.

Compact form of *Townsendia incana* in cultivation.

with stemless, pale lavender to white flowers in March and April. I do not see seed of this species offered often, which is unfortunate as it is so lovely. It is a must for the trough.

*Townsendia mensana* is endemic to Uinta Basin, Utah, among sagebrush, pinyon, and juniper, particularly on barren and semibarren sites, at 1705–2880 m (5540–9360 ft.). A tiny, beautiful species, it forms a tight silver ball 3–5 cm (1¼–2 in.) high with very small, narrow leaves. This ball is completely covered with white, sometimes lemon, stemless flowers to 2 cm (¾ in.) wide nestling in the foliage. In cultivation it is susceptible to rotting off but in the wild it survives dry, hot summers as well as winters with below freezing temperatures. Seed rarely, if ever, appears in lists.

*Townsendia montana* (synonym *T. alpigena*) grows in Utah and northeast Oregon, Idaho, Montana, and Wyoming at 2150–3330 m (6990–10,815 ft.). No *Townsendia* species can be more colorful as its flowers range from white to pink, dark purple, or pale blue. However, the specimen I grow and the one that appears most in cultivation has rich, dark purple flowers. Among the smaller species, it forms an attractive mound with short stems to 2.5 cm (1 in.), and because it is easy to grow, it is well suited to a trough or pot if intended for exhibition.

Variety *caelilinensis* is endemic to the Wasatch Plateau area in Utah, where it grows at an elevation of 2150–2770 m

Close-up of *Townsendia montana* in cultivation.

*Townsendia mensana* in cultivation.

*Townsendia montana*, Medicine Wheel, Wyoming. Photo Peter Downe.

*Townsendia montana* var. *caelilinensis*, Wasatch Plateau. Photo Ron Ratko.

(6990–9000 ft.) in pinyon and juniper as well as spruce and fir communities. A choice but rarely seen variety, it has a low cushion of huge white flowers. Welsh, et al. (1987) record it as a variety of *Townsendia montana* though it looks very different. The plant I grew from seed took three years to flower from germination, then died shortly thereafter.

Variety *minima* is endemic to Garfield and Kane counties of Utah at an altitude of 2375–3115 m (7720–10,120 ft.) among ponderosa and western bristlecone pine communities. It is completely different from the type in that the mound is 12.5–15 cm (5–6 in.) high with branched stems and small white flowers. Although slow to set viable seed (it may require a companion for successful pollination), it is an excellent plant for pot culture.

*Townsendia nuttallii* grows in Montana and Wyoming at 2770–3075 m (9000–10,000 ft.) on exposed limestone ridges. It forms a mound 2.5–5 cm (1–2 in.) high from dense tufts of smooth, silvery leaves that are less spatulate than *T. spathulata*, a species with which it is often confused because of the leaf shape. Stemless white, pink, or pale lavender flowers are also larger than *T. spathulata*. Although very slow growing, this is another species that is excellent in a trough or for pot culture.

*Townsendia parryi* grows at 2460–2923 m (8000–9500 ft.) in Idaho, Montana, Nevada, and Wyoming. It has lavender to purple flowers 5–8 cm (2–3 in.)

*Townsendia montana* var. *minima* on the road to Capitol Reef, Utah. Photo Ron Ratko.

*Townsendia nuttallii* in cultivation.

*Townsendia parryi*, Schuler Park, Big Horn Mountains, Wyoming. Photo Chris Norton.

across on stems growing from a basal rosette to 30 cm (12 in.) tall. Many plants growing at a higher altitude, however, are only 5 cm (2 in.) tall. The central stem is branched and may bear many flowers. A lovely townsendia for the garden, it flowers throughout the summer and is worth maintaining from seed as it is a short-lived perennial.

*Townsendia rothrockii* comes from the snow melt areas of Colorado at 3690–4000 m (12,000–13,000 ft.). It grows as a low cushion of dense, tight rosettes with glaucous green leaves stained purple. The huge, pale lilac, daisylike flowers on stems to 2.5 cm (1 in.) tall are almost cup-shaped. An excellent plant for a scree area in the rock garden, it will, like other cushion plants, grow much tighter there. This species makes an excellent pot plant in the alpine house if you can keep the aphids away.

*Townsendia scapigera* grows at 1525–3175 m (4955–10,320 ft.) on the volcanic gravel slopes of Idaho, Utah, California, and Nevada. Short shoots from a woody base form a small mound of gray spatulate leaves covered with tiny stiff hairs. White to pale violet or pink flowers 2.5 cm (1 in.) across are on 5–8-cm (2–3-in.) tall stems. A biennial or short-lived perennial, it is unfortunately rarely seen.

*Townsendia spathulata* grows in Wyoming and Montana at 2155–3075 m (7000–10,000 ft.) and is often confused with *T. nuttallii*. It is mound forming to 2.5 cm (1 in.) high and has silver, hairy, spatulate leaves with stemless pink to lavender flowers. In cultivation it blooms in March through April. There seem to be two forms in cultivation, one that is commonly grown from seed available from commercial lists, and another from the Pryor Mountains of Montana that is rarely cultivated. Where wild horses roam, hundreds of these plants grow in the limestone tufa screes with *Phlox bryoides*.

Although Beaman's (1957) townsendia monograph recognized *Townsendia spathulata* as only growing in the Fremont,

*Townsendia scapigera*, White Mountains, California. Photo Chris Norton.

*Townsendia rothrockii* in cultivation.

Usual form of *Townsendia spathulata* in cultivation.

Natrona, and Sweetwater counties of Wyoming, Ev Whittemore found one—the most beautiful by far—growing in the Pryor Mountains of Montana at around 2155 m (7000 ft.). It remained an unidentified *Townsendia* species for many years until 1998 when John Grimshaw, an English botanist, took samples to Royal Botanic Gardens, Kew, and identified it from original material as *T. spathulata*. As is the case with many desirable plants, propagation of this species remains difficult. The plants are in seed in mid-May, and although seedlings are common in the area, there has been little germination from several collections.

A similar thing has happened in cultivation, and although I hand pollinated the three or four plants that were in flower at the same time, the seed I collected from these plants was unviable. Perhaps the myriads of horse-flies in the area where the townsendias grow are not there only to invade our eyes, ears, and noses, but also to act as pollinators.

**Propagation**

Since most species set seed, it is best to propagate townsendias by seed even if you have only one plant. If you sow seed as soon as it is ripe, it will usually germinate within four to six weeks. My plants typically flower in March through May, so I sow seed in June through July. I once sowed seed of an early flowering *Townsendia montana* and it produced a couple of plants that flowered the same year. This does not happen very

*Townsendia spathulata* habitat, Pryor Mountains, Montana. Photo Ev Whittemore.

Foliage of *Townsendia spathulata*, Pryor Mountains, Montana.

Wild horses of Pryor Mountain. Photo Ev Whittemore.

*Townsendia spathulata* in flower.

often but it shows how quickly these plants grow. I propagate *T. leptotes* each year from seed collected from my own plants; it is very slow growing.

Before you sow townsendia seed, however, examine it to ensure that it is fertile. For many years I sowed all the "seed" that I collected from my plants and often wondered why germination of some species was so poor. Only after I emptied a large bag of this "seed" onto a piece of white paper did I realize that although each one had the usual hairy tuft at one end, the achene of most seed was thin and transparent. Only a tiny fraction of what I thought was good, fertile seed had a plump, brown achene. Once you see fertile and nonfertile townsendia seed together, you too will make no more sowing mistakes.

Although I have had some success taking rosettes as cuttings in spring and inserting them in sand, I do this only if I want to propagate a particularly good form or grow a plant that does not set fertile seed.

## Cultivation

Townsendias have a long taproot, which means that pricking out seedlings can be tricky since you have to be very careful not to break the root. Most autumn-sown seed germinates in spring and results in plants that flower the following year. If seed you sowed in late summer resulted in early autumn germination, you can start pricking out the seedlings soon after. They grow quite rapidly once pricked out, and by the autumn of the following year buds will appear. (Townsendias normally form their buds in autumn prior to the year in which they flower.) After flowering has occurred, new rosettes immediately start to form; in some species the rosettes even start this process prior to flowering. As these rosettes increase in size, new bud growth also begins. By autumn the buds are ready to rest until the following spring.

If you plan to grow townsendias outside they must be in full sun in a scree or trough—or at least in soil with a great deal of grit mixed in. Although perfectly hardy, most species do not do well if there is winter wet constantly around the neck of the plant, and by the following spring they could look like a sorry, mushy mess if you have not taken appropriate care.

Even in winter you should not allow pot-grown plants to dry out. Remember that in nature the long taproots continually have access to moisture that enables them to stay cool, both in summer when the surrounding soil is bone dry and in winter when growth is at a standstill and plants are resting. Many *Townsendia* species are excellent exhibition plants when grown in pots, but you must approach pot cultivation very differently. Since there is still a little growth over winter, if you let the soil mix become too dry the plant goes into a resting period. From this moment on you must take great care when applying water. *Softly, softly* is the way to operate. If you give too much water too soon early in the spring, the stem will rot off almost immediately. You will have much better luck keeping the plant growing if you lightly water it throughout the winter. Plants growing outside in the rock garden or trough are, of course, naturally moist at the roots.

Another effect of giving insufficient water to pot-grown townsendias is that the buds go blind. That is to say that buds formed in autumn appear alright until the following spring when, instead of fattening up ready to flower, they gradually turn brown and eventually look dead. You must remove these dead buds to stop infection reaching other parts of the plant.

Excluding slugs (which can be pests anywhere), aphids and red spider mite affect mainly pot-grown specimens in the alpine house. On a species like *Townsendia hookeri*, for example, that has long, thin leaves, you can easily spot aphids, but on the compact cushion species, such as *T. rothrockii*, it is difficult to see the aphids congregating under the cushions until the telltale signs of the sticky black excretion form on the leaves. Regarding the effects of red spider, it seems that the more silvery the leaf the more mottled it becomes. Hot, dry conditions in the alpine house mean pests will do their worst, so make sure you keep the air moist on hot days.

## TRIFOLIUM
Leguminosae, or Fabaceae
*clovers*

Almost 300 clover species exist throughout the world, and about 40 are native to the Rockies. *Trifolium* means "having three leaves or leaflets," and the dense, globular heads of pea-like flowers on plants in this genus make them stand out from other alpines. The five species I describe are all available in commercial seed lists.

*Trifolium brandegei* occurs only in Colorado and New Mexico. Large flower heads of pale pink grow on stems 10–15 cm (4–6 in.) tall.

*Trifolium dasyphyllum* is a very common species in the Rockies of southern Montana, Wyoming, eastern Utah, Colorado, and New Mexico, usually growing among rocks in alpine zones and occasionally at subalpine levels. Tufted, clumped, and mat forming, it is from 3 to 15 cm (1¼ to 6 in.) high. Whitish yellow flowers in July through September have purple-red tips and sometimes a deep rose keel. The leaves are blue-gray.

*Trifolium haydenii* is supposedly endemic to the subalpine and alpine meadows of the Beartooth-Yellowstone Park area in southern Montana and northwest Wyoming, but it reputedly also grows in eastern Idaho. A sprawling plant that is usually tufted, it occasionally forms mats. More typically, however, it grows in loose patches with stems 2.5–5 cm (1–2 in.) tall. It has reddish to cream flowers in July through August.

*Trifolium macrocephalum* grows in Washington at approximately 925 m (3000 ft.). A mat-forming species, it has decumbent stems 15–25 cm (6–10 in.) long with deep blue-green leaves. Large heads of flowers vary from pink or rose to a grayish white, and each petal is tipped with rose-violet. Spreading rhizomes may make this species invasive.

*Trifolium nanum* is a Rocky Mountain species growing in the subalpine and alpine meadows and fell-fields in Montana, southern Idaho, to New Mexico. This species is unmistakable and must be the best in the

Habitat of *Trifolium nanum* in Loveland Pass, Colorado.

genus. It forms dense mats and cushions, and although the almost stemless heads of flowers are smaller than the other species, they are so tightly packed against each other you would not think so. Flowers range from a bright red to very pale pink.

*Trifolium parryi* grows in alpine or sub-alpine rocky meadows and stream banks from southern Idaho to Montana and New Mexico. Although a spreading plant, it grows more upright than either *T. haydenii* or *T. dasyphyllum* with 2.5–5-cm (1–2-in.) tall stems. It is a beautiful species with dense heads of fragrant deep pink, reddish purple to rose flowers from midsummer.

## Propagation

Plants of the more choice species are propagated by seed, which is now available in many commercial seed lists. Like others in the pea family, trifoliums germinate quickly when exposed to cold and moist conditions in the open air, but they easily damp off unless you bring them under cover as soon as you notice that germination has begun. I have not yet tried propagating any species by cuttings.

## Cultivation

As with any other plant grown from wild seed, trifoliums show color variation, and some of my plants are not nearly as vivid as those I saw on Loveland Pass in Colorado. I am therefore growing on many seedlings from which I plan to select the best color forms. Apart from providing a well-drained soil or soil mix and limiting the amount of moisture during winter, I have not found these plants to have too many requirements in cultivation. Since they are high alpine plants that receive winter snow cover in the wild, they do better with a relatively dry rest period in winter. They die back to brown-black tufts at this time but must have some moisture at the roots if they grow in a pot.

Whitefly is a problem in the alpine house especially if the temperature during winter rest periods is not low enough to kill these pests. Slugs are the usual predators in the garden or trough.

*Trifolium nanum* and *Eritrichium nanum* growing together, Loveland Pass, Colorado.

*Trifolium nanum* on Loveland Pass, Colorado.

*Trifolium nanum*, Mount Evans, Colorado. Photo Chris Norton.

# V

## VIOLA
Violaceae
*violets*

Most gardeners delight in growing pansies in their gardens, and violas are just smaller and more dainty delights. Violas grow in clumps throughout the West and light up the ground with their yellow, white, or blue flowers. The folding petals have given rise to the phrase "shrinking violet." Many species hybridize with one another, and the resulting intermediate forms make identification difficult. Some species go dormant in summer soon after blooming.

I describe the more popular species in greater detail than those that are less well known, but all are worth growing.

*Viola adunca* grows in meadows, open moist woodland, and rocky slopes to 3450 m (11,210 ft.) in Alaska and the Yukon to southern California, Arizona, New Mexico, and the northern Great Plains. A tufted to clump-forming plant, it has thick, dark green leaves that are finely crenulate and ovate to heart shaped. Lavender-violet to deep violet flowers in March through August are somewhat small at 1.2–2 cm (½–¾ in.) across. The bottom three petals are white at the base, and all the petals have darker veins. A slender spur extends backward from the petals. Early in the growing season the stems are 2.5–5 cm (1–2 in.) tall, later becoming 5–12.5 cm (2–5 in.) tall and ascending to prostrate. It produces flowers that are self-pollinating without opening. Forma *albiflora* is a white form.

Variety *bellidifolia*, a dwarf variety, grows in high elevations of the Rockies.

*Viola beckwithii* grows in northeast Oregon, southeast California, Idaho, Nevada, and Utah in vernally moist sagebrush and open pine woods at 1370–1680 m (4450–5460 ft.). It forms a small clump 5–12.5 cm (2–5 in.) tall. The long-stalked, gray-green leaves grow to 2.5 cm (1 in.) long and are trilobed and then pinnatifid. The flowers bloom in March through May and are beautiful. They are 1.2–2 cm (½–¾ in.) across with the upper two petals a reddish purple and the lower three petals lilac to almost white. Near the yellow base of these three petals are reddish purple veins. The plants are dormant in summer.

*Viola canadensis* is widespread in moist woodlands, ranging from Canada to Oregon, Arizona, and east to the Rockies. The leaves are 2.5–7.5 cm (1–3 in.) long on slender stems to 30 cm (12 in.) long. In May through July white flowers that are yellow at the base grow on stems 10–40 cm (4–15¾ in.) tall. Unlike other white-flowered species, the flowers grow from the axils of the upper leaves as well as having yellow petal bases.

*Viola cuneata* grows in Oregon and California. Stems 10–20 cm (4–8 in.) tall bear white flowers in spring to summer that are finely speckled with purple. The plant goes dormant after blooming.

*Viola douglasii* occurs in Oregon and California. It is 5–15 cm (2–6 in.) tall with deeply divided leaves and large, bright yellow flowers in March through May.

*Viola flettii* inhabits alpine stony slopes, rock crevices, and screes in the Olympics of Washington. It is tufted to clump forming (the clumps are small), and is instantly recognizable with deep purple, kidney-shaped leaves 1.2–3.8 cm (½–1½ in.) across. Stems grow 2.5–15 cm (1–6 in.) tall with purplish violet flowers to 2.5 cm (1 in.) across in June through August. The lower lip petal is long and narrow with a large yellow basal spot, and the lower lateral petals are yellow bearded. It becomes dormant in autumn and commences growth very late in spring.

*Viola glabella* grows in Alaska to California and Montana. It is 10–30 cm (4–12 in.) tall with heart-shaped leaves and deep yellow flowers in March through July.

*Viola hallii* occurs in Oregon and California in forests and rocky open areas at 300–2000 m (975–6500 ft.). Although very

similar to *V. beckwithii* in size and habit, it is less hairy with leaf segments that are quite often lanceolate. The flower is very attractive with three cream-colored lower petals, a yellow, purple-striped eye, and two, deep reddish violet upper petals. After it blooms in spring to summer it becomes dormant.

*Viola lobata* grows in Oregon and California. Similar to *V. glabella*, it is 10–30 cm (4–12 in.) tall with deep yellow flowers in April through July. The flowers are sometimes purple veined.

*Viola nuttallii* grows in meadows and dry mountain forests of Washington, Oregon, and California. This very pretty violet grows 2.5–7.5 cm (1–3 in.) high with hairy, lanceolate to ovate leaves and glabrous seed capsules. The flowers in May through June have deep yellow petals and the veins on the lower three are brown-purple.

*Viola odorata*, the English violet, grows in Utah and around some of California's old towns. An introduction from Europe, it has naturalized in many places in the United States. A mat-forming species, it spreads by thick rhizomes that grow along the soil's surface. The crenate and short-pediceled

*Viola flettii*, Mount Townsend, Washington.

*Viola nuttallii*, Oregon.

leaves are 2.5–6.3 cm (1–2½ in.) long and either kidney shaped or ovate to orbicular. Stems 5–10 cm (2–4 in.) tall bear fragrant, dark violet-purple or white flowers in spring that have four narrow, twisted petals and a single flat lip.

*Viola pedatifida* grows in Arizona, Colorado, and New Mexico and is 7.5–20 cm (3–8 in.) tall. Blue-violet flowers in May through June are outward facing, and the leaves are deeply divided.

*Viola purpurea* ranges from Montana to Arizona and from Washington to California growing from montane to alpine scree slopes. It is clump forming with some or all of the leaves starting from below ground level. The leaves are variable in shape; they may be entire or round-toothed, are often tinged with purple, and are always heavily veined. Stems 5–20 cm (2–8 in.) long are prostrate in the sun and semi-erect in the shade. Yellow flowers in May through August are to 2 cm (¾ in.) across with a purple tinge on the back of the upper petals and purple or brown veining on the lower three. The lowest petal has a very short spur that extends beneath the flower.

*Viola sheltonii* grows in Washington, Oregon, Idaho, California, and Colorado. It is 2.5–5 cm (1–2 in.) tall with deep lemon-yellow flowers in April through July and fan-shaped pinnate leaves.

### Propagation

You can propagate violas by seed, division, or cuttings. If you want to collect seed from your own plants, be aware that the seed capsules explode. It is particularly important to put some form of seed containment over the capsule to catch the seed of a rare species. Seed of more difficult species, such as *Viola beckwithii* and *V. flettii*, can take two to three years to germinate. It is also important to take great care when pricking out the seedlings as you must ensure that they are buried to the same depth as they were in the seed pot. Cuttings usually root fairly easily, and some species, such as *V. flettii*, can be propagated by root cuttings.

### Cultivation

Most violas grow well in the open garden but species like *Viola flettii* and *V. beckwithii* require alpine house treatment in areas of heavy rainfall.

Pest problems include aphids and red spider on plants that are growing under glass and slugs in the open garden.

# Z

## ZAUSCHNERIA
Onagraceae
*California fuchsias, hummingbird flowers*

*Zauschneria* is an extremely drought-tolerant, California native that blooms late in the season after the summer heat has turned grasses brown and most wildflowers have set seed. With color so late in the year, zauschnerias are a welcome addition to the rock garden, though it is inclined to spread when grown in rich soil and in the sun. It has funnel-shaped, red-orange flowers with four, two-cleft petals, four red sepals, and eight red stamens that protrude from the end of the flower. The size and shape of the flowers give rise to one common name, California fuchsia. An alternative common name, hummingbird flower, reveals how attractive it is to these most beautiful and delicate of visitors who feed on the nectar before beginning their southward migration. Zauschnerias are more or less herbaceous perennials that usually retreat underground during winter. Shoots emerge again in the spring from the plant's base.

*Zauschneria californica* (synonyms *Epilobium californicum, E. canum*) grows in stony places from sea level to about 3300 m (10,725 ft.) in California. It is limited to lower altitudes, which can made it susceptible to frost in cultivation. It is a clump-forming, woody-based, deciduous species to 50 cm (20 in.) across that spreads by rhizomes. Green to gray hairy leaves that are linear to lance shaped grow on stems 30–60 cm (12–24 in.) tall. Terminal racemes of brilliant scarlet, tubular flowers in late summer to autumn are 2.5–4 cm (1–1½ in.) long.

Subspecies *angustifolia* grows in California in sagebrush below 600 m (1950 ft.); it has linear leaves and smaller flowers. It is also slightly shorter at 50 cm (20 in.).

Subspecies *latifolia* (synonyms *Zauschneria arizonica, Z. latifolia*) has the largest range of all, from southwest Oregon to California, Baja California in Mexico, Idaho, Wyoming, Nevada, Arizona, and Utah. Its habitat varies from damp canyons to rock outcrops and talus slopes among juniper and ponderosa pine, and from sea level to about 3300 m (10,725 ft.). This shrubby subspecies makes a clump 5–90 cm (2–36 in.) tall, depending on altitude, and is glandular-puberulent. It occasionally has gray-white hairs, and the lanceolate to elliptic or ovate leaves grow to 4 cm (1½ in.) long. The flowers in August through October are from 2.5 to 6.3 cm (1 to 2½ in.) long.

'Alba' is a white form with fresh green foliage that grows to 20 cm (8 in.) tall and 60 cm (24 in.) across. 'Dublin' (synonym 'Glasnevin') is green-leaved with large flowers, and as it originates at high altitude, it is much hardier and more compact, growing to 25 cm (10 in.) tall and to 30 cm (12 in.) across.

'Solidarity Pink' was found at the Solidarity Mine in the Sierra Nevada foothills. The pale pink flowers are less floriferous than 'Dublin', and it has a sprawling habit to 60 cm (24 in.). 'Wayne's Silver' is a selection from Wayne Roderick that came out of his work at the University of California in Berkeley. It has very silver foliage and slightly larger scarlet flowers on erect stems to 30 cm (12 in.) tall, spreading to 90 cm (36 in.) across.

*Zauschneria cana* (synonyms *Z. californica* var. *cana, Z. californica* var. *microphylla*) grows at a lower elevation than *Z. californica* and is more compact. It has small linear to lanceolate silver-gray leaves and grows 45–60 cm (18–24 in.) tall. The red flowers are similar to *Z. californica* but with shorter petals.

*Zauschneria garrettii* comes from California, Idaho, Wyoming, and Utah, where its habitat at around 1800–2460 m

Close-up of *Zauschneria californica* 'Dublin'.

(5850–8000 ft.) is dry woodland and rocky, sandy areas. It grows to 38 cm (15 in.) tall and is quick spreading to 45 cm (18 in.). It has green leaves and glowing, orange-red flowers.

*Zauschneria septentrionalis* is from California, where it grows in dry, sandy places below 830 m (2700 ft.). An herbaceous species, it has lanceolate to oval leaves to 2.5 cm (1 in.) that are silver-gray and very hairy. The prostrate stems grow 10–20 cm (4–8 in.) long and have terminal clusters of 2.5–3.2-cm (1–1¼-in.) long red flowers.

## Propagation

Propagate zauschnerias by seed when and if it is available. Cuttings that you take in late spring or late summer will root fairly easy. You can also carefully divide the clumps in spring.

## Cultivation

Zauschnerias do well in ordinary garden soil in a sunny spot. *Zauschneria californica* may be too tender for most gardens but I had no problems in my Timsbury garden with *Z. californica* 'Dublin' or *Z. septentrionalis*, both of which survived the wet winters. Other growers, though, told me that *Z. septentrionalis* did not survive winter damp in their area, so perhaps it would safer to give them some protection from the rain during winter. Do not give zauschnerias a too rich or gravel-based soil as they tend to spread very quickly in this medium. They make attractive patio plants for a while but need continuous potting on.

Aphids are a problem for plants cultivated under glass, and slugs eat out the new growing tips of plants that grow in the garden.

# CULTIVATION

IN ATTEMPTING TO GROW western North American alpine plants you face one of the biggest challenges in the horticultural world. You can, however, meet and overcome this challenge with a little thought, care, and planning. Before I explain some methods of cultivation that I have found helpful, I describe some of the natural habitats of alpine plants you may need to take into account.

The harsh, sea-level conditions of Alaska in which alpines grow may be similarly harsh in a high mountain habitat further south in the Rockies. In mountain meadows at low elevation, plants grow taller and have much richer soil in which to thrive, and yet at alpine levels they grow in fast draining screes or a "soil" of stone, grit, pumice, or bare rock. Plants that are covered by snow for six months to almost a year may have six weeks or less to grow, flower, and set seed before the first snows of winter cover them again. The only nutrients these plants have come from whatever chemicals are in the rocks, the droppings from the variety of animals that live in the area, or the organic matter from dead plants. These high alpines receive moisture from thunderstorms or the snowmelt that may run deep underground (wetter areas will of course support a different kind of plant).

Not all the "alpines" we try to grow come from mountainous regions. Many are from the plains and intermountain regions, where conditions are more desertlike and where xeric plants grow and flourish in high summer temperatures with very little moisture. Plants in such xeric areas have long taproots or succulent leaves, among other adaptations, that enable them to survive in the "soil," which varies only in the rocks that go into its makeup.

In the Pacific Northwest some areas receive up to 152 cm (60 in.) of precipitation between mid-October and June; the Cascades and Olympics provide an altogether different habitat and support plants that need more moisture and can survive damp winters in cultivation. The "soil" in which alpines are growing on those mountain ranges consists mainly of volcanic rubble and pumice, and winter snow cover keeps them dry.

Having briefly summarized the typical alpine plant habitats, I am sure you have an idea of some of the problems that lie ahead as you try growing these plants for yourself. Although it is impossible for me to provide full details here of the various ways to grow alpines—and, of course, it is equally impossible to simulate the exact habitats of every alpine plant in your own garden or alpine house—I can suggest methods of cultivation that will help overcome the more frequently encountered problems. I also recommend that you read some of the many publications that detail all methods of alpine cultivation.

## Containers

Alpines will grow in any sort of container, from the tiny ornamental pot brought back from a holiday, to an elegant, top-of-the-line trough purchased from a deluxe garden center, to the ultimate container, a 1500-year-old stone coffin. Containers made from a variety of materials and by a variety of methods and construction techniques can be found in many specialist publications. They all require one thing though—drainage holes!

When you plant up a container cover the drainage holes with small pieces of plastic mesh and cover that with a layer of fast draining material, such as coarse grit. Set the plants in as you fill the container with soil mix and insert pieces of rock (if required) as you go. Top-dress with a 1.2–2.5-cm (½–1-in.) layer of grit to act as a mulch and facilitate the picking out of weed seedlings. Finally, position the container so it is raised slightly above the ground and water in the plants. Do not place your container in permanent shade or plant up a large trough too far from where you intend to place it as a heavy trough means an aching back.

Collection of containers at Leach Botanical Garden, Portland, Oregon.

Miniature alpine garden at an Alpine Garden Society show.

Trough at Wisley Gardens, England.

A 1500-year-old Roman stone coffin used as an alpine trough.

## Alpine Beds or Rock Gardens

Alpine beds and rock gardens involve a great deal of hard and heavy work, many rocks, and a lot of soil. All your work and effort can result in a disaster if the rock work does not look natural. Many rock gardens have that "currant bun" look about them with rocks perched on top of the bed. Rocks in an alpine bed should look like icebergs, meaning that nine-tenths of the rock is buried out of sight.

Betty and Ned Lowry's alpine bed at Renton, Washington.

David Hale's alpine bed at Arch Cape, Oregon.

Rock garden at Royal Botanical Gardens, Kew.

### Sand Beds

Site the sand bed in the sun and then kill off all perennial weeds growing on the site either with a weed killer or by digging the plot over. An alpine sand bed should be a minimum of 30 cm (12 in.) deep but can be up to 75 cm (29½ in.) deep. Build the walls as you would for any raised bed using materials such as concrete building blocks or rock. (I have seen a large successful bed made from numerous truck loads of stone chippings) Before you fill the enclosure, lay a

Circular sand bed at Mt. Tahoma Nursery.

Part of a long narrow sand bed at Mt. Tahoma Nursery.

permeable liner along the bottom to prevent earthworms from carrying humus up into the sand.

Fill the bed with a coarse grade of building sand or horticultural grit. You can create narrow crevices with carefully positioned rocks, so providing appropriate habitats for the more demanding alpine plants. Since sand beds provide an environment that is fast draining with a quickly drying surface, you will find that the more difficult alpines survive in these beds much better than they do in the ordinary rock garden, particularly in areas with damp autumns and winters. Apply a slow release fertilizer in early spring.

### Raised Beds

A raised bed is very similar to the sand bed except that it is filled with a different mixture. What that mixture is may be governed by the type of plants you want to cultivate, but usually it is a mix that suits a wide range of plants. My raised beds are filled with a 50/50 mixture of coarse grit and garden soil and used soil mixture from pots. The plants thrive in this gritty mix. After I have finished planting, I mulch the surface with coarse grit.

Not all gardens have suitable soil, and quite often the mixture is made up of peat, grit, leaf mold, and decayed organic matter such as bark. Such a mixture in a raised bed allows you to cultivate plants that will not survive in the ordinary alpine or rock garden. A raised bed may also be a kind of tabletop structure with concrete slabs laid across brick or stone piers. Both sand and raised beds are excellent for any alpine gardener who cannot bend down or for those who garden from a wheelchair. At the Cheshire Home in Timsbury, a residential home for disabled (differently abled) people, a great deal of the garden is made up of raised beds, and I regularly give demonstrations on how to plant up raised beds and containers with alpine plants.

Another reason to build a raised bed is if the ground where you garden cannot be dug up. Sonia Lowzow in Lakeside, Arizona, could garden only by building up since the ground was so hard that even a pickaxe had no effect.

Raised and alpine beds in the author's garden with another under construction.

Raised bed of the late Sonia Lowzow, Lakeside, Arizona.

## Alpine Houses

What is an alpine house? Simply put, it is a structure that protects the plants from excessive moisture and ill-timed frosts. It can be anything from a small lean-to construction, to a greenhouse with the panes of glass removed for extra ventilation, to the most up-to-date, expensive, custom-built unit. It may be built of brick, wood, or aluminum—it may even be a polythene tunnel (also called a hoop house). In fact, any construction that keeps the winter rain off the plants and allows a free flow of air will do.

Perhaps you are asking if you need an alpine house if you do not show plants. Or perhaps you are asking if you need an alpine house if you want to grow plants only in the garden. How many times have I heard those questions? Just because exhibitors use alpine houses does not mean that their only use is for growing show plants. Growing alpines in the garden is perfectly natural and we all do that, of course, but if you want to try some of the more difficult species, it is essential that you protect them from the wet or humid winter weather. Having an alpine house allows you to grow many plants that would otherwise die in the open garden. You can build raised beds or small mountain scenes in your alpine house if you prefer not to use pots. Plants inside an alpine house are likely to get individual attention, and when they bloom you will appreciate flowers that have not been torn to pieces by last night's storm. Of course there is the added benefit that you too remain snug and protected from the wind and rain during inclement weather.

Some of you may worry that in summer the temperature is much too high and the plants will burn. You could erect some form of shading for the alpine house, but keep in mind that most plants do not need to remain under glass all year and can be moved outside into the fresh air during early summer, especially since summer rain has no ill effect. You can leave the plants outside until autumn before bringing them under cover again.

## Soil Mixtures

For the most part, soil mixture come in two forms, peat based and soil based. Many nurseries make their own peat-based mix with added, slow release fertilizer for growing plants in pots. Although this mixture helps establish a good root system and makes the plants grow fast, weaning the plants off the peat mix for later planting in a soil-based mix or in the garden can pose problems as the roots will often not grow out into the soil. You should be aware that the ready-made, peat-based mixes you buy have only enough fertilizer to last approximately six weeks; thereafter you have to feed the plants yourself.

In the early days of my nursery I used a peat-based mixture, but that changed very quickly when I lost more than 600 plants one very hot day when the peat dried out and became impossible to wet again. Experience has also shown that plants are more prone to attack by vine weevil grubs if I grow them in a peat-based mix. I use only a soil-based mixture now, which, although heavier to carry, has never posed any problems. I usually use the John Innes composts (these are mixes that have been produced after much experimentation by the John Innes Institute and that, in theory, will result in a standardized product), and have included a recipe of the basic neutral soil mix that is so well suited to alpine plants. In practice there is some variation in the origin of the sterilized soil and in the maker's interpretation of "grit": some soil mixes contain too much peat, and others contain grit that is almost like fine builders' sand. I am lucky in Somerset because the local manufacturer uses top quality soil from the Mendip Hills near Timsbury and lime-free Cornish grit (neutral horticultural grit), which is crushed granite. If you decide to make your own soil mixes, you can be assured that the chemicals used are standard and can be obtained from most garden centers, as can a complete base fertilizer that also contains trace elements. All ingredients are for 0.76 cubic m (1 cubic yard) of soil mix.

*John Innes seed mix*
2 parts sterilized soil
1 part moss peat
1 part lime-free coarse grit
1 kg (2 lb) superphosphate
500 g (1 lb) chalk

*John Innes potting compost number 1*
7 parts sterilized soil
3 parts moss peat
2 parts lime-free coarse grit
2.2 kg (5 lb) complete base fertilizer
500 g (1 lb) chalk

For plants that are hungry feeders, such as campanulas and lewisias, I recommend using double the amount of base fertilizer. (Note that John Innes compost number 2 has twice the amount of base fertilizer as number 1, or 4.5 kg [10 lb], and that number 3 has three times the amount, or 6.8 kg [15 lb].) The makers of John Innes composts near Timsbury, on hearing that chalk is not available in the United States, recommend using gypsum, although they are not sure how much you should use. I suggest you carefully check the pH to ensure you have a neutral soil mixture.

You can steam sterilize soil using the appropriate apparatus or the microwave if your spouse will let you. If you do use the microwave you will need a thick-walled plastic container with a translucent snap-on lid. Place the soil inside these containers either loose or in the plastic flower pots you intend to use for your alpine plants (if you microwave the pots as well you will also be sterilizing them) and secure the lid in a way that allows some air to escape. Be sure to leave one corner of the lid unsealed (unless you are using a "breathable" storage container that is not airtight) or else the lid will be blown off the container. I also recommend pots of rigid plastic rather than of flimsy, thin-walled plastic that could melt. Microwave the soil on full power for about 45 seconds for each 5-cm (2-inch) square plastic pot. For example, if you have 15 soil-filled pots or the equivalent amount of soil, set the microwave for 10–12 minutes. If your microwave does not have a rotating platform you will need to manually rotate the container in the microwave every three minutes to ensure uniform heating. Allow the soil to cool completely—ideally, the soil temperature should be 20°C (68°F) or slightly cooler—before you use it.

If you cannot obtain John Innes composts or do not wish to make anything similar to those composts, you could follow the standard recipe of Rick Lupp at Mt. Tahoma Nursery.

*Rick Lupp's potting compost*
9 parts coarse sand
5 parts coarse peat
4 parts pumice or grit

If you use Rick Lupp's recipe, you will need to feed your plants with encapsulated slow-release fertilizer. You should also adjust the mix for certain plants; for example, add more grit for *Primula allionii* and more peat for gentians. The soil mixtures I have seen at garden centers in the United States are almost all peat based with a small amount of perlite and vermiculite, and they hold water like a sponge unless you add more grit.

In spite of everything I say about soil mixes, if you are succeeding with your own mix, then stick to it. Remember, however, that grit is a necessity.

## Propagation

If you are growing alpine plants from seed, fill a 7-cm (2¾-in.) pot with soil mix to just below the brim and sow the seed on the surface. Cover the seed with a layer of grit and place it outside to face all weather conditions. The only time I would not do this is when you have fine seed, such as from campanulas, in which case you should sow the seed on top of the grit and stand the pots in a saucer of water to allow the seed to be drawn down into the grit. Once germination has occurred, take the pot into the alpine house or place it in a frame for the seedlings to grow on. Rather than sow seed from ericaceous plants on the surface of the soil mixture, sow it instead on peat that has been sterilized (you can do that by pouring boiling water over it). Closely cover the pot with polythene until germination. Take cuttings all year round and insert them into very fine, sandlike grit in a closed, plastic propagator.

As I emphasized in the discussion on soil mixtures, if your own propagation methods are working well, then you should not change them. Although I suggest specific propagation methods for each genus, I am more interested in encouraging you to continually propagate your plants any way you can. How many times have you bought or been given a plant and not propagated it, only to have it die? Even if you become the sole owner of the rarest plant ever, *propagate* it as soon as possible; if you lose it, it will quite likely become lost forever.

Grow and enjoy your alpines!

# GLOSSARY

**Achene.** A small, dry, hard, one-seeded indehiscent fruit developing from a single ovary.

**Alpine.** Referring to plants growing at or above timberline in subalpine and alpine zones in mountainous regions.

**Ascending.** Growing obliquely upward, often curving.

**Banner.** The upper petal of a papilionaceous flower, as in the sweet pea.

**Bipinnate.** Doubly or two-pinnate, as in many compound leaves.

**Blade.** The expanded part of a leaf or petal.

**Boreal.** Relating to the northern plant life characterized by coniferous forests and tundra. Applied to plants of northern origin.

**Bract.** A reduced leaf subtending a flower, usually associated with the inflorescence.

**Caespitose.** Growing in tufts.

**Calcareous.** Containing chalk. Growing on limestone or in lime-based soil.

**Calyx.** Outer whorl of flowering parts; a collective term for all the sepals of the flower.

**Capitate.** Forming dense, headlike clusters.

**Carinate.** Keeled, with a sharp, longitudinal ridge.

**Caudex.** The woody base of an otherwise herbaceous perennial.

**Ciliate.** Fringed with marginal hairs.

**Circumboreal.** Occuring around the earth in the northern part of the Northern Hemisphere south of the circumpolar region.

**Circumpolar.** Occuring around or surrounding the north pole in the cool temperate zone adjacent to the arctic.

**Compost.** As used here, the term refers to the wider sense of "growing medium" or "soil medium," not to the more narrow definition of partially rotted organic matter.

**Connate.** The union of like structures.

**Cordate.** Shaped like a heart.

**Corolla.** Inner whorl of floral parts; collective name for petals.

**Crenate.** Having margins with rounded teeth.

**Cuneate.** Wedge shaped, narrowing at the base.

**Cyme.** A flat-topped or convex paniculate flower cluster, with the central flowers opening first.

**Deciduous.** Falling off or shedding leaves seasonally; not evergreen.

**Decumbent.** Resting on the ground, but with the tip of the stems ascending.

**Deltoid.** Equilaterally triangular; shaped like a capital Greek letter delta.

**Dentate.** Having margins with sharp teeth that are not directed forward.

**Denticulate.** Minutely dentate or toothed.

**Dioecious.** Having staminate and pistillate flowers on different plants.

**Divided.** Of leaves, separated to the base.

**Efarinose.** Lacking farina.

**Emarginate.** Having a small notch at the apex.

**Entire.** Having undivided, continuous margins that are not incised or toothed.

**Erect.** Upright in relation to the ground; perpendicular to the surface of attachment.

**Ericaceous.** Acid loving.

**Exserted.** Protruding beyond an organ or part, as stamens from the corolla.

**Farina.** A mealy, floury, or sometimes waxy powder.

**Farinose.** Coated with farina.

**Fell-field.** Very rocky, usually exposed sites; common on windswept ridges and slopes.

**Foliolate.** Having leaflets.

**Glabrous.** Without hairs.

**Gland.** A depression, protuberance, or appendage that usually secretes a sticky fluid.

**Glandular.** Bearing glands.

**Glaucous.** Covered or whitened with a waxy bloom, as in a cabbage leaf.

**Globose.** Spherical or nearly so.

**Herb.** A nonwoody plant or one that is not woody above ground level.

**Herbaceous.** Not woody.

**Indehiscent.** Not splitting open at maturity.

**Inflorescence.** The flower cluster of a plant.

**Involucral bracts.** Free or various connate bracts, usually green, that subtend and often enclose the florets.

**Keel.** A prominent dorsal ridge like the keel of a boat. In a pea flower, the two lower petals that are pressed together around the stamens and pistil.

**Lanceolate.** Shaped like a lance-head, tapering to an apex and sometimes a base.

**Ligule.** The little tongue in the ray florets of a daisy; also the collarlike outgrowth at the junction of the sheath and blade of a grass leaf.

**Linear.** Resembling a line; long and narrow, of uniform width, as in leaf blades of grass.

**Lobe.** A division or segment of an organ, as of a leaf.

**Locule.** A small cavity or compartment such as those in a plant's ovary.

**Margin.** The edge or border of a leaf.

**Montane.** Growing in the mountains.

**Monocarpic.** A plant that bears fruit once before dying. Usually an annual or biennial, but can apply to plants that take many years to mature.

**Moraines.** A mass of rocks, gravel, or sand carried and finally deposited by a glacier.

**Oblanceolate.** Inversely lanceolate.

**Obovate.** Egg-shaped with the point of attachment at the narrowest end.

**Opposite.** Plant parts situated diametrically opposed to each other at the same node.

**Orbicular.** Approximately circular in outline.

**Ovate.** Egg-shaped with the point of attachment at the broadest end.

**Palmate.** Having lobes or veins radiating from a common point, like the fingers of a hand.

**Panicle.** (adj. paniculate). A compound racemose inflorescence.

**Papilionaceous.** Having the butterfly-like corolla of the pea, with banner, wings, and keel.

**Parted.** Of leaves. Deeply cleft nearly to the base.

**Pedicel.** The stalk of a single flower in a flower cluster.

**Perianth.** The floral envelope of the calyx and corolla.

**Petiole.** A leaf stalk.

**Pinnate.** A compound leaf consisting of several leaflets arranged on each side of a compound petiole; featherlike.

**Pin.** A flower form in which the style is long so that the stigma appears at the mouth of the corolla and the anthers are inserted in the corolla tube.

**Pinnatifid.** Pinnately cleft into narrow lobes that do not reach the midrib.

**Pistil.** The ovule-bearing organ of a flower consisting of stigma and ovary, usually with a style in between.

**Placenta.** (pl placentae) The ovule-bearing part of an ovary.

**Pricking out.** The careful removal of a seedling from a germination medium for potting in a soil mixture.

**Puberulent.** Minutely pubescent.

**Pubescent.** Covered with short, soft hairs; downy.

**Pulvinate.** Cushion shaped.

**Raceme.** An inflorescence formed of a usually erect stem bearing few to many flowers on a short pedicel.

**Racemose.** Having racemes; racemelike.

**Ray.** A primary branch of an umbel; in Compositae, the ligule of a ray flower.

**Revolute.** Rolled backward from both margins toward the underside.

**Rhizome.** An underground stem or root-stock with scales, leaves, and buds at the nodes.

**Rhombic.** Diamond shaped.

**Rosette.** A crowded cluster of radiating leaves arising from a shortened stem at or near ground level.

**Scape.** A leafless peduncle rising from the ground in acaulescent plants.

**Scapose.** With the flowers borne on a scape.

**Scree.** A site consisting mostly of rocky debris, usually broken from and accumulating at the base of large rock masses. A small amount of decayed vegetable matter is mixed in with the broken rock.

**Seep.** A moist location where underground water comes to the surface.

**Sepal.** A segment of a calyx or a segment of a perianth where only one whorl is present.

**Septum.** A partition between the cavities, as in an ovary.

**Serrate.** Saw-toothed with the teeth pointed forward.

**Sessile.** Attached directly by the base, not stalked, as in a leaf without a petiole.

**Silique.** A many-seeded capsule of the Cruciferae, with two valves splitting from the bottom and leaving a false petition between the placentae, typically more than twice as long as wide.

**Snowbed.** An area where deep snow accumulates in winter and persists at least to midsummer.

**Spatulate.** A blade that is rounded above and gradually tapering to the base; spatula-like.

**Stellate.** Star shaped.

**Stigma.** The receptive part of the pistil on which the pollen germinates.

**Stipule.** The part of the leaf where it attaches to the stem (common in the rose and pea families); a broadening on either side of the stem that could be mistaken for a bract.

**Stolon.** A modified stem that bends over or creeps, rooting and also producing a new plant at the tip or nodes.

**Stoloniferous.** Having stolons.

**Style.** The contracted portion of the pistil between the ovary and the stigma.

**Subalpine.** Nearly alpine; a forested region below the timberline that is somewhat less severe in climate than the alpine region but still affected by cold temperatures and short growing seasons.

**Subspecies.** A geographic variant within a species. A unit of classification below the rank of species consisting of two or more varieties.

**Subtend.** To be below and close to the axil, as in a leaf that subtends the shoot borne in the axis.

**Synonym.** An outmoded systematic name, as with a species published superflously.

**Talus.** The accumulated mass of rock debris at the foot of a cliff; a smaller, often more earthy version of a scree.

**Taxon.** (pl taxa) A taxanomic group of any category, such as the species within the same genus or a group of variable hybrids, with the same parentage; a group at any rank in the taxonomic hierarchy.

**Ternate.** Arranged in threes, as a leaf consisting of three leaflets.

**Thrum.** A flower form in which the style is short so that the stigma is included in the corolla tube and the anthers are positioned at the mouth of the flower.

**Type.** The specimen on which the name of plant is based.

**Triternate.** Thrice or three times ternate.

**Villous.** Bearing long, soft, and unmatted hairs; shaggy.

**Xeric.** Of or adapted to dry places.

# APPENDIX 1
## Alpine Plant Distribution by State

I DO NOT INTEND what follows to be a comprehensive checklist of all the alpine species that grow in each state. Rather, I offer this list as a convenient guide for readers traveling to a particular state who may want to know which alpines they are likely to see there.

**ALASKA**

*Androsace chamaejasme*
*Anemone drummondii*
*Anemone globosa*
*Anemone multiceps*
*Anemone multifida*
*Anemone narcissiflora*
*Anemone parviflora*
*Anemone richardsonii*
*Aquilegia brevistyla*
*Aquilegia formosa*
*Astragalus nutzotinensis*
*Astragalus polaris*
*Astragalus umbellatus*
*Campanula lasiocarpa*
*Campanula rotundifolia*
*Campanula scouleri*
*Campanula uniflora*
*Castilleja elegans*
*Castilleja miniata*
*Castilleja unalaschensis*
*Claytonia acutifolia*
*Claytonia sarmentosa*
*Claytonia scammaniana*
*Claytonia tuberosa*
*Delphinium brachycentrum*

*Dodecatheon frigidum*
*Dodecatheon jeffreyi*
*Dodecatheon pulchellum*
*Douglasia alaskana*
*Douglasia arctica*
*Douglasia beringensis*
*Douglasia gormanii*
*Douglasia ochotensis*
*Draba alpina*
*Draba densifolia*
*Draba incerta*
*Draba lanceolata*
*Draba macrocarpa*
*Draba stenopetala*
*Dryas × suendermannii*
*Dryas integrifolia*
*Dryas octopetala*
*Erigeron compositus*
*Erigeron eriocephalus*
*Erigeron humilis*
*Erigeron hyperboreus*
*Erigeron purpuratus*
*Eritrichium aretioides*
*Eritrichium chamissonis*
*Eritrichium splendens*
*Gentiana algida*

*Gentiana douglasiana*
*Gentiana glauca*
*Gentiana platypetala*
*Gentiana prostrata*
*Gentianella amarella*
*Gentianella propinqua*
*Gentianopsis thermalis*
*Lesquerella arctica*
*Lewisia pygmaea*
*Lupinus arcticus*
*Lupinus nootkatensis*
*Oxytropis deflexa*
*Oxytropis maydelliana*
*Oxytropis mertensia*
*Oxytropis nigrescens*
*Oxytropis scammaniana*
*Oxytropis splendens*
*Penstemon procerus*
*Phacelia sericea*
*Phlox alaskensis*
*Phlox borealis*
*Phlox richardsonii*
*Phlox sibirica*
*Polemonium boreale*
*Polemonium pulcherrimum*
*Primula anvilensis*

Primula borealis
Primula cuneifolia
Primula egaliksensis
Primula eximia
Primula incana
Primula mistassinica
Primula nutans
Primula tschuktchorum
Pulsatilla patens
Ranunculus eschscholtzii
Ranunculus gelidus
Ranunculus nivalis
Ranunculus pygmaeus
Ranunculus verecundus
Saxifraga bronchialis
Saxifraga cernua
Saxifraga davurica
Saxifraga eschscholtzii
Saxifraga ferruginea
Saxifraga lyallii
Saxifraga mertensiana
Saxifraga odontoloma
Saxifraga oppositifolia
Saxifraga rivularis
Saxifraga serpyllifolia
Saxifraga tolmiei
Saxifraga unalaschcensis
Silene acaulis
Synthyris borealis
Viola adunca
Viola glabella

## ARIZONA

Anemone multifida
Anemone tuberosa
Aquilegia caerulea
Aquilegia chrysantha
Aquilegia micrantha
Astragalus amphioxys
Astragalus calycosus
Astragalus ceramicus
Astragalus kentrophyta

Astragalus newberryi
Astragalus zionis
Campanula parryi
Castilleja chromosa
Castilleja miniata
Claytonia lanceolata
Collomia grandiflora
Delphinium andersonii
Delphinium nuttallianum
Dodecatheon alpinum
Erigeron compactus
Erigeron compositus
Erigeron flagellaris
Erigeron scopulinus
Erigeron simplex
Eriogonum ericifolium
Eriogonum fasciculatum
Eriogonum ovalifolium
Eriogonum shockleyi
Eriogonum umbellatum
Eriogonum wrightii
Gentiana affinis
Gentiana calycosa
Gentiana parryi
Gentianella amarella
Gilia aggregata
Gilia congesta
Gilia subnuda
Hymenoxys acaulis
Hymenoxys cooperi
Hymenoxys richardsonii
Hymenoxys subintegra
Ivesia sabulosa
Lesquerella arizonica
Lesquerella fendleri
Lesquerella goodingii
Lesquerella intermedia
Lesquerella ludoviciana
Lewisia brachycalyx
Lewisia pygmaea
Lewisia rediviva
Lupinus argenteus

Oxytropis lambertii
Oxytropis oreophila
Penstemon barbatus
Penstemon caespitosus
Penstemon eatonii
Penstemon linarioides
Penstemon ophianthus
Penstemon pinifolius
Penstemon rydbergii
Penstemon thompsoniae
Penstemon utahensis
Penstemon whippleanus
Petrophytum caespitosum
Phlox amabilis
Phlox austromontana
Phlox grayi
Phlox longifolia
Phlox speciosa
Phlox tenuifolia
Phlox viscida
Physaria chambersii
Physaria newberryi
Polemonium pauciflorum
Polemonium pulcherrimum
Polemonium viscosum
Primula parryi
Primula rusbyi
Primula specuicola
Ranunculus andersonii
Saxifraga caespitosa
Saxifraga davurica
Saxifraga flagellaris
Silene acaulis
Talinum brevifolium
Talinum pulchellum
Townsendia exscapa
Townsendia formosa
Townsendia glabella
Townsendia grandiflora
Viola adunca
Viola canadensis
Viola pedatifida

## ARIZONA (cont.)
*Viola purpurea*
*Zauschneria californica*

## CALIFORNIA
*Anemone drummondii*
*Anemone globosa*
*Anemone multifida*
*Anemone tuberosa*
*Aquilegia formosa*
*Aquilegia pubescens*
*Aquilegia shockleyi*
*Astragalus austinae*
*Astragalus bolanderi*
*Astragalus calycosus*
*Astragalus coccineus*
*Astragalus kentrophyta*
*Astragalus lentiginosus*
*Astragalus newberryi*
*Astragalus purshii*
*Astragalus whitneyi*
*Calyptridium umbellatum*
*Campanula prenanthoides*
*Campanula rotundifolia*
*Campanula scabrella*
*Campanula scouleri*
*Campanula shetleri*
*Castilleja applegatei*
*Castilleja arachnoidea*
*Castilleja chromosa*
*Castilleja cinerea*
*Castilleja latifolia*
*Castilleja miniata*
*Castilleja nana*
*Claytonia exigua*
*Claytonia lanceolata*
*Claytonia nevadensis*
*Collomia debilis*
*Collomia grandiflora*
*Delphinium andersonii*
*Delphinium decorum*
*Delphinium hesperinum*

*Delphinium menziesii*
*Delphinium nudicaule*
*Delphinium nuttallianum*
*Delphinium patens*
*Delphinium pratense*
*Delphinium variegatum*
*Dicentra chrysantha*
*Dicentra formosa*
*Dicentra ochroleuca*
*Dicentra pauciflora*
*Dicentra uniflora*
*Dodecatheon alpinum*
*Dodecatheon clevelandii*
*Dodecatheon conjugans*
*Dodecatheon hansenii*
*Dodecatheon hendersonii*
*Dodecatheon jeffreyi*
*Dodecatheon redolens*
*Dodecatheon subalpinum*
*Draba aureola*
*Draba breweri*
*Draba corrugata*
*Draba cruciata*
*Draba densifolia*
*Draba howellii*
*Draba lemmonii*
*Draba oligosperma*
*Draba paysonii*
*Draba sierrae*
*Epilobium glaberrimum*
*Epilobium glandulosum*
*Epilobium obcordatum*
*Erigeron chrysopsidis*
*Erigeron compactus*
*Erigeron compositus*
*Erigeron vagus*
*Eriogonum breedlovei*
*Eriogonum caespitosum*
*Eriogonum compositum*
*Eriogonum douglasii*
*Eriogonum fasciculatum*
*Eriogonum gracilipes*

*Eriogonum heracleoides*
*Eriogonum incanum*
*Eriogonum kellogii*
*Eriogonum kennedyi*
*Eriogonum latifolium*
*Eriogonum libertini*
*Eriogonum lobbii*
*Eriogonum marifolium*
*Eriogonum niveum*
*Eriogonum ochrocephalum*
*Eriogonum ovalifolium*
*Eriogonum parvifolium*
*Eriogonum rosense*
*Eriogonum saxatile*
*Eriogonum shockleyi*
*Eriogonum siskiyouense*
*Eriogonum sphaerocephalum*
*Eriogonum strictum*
*Eriogonum umbellatum*
*Eriogonum ursinum*
*Eriogonum wrightii*
*Gentiana affinis*
*Gentiana calycosa*
*Gentiana newberryi*
*Gentiana prostrata*
*Gentiana sceptrum*
*Gentiana setigera*
*Gentianella amarella*
*Gentianopsis thermalis*
*Gilia aggregata*
*Gilia congesta*
*Hulsea algida*
*Hulsea nana*
*Hulsea vestita*
*Hymenoxys cooperi*
*Ivesia argyrocoma*
*Ivesia gordonii*
*Ivesia kingii*
*Ivesia lycopodioides*
*Ivesia muirii*
*Ivesia pymaea*
*Ivesia santolinoides*

Ivesia shockleyi
Keckiella cordifolia
Keckiella corymbosa
Keckiella ternata
Leptodactylon californicum
Leptodactylon pungens
Lesquerella kingii
Lesquerella occidentalis
Lewisia brachycalyx
Lewisia cantelovii
Lewisia congdonii
Lewisia cotyledon
Lewisia disepela
Lewisia kelloggii
Lewisia leeana
Lewisia longipetala
Lewisia nevadensis
Lewisia oppositifolia
Lewisia pygmaea
Lewisia rediviva
Lewisia serrata
Lewisia sierrae
Lewisia stebbinsii
Lewisia triphylla
Lupinus argenteus
Lupinus breweri
Lupinus lepidus
Monardella cinerea
Monardella macrantha
Monardella nana
Monardella odoratissima
Monardella palmeri
Monardella villosa
Oxytropis deflexa
Oxytropis oreophila
Oxytropis parryi
Oxytropis viscida
Penstemon californicus
Penstemon centranthifolius
Penstemon davidsonii
Penstemon eatonii
Penstemon heterodoxus

Penstemon heterophyllus
Penstemon humilis
Penstemon janishiae
Penstemon newberryi
Penstemon parvulus
Penstemon procerus
Penstemon purpusii
Penstemon rupicola
Penstemon rydbergii
Penstemon speciosus
Penstemon tracyi
Penstemon utahensis
Petrophytum caespitosum
Phacelia argentea
Phacelia bolanderi
Phacelia corymbosa
Phacelia hastata
Phacelia heterophylla
Phlox adsurgens
Phlox austromontana
Phlox covillei
Phlox diffusa
Phlox dolichantha
Phlox douglasii
Phlox grayi
Phlox hirsuta
Phlox hoodii
Phlox lanata
Phlox longifolia
Phlox speciosa
Phlox stansburyi
Phlox superba
Physaria chambersii
Polemonium californicum
Polemonium chartaceum
Polemonium eximium
Polemonium pulcherrimum
Primula suffrutescens
Pulsatilla occidentalis
Ranunculus alismaefolius
Ranunculus andersonii
Ranunculus californicus

Ranunculus eschscholtzii
Ranunculus glaberrimus
Ranunculus hystriculus
Ranunculus populago
Saxifraga aprica
Saxifraga bryophora
Saxifraga californica
Saxifraga davurica
Saxifraga ferruginea
Saxifraga fragarioides
Saxifraga mertensiana
Saxifraga odontoloma
Saxifraga tolmiei
Scutellaria angustifolia
Scutellaria antirrhinoides
Scutellaria austiniae
Scutellaria bolanderi
Scutellaria californica
Scutellaria nana
Scutellaria tuberosa
Silene californica
Silene campanulata
Silene douglasii
Silene hookeri
Silene parishii
Silene sargentii
Synthyris missurica
Synthyris reniformis
Townsendia condensata
Townsendia grandiflora
Townsendia scapigera
Viola adunca
Viola beckwithii
Viola cuneata
Viola douglasii
Viola glabella
Viola hallii
Viola lobata
Viola nuttallii
Viola odorata
Viola purpurea
Viola shetlonii

## CALIFORNIA (cont.)
*Zauschneria californica*
*Zauschneria garrettii*
*Zauschneria septentrionalis*

## COLORADO
*Androsace chamaejasme*
*Anemone canadensis*
*Anemone globosa*
*Anemone narcissiflora*
*Anemone parviflora*
*Aquilegia brevistyla*
*Aquilegia caerulea*
*Aquilegia chrysantha*
*Aquilegia elegantula*
*Aquilegia flavescens*
*Aquilegia micrantha*
*Aquilegia saximontana*
*Astragalus asclepiadoides*
*Astragalus chamaeleuce*
*Astragalus detritalis*
*Astragalus gilviflorus*
*Astragalus hyalinus*
*Astragalus kentrophyta*
*Astragalus lutosus*
*Astragalus purshii*
*Astragalus sericoleucus*
*Astragalus spatulatus*
*Astragalus tridactylicus*
*Campanula parryi*
*Campanula rotundifolia*
*Campanula uniflora*
*Castilleja haydenii*
*Castilleja occidentalis*
*Castilleja rhexifolia*
*Castilleja scabrida*
*Castilleja sulphurea*
*Claytonia lanceolata*
*Claytonia megarrhiza*
*Delphinium alpestre*
*Delphinium andersonii*
*Delphinium nelsonii*

*Dodecatheon pulchellum*
*Draba crassa*
*Draba lanceolata*
*Draba oligosperma*
*Dryas octopetala*
*Epilobium latifolium*
*Erigeron compositus*
*Erigeron flagellaris*
*Erigeron leiomerus*
*Erigeron vagus*
*Eriogonum brevicaule*
*Eriogonum caespitosum*
*Eriogonum flavum*
*Eriogonum jamesii*
*Eriogonum pauciflorum*
*Eriogonum shockleyi*
*Eriogonum tumulosum*
*Eriogonum umbellatum*
*Eritrichium nanum*
*Gentiana affinis*
*Gentiana algida*
*Gentiana parryi*
*Gentiana prostrata*
*Gentianopsis thermalis*
*Gilia aggregata*
*Gilia congesta*
*Gilia globularis*
*Gilia pinnatifida*
*Gilia roseata*
*Gilia spicata*
*Gilia subnuda*
*Hymenoxys acaulis*
*Hymenoxys brandegii*
*Hymenoxys grandiflora*
*Hymenoxys richardsonii*
*Hymenoxys scaposa*
*Ivesia gordonii*
*Leptodactylon caespitosum*
*Leptodactylon watsonii*
*Lesquerella alpina*
*Lesquerella fendleri*
*Lesquerella ovalifolia*

*Lesquerella subumbellata*
*Lewisia pygmaea*
*Lewisia rediviva*
*Lewisia triphylla*
*Lupinus argenteus*
*Lupinus lepidus*
*Oxytropis campestris*
*Oxytropis deflexa*
*Oxytropis lambertii*
*Oxytropis multiceps*
*Oxytropis parryi*
*Oxytropis podocarpa*
*Oxytropis sericea*
*Oxytropis splendens*
*Oxytropis viscida*
*Paronychia pulvinata*
*Penstemon acaulis*
*Penstemon barbatus*
*Penstemon caespitosus*
*Penstemon crandallii*
*Penstemon eatonii*
*Penstemon eriantherus*
*Penstemon fremontii*
*Penstemon grahamii*
*Penstemon hallii*
*Penstemon humilis*
*Penstemon jamesii*
*Penstemon laricifolius*
*Penstemon linarioides*
*Penstemon ophianthus*
*Penstemon procerus*
*Penstemon procumbens*
*Penstemon rydbergii*
*Penstemon secundiflorus*
*Penstemon teucrioides*
*Penstemon virens*
*Penstemon whippleanus*
*Phacelia hastata*
*Phacelia sericea*
*Phlox amabilis*
*Phlox andicola*
*Phlox bryoides*

Phlox caespitosa
Phlox caryophylla
Phlox hoodii
Phlox kelseyi
Phlox muscoides
Phlox variabilis
Physaria acutifolia
Physaria alpina
Physaria bellii
Physaria obcordata
Physaria vitulifera
Polemonium brandegei
Polemonium pulcherrimum
Polemonium viscosum
Primula angustifolia
Primula egaliksensis
Primula incana
Primula parryi
Pulsatilla patens
Ranunculus adoneus
Ranunculus alismaefolius
Ranunculus eschscholtzii
Ranunculus gelidus
Ranunculus glaberrimus
Ranunculus macaulayi
Ranunculus pedatifidus
Ranunculus pygmaeus
Saxifraga adscendens
Saxifraga cernua
Saxifraga chrysantha
Saxifraga flagellaris
Saxifraga hirculus
Saxifraga odontoloma
Saxifraga oregana
Saxifraga rhomboidea
Saxifraga rivularis
Scutellaria brittonii
Silene acaulis
Telesonix jamesii
Townsendia eximea
Townsendia exscapa
Townsendia glabella

Townsendia grandiflora
Townsendia hookeri
Townsendia incana
Townsendia leptotes
Townsendia rothrockii
Trifolium brandegei
Trifolium dasyphyllum
Trifolium nanum
Trifolium parryi
Viola adunca
Viola nuttallii
Viola pedatifida
Viola purpurea

## IDAHO

Anemone drummondii
Anemone globosa
Anemone parviflora
Aquilegia caerulea
Aquilegia jonesii
Astragalus calycosus
Astragalus ceramicus
Astragalus kentrophyta
Astragalus spatulatus
Astragalus utahensis
Campanula scabrella
Castilleja applegatei
Castilleja pulchella
Castilleja rhexifolia
Castilleja sulphurea
Collomia debilis
Delphinium bicolor
Delphinium nelsonii
Dicentra uniflora
Dodecatheon dentatum
Douglasia idahoensis
Douglasia montana
Draba densifolia
Draba sphaerocarpa
Dryas integrifolia
Dryas octopetala
Epilobium glaberrimum

Epilobium latifolium
Epilobium obcordatum
Erigeron compositus
Erigeron leiomerus
Erigeron linearis
Erigeron simplex
Eriogonum brevicaule
Eriogonum caespitosum
Eriogonum chrysocephalum
Eriogonum compositum
Eriogonum flavum
Eriogonum mancum
Eriogonum niveum
Eriogonum ovalifolium
Eriogonum shockleyi
Eriogonum thymoides
Gentiana affinis
Gentiana calycosa
Gentiana prostrata
Gentianella propinqua
Gilia aggregata
Gilia congesta
Gilia spicata
Hulsea algida
Hymenoxys acaulis
Hymenoxys grandiflora
Hymenoxys richardsonii
Kelseya uniflora
Leptodactylon watsonii
Lesquerella alpina
Lesquerella carinata
Lesquerella douglasii
Lesquerella occidentalis
Lesquerella paysonii
Lewisia kelloggii
Lewisia nevadensis
Lewisia pygmaea
Lewisia rediviva
Lupinus argenteus
Lupinus lepidus
Monardella odoratissima
Oxytropis campestris

## IDAHO (cont.)

*Oxytropis lagopus*
*Oxytropis lambertii*
*Oxytropis parryi*
*Oxytropis sericea*
*Penstemon aridus*
*Penstemon eriantherus*
*Penstemon fruticosus*
*Penstemon gairdneri*
*Penstemon humilis*
*Penstemon janishiae*
*Penstemon nitidus*
*Penstemon procerus*
*Penstemon rydbergii*
*Penstemon speciosus*
*Penstemon venustus*
*Penstemon whippleanus*
*Petrophytum caespitosum*
*Phacelia hastata*
*Phacelia lyallii*
*Phacelia sericea*
*Phlox aculeata*
*Phlox bryoides*
*Phlox diffusa*
*Phlox kelseyi*
*Phlox longifolia*
*Phlox mollis*
*Phlox muscoides*
*Phlox viridis*
*Phlox viscida*
*Physaria didymocarpa*
*Physaria integrifolia*
*Physaria oregana*
*Polemonium pulcherrimum*
*Polemonium viscosum*
*Primula alcalina*
*Primula cusickiana*
*Primula incana*
*Primula parryi*
*Ranunculus adoneus*
*Ranunculus alismaefolius*
*Ranunculus andersonii*

*Ranunculus eschscholtzii*
*Ranunculus gelidus*
*Ranunculus populago*
*Ranunculus verecundus*
*Saxifraga bronchialis*
*Saxifraga lyallii*
*Saxifraga mertensiana*
*Saxifraga occidentalis*
*Saxifraga odontoloma*
*Saxifraga oppositifolia*
*Saxifraga oregana*
*Saxifraga rhomboidea*
*Saxifraga tolmiei*
*Scutellaria angustifolia*
*Scutellaria antirrhinoides*
*Scutellaria nana*
*Silene acaulis*
*Silene douglasii*
*Synthyris missurica*
*Synthyris pinnatifida*
*Telesonix jamesii*
*Townsendia condensata*
*Townsendia florifer*
*Townsendia montana*
*Townsendia parryi*
*Trifolium haydenii*
*Trifolium nanum*
*Trifolium parryi*
*Viola beckwithii*
*Viola canadensis*
*Viola purpurea*
*Zauschneria californica*
*Zauschneria garrettii*

## MONTANA

*Androsace chamaejasme*
*Anemone drummondii*
*Anemone globosa*
*Aquilegia brevistyla*
*Aquilegia caerulea*
*Aquilegia flavescens*
*Aquilegia formosa*

*Aquilegia jonesii*
*Astragalus aretioides*
*Astragalus barrii*
*Astragalus ceramicus*
*Astragalus gilviflorus*
*Astragalus hyalinus*
*Astragalus kentrophyta*
*Astragalus purshii*
*Calyptridium umbellatum*
*Campanula rotundifolia*
*Campanula scabrella*
*Campanula uniflora*
*Castilleja occidentalis*
*Castilleja pulchella*
*Castilleja rhexifolia*
*Castilleja sulphurea*
*Claytonia lanceolata*
*Collomia debilis*
*Collomia grandiflora*
*Delphinium andersonii*
*Delphinium bicolor*
*Dodecatheon conjugans*
*Dodecatheon pulchellum*
*Douglasia montana*
*Draba crassa*
*Draba densifolia*
*Dryas drummondii*
*Epilobium glaberrimum*
*Epilobium latifolium*
*Erigeron montanensis*
*Erigeron rydbergii*
*Erigeron simplex*
*Eriogonum caespitosum*
*Eriogonum heracleoides*
*Eriogonum strictum*
*Eriogonum umbellatum*
*Eritrichium howardii*
*Eritrichium nanum*
*Gentiana affinis*
*Gentiana algida*
*Gentiana calycosa*
*Gentiana glauca*

Gentiana prostrata
Gentianella propinqua
Gentianopsis thermalis
Gilia aggregata
Gilia congesta
Gilia spicata
Hulsea algida
Hymenoxys acaulis
Hymenoxys grandiflora
Hymenoxys richardsonii
Ivesia gordonii
Kelseya uniflora
Leptodactylon pungens
Lesquerella alpina
Lesquerella carinata
Lesquerella ludoviciana
Lesquerella paysonii
Lewisia nevadensis
Lewisia pygmaea
Lewisia rediviva
Lewisia triphylla
Lupinus argenteus
Oxytropis campestris
Oxytropis lagopus
Oxytropis lambertii
Oxytropis podocarpa
Oxytropis sericea
Oxytropis splendens
Paronychia pulvinata
Penstemon aridus
Penstemon confertus
Penstemon eriantherus
Penstemon fruticosus
Penstemon laricifolius
Penstemon nitidus
Penstemon rydbergii
Penstemon whippleanus
Petrophytum caespitosum
Phacelia hastata
Phacelia lyallii
Phlox albomarginata
Phlox andicola

Phlox bryoides
Phlox diffusa
Phlox douglasii
Phlox hoodii
Phlox kelseyi
Phlox longifolia
Phlox muscoides
Phlox speciosa
Phlox variabilis
Phlox viridis
Physaria didymocarpa
Polemonium pulcherrimum
Polemonium viscosum
Primula egaliksensis
Primula incana
Primula parryi
Pulsatilla patens
Ranunculus alismaefolius
Ranunculus eschscholtzii
Ranunculus gelidus
Ranunculus glaberrimus
Ranunculus pedatifidus
Ranunculus populago
Ranunculus pygmaeus
Saxifraga adscendens
Saxifraga bronchialis
Saxifraga cernua
Saxifraga flagellaris
Saxifraga lyallii
Saxifraga mertensiana
Saxifraga occidentalis
Saxifraga odontoloma
Saxifraga oppositifolia
Saxifraga oregana
Saxifraga rhomboidea
Saxifraga tolmiei
Shoshonea pulvinata
Silene acaulis
Silene douglasii
Synthyris missurica
Synthyris pinnatifida
Telesonix jamesii

Townsendia condensata
Townsendia hookeri
Townsendia leptotes
Townsendia montana
Townsendia parryi
Townsendia spathulata
Trifolium dasyphyllum
Trifolium haydenii
Trifolium nanum
Trifolium parryi
Viola adunca
Viola glabella
Viola nuttallii
Viola purpurea

## NEVADA

Anemone globosa
Anemone multifida
Aquilegia formosa
Aquilegia scopulorum
Astragalus amphioxys
Astragalus austinae
Astragalus calycosus
Astragalus kentrophyta
Astragalus lentiginosus
Astragalus newberryi
Astragalus piutensis
Astragalus purshii
Astragalus uncialis
Astragalus utahensis
Astragalus whitneyi
Castilleja applegatei
Castilleja chromosa
Castilleja nana
Castilleja scabrida
Claytonia megarrhiza
Collomia debilis
Delphinium andersonii
Dodecatheon redolens
Draba densifolia
Draba lanceolata
Draba oligosperma

## NEVADA (cont.)

Draba sphaeroides
Epilobium obcordatum
Erigeron chrysopsidis
Erigeron flagellaris
Erigeron leiomerus
Erigeron linearis
Erigeron simplex
Erigeron uncialis
Erigeron vagus
Eriogonum argophyllum
Eriogonum brevicaule
Eriogonum douglasii
Eriogonum fasciculatum
Eriogonum heracleoides
Eriogonum holmgrenii
Eriogonum lobbii
Eriogonum marifolium
Eriogonum ochrocephalum
Eriogonum ovalifolium
Eriogonum rosense
Eriogonum shockleyi
Eriogonum sphaerocephalum
Eriogonum strictum
Eriogonum umbellatum
Eriogonum villiflorum
Eriogonum wrightii
Gentiana affinis
Gentiana newberryi
Gentiana prostrata
Gilia aggregata
Gilia congesta
Hulsea vestita
Hymenoxys acaulis
Hymenoxys cooperi
Ivesia argyrocoma
Ivesia kingii
Ivesia lycopodioides
Ivesia rhypara
Ivesia sabulosa
Ivesia setosa
Ivesia shockleyi

Lepidium nanum
Leptodactylon caespitosum
Leptodactylon pungens
Leptodactylon watsonii
Lesquerella kingii
Lesquerella ludoviciana
Lesquerella occidentalis
Lewisia brachycalyx
Lewisia maguirei
Lewisia nevadensis
Lewisia pygmaea
Lewisia rediviva
Lewisia triphylla
Lupinus argenteus
Lupinus lepidus
Oxytropis oreophila
Oxytropis viscida
Penstemon eatonii
Penstemon humilis
Penstemon janishiae
Penstemon leiophyllus
Penstemon linarioides
Penstemon newberryi
Penstemon petiolatus
Penstemon procerus
Penstemon rydbergii
Penstemon speciosus
Penstemon thompsoniae
Penstemon utahensis
Petrophytum caespitosum
Phacelia sericea
Phlox austromontana
Phlox caespitosa
Phlox covillei
Phlox gladiformis
Phlox griseola
Phlox muscoides
Phlox superba
Phlox tumulosa
Phlox viridis
Physaria chambersii
Polemonium brandegei

Polemonium pulcherrimum
Polemonium viscosum
Primula capillaris
Primula nevadensis
Primula parryi
Pulsatilla occidentalis
Ranunculus adoneus
Ranunculus andersonii
Ranunculus eschscholtzii
Saxifraga caespitosa
Saxifraga occidentalis
Scutellaria antirrhinoides
Scutellaria nana
Scutellaria sapphirina
Silene douglasii
Silene sargentii
Telesonix jamesii
Townsendia exscapa
Townsendia florifer
Townsendia incana
Townsendia jonesii
Townsendia scapigera
Viola beckwithii
Zauschneria californica

## NEW MEXICO

Androsace chamaejasme
Anemone canadensis
Anemone globosa
Anemone multifida
Anemone tuberosa
Aquilegia caerulea
Aquilegia chaplinii
Aquilegia chrysantha
Aquilegia elegantula
Aquilegia longissima
Astragalus amphioxys
Astragalus ceramicus
Astragalus kentrophyta
Astragalus newberryi
Campanula parryi
Campanula rotundifolia

Castilleja chromosa
Castilleja haydenii
Castilleja miniata
Castilleja occidentalis
Castilleja rhexifolia
Castilleja scabrida
Castilleja sulphurea
Claytonia lanceolata
Delphinium alpestre
Delphinium andersonii
Delphinium nuttallianum
Erigeron leiomerus
Erigeron simplex
Eriogonum ovalifolium
Eriogonum shockleyi
Eriogonum wrightii
Gentiana affinis
Gentiana algida
Gentiana parryi
Gentianella amarella
Gilia aggregata
Gilia congesta
Gilia formosa
Gilia pinnatifida
Gilia spicata
Gilia subnuda
Hymenoxys acaulis
Leptodactylon pungens
Lesquerella fendleri
Lesquerella goodingii
Lesquerella intermedia
Lesquerella ovalifolia
Lewisia brachycalyx
Lewisia pygmaea
Lupinus argenteus
Monardella odoratissima
Oxytropis deflexa
Oxytropis lambertii
Oxytropis parryi
Oxytropis sericea
Oxytropis splendens
Penstemon alamosensis

Penstemon barbatus
Penstemon crandallii
Penstemon eatonii
Penstemon jamesii
Penstemon linarioides
Penstemon ophianthus
Penstemon pinifolius
Penstemon rydbergii
Penstemon secundiflorus
Penstemon whippleanus
Petrophytum caespitosum
Phacelia sericea
Phlox amabilis
Phlox caryophylla
Phlox grayi
Phlox longifolia
Phlox viridis
Physaria newberryi
Polemonium brandegei
Polemonium pauciflorum
Polemonium pulcherrimum
Polemonium viscosum
Primula angustifolia
Primula parryi
Primula rusbyi
Pulsatilla patens
Ranunculus eschscholtzii
Ranunculus glaberrimus
Ranunculus macaulayi
Saxifraga bronchialis
Saxifraga caespitosa
Saxifraga cernua
Saxifraga chrysantha
Saxifraga davurica
Saxifraga flagellaris
Saxifraga odontoloma
Saxifraga rhomboidea
Scutellaria brittonii
Silene acaulis
Silene laciniata
Silene wrightii
Talinum brachypodium

Talinum brevifolium
Talinum pulchellum
Telesonix jamesii
Townsendia exscapa
Townsendia formosa
Townsendia glabella
Townsendia grandiflora
Townsendia incana
Trifolium brandegei
Trifolium dasyphyllum
Trifolium nanum
Trifolium parryi
Viola adunca
Viola canadensis
Viola nuttallii
Viola pedatifida

## OREGON

Anemone drummondii
Anemone globosa
Anemone multifida
Anemone oregana
Anemone parviflora
Aquilegia flavescens
Aquilegia formosa
Astragalus kentrophyta
Astragalus newberryi
Astragalus purshii
Astragalus whitneyi
Calyptridium umbellatum
Campanula prenanthoides
Campanula rotundifolia
Campanula scabrella
Campanula scouleri
Castilleja applegatei
Castilleja arachnoidea
Castilleja chromosa
Castilleja rhexifolia
Claytonia megarrhiza
Claytonia nevadensis
Claytonia nevadensis
Collomia debilis

**OREGON (cont.)**

Collomia grandiflora
Delphinium andersonii
Delphinium decorum
Delphinium menziesii
Dicentra cuccularia
Dicentra formosa
Dicentra pauciflora
Dicentra uniflora
Dodecatheon alpinum
Dodecatheon conjugans
Dodecatheon dentatum
Dodecatheon hendersonii
Dodecatheon jeffreyi
Dodecatheon poeticum
Douglasia laevigata
Draba aureola
Draba densifolia
Draba howellii
Draba paysonii
Draba sphaeroides
Dryas drummondii
Dryas octopetala
Epilobium alpinum
Epilobium glaberrimum
Epilobium glandulosum
Epilobium latifolium
Epilobium obcordatum
Epilobium rigidum
Erigeron chrysopsidis
Erigeron compositus
Erigeron flagellaris
Erigeron linearis
Erigeron simplex
Eriogonum caespitosum
Eriogonum compositum
Eriogonum diclinum
Eriogonum douglasii
Eriogonum latifolium
Eriogonum marifolium
Eriogonum ovalifolium
Eriogonum sphaerocephalum

Eriogonum strictum
Eriogonum thymoides
Eriogonum umbellatum
Eritrichium nanum
Gentiana affinis
Gentiana bisetaea
Gentiana calycosa
Gentiana newberryi
Gentiana sceptrum
Gentiana setigera
Gentianella amarella
Gilia aggregata
Gilia congesta
Hulsea algida
Hulsea nana
Ivesia argyrocoma
Ivesia gordonii
Ivesia rhypara
Leptodactylon pungens
Lesquerella douglasii
Lesquerella kingii
Lesquerella occidentalis
Lewisia columbiana
Lewisia cotyledon
Lewisia leeana
Lewisia nevadensis
Lewisia oppositifolia
Lewisia pygmaea
Lewisia rediviva
Lewisia triphylla
Lupinus argenteus
Lupinus breweri
Lupinus lepidus
Oxytropis campestris
Oxytropis deflexa
Oxytropis oreophila
Oxytropis viscida
Penstemon cardwellii
Penstemon confertus
Penstemon davidsonii
Penstemon eriantherus
Penstemon fruticosus

Penstemon gairdneri
Penstemon heterophyllus
Penstemon humilis
Penstemon janishiae
Penstemon ovatus
Penstemon parvulus
Penstemon procerus
Penstemon richardsonii
Penstemon rupicola
Penstemon rydbergii
Penstemon serrulatus
Penstemon speciosus
Penstemon venustus
Petrophytum caespitosum
Phacelia argentea
Phacelia corymbosa
Phacelia hastata
Phacelia heterophylla
Phacelia lutea
Phacelia sericea
Phacelia verna
Phlox adsurgens
Phlox diffusa
Phlox douglasii
Phlox hoodii
Phlox lanata
Phlox longifolia
Phlox mollis
Phlox muscoides
Phlox peckii
Phlox speciosa
Phlox viridis
Phlox viscida
Physaria chambersii
Physaria oregana
Polemonium pulcherrimum
Primula cusickiana
Pulsatilla occidentalis
Ranunculus alismaefolius
Ranunculus andersonii
Ranunculus californicus
Ranunculus eschscholtzii

Ranunculus glaberrimus
Ranunculus populago
Ranunculus reconditis
Ranunculus verecundus
Saxifraga adscendens
Saxifraga aprica
Saxifraga bronchialis
Saxifraga caespitosa
Saxifraga californica
Saxifraga davurica
Saxifraga ferruginea
Saxifraga fragarioides
Saxifraga hitchcockiana
Saxifraga integrifolia
Saxifraga occidentalis
Saxifraga odontoloma
Saxifraga oppositifolia
Saxifraga oregana
Saxifraga tolmiei
Scutellaria angustifolia
Scutellaria antirrhinoides
Scutellaria nana
Scutellaria tuberosa
Silene acaulis
Silene californica
Silene campanulata
Silene douglasii
Silene hookeri
Silene suksdorfii
Synthyris missurica
Synthyris reniformis
Synthyris schizantha
Synthyris stellata
Talinum spinescens
Townsendia florifer
Viola beckwithii
Viola canadensis
Viola cuneata
Viola douglasii
Viola glabella
Viola hallii
Viola lobata

Viola nuttallii
Viola purpurea
Viola shetlonii

## UTAH

Androsace chamaejasme
Anemone globosa
Anemone parviflora
Anemone tuberosa
Aquilegia barnebyi
Aquilegia caerulea
Aquilegia chrysantha
Aquilegia elegantula
Aquilegia flavescens
Aquilegia formosa
Aquilegia grahamii
Aquilegia micrantha
Aquilegia scopulorum
Astragalus amphioxys
Astragalus aretioides
Astragalus asclepiadoides
Astragalus ceramicus
Astragalus chamaeleuce
Astragalus cymboides
Astragalus detritalis
Astragalus kentrophyta
Astragalus lentiginosus
Astragalus loanus
Astragalus lutosus
Astragalus musiniensis
Astragalus newberryi
Astragalus piutensis
Astragalus purshii
Astragalus simplicifolius
Astragalus uncialis
Astragalus utahensis
Astragalus zionis
Calyptridium umbellatum
Campanula parryi
Campanula uniflora
Castilleja applegatei
Castilleja chromosa

Castilleja miniata
Castilleja nana
Castilleja occidentalis
Castilleja pulchella
Castilleja rhexifolia
Castilleja scabrida
Castilleja sulphurea
Claytonia lanceolata
Claytonia megarrhiza
Collomia debilis
Delphinium andersonii
Delphinium nelsonii
Delphinium nuttallianum
Dicentra uniflora
Dodecatheon alpinum
Dodecatheon dentatum
Dodecatheon pulchellum
Dodecatheon redolens
Draba asprella
Draba crassa
Draba densifolia
Draba incerta
Draba lanceolata
Draba oligosperma
Draba subalpina
Draba ventosa
Epilobium glaberrimum
Erigeron compactus
Erigeron compositus
Erigeron flagellaris
Erigeron leiomerus
Erigeron linearis
Erigeron simplex
Erigeron vagus
Eriogonum bicolor
Eriogonum brevicaule
Eriogonum caespitosum
Eriogonum heracleoides
Eriogonum ovalifolium
Eriogonum panguicense
Eriogonum shockleyi
Eriogonum soredium

## UTAH (cont.)

Eriogonum tumulosum
Eriogonum umbellatum
Eriogonum villiflorum
Eriogonum wrightii
Gentiana affinis
Gentiana algida
Gentiana calycosa
Gentiana parryi
Gentiana prostrata
Gentianopsis thermalis
Gilia aggregata
Gilia caespitosa
Gilia congesta
Gilia pinnatifida
Gilia roseata
Gilia spicata
Gilia stenothyrsa
Gilia subnuda
Gilia tridactyla
Hymenoxys acaulis
Hymenoxys cooperi
Hymenoxys grandiflora
Hymenoxys lapidicola
Hymenoxys richardsonii
Hymenoxys scaposa
Hymenoxys subintegra
Hymenoxys torreyana
Ivesia gordonii
Ivesia kingii
Ivesia sabulosa
Ivesia sabulosa
Ivesia setosa
Ivesia shockleyi
Ivesia utahensis
Lepidium barnebyanum
Lepidium ostileri
Leptodactylon caespitosum
Leptodactylon pungens
Leptodactylon watsonii
Lesquerella alpina
Lesquerella arizonica

Lesquerella fendleri
Lesquerella garretti
Lesquerella hemiphysaria
Lesquerella intermedia
Lesquerella kingii
Lesquerella ludoviciana
Lesquerella occidentalis
Lesquerella rubicundula
Lesquerella subumbellata
Lesquerella tumulosa
Lesquerella wardii
Lewisia brachycalyx
Lewisia pygmaea
Lewisia rediviva
Lewisia triphylla
Lupinus argenteus
Lupinus lepidus
Monardella odoratissima
Oxytropis campestris
Oxytropis deflexa
Oxytropis lambertii
Oxytropis multiceps
Oxytropis sericea
Oxytropis viscida
Penstemon acaulis
Penstemon barbatus
Penstemon caespitosus
Penstemon crandallii
Penstemon duchesnensis
Penstemon eatonii
Penstemon fremontii
Penstemon grahamii
Penstemon humilis
Penstemon leiophyllus
Penstemon linarioides
Penstemon nanus
Penstemon ophianthus
Penstemon petiolatus
Penstemon procerus
Penstemon rydbergii
Penstemon speciosus
Penstemon thompsoniae

Penstemon uintahensis
Penstemon utahensis
Penstemon whippleanus
Petrophytum caespitosum
Phacelia hastata
Phacelia sericea
Phlox amabilis
Phlox austromontana
Phlox bryoides
Phlox caespitosa
Phlox gladiformis
Phlox grayi
Phlox griseola
Phlox longifolia
Phlox muscoides
Phlox tumulosa
Phlox variabilis
Physaria acutifolia
Physaria chambersii
Physaria didymocarpa
Physaria newberryi
Polemonium brandegei
Polemonium pulcherrimum
Polemonium viscosum
Primula domensis
Primula incana
Primula maguirei
Primula parryi
Primula specuicola
Pulsatilla patens
Ranunculus adoneus
Ranunculus alismaefolius
Ranunculus andersonii
Ranunculus eschscholtzii
Ranunculus gelidus
Ranunculus glaberrimus
Ranunculus pedatifidus
Saxifraga adscendens
Saxifraga bronchialis
Saxifraga caespitosa
Saxifraga chrysantha
Saxifraga flagellaris

Saxifraga hirculus
Saxifraga odontoloma
Saxifraga rhomboidea
Scutellaria antirrhinoides
Scutellaria sapphirina
Silene acaulis
Silene douglasii
Silene petersonii
Silene scouleri
Synthyris pinnatifida
Talinum brevifolium
Telesonix jamesii
Townsendia aprica
Townsendia condensata
Townsendia exscapa
Townsendia florifer
Townsendia glabella
Townsendia hookeri
Townsendia incana
Townsendia jonesii
Townsendia mensana
Townsendia montana
Townsendia scapigera
Trifolium dasyphyllum
Trifolium nanum
Trifolium parryi
Viola adunca
Viola beckwithii
Viola canadensis
Viola nuttallii
Viola odorata
Viola purpurea
Zauschneria californica
Zauschneria garrettii

## WASHINGTON
Anemone drummondii
Anemone globosa
Anemone multifida
Anemone oregana
Aquilegia flavescens
Aquilegia formosa

Astragalus purshii
Astragalus whitneyi
Calyptridium umbellatum
Campanula lasiocarpa
Campanula parryi
Campanula piperi
Campanula rotundifolia
Campanula scabrella
Campanula scouleri
Castilleja parviflora
Castilleja thompsonii
Claytonia lanceolata
Claytonia megarrhiza
Collomia debilis
Collomia grandiflora
Delphinium glareosum
Delphinium menziesii
Dicentra cuccularia
Dicentra formosa
Dicentra uniflora
Dodecatheon conjugans
Dodecatheon dentatum
Dodecatheon hendersonii
Dodecatheon jeffreyi
Dodecatheon poeticum
Douglasia laevigata
Douglasia nivalis
Draba aureola
Draba densifolia
Draba paysonii
Dryas drummondii
Dryas octopetala
Epilobium alpinum
Epilobium glaberrimum
Epilobium glandulosum
Epilobium latifolium
Erigeron aureus
Erigeron chrysopsidis
Erigeron compactus
Erigeron compositus
Erigeron flagellaris
Erigeron flettii

Erigeron linearis
Erigeron poliospermus
Eriogonum compositum
Eriogonum douglasii
Eriogonum heracleoides
Eriogonum ovalifolium
Eriogonum sphaerocephalum
Eriogonum strictum
Eriogonum thymoides
Eriogonum umbellatum
Gentiana affinis
Gentiana calycosa
Gentianella amarella
Gilia aggregata
Hulsea nana
Ivesia gordonii
Ivesia shockleyi
Leptodactylon pungens
Lesquerella douglasii
Lewisia columbiana
Lewisia nevadensis
Lewisia pygmaea
Lewisia rediviva
Lewisia triphylla
Lewisia tweedyi
Lupinus argenteus
Lupinus latifolius
Lupinus lepidus
Monardella odoratissima
Oxytropis campestris
Oxytropis deflexa
Oxytropis viscida
Penstemon cardwellii
Penstemon confertus
Penstemon davidsonii
Penstemon eriantherus
Penstemon fruticosus
Penstemon gairdneri
Penstemon humilis
Penstemon ovatus
Penstemon procerus
Penstemon pruinosus

## WASHINGTON (cont.)

*Penstemon richardsonii*
*Penstemon rupicola*
*Penstemon rydbergii*
*Penstemon serrulatus*
*Penstemon speciosus*
*Penstemon venustus*
*Penstemon washingtonensis*
*Petrophytum cinerascens*
*Petrophytum hendersonii*
*Phacelia hastata*
*Phacelia heterophylla*
*Phacelia sericea*
*Phlox diffusa*
*Phlox douglasii*
*Phlox hendersonii*
*Phlox hoodii*
*Phlox longifolia*
*Phlox mollis*
*Phlox muscoides*
*Phlox speciosa*
*Phlox viridis*
*Phlox viscida*
*Physaria alpestris*
*Physaria oregana*
*Polemonium elegans*
*Polemonium pulcherrimum*
*Polemonium viscosum*
*Pulsatilla occidentalis*
*Pulsatilla patens*
*Ranunculus alismaefolius*
*Ranunculus eschscholtzii*
*Ranunculus glaberrimus*
*Ranunculus populago*
*Ranunculus reconditis*
*Ranunculus verecundus*
*Saxifraga adscendens*
*Saxifraga bronchialis*
*Saxifraga caespitosa*
*Saxifraga davurica*
*Saxifraga ferruginea*
*Saxifraga integrifolia*

*Saxifraga lyallii*
*Saxifraga occidentalis*
*Saxifraga odontoloma*
*Saxifraga oppositifolia*
*Saxifraga oregana*
*Saxifraga tolmiei*
*Scutellaria angustifolia*
*Silene acaulis*
*Silene douglasii*
*Silene parryi*
*Silene suksdorfii*
*Synthyris missurica*
*Synthyris pinnatifida*
*Synthyris reniformis*
*Synthyris schizantha*
*Talinum okanoganense*
*Talinum spinescens*
*Townsendia florifer*
*Trifolium macrocephalum*
*Viola canadensis*
*Viola flettii*
*Viola glabella*
*Viola nuttallii*
*Viola purpurea*

## WYOMING

*Androsace chamaejasme*
*Anemone globosa*
*Anemone multifida*
*Anemone narcissiflora*
*Aquilegia flavescens*
*Aquilegia jonesii*
*Aquilegia laramiensis*
*Astragalus aretioides*
*Astragalus barrii*
*Astragalus calycosus*
*Astragalus chamaeleuce*
*Astragalus gilviflorus*
*Astragalus hyalinus*
*Astragalus kentrophyta*
*Astragalus purshii*
*Astragalus sericoleucus*

*Astragalus tridactylicus*
*Calyptridium umbellatum*
*Campanula rotundifolia*
*Campanula uniflora*
*Castilleja applegatei*
*Castilleja chromosa*
*Castilleja pulchella*
*Claytonia lanceolata*
*Collomia debilis*
*Collomia grandiflora*
*Delphinium bicolor*
*Delphinium nelsonii*
*Dicentra uniflora*
*Dodecatheon conjugans*
*Dodecatheon pulchellum*
*Douglasia montana*
*Draba crassa*
*Draba densifolia*
*Draba incerta*
*Draba oligosperma*
*Draba ventosa*
*Erigeron flagellaris*
*Erigeron leiomerus*
*Erigeron linearis*
*Erigeron rydbergii*
*Eriogonum acaule*
*Eriogonum brevicaule*
*Eriogonum flavum*
*Eriogonum heracleoides*
*Eriogonum jamesii*
*Eriogonum ovalifolium*
*Eritrichium howardii*
*Eritrichium nanum*
*Gentiana algida*
*Gentiana calycosa*
*Gentiana parryi*
*Gentiana prostrata*
*Gentianella propinqua*
*Gentianopsis thermalis*
*Gilia aggregata*
*Gilia congesta*
*Gilia pinnatifida*

*Hymenoxys acaulis*
*Hymenoxys richardsonii*
*Hymenoxys torreyana*
*Ivesia gordonii*
*Kelseya uniflora*
*Leptodactylon caespitosum*
*Leptodactylon watsonii*
*Lesquerella alpina*
*Lesquerella carinata*
*Lesquerella paysonii*
*Lesquerella subumbellata*
*Lewisia pygmaea*
*Lewisia rediviva*
*Lewisia triphylla*
*Lupinus argenteus*
*Monardella odoratissima*
*Oxytropis campestris*
*Oxytropis lagopus*
*Oxytropis lambertii*
*Oxytropis multiceps*
*Oxytropis nana*
*Oxytropis parryi*
*Oxytropis podocarpa*
*Oxytropis sericea*
*Paronychia pulvinata*
*Penstemon acaulis*
*Penstemon aridus*
*Penstemon caespitosus*
*Penstemon fremontii*
*Penstemon fruticosus*
*Penstemon laricifolius*
*Penstemon nitidus*
*Penstemon paysoniorum*
*Penstemon rydbergii*

*Penstemon secundiflorus*
*Penstemon virens*
*Penstemon whippleanus*
*Petrophytum caespitosum*
*Phlox alyssifolia*
*Phlox bryoides*
*Phlox caespitosa*
*Phlox diffusa*
*Phlox hoodii*
*Phlox kelseyi*
*Phlox longifolia*
*Phlox muscoides*
*Phlox pungens*
*Phlox variabilis*
*Physaria acutifolia*
*Physaria condensata*
*Physaria didymocarpa*
*Physaria dornii*
*Physaria eburniflora*
*Physaria integrifolia*
*Physaria saximontana*
*Polemonium brandegei*
*Polemonium pulcherrimum*
*Polemonium viscosum*
*Primula egaliksensis*
*Primula incana*
*Primula parryi*
*Pulsatilla patens*
*Ranunculus adoneus*
*Ranunculus alismaefolius*
*Ranunculus eschscholtzii*
*Ranunculus gelidus*
*Ranunculus pedatifidus*
*Ranunculus pygmaeus*

*Ranunculus verecundus*
*Saxifraga bronchialis*
*Saxifraga cernua*
*Saxifraga chrysantha*
*Saxifraga flagellaris*
*Saxifraga occidentalis*
*Saxifraga odontoloma*
*Saxifraga oppositifolia*
*Saxifraga rhomboidea*
*Scutellaria brittonii*
*Shoshonea pulvinata*
*Silene acaulis*
*Synthyris pinnatifida*
*Telesonix jamesii*
*Townsendia condensata*
*Townsendia grandiflora*
*Townsendia hookeri*
*Townsendia incana*
*Townsendia leptotes*
*Townsendia montana*
*Townsendia nuttallii*
*Townsendia parryi*
*Townsendia spathulata*
*Trifolium dasyphyllum*
*Trifolium haydenii*
*Trifolium nanum*
*Trifolium parryi*
*Viola adunca*
*Viola nuttallii*
*Viola purpurea*
*Zauschneria californica*
*Zauschneria garrettii*

# APPENDIX 2
## Societies and Mail-Order Sources

**Plant Societies**

A number of specialist societies deal specifically with the cultivation of alpine plants, and I encourage all enthusiasts to join at least one. Regular bulletins, an annual seed list, and regular shows are only some of the benefits of membership. Interested readers should contact the societies directly.

**Alpine Garden Club of British Columbia**
Dana Cromie
c/o 2208 Alder Street
Vancouver, British Columbia
Canada V6H 2R9

**The Alpine Garden Society**
AGS Center
Avon Bank
Pershore, Worcestershire WR10 3JP
United Kingdom

**American Penstemon Society**
Ann Bartlett
1569 S. Holland Court
Lakewood, Colorado 80232

**The Androsace Society**
David Mowle
16 Peacock Lane
Hest Bank, Lancaster LA2 6EN
United Kingdom

**The North American Rock Garden Society**
Jacques Mommens, Executive Secretary
P.O. Box 67
Millwood, New York 10546

**The Scottish Rock Garden Club**
Hazel Smith, Subscription Secretary
Harrglayock, Salsgirth
Dollar, Fife
Scotland FK14 7NE

**Vancouver Island Rock and Alpine Garden Society**
P.O. Box 6507 Station C
Victoria, British Columbia
Canada V8P 5M4

## Seed Lists

The following businesses offer seed of western North American alpines. Most seed has been collected in the wild.

**Alplains**
32315 Pine Crest Court
Kiowa, Colorado 80117

**Jim and Jenny Archibald**
Bryn Collen
Ffostrasol, Llandsul
Dyfed
Wales SA44 5SB

**Beaver Creek Greenhouses**
P.O. Box 129
Fruitvale, British Columbia
Canada V0G IL0

**Northwest Native Seed**
17595 Vierra Canyon Road # 172
Prunedale, California 93907

**Rocky Mountain Rare Plants**
1706 Deerpath Road
Franktown, Colorado 80116-9462

**Rogue House Seed**
250 Maple Street
Central Point, Oregon 97502

**Southwestern Native Seed**
P.O. Box 50503
Tuscon, Arizona 85703

## Mail-Order Nurseries

The following nurseries sell western North American plants.

**Arrowhead Alpines**
P.O. Box 857
Fowlerville, Michigan 48836

**Ashwood Nurseries** (lewisias)
Greensforge
Kingswinford, West Midlands, DY6 0AE
United Kingdom

**Graham's Hardy Plants**
'Southcroft'
North Road
Timsbury, Bath BA2 0JN
United Kingdom

**Lingen Nursery and Garden**
Lingen
Nr. Bucknell, Shropshire SY7 0DY
United Kingdom

**Parham Bungalow Plants**
Parham Lane
Market Lavington
Devizes, Wiltshire SN10 4QA
United Kingdom

**Mt. Tahoma Nursery**
28111 112th Avenue E.
Graham, Washington 98338

**Siskiyou Rare Plant Nursery**
2825 Cummings Road
Medford, Oregon 97501

**Wrightman Alpines**
RR#3, 1503 Napperton Dr.
Kerwood
Ontario, Canada N0M 2B0

# BIBLIOGRAPHY

Albee, B. J., L. M. Shultz, and S. Goodrich. 1988. *Digital Atlas of the Vascular Plants of Utah*. Salt Lake City: Utah Museum of Natural History. Retrieved September 2001 from the World Wide Web: <http://www.gis.usu.edu/Geography-Department/utgeog/utvatlas/ut-vascatlas.html>

Alpine Garden Society. 1993. *Encyclopaedia of Alpines*. Pershore, England: Alpine Garden Society.

American Rock Garden Society. 1976. *Alpines of the Americas*. Report of the First Interim International Rock Garden Conference.

American Rock Garden Society and Denver Botanic Gardens. 1986. *Rocky Mountain Alpines*. Portland, Oregon: Timber Press.

Andrews, J. 1990. "Plant Gems of the Golden State." *Bulletin of the American Rock Garden Society* 48 (1): 35–36, 45–46.

Archibald, J. 1989–1990. Seed List.

Barneby, R., and H. D. Ripley. 1947. *Leaflets of Western Botany* 5 (4): 65.

Barneby, R. 1964. *Atlas of North American Astragalus*, Part II. The *Ceridothrix*, *Hypoglottis*, *Piptolodoid*, *Trimeniaeus*, and *Orophaca* Astragali. Memoirs of the New York Botanical Garden 13: 597—1188.

Barr, C. A. 1983. *Jewels of the Plains*. Minneapolis: University of Minnesota Press.

Beaman, J. H. 1957. "The Systematics and Evolution of *Townsendia* (Compositae)." Contributions from the Gray Herbarium of Harvard University 183: 1–151.

Belzer, T. J. 1984. *Roadside Plants of Southern California*. Missoula, Montana: Mountain Press.

Buchanan, H. 1992. *Wildflowers of Southwestern Utah*. Helena, Montana: Falcon Press.

Colorado Native Plant Society. 1989. *Rare Plants of Colorado*. Estes Park, Colorado: Rocky Mountain Nature Association.

Craighead, J. J., F. C. Craighead, and R. J. Davis. 1963. *Field Guide to Rocky Mountain Wildflowers*. Boston, Massachusetts: Houghton Mifflin.

Dannen, K., and D. Dannen. 1981. *Rocky Mountain Wildflowers*. Estes Park, Colorado: Tundra.

Davidson, B. L. 2000. *Lewisias*. Portland, Oregon: Timber Press.

Day-Skowron, R. 1996. Rocky Mountain Rare Plants seed catalog.

Deno, N. 1991. *Seed Germination Theory and Practice*. State College, Pennsylvania: Norman Deno.

DeSanto, J. 1991. "Variations in Aquilagia jonesii." *Bulletin of the American Rock Garden Society* 49 (1): 60–65.

———. 1993. *Bitterroot*. Babb, Montana: Lere Press.

Dierig, D. A. 1995. "Lesquerellas." *New Crop FactSHEET*, Center for New Crops and Plants Products, Purdue University: Indiana.

Duft, J. F., and R. K. Mosely. 1989. *Alpine Wildflowers of the Rocky Mountains*. Missoula, Montana: Mountain Press.

Eastman, D. 1990. *Rare and Endangered Plants of Oregon*. Woodburn, Oregon: Beautiful America.

Elliott, R. C. 1966. *The Genus Lewisia*. London: Alpine Garden Society. 2d ed. 1978; originally published 1966 in the *Quarterly Bulletin of the Alpine Garden Society* 34: 1–76.

Foster, H. L. 1968. *Rock Gardening: A Guide to Growing Alpines and Other Wildflowers in the American Garden*. Boston, Massachusetts: Houghton Mifflin.

Goodrich, S., and E. Neese. 1986. *Uinta Basin Flora*. Ogden, Utah: U.S.D.A. Forest Service-Intermountain Region.

Great Plains Flora Association. 1986. *Flora of the Great Plains*. Lawrence: University Press of Kansas.

Griffiths, A. 1964. *Collins Guide to Alpines and Rock Garden Plants*. London: Chancellor Press.

Guppy, A. 1997. "Cultivation of *Castilleja*." *Botanical Electronic News* 156 (February): 2–4. Retrieved 2000 from the World Wide Web: <http://www.ou.edu/cas/botany-micro/ben156.html>

Harris, C. O., and B. E. Willard. 1976. *Alpine Wildflowers of the Rocky Mountains*. Estes Park, Colorado: Rocky Mountain Nature Association.

Heath, R. E. 1964. *Collectors Alpines*. London: Collingridge Books.

Herder, F. 1872. *Acta Horti Petropalitanus* 1: 535.

Hogan, S. 1990. "Lewisias, Wild and Cultivated." *Bulletin of the American Rock Garden Society* 48 (1): 47–52.

Holmgren, N. 1994. *Brittonia* 46: 91

Hultén, E. 1968. *Flora of Alaska and Neighboring Territories*. Standford, California: Stanford University Press.

Idaho Fish and Game. 2001. Idaho Conservation Data Center. Retrieved 2000 from the World Wide Web: <http://www2.state.id.us/fishgame/info/cdc/cdc.htm>.

Ingwersen, W. 1978. *Ingwersen's Manual of Alpine Plants.* Eastbourne, England: Will Ingwersen and Dunnsprint.

Joyner, D. 1995. "The Genus Castilleja in Utah." *Rock Garden Quarterly* 53 (4): 245–258.

Kelaidis, G. 1993. Rocky Mountain Rare Plants seed catalog.

Kelaidis, P. 1990. "Physarias: April's Garden Gold." *Bulletin of the American Rock Garden Society* 48 (2): 111-116.

———. 1991. "Dwarf *Phlox* and *Penstemon*." In The Alpine Garden Society and the Scottish Rock Garden Club. *A Century of Alpines.* Pershore, England: Sixth International Rock Garden Plant Conference. 88–104.

———. 1998. "Townsendias: Halcyon Daisies of the Rockies." *Rock Garden Quarterly* 56 (2): 99–118.

———. 2000. "Book Review of *Rock Garden Plants: A Color Encyclopedia by Baldassare Mineo*." *Rock Garden Quarterly* 58 (2): 155.

Kelso, S. 1987a. "*Primula anvilensis* (Primulaceae): A New Species from Northwestern Alaska." *Systematic Botany* 12 (1): 9–13.

———. 1987b. "*Primula tschuktschorum* and *Primula eximia* (Primulaceae: Section *Crystallophlomis*): A Distylous Species and Its Homostylous Derivative from the Bering Region, Alaska." *Brittonia* 39 (1): 63–72.

———. 1991a. "Taxonomy and Biogeography of *Primula* sect. *Cuneifolia* (Primulaceae) in North America." *Madroño* 38 (1): 37–44.

———. 1991b. "Taxonomy of *Primula* sects. *Aleuritia* and *Armerina* in North America." *Rhodora* 93 (873): 67–99.

Kelso, S., B. A. Yurtsev, and D. F. Murray. 1994. "*Douglasia beringensis* (Primulaceae): A New Species from Northwestern Alaska." *Novon* 4 (4): 381–385.

Klise, N. 1989. "The Dodecatheon Newsletter." *Delaware Valley Chapter* 13 (5).

Lodewick, K., and R. Lodewick. 1970. *Penstemon Field Identifier.* Supplement to the *American Penstemon Society Bulletin* No. 29.

———. 1971. *Penstemon Field Identifier Part 2.* Supplement to the *American Penstemon Society Bulletin* No. 30.

———. 1972. *Penstemon Field Identifier Part 3.* Supplement to the *American Penstemon Society Bulletin* No. 31.

———. 1973. *Penstemon Field Identifier Part 4.* Supplement to the *American Penstemon Society Bulletin* No. 32.

———. 1974. *Penstemon Field Identifier Part 5.* Supplement to the *American Penstemon Society Bulletin* No. 33.

———. 1975. *Penstemon Field Identifier Part 6.* Supplement to the *American Penstemon Society Bulletin* No. 34.

———. 1976. *Penstemon Field Identifier Part 7.* Supplement to the *American Penstemon Society Bulletin* No. 35.

———. 1977. *Penstemon Field Identifier Part 8.* Supplement to the *American Penstemon Society Bulletin* No. 36.

———. 1983. *Penstemon Field Identifier Part 9.* Supplement to the *American Penstemon Society Bulletin* No. 41–42.

Lowe, D. 1991. *Growing Alpines in Raised Beds, Troughs, and Tufa.* London: Batsford.

Lunn, J. G. 1991. "Native *Primula* of Western America." *Bulletin of the American Rock Garden Society* 49 (2):

Mathew, B. 1989. *The Genus Lewisia.* Bromley, Kent: Christopher Helm; Portland, Oregon: Timber Press, in association with the Royal Botanic Gardens, Kew.

Nelson, R. A. 1976. *Plants of Rocky Mountain National Park.* 3d ed. Rocky Mountain Nature Association.

Niehaus, T. F. 1974. *Sierra Wildflowers Mount Lassen to Kern Canyon.* Berkeley: University of California Press.

Niehaus, T. F., and C. L. Ripper. 1976. *Pacific States Wildflowers.* Boston, Massachusetts: Houghton Mifflin.

Nold, R. 1999. *Penstemons.* Portland, Oregon: Timber Press.

North American Rock Garden Society. 1996. *Rock Garden Plants of North America.* Portland, Oregon: Timber Press.

Northington, D. 1995. "Flowers for the Future." *The Garden* (May): 174–178.

Pratt, V. E. 1989. *Alaskan Wildflowers.* Anchorage: Alaskakrafts.

Pratt, V. E., and F. G. Pratt. 1993. *Wildflowers of Denali National Park.* Anchorage: Alaskakrafts.

Richards, J. 1993. *Primula.* Portland, Oregon: Timber Press.

Rolfe, R. 1990. *The Alpine House.* Portland, Oregon: Timber Press.

Ross, R. A., and H. L. Chambers. 1988. *Wildflowers of the Western Cascades.* Portland, Oregon: Timber Press.

Shaw, R. 1981. *Plants of Yellowstone and Grand Teton National Parks.* Salt Lake City, Utah: Wheelwright Press.

Sherman, K. 1996. "Castillejas: Meeting the Challenge." *Rock Garden Quarterly* 54 (2): 133–138.

Smith, G., and D. Lowe. 1997. *The Genus* Androsace*: A Monograph for Gardeners and Botanists.* Pershore, England: Alpine Garden Society.

Spellenberg, R. 1979. *The Audubon Society Field Guide to North American Wildflowers*, Western Region. New York: Alfred A. Knopf.

Strickler, D. 1990. *Alpine Wildflowers.* Columbia Falls, Montana: Flower Press.

Weber, W. A. 1987. *Colorado Flora Western Slope.* Boulder, Colorado: Colorado Associated University Press.

Welsh, S. L., N. D. Atwood, L. C. Higgins, and S. Goodrich. 1987. *A Utah Flora.* Provo, Utah: Brigham Young University.

Wilson, L., J. Wilson, and J. Nicholas. 1987. *Wildflowers of Yosemite.* New York: Sunrise Productions.

# INDEX OF PLANT NAMES